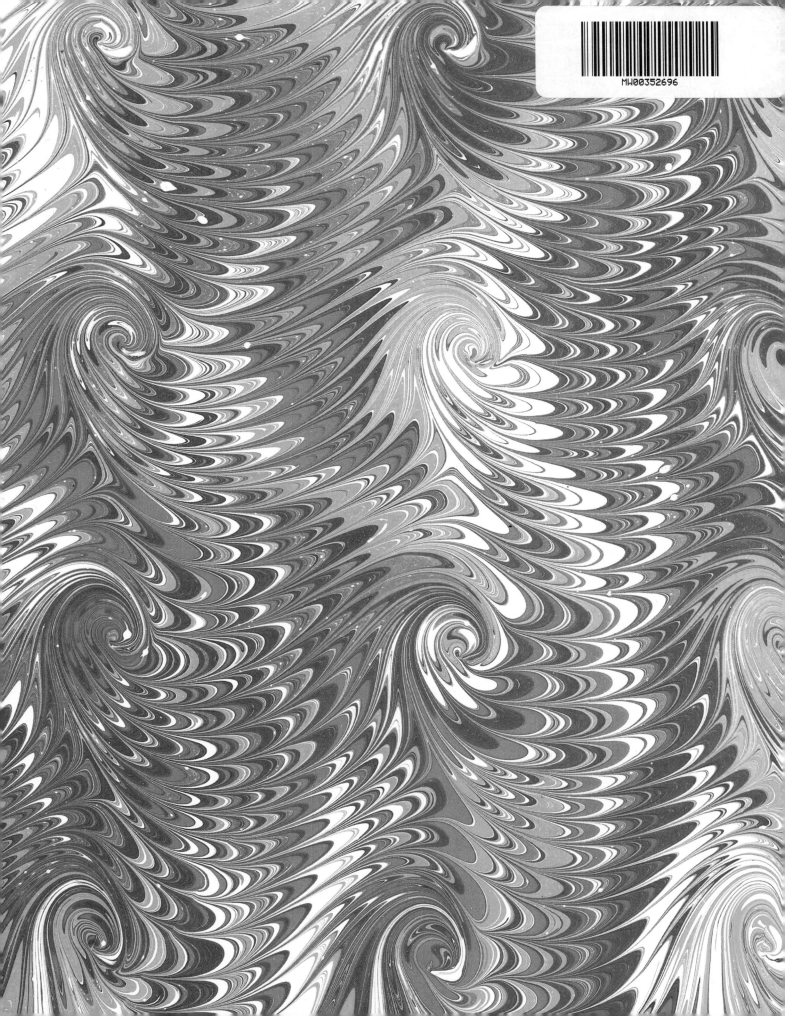

MW00352696

WAFFEN-SS COMMANDERS

Also by the Author
ALLGEMEINE-SS: THE COMMANDS, UNITS AND LEADERS OF THE GENERAL SS
IMAGES OF THE WAFFEN-SS: A PHOTO CHRONICLE OF GERMANY'S ELITE TROOPS
RIDING EAST: THE SS CAVALRY BRIGADE IN POLAND AND RUSSIA 1939-1942
SS-STURMBANNFÜHRER ERNST AUGUST KRAG

WAFFEN-SS COMMANDERS

THE ARMY, CORPS AND DIVISIONAL LEADERS OF A LEGEND

AUGSBERGER to KREUTZ

MARK C. YERGER

Schiffer Military History
Atglen, PA

This volume is sincerely dedicated to the following for their help
and valued friendship:

Otto Baum
Leslie DiNizo
Kurt Imhoff
Hans Kempin (†)
Ernst August Krag (†)
Karl Kreutz
Otto Kumm
Josef Lainer
Fritz Langanke
James Lucas
Jess Lukens
John Moore
George Nipe
Phil A. Nix
Ruth Sommers
Otto Weidinger (†)
and
Truppenkameradschaft
"DF"

Book Design by Robert Biondi.

Printed in the United States of America.
ISBN: 0-7643-0356-2

We are interested in hearing from authors with book ideas on related topics.

Published by Schiffer Publishing Ltd.
4880 Lower Valley Road
Atglen, PA 19310
Phone: (610) 593-1777
FAX: (610) 593-2002
E-mail: Schifferbk@aol.com.
Please write for a free catalog.
This book may be purchased from the publisher.
Please include $3.95 postage.
Try your bookstore first.

FOREWORD

This is the story of the divisional commanders of the Waffen-SS, a part of the German Wehrmacht. These nearly one million soldiers have been defamed in an unimaginable way since the end of World War II and this continues today.

Service in the Waffen-SS, and its heroic combats on many fronts, was and is according to the Federal Republic of Germany, not valued as military service. We ask what our almost 300,000 men killed in action served as, if not as soldiers. We fought for Germany. Germany is our country and from it we ask nothing more than justice.

We are bound in gratitude to my close friend Mark C. Yerger for writing this series of biographies of the senior commanders, as well as for writing his other books. Many of the commanders characterized the image of the Waffen-SS in an outstanding manner.

Many commanders came from our youth, having not seen World War I or had been just children at the time. By the end of the Second World War they had to bear the highest responsibilities for the men of their commands while still only in their 30s.

I hope this book will aid in correcting the distorted image of the brave soldiers of the Waffen-SS that has existed since the end of the war.

Otto Kumm
SS-Brigadeführer a.D.

CONTENTS

ACKNOWLEDGEMENTS

The list of people I owe a debt of gratitude for assisting with this volume is lengthy. Each contributed not only knowledge, but time, patience and much appreciated friendship. The reader also owes each of them a debt of thanks, for their help leaves a signature of detail, accuracy and desire to see history recorded as accurately as possible.

My mentor Otto Weidinger (†) still provides personal motivation for me more than half a decade after his death. This series was conceived during a lengthy walk with him in Aalen, during which we outlined the topics of Waffen-SS books that needed to be written. I hope this is how he envisioned the presentation, and his personal insights into the divisional commanders of "Das Reich" provided the first separation of fact from fiction.

Otto Baum has been a friend, mentor and sounding board for me during the past decade. His help with this and numerous other volumes, in addition to my continuous research into "Das Reich" and his own military career, continues to be a priceless gift. His efforts on my behalf have been far more than I could ever have wished for or expected. My deepest thanks to both him and his wife.

I want to thank Otto Kumm for writing the foreword and for his assistance with his biography. He has proved to be unwavering in both support and contribution as an historian. Few other veterans have campaigned for the historical and social rights of their former troops as has he. His own contributions to numerous texts, being the creator of HIAG and serving as the anchor of numerous individual veteran groups, make him an acknowledged leader of great character throughout his lifetime. As commander of "Prinz Eugen" and later the last commander of the "Leibstandarte," his biography will appear in volume 2.

Ruth Sommers hears everything, reads everything and provides the balanced advice needed in all phases of my work. Without her support and help this book, as well as the last four, would never have been written.

Kurt Imhoff helped immensely with support, photographic material and suggestions. A prolific author on the combat engineer units of the Waffen-SS, his friendship is a prized possession as is my ability to help him with his research.

My friend John Moore helps more than any other historian with every project. He tirelessly assists with information and material as well as often-needed advice. His published study of Waffen-SS signals officers is definitive. Our partnership in another large Waffen-SS project hopefully will provide a new standard of research with a previously unexamined topic. Now that he's pushed me into the second phase of computer use, I am all the more terrified of the electronic age.

Despite a hectic professional schedule, Ignacio Arrondo made his own extensive reference library and detailed knowledge available, making numerous corrections and suggestions with the manuscript data. He also enabled me to see where clarity was less than I wished and eliminate those problems. His contribution was both priceless and deeply appreciated.

Karl Kreutz not only helped with his own biography, which he considered of less importance than the story of his unit, but also assisted tremendously with all facets of my ongoing study of the artillery regiment of "Das Reich."

Hans Kempin (†), despite a then time-consuming business of his own, allowed me the privilege of being the only historian he started and maintained contact with. His dozens of lengthy letters in reply to my questions are a priceless insight into his career and commands. Having met him was also my good fortune and pleasure.

George Nipe has continued to assist the author, who can't draw a straight line using a ruler, with drawings and maps. His skills provided the tactical symbol explanations and the map illustrating the tactical situation resulting in Otto Baum's award of the Knight's Cross. His study of the Mius battles, "Decision in the Ukraine," is definitive and has made previous texts covering the topic obsolete.

Over the years, I had the privilege of meeting and/or corresponding with several other divisional commanders. I would like to thank Arthur Silgailis, Sylvester Stadler (†), Karl Ullrich (†), Richard Schulze-Kossens (†), Theodor Wisch (†), Heinz Harmel and Gustav Lombard (†) for their patience and time in replying to numerous inquiries. All provided additional documentation, information and photographs.

Al Brandt started as a militaria collector and developed into a higher species: historian. His linguistic skills, dedication to historical preservation and thirst for knowledge are total. Aside from helping me in all phases of research, his own full-length study of Knight's Cross holder Remy Schrijnen will be a welcome biographical account in the history of the Waffen-SS when it is released. I hope his horrendous workload still allows him to consider co-authoring a divisional history with me in the future.

A special thanks goes to James Lucas who provided warmth, encouragement and much welcome linguistic humor when desperately needed. His second volume of "Hitler's Enforcers" is eagerly awaited by this author. I also want to thank Roger James Bender, Jost W. Schneider, Munin Verlag, the Berlin Document Center and Ullstein for photographic help. The patience of Bob Biondi in this project and its design has eased potential stress in that area.

As always, Jess Lukens made his photographic collection available and this allows a more complete presentation than would have been possible otherwise. I'd also like to thank Bob Ruman and "Articles of War" for handling my necessary reference book needs and allowing me the time saved with the ability to get all my text needs from a single source.

Henry Deemer read the manuscript and added much in the form of grammatical corrections and suggestions despite a horrendous personal schedule. He is also a source of constant humor that eases some of the normal stress in my occupation. If any readers are glad I write, a word of thanks is due Hank since he was my first mentor.

Phil Nix helped with his own notes, corrections and suggestions, despite being heavily involved in his own book on another facet. Since I'm involved with that project as well, his efforts are doubly appreciated.

Many thanks are due to my mother and younger sister for a variety or reasons. Without the help of Dawn Sheffield, I'd still be refiling the research material for my last four books. For that and more she is adored. Likewise appreciated is the friendships extended to me by Mark Burkholder and Linda Lease. Peter Schiffer and Bob Biondi allow me the freedom of subject choice, as well as design input with all my books, both of which are deeply appreciated along with their support. Also enjoyed were the many kind letters from the readership regarding the other recent texts released. The many others who offered help, advice or suggestions are thanked as well.

Fred, my cat, continued his unique contribution. On the advice of several colleagues, I obtained a second feline in the hope Fred would be more occupied during my absence for research. The result is the addition of Ralph to a crowded work area. Together they constitute a conspiracy against my sanity at regular intervals. However, I prefer their company to a variety of my fellow humans.

Mark C. Yerger

INTRODUCTION

The essence of this two-volume series will allow the reader to examine the individuals who were higher unit commanding officers in some of the most successful and influential combat formations produced by any country in this century. The abilities and accomplishments of the units of the Waffen-SS, in both defense and offense, remain legendary. I hope to add to the recorded knowledge of these units by examining their commanders. Perhaps I can also clarify some incorrect concepts that linger more than half a century after the Second World War has ended.

The subject of the entire SS being judged as a criminal organization has been examined in depth previously to the point where the reader most likely already has an opinion. That opinion, be it partly or totally negative or positive, can only be reinforced or changed by continually assimilating all possible texts and period documentation. An open-minded approach, void of any emotional or political connection, is also essential. With regard to published texts, that open-mindedness and a more knowledgeable approach seems to be most often obtained from those researching due to interest in the field versus those using the subject solely in pursuit of scholastic qualifications. Academically acquired credentials have not always been matched by equal amounts of *knowledge*.

Individuals in any type of study should be judged as such. A collective judgment by any historian, regardless of perspective, serves no worthwhile contribution to understanding. The majority of soldiers in all countries during all wars are living and striving for the same goals: to serve their country, to attain victory and to survive.

The collective judgment arrived upon by the Allied trial system designating the entire SS as a criminal organization did not decree automatic guilt of unlawful acts by *all* member individuals.

This blanket verdict of organizational guilt created flaws both in the legal and moral sense, which can be expected of a victor punishing a vanquished. A desire for a prompt trial also allowed insufficient time for all facts and perspectives to be considered. This was the case for the SS as well as other groups and numerous specific individuals.

Among these faults was the exclusion of obviously guilty components, such as not indicting the entire Ordnungspolizei (Order Police or Orpo) for closer examination of its activities. While civilian municipal police have the same duties in any country, numerous independent Orpo units in Russia, subordinated to Higher SS and Police Leaders, carried out illegal acts. The police were, however, needed in the post-war period for normal civil operations, so its wartime subordination to Himmler (and thus the SS) was overlooked. The singling out of individuals to represent groups exonerated from prosecution, such as Alfred Jodl and Wilhelm Keitel, who were executed, while the High Command of the Army and High Command of the Armed Forces were not indicted, was obviously unjust regardless of one's opinion or perspective. A counter to this statement might be that these two men were next under Hitler within the military chain of command and were available for trial. However, in trials held in recent times (Vietnam and My Lai) the actual perpetrator (a junior field grade officer) was tried for a crime and his superiors not held accountable. This involves those responsible for crimes in the field during wartime. Instigating war, a crime against humanity, was not the decision of those senior Army officers. Hitler's total control and authority makes it questionable as to whether these two men had any actual decision-making authority without a directive from their Führer. Also, as is historically known, it was Hitler who wished to pursue a European war which he did as the undisputed and singular elected civil authority of Germany. The actions of persons subordinate to a legally-elected , then dictatorship, as far as being responsible for the decisions, decrees or actions of that leader, remains a legal argument for the crimes against humanity charges against many individuals.

Finally, the dismissal of charges against, or pardoning of, obviously guilty individuals (such as numerous commanders of the Einsatzgruppen in the early 1950s) leaves open to question why justice was to be served only if politically advantageous instead of always. Numerous persons considered criminal by the legal precedents laid down at the primary trials were protected by various Allied intelligence, scientific and military groups due to their value in the post-war years, out-weighing the less perceived need to see justice fulfilled. A study of the legal proceedings, to include persons or groups punished as well as those excluded from indictment, shows the post-war trial system against Germans accused of war crimes to be flawed in numerous instances. This is especially true when punishment was handed down only due to membership in a group despite no crimes having been committed by that individual. These ranged from fines and longer-than-normal prisoner of war status, to being denied equal job or career opportunities in post-war Germany.

Former Waffen-SS men tried by communist judicial authorities, particularly in Russia, Poland and Yugoslavia, received infinitely harsher (often death) sentences than were recommended for the same persons by counterpart Western legal systems prior to their being extradited, such as in the case of Jürgen Wagner. In several instances, examination of the facts in these trials shows justice came in the form of simple revenge by a former adversary who had been previously defeated in combat. Accounts of the fighting style in Yugoslavia, while extremely harsh, were historically typical in that sphere of society and its methods were used by both opponents. It was the sole area where large scale (divisional size) anti-partisan warfare was conducted with material support for Tito's partisans being provided by the Allies. The fate of Waffen-SS men captured or extradited to that country, primarily from the "Prinz Eugen" Division, was abnormally harsh and no account was taken of similar fighting methods employed by opposition partisan forces. That excesses occurred in this theater by both sides is unfortunate but a trait and reality of that style of combat. However, no Yugoslavian partisan leaders were ever tried by German courts for actions of a similar nature. Anti-partisan warfare is illegal by international agreement and only the German response to that type of action was tried by courts of law. An unbalanced pursuit of justice is a cloud on the democratic process.

A constant effort has existed to continue making some group or individual newsworthy (and potentially punishable) as being responsible for the millions of non-combat related deaths during the Third Reich. The concentration camp system was a separately-run entity within the SS. Unfortunately, when individuals were available to be prosecuted who had been directly connected to the horrific crimes of the Holocaust, they often escaped prosecution or punishment. The reasons for this were varied. Among the primary reasons were what was politically expedient at that time and legal developments in the countries involved with jurisdiction for the individual cases. Persons connected to military service within the SS (Waffen-SS) have often been targeted as the emotional substitute of the directly Holocaust-related group of perpetrators. Approximately 60,000 men served in the concentration camp system, most of whom never saw any military service. More than 900,000 men served in the Waffen-SS during its existence. This latter group being condemned is due in part because of their visibility since they have the legal right to meet at military veteran reunions in post-war Germany, the same as other armed forces units of the period. Being acknowledged by military historians as elite combat troops does not deter those who automatically categorize all who served in the SS as automatically connected to the concentration camp system. The fact that these units are admired and respected, and a constant source of interest to readers, historians and scholars, fuels the fire of agitation burning in those seeking revenge for the non-military actions that resulted in so many millions of deaths during the Third Reich period. While it is understandable to direct hatred towards the perpetrators of the Holocaust, it is wrong to channel that anger towards others not directly responsible. Those groups or individuals guilty of massive deaths or suffering inflicted on innocent people should be punished. At the same time, those unconnected and *innocent* of such horrible acts should not be made the emotional substitute for others who *were* guilty. This happens often, especially in current day Germany due to actions of the press, anti-German activists, war crimes researchers and others.

There is the question of acts of an illegal nature perpetrated by units in the field, such as the Malmedy incident. Though these actions occurred, are not denied, and are regrettable, such acts were not done by the majority of Waffen-SS troops. Some historical question still exists of the validity of certain examples of this. Also, we will never know the number of Allied illegal acts of a similar nature. These did occur as well and in far more than one instance. Such action cannot be considered acceptable by victor or vanquished but, likewise, the limited percentage of persons involved, most often young and emotionally charged younger troops on both sides, should be kept in perspective.

One of the results of this post-war necessity to blame all was the elimination of various aspects of veterans benefits for former members of the Waffen-SS. An argument for this civil rights exclusion was put forth that only three armed forces existed and were divided by element: land/army, sea/navy, air/air force. Using that logic, veterans of the Waffen-SS were not allowed civil rights (pensions, etc.) granted to other men of Germany's armed forces and police. In logical response to that, the United States has four armed services, the fourth being our elite U.S. Marines.

Many of the men in this series could have written historically significant and valuable personal memoirs: Paul Hausser, Felix Steiner, Herbert Otto Gille, Georg Keppler and Josef Dietrich among many others. In the initial post-war decade, the recollections of former German Army commanders made acceptable and popular publishing matter. Unfortunately, that initial wave of Army memoirs, in order to alienate themselves from the SS in any way, often negated or forgot the military contributions of Waffen-SS formations. Proof of those sacrifices, and the comments by Army commanders in period documentation, show a different opinion at that time in the eyes of Army leaders begging for Waffen-SS formations. Army commanders submitted and/or concurred with the granting of major awards to men in this series for their military contribution as well as that of their units. In addition, it was Army corps or higher commanders who provided the evaluations partly resulting in promotions at divisional commander level. Some of the better Army commanders have acknowledged the excellence of Waffen-SS units in their recollections including von Manstein, von Mellenthin and Guderian.

In the case of the Waffen-SS, the senior commanders were involved in the immediate post-war period with simply trying to write the introductory texts on the group itself (Paul Hausser and Felix Steiner) or organizing veterans to seek compensation for unavailable post-war soldier's benefits such as Otto Kumm's forming the basis of HIAG (the reciprocal aid society of former members of the Waffen-SS) in Hamburg during 1950. Herbert Otto Gille created "Wiking Ruf" magazine (which developed into "Der Freiwillige") and still serves as the official periodical of Waffen-SS veterans after almost fifty years of publication.[1] The more personal recollections and unique perspectives of individual military leaders or events are forever lost and that is a tragedy. The obvious personal modesty of those military commanders and decorated officers I have met or corresponded with, leads this author to conclude most felt their individual biographies were of little importance in comparison to the overall history of the actual units and the men under their command. Of the more than a dozen divisional commanders I have known, all were adamant in their belief the men under them earned them their positions, rank and decorations rather than their own individual performance. This opinion was also evident in the other ranks, judging from my contact with more than two hundred Knight's Cross holders or commanders of units less than divisional in size.

Several higher formation leaders contributed detailed written histories of units they served with or commanded, laying the groundwork for future military researchers. Among these authors are Rudolf Lehmann ("Leibstandarte"), Otto Kumm ("Prinz Eugen"), Sylvester Stadler (II.SS-Panzer-Korps at Kursk), Karl Ullrich ("Totenkopf"),

Arthur Silgailis (Latvian Waffen-SS units), Franz Schreiber ("Nord"), Richard Schulze-Kossens (SS Officer Schools), and Hubert Meyer ("Hitlerjugend"). A special note of acknowledgment is owed to Walter Harzer ("SS-Polizei-Division") for his many years of objective research and gathering of historical information while official HIAG historian.

In some areas of academic snobbery these books are rejected since they do not follow the current trend of acceptably documented format. Persons with a more intelligent and open-minded desire to learn have accepted them as priceless since they are compiled by the men *who were actually there* and also take advantage of privately-held documentation of Waffen-SS veterans. They felt no need to prove the facts since they *participated* in the events, unlike historians of a later period who must prove statements with paper documentation.

Though each person in this series is an individual, most fall within basic groups depending upon their age and background. Many were well-educated. Having passed their Abitur, they were allowed to pursue advanced education or higher technical training. The most senior commanders, who comprise the first group, were officers in World War I and/or had graduated from cadet training in the pre-World War I era. The second group worked their way through the ranks by their deeds and individual performances, a somewhat more difficult task in the more class-conscious Army of that time. This was a primary factor that led many men to chose the SS-Verfügungstruppe, and later the Waffen-SS, as their career or service option. The third group were the graduates of the SS officer schools in the pre-war years who became senior staff officers or regimental commanders before obtaining a divisional command.[2] Professional civil police officers with additional military training formed a smaller fourth group.[3] Another group, though probably the smallest, was composed of trained Army officers who transferred to the Waffen-SS. Similarly, some men with high rank in other branches of the SS also served in combat with the Waffen-SS. These men normally accepted an initially lower rank as reserve officers (designated with the suffix d.R.) before eventually seeing fully active service and earning a command. As reserve officers they were to retain their Waffen-SS rank until the end of the war while fully active ranks would retain the rank permanently.

The final small classification group were the high-ranking police generals who attained their rank and position solely within the pre-war and wartime Allgemeine-SS. These were primarily former Higher SS and Police Leaders at corps command level.[4] Himmler

---

[1] The magazine contains historical articles, death notices and current day commentary, the latter being the views of the editorial and questionable if the thoughts of all former members.

[2] The two primary officer schools were at Braunschweig and Bad Tölz, though the SS military training system expanded far beyond those facilities. See Schulze-Kossens, Richard: "Die Junkerschulen."

[3] These men are found throughout the formations and are not restricted as one may believe to the SS-Polizei-Division. For data on the units of the Ordnungspolizei see the Bundesarchiv publication "Die Geschichte der Ordnungspolizei, 1933-1945."

[4] For the units of the Allgemeine-SS, in which some men served at lower rank prior to the SS/Verfügungstruppe being formed, commanded units or held posts, see Yerger, Mark "Allgemeine-SS, The Commands, Units and Leaders of the General

appointed these men in the final year of the war due to their rank and, as the Reichsführer-SS felt it necessary, their brutality in order to curb a catastrophic and collapsing front-line situation. These later Waffen-SS Generals, though officially commanders, lacked the leadership qualities, skills or combat experience to perform their commands effectively. They were quickly given Waffen-SS rank during the summer of 1944, initially to allow them to undertake the responsibilities of overseeing prisoners-of-war under the terms laid down in the Hague Convention. They were neither professional soldiers nor part of the pre-war tradition developed by Paul Hausser and others and their contribution was almost totally negative with regard to tactical skills, leadership, and accomplishments in the field. Of these only Heinz Reinefarth was acknowledged for bravery in combat against front line troops by winning the Knight's Cross in 1940 while serving with the Army as an NCO, a rarity at that point in time. It was Himmler's penchant for technically connecting individuals or groups such as this that resulted in a collective opinion or judgment by many authors, historians and legal experts. While officers in this category were *technically* members of the Waffen-SS, they cannot logically be compared to the regular career military-oriented officers that comprised the majority of those within the Waffen-SS, per se. These individuals constitute a "gray area" of commanders who affected the reputation of the majority and must be examined as such. This small group, aside from Reinefarth, includes Erich von dem Bach, Friedrich Jeckeln and Curt von Gottberg. While they had some success against lesser partisan formations, they were less than competent as higher formation commanders. All armies produce a small percentage of incompetent officers who attain high rank or position by means other than the possession of military skills.

Retrospective historical categorization exists for units as well. While the "Totenkopf" Division was formed from armed unit cadre existing in the pre-war concentration camp guard unit system, by the end of the war losses had turned over the manpower of the division several times over with men that were in no way connected to or trained in the system developed prior to 1939 by Theodor Eicke, the first commander of the division.

Logic dictates that there is an obvious difference between the composition of this unit from its start until its dissolution in 1945. While a knowledgeable and objective reader is aware that Theodor Eicke headed the pre-war concentration camp system, not every man who served in "Totenkopf" from 1939 to 1945 was a concentration camp guard. Eicke did use the camp system as punishment during his command tenure, sending those who incurred his wrath to guard positions, or in some instances, as inmates. A percentage of those recruited in the pre-war camp system survived through the

war, serving in both Waffen-SS and Army units. Although this division's formation is unique, its beginnings are used for much negative bias against all Waffen-SS formations. From a military standpoint, this was also among the best offensive and defensive formations that fought on the Eastern Front. The unit suffered heavy losses and its original personnel complement replaced several times over during the war with recruits or draftees in no way connected to its earlier development. Again, individuals, as well as actions or units, should be judged on an individual basis.

The success and reputation of a commander depends on the same factors in any war: the training and morale of his troops, their equipment and condition, quality of the opposition, supply, knowledge of the enemy and simple luck. Paul Hausser is to be credited for the excellent training of the early formations and developing the SS officer school system. Some excellent commanders were not always a success, while the reverse is also feasible. Herbert Otto Gille and Georg Keppler were among the finest corps commanders of the Waffen-SS, but their multiple skills could do nothing in the final months of the war to reverse the situation at the front. Despite Fritz Freitag's narrow scope of understanding of foreign troops and mediocre at best leadership skills at divisional level, his units did surprisingly well in combat. Likewise, a man can be a great or effective leader (there is a difference) without being an able strategist or tactician. Theodor Eicke was an effective leader whose personality and will were imposed, at times brutally, on his command. His reputation as an abnormally harsh disciplinarian and poor strategist does not detract from the reputation for toughness his command earned in battle. Josef Dietrich also lacked the tactical skills, but was a great commander of men with true concern for those he led. He also had seen a great deal of combat in World War I. In many cases, much credit for the commander's success and reputation must be given to the divisional 1a (1.Generalstabsoffizier or First General Staff Officer) or Chief of Staff at corps level. In all cases, these men contributed highly to the achievements of these various commanders, most of whom maintained the lead-from-the-front style of German officers that made them so popular (and effective) with their men. Many men who served in a senior staff post eventually rose to command a division or corps, such as Fritz Freitag, Matthias Kleinheisterkamp, Otto Kumm, Rudolf Lehmann, Karl Gesele and Werner Ostendorfff.

Next, there is the question of whom to include within the study. While this is obvious in many cases, another gray area exists in qualifying an individual for inclusion with the later units formed. In some cases it became a matter of judgment or opinion, such as Jakob Fick being excluded for his two-day command of "Götz von Berlichingen" while Christian Tychsen's similar length leadership of "Das Reich" is within the series, as this author is convinced Tychsen would have become a permanent commander had he not been killed. Some held only divisional formation staff posts and these are not included, unless, of course, they continued or com-

SS." This volume includes the Higher SS and Police Leaders, SS and Police Leaders, Main Districts (Oberabschnitte), Districts (Abschnitte) and Standarten (Regiments) for both foot as well as riding units.

manded elsewhere.[5] An exception to this is made in rare instances, such as the case of Peter Hansen, who is included due to his influence with the Latvian and Italian units (as well as the Waffen-SS artillery). With the exception of Kampfgruppe "Nord," due to being the initial large Waffen-SS mountain formation, precursor formation commanders prior to a division being formed, are excluded. One example is Conrad Schellong's command of the 6.SS-Sturmbrigade "Langemarck." In this instance, the eventual 27.SS-Freiwilligen-Grenadier-Division "Langemarck," only Thomas Müller is considered the actual divisional commander and included as such. Likewise, Michael Broser and Zoltan von Pisky, having only been assigned to formation staff duties with the two Hungarian divisional units, excludes them. Other examples excluded within the same general limitations are Viktor Knapp, Albert Doerheit and Martin Kohlroser, as they only commanded the SS-Freiwilligen-Grenadier-Brigade "Landstorm Nederland." Michael Lippert is included as the only leader of the 34.SS-Grenadier-Division "Landstorm Nederland." Likewise, Dr. Oskar Dirlewanger is considered the commander of the "Dirlewanger" Brigade, while Fritz Schmedes will be considered the tactical leader and actual ranking authority of the 36.Waffen-Grenadier-Division der SS.

The same rules apply to corps commands existing on paper and their respective commanders, such as Franz Vitez Feketehalmy-Czeydner, Eugen Vitez Ruszakay-Ranzenberger and the Hungarian SS corps.[6] Again, men whose command excludes them in one instance will often be within the series due to other commands. Most commanders of the independent SS brigades are found due to other commands.[7] Some are deleted, as subordinates actually held the command while they were only titular or technically commanders, such as Karl Wolff (Supreme SS and Police Leader, as well as senior military commander in Italy) with the 29.Waffen-Grenadier-Division der SS (italienische Nr. 1).[8] In instances where command-

ers were killed and command position was briefly vacant before a replacement arrived, normally the 1a (division) or chief of staff (corps) handled the day-to-day operations. In some rare cases, these became officially assigned temporary commanders for extended periods and are included as combat formation commanders, such as Hubert Meyer's command of the 12.SS-Panzer-Division "Hitlerjugend" after the capture of Kurt Meyer. Briefer instances, such as Hans-Joachim Mützelfeldt, are excluded.[9] In all cases the divisional 1a, corps Chief of Staff or a senior regimental commander held temporary command when the unit leader attended strategy sessions, meetings, ceremonies, etc.

Dual commands were possible for a single unit within the same period. One such example is Heinz Lammerding and his command of "Das Reich." While officially divisional commander, he led a Kampfgruppe of divisional elements in Russia while Sylvester Stadler commanded the reforming portions of the division in France. Similar were the movements and dividing of the SS-Polizei Division in 1944, in which case all commanders are within the series, and the divisional expansion of "Nord" while the original Kampfgruppe existed.

Another unique situation was the 33.Waffen-Grenadier-Division der SS "Charlemagne." Because a German formation had to have a German as its senior authority, since he had the powers of a judge within the unit, this division had a French commander (Edgar Puaud), as well as an overseeing German Inspector (Gustav Krukenberg and later Walter Zimmermann). In this instance, all three are included.

Likewise unique was the establishment of a post and appointment of an Infanterieführer (Arthur Silgailis) with the Latvian corps (VI.Waffen-Armee-Korps der SS (lettische). Although Silgailis' single week command of the 19.Waffen-Grenadier-Division der SS (lettische Nr. 2) alone technically allows his inclusion, he is equally included for holding that unique post within among the best of the foreign formations. Had a Latvian been allowed to officially and permanently command at divisional (or corps) level, it would no doubt have been Silgailis or the Inspector General of the Latvian Legion, Rudolf Bangerskis.

Temporary Army commanders at corps level are not included, since they were not given Waffen-SS rank and their story is already being written in detail by another series.[10] The dates of command

---

[5] Among this category are Dr. Hans Brand, Josef Berschneider and Carl Marks, who commanded the formation staff of the 24.Waffen-Gebirgs-(Kartsjäger) Division der SS. For this unit (among the most questionable as to actually being operational as a designated division), Werner Hahn is considered the sole commander with the final formation leader, Heinz Wagner, in command of the reduced and retitled Waffen-Gebirgs-(Karstjäger)Brigade der SS. Christoph Diehm held a similar formation staff post with the 29.Waffen-Grenadier-Division der SS (russische Nr.1). Diehm's command was absorbed by the 30.Waffen-Grenadier-Division der SS (russische Nr. 2) and the divisional number designation given to the Italian SS division. As such, Hans Siegling is given as the sole commander of a Russian volunteer division. For Diehm's career and photograph see Yerger, "Allgemeine-SS." The commander of the Kaminski Brigade, Bronislav Kaminski, is likewise excluded, since his unit staff was executed after the Warsaw trial by the SS and not used as cadre for Diehm's formation staff.

[6] Both men commanded the paper-only existing XVII.Waffen-Armee-Korps der SS (ungarisches). Bender/Taylor, "Uniforms, Organazation and History of the Waffen-SS," volume 5, page 241.

[7] Among those within that catagory are Karl Gesele, Carl-Maria Demelhuber, Karl von Treuenfeld, Fritz von Scholz, Richard Hermann, Hermann Fegelein, Fritz Freitag and Wilhelm Trabandt. The primary four separate brigades were the SS-Sturmbrigade "Reichsführer-SS," the SS-Kavallerie-Brigade and the 1. and 2.SS-Infanterie-Brigaden (mot). All were eventually incorporated into Waffen-SS divisions.

[8] As Supreme SS and Police Leader and Senior Military Commander in Italy, Wolff was technically commander of the 29.Waffen-Grenadier-Division der SS (italienische Nr. 1) but actual formation, then command, was handled by subordinates and deputies Peter Hansen, Constantin Heldmann and Otto Jungkunz.

[9] Mützelfeldt, a German Cross in Gold holder with the Flak Abteilung of "Das Reich," briefly oversaw the daily operational running of the 20.Waffen-Grenadier-Division der SS (estnische Nr.1) while its 1.Generalstabsoffizier (1a), between the death of Franz Augsberger and the arrival of his replacement, Berthold Maack.

[10] Though a few Army commanders briefly led Waffen-SS divisions due to field events, this was primarily done at corps level, including Martin Unrein (III.(germanisches)SS-Panzer-Korps), Günther Krappe (X.SS-Armee-Korps), Günther Blumentritt (XII.SS-Armee-Korps) and Eduard Crasemann (also XII.SS-Armee-Korps). The XV.Kosaken-Kavallerie-Korps, which came under SS control in November, 1944, and was led by Helmuth von Pannwitz, is not included due to its being an Army formation. Some texts incorrectly give several of these commanders SS rank (Pannwitz's staff was also entirely Army). Heinrich Himmler's disastrous periods as the commander of Heeresgruppen "Oberrhein" (Upper Rhine) and "Vistula" are not included as they were Army formations. Any normal function-

stated must be taken as worded since three dates can exist: the date a man was assigned command, the date he arrived at his command, and the day his command actually commenced. The terms temporary, substitute and full commander are somewhat academic. The man commanding was the commander. However, there is an overlap in some instances where a person was the "official" commander while another officer served as a "temporary" leader or "designated deputy" while the "official" commander was ill, wounded, in transit or reassigned.

Older commanders who served in units created and supported by a Land (state) or Kreis (province) in World War I and earlier will have these areas mentioned (kingdom or state) and the unit type with numerical designation within the Imperial German Army units list. In the case of the Austro-Hungarian Empire's units it will be explained when known if Common, Austrian or Hungarian wherever possible.[11] As this topic and its terminology is generally outside the scope of the WWII era reader, these units are given in English as are all decorations of individual Länder and foreign countries for both World Wars. In addition, equivalents are provided in the glossary. Third Reich unit terms and all ranks, more familiar to the reader though also within the glossary, are given in German. An individual could be promoted on one date but have the advance in rank be retroactive for purposes of seniority. Third Reich decorations are included where known with the exception of base-required qualification badges such as the SA Sports Badge in Bronze. Consulting the numerous volumes on the topic of awards and badges of honor will familiarize the reader with additional illustrations and

data for a given award aside from that provided within this volume.

The two primary Third Reich decorations relevant for bravery, leadership and contribution to the war effort were the Knight's Cross and its higher grades (Oakleaves, Swords and Diamonds) and the German Cross. While the Knight's Cross could be awarded for a single instance of personal bravery or military contribution (leadership), the German Cross was divided into two grades. The award in gold was applicable for multiple displays of bravery while the version in silver was awarded for contributions to the war effort. The latter was rarely awarded in comparison to the former throughout all German units and organizations. It is interesting to note that many men who qualified for the various grades of the SS Long Service Award, given for 4, 8, 12 and 25 years service, never received their award. A similar situation arises with the Long Service Award of the NSDAP, given for 10, 15 and 25 years service. The date of an award is the date it was approved with the actual presentation of the decoration coming normally sometime shortly afterwards when it was bestowed. While most award recommendations were placed within a short period of time after the events, in some rare cases this could be years later, such as in the case of Fritz Klingenberg's German Cross in Gold.

Men could hold ranks in several groups including primarily the Allgemeine-SS, Polizei, NSDAP and Waffen-SS. Likewise, dual commands were common, though most Allgemeine-SS, civil and Polizei posts were performed by substitutes while men served at the front in another capacity.

I have refrained from including the actual combat history of individual units as much as possible to concentrate on the individuals or combats in which they participated that resulted in the granting of recommendations for decorations. Where deemed necessary the numerous structural and title changes of various commands and units are noted. A simplified list of the primary commands is included, as well as an explanation of tactical symbols used in compiling Order of Battle charts for the various commands by the SS-Führungshauptamt. The charts themselves are within the biography an individual who commanded the unit (or one of its primary components) during the time frame of the specific chart. The appendix also provides the corps and divisional composition within the SS Field Post number list for 1943 in order to allow the reader to further envision the size and composition of the command itself. Additional charts and another Field Post list will be included in the second, concluding volume. Books on individual Waffen-SS units are numerous and growing, so consulting the bibliography, in which many entries include additional recommended reading, will allow the reader to cover the actions of a unit under a given commander.

The comments in some individual biographies hopefully give the reader a small basis to begin formulating an opinion on a given commander. These conclusions have been arrived at through period documentation, recollections or writings by subordinates, peers, and in some cases the individuals themselves.

---

ing of Himmler's two Army Group commands resulted from the efforts of his Chiefs of Staff, Werner Ostendorffff and Heinz Lammerding, who are included for their Waffen-SS divisional commands. For data on the General rank commanders of the German Army see "Deutschlands Generale und Admirale" being compiled by German publisher Biblio-Verlag. Teil IV of the series, "Die Generale des Heeres 1921-1945," covers the Army in twelve volumes, of which four have been released at the time of this writing.

[11] Many of the Waffen-SS commanders, including non-divisional leaders and staff, saw service in World War I (or earlier) with units of the Austro-Hungarian military. For that reason a brief description is necessary, since titles of units in that army, as seen in the biographies, was more defined by composition. In the Austro-Hungarian Empire's army, units composed of men from both Austria and Hungary were listed as the Common Army, solely from Austria as Landwehr units and solely from Hungary as Landwehr (Honved) in the case of infantry, for example. In pre-1914 units of Imperial Germany and the Austro-Hungarian Empire there were variations of infantry and cavalry. For example, Hussar were light cavalry with brilliant uniforms, Dragoner were heavily armed cavalry, Kürassier were cavalry wearing a cuirass or breast plate, Uhlan were cavalry with a lance (as were Lancers as a more general term). States raised, financially supported and originally garrisoned units with the names remaining part of the traditional title even when the states themselves changed. For unit structure and composition of pre-1918 units of the Imperial German Army see the four volumes by Wegner, Günther, "Stellenbesetzung der deutschen Heeres 1815-1939." For similar information on the Reichswehr, Freikorps and Landespolizei prior to absorption by the Wehrmacht, see Tessin, Georg, "Verbande und Truppen des Deutschen Heeres 1918-1939." The Austro-Hungarian Empire's units, their history, flags and traditions are exceptionally covered by James Lucas in "Fighting Troops of the Austro-Hungarian Army 1868-1914." The Austro-Hungarian monarchy consisted of the Imperial lands (Austria proper, Bohemia, Moravia, Austrian Silesia and Austrian Poland) and the Royal lands (Hungary, Transalvania, Croatia, Slovenia and part of Dalmatia). Ruled by the Emperor of Austria and the King of Hungary (the same individual), the Empire existed from 1867 to the end of World War I, when it broke up due to the aspirations of its numerous minorities.

The two primary SS officer training academies, Bad Tölz (above) and Braunschweig. Bad Tölz commenced its first class in 1934 under Paul Lettow, Braunschweig the following year under the supervision of Paul Hausser. Braunschweig was formerly a Prussian cadet school while Tölz was especially built for the SS and was the only one of the two buildings to survive the war. Braunschweig was destroyed in a 1944 air-raid.

It is impossible to say who was the greatest commander and each reader has an individual they consider the best, the bravest, or most interesting. However, with regard to overall influence and development of the Waffen-SS, there can be little doubt that Paul Hausser deservedly is referred to as the "Father of the Troop" by veterans of all units. A full-length biographical study of this largest-sized formation leader with Waffen-SS rank should be written and this author would be more than willing to contribute all the material he has. Naturally, arguments could be put forth for other leaders for their contribution to technical, tactical, and other advances initiated by the Waffen-SS.

My primary research interests being unit structural development and biographical, I have been queried by readers as to who I thought was a best commander (for the variety of reasons possible) or most interesting. My best response, though only a personal opinion, would be those commanders who served some aspect of their military service in "Das Reich" and its predecessor units of the SS-Verfügungstruppe. That categorization saves space in compiling what would no doubt be a lengthy list of individuals for various reasons, though it does not include all the commanders I consider to have been excellent. Additionally, many commanders are overlooked or unknown outside their individual units and rectifying that is a primary goal of this series.

These men are almost all deceased, both commanders and their former subordinates. I, myself, am of the last generation that had the opportunity to meet some of them and hear *their* side, *their* perspectives and *their* opinions. Their understandable initial hesitance with a foreign historian and researcher resulted from previous nuisance harassment by obsessive memorabilia collectors or the more serious concern that they should be rightfully studied as soldiers rather than criminals.

Granted, with so many individuals from a variety of backgrounds having lived through such diverse and tumultuous experiences, there are understandably a variety of personal political opinions. The vast majority of Waffen-SS veterans I have met personally or corresponded with were totally objective in their recollections of experiences, events or other individuals. Readers of my previous books are aware that I have no interest in the boredom of politics. However, to reply to several inquiries as to whether I have ever been engaged in political discussion or questioned regarding the same, the answer is a flat no. My purpose and interest with this subject is strictly that of the historian who has been understood and accepted even by the tiny minority that are motivated politically. With regard to honorable character, courage, loyalty of friendship and desire for knowledge, there are no better examples this author can name than some of the individuals he has met who served in these formations. However, that is only my own opinion based on research and personal contact.

Emotion, revenge and politics in the post-war years seem to remain a cloud covering many of the facts for some historians. Those who condemn the entire Waffen-SS as criminals offer as little knowledge contribution as those who are motivated with blanket opposite opinions inspired by purely political interests. Neither offers any neutral educational contribution. Logical consumption of facts is a far more constructive time expenditure. In doing this, one eventually sees the mass majority of these men and the troops under their command for what they were, a group of field combat soldiers who greatly influenced the development of modern warfare.

Finally, I would hope that perhaps this volume might motivate others to undertake the research and writing of a text in this field. Though not a financially lucrative undertaking, as any who have compiled a book can attest, the intangible rewards are priceless. One learns, comprehends, and, at least in my experience, meets a wonderful group of fellow researchers. Equally satisfying for myself has been the opportunity to know many of the actual personalities involved in the topic. That has been a priceless experience.

As always, I welcome contact with other SS researchers and the readership. Any additional information, either photographic or factual, sent to me will be added to an addendum in the concluding volume. Especially needed at this time for the concluding volume, aside from those not illustrated in this volume, are photographs of the following divisional commanders: Thomas Müller, Karl von Treuenfeld, Michael Lippert, Herbert von Obwurzer, Rudiger Pipkorn, and Hans Siegling.

Mark C. Yerger
P.O. Box 4485
Lancaster, PA 17604 U.S.A.

THE COMMANDS

Though the first division of the Waffen-SS was formed in October, 1939, the first corps formation did not exist until mid-1942. The actual major expansion of the divisional units began in 1943, with ten being in existence by the time of the 1943 Field Post list compilation (see appendix) and a total of nine being formed in that year alone. Many units saw a progression of name designations and by October, 1943, a renumbering system allotted a numerical designation for each corps, division and the primary regiments (infantry, cavalry or mountain within each division). That system started with the "Leibstandarte" as the first division and containing the first two regiments. All divisions had designated names with many being accorded these as honor titles which appeared as a uniform cufftitle. Additionally, some regiments and, in rare instances, other units also had a similar title. Among these were

regiments "Deutschland," "Germania," and "Der Führer" from the pre-war period. Titles given to units during war-time most often honored fallen commanders or prominent names associated with the Nazi Party. Most divisions contained two regiments of primary troops by mid-war, either infantry, mountain or cavalry. Foreign units with three primary regiments were most often severely understrength. In general, units with a "Freiwilligen" (volunteer) prefix in their title constitute primarily foreign "volunteer" units while those with "Waffen" (armed) were of what was determined to be those of lesser quality foreign conscripts. Panzergrenadier (armored infantry) were in both armor as well as motorized infantry units.[1] The following list shows the Armies, Corps and Divisions at their peak (not necessarily final) designation followed by their original activation period and, where applicable, cufftitle:

6.SS-Panzer-Armee	(October 1944)
Armeegruppe "Steiner"-Armeeoberkommando 11[2]	(March 1945)
I.SS-Panzer-Korps "Leibstandarte"	(July 1943)
II.SS-Panzer-Korps[3]	(May 1942)
III.(germ.)SS-Panzer-Korps	(April 1943)
IV.SS-Panzer-Korps[4]	(June 1943)
V.SS-Freiwilligen-Gebirgs-Korps	(July 1943)
VI.Waffen-Armee-Korps der SS (lettische)	(October 1943)
VII.SS-Panzer-Korps[5]	(October 1943)
IX.Waffen-Gebirgs-Korps der SS	(June 1944)
X.Armee-Korps der SS[6]	(January 1945)

[1] The first four divisions to receive tanks were still designated as Panzer-Grenadier units more than a year after the addition of an armored regiment had actually made them Panzer Divisions (their titles were changed later in all cases).
[2] Staffed only with a far-less-than-Armee-sized number of attached units.
[3] Formed as SS-Generalkommando, it was actually the first corps formed.
[4] Formation suspended from end of August, 1943, to June, 1944. Formation continued from elements of the headquarters of VII.SS-Panzer-Korps.
[5] Ordered absorbed by the IV.SS-Panzer-Korps on June 30, 1944.
[6] Formed from the staff of the XIV.SS-Armee-Korps.

XI.SS-Armee-Korps[7]	(July 1944)
XII.SS-Armee-Korps	(August 1944)
XIII.SS-Armee-Korps	(August 1944)
XIV.SS-Armee-Korps	(November 1944)
XV.Kosaken-Kavallerie-Korps[8]	(November 1944)
XVI.SS-Armee-Korps	(January 1945)
XVII.Waffen-Armee-Korps der SS (ungarische)[9]	(January 1945)
XVIII.SS-Armee-Korps	(February 1945)

Final Divisional Designation	**Divisional Status First Assigned**	**Divisional Cufftitle**
1.SS-Panzer-Division "Leibstandarte"[10]	(June 1941)[11]	Adolf Hitler
2.SS-Panzer-Division "Das Reich"[12]	(October 1939)	Das Reich
3.SS-Panzer-Division "Totenkopf"[13]	(October 1939)	Totenkopf
4.SS-Polizei-Panzer-Grenadier-Division[14]	(October 1939)	SS-Polizei-Division[15]
5.SS-Panzer-Division "Wiking"[16]	(December 1940)	Wiking
6.SS-Gebirgs-Division "Nord"	(June 1941)[17]	Nord
7.SS-Freiwilligen-Gebirgs-Division "Prinz Eugen"[18]	(March 1942)	Prinz Eugen
8.SS-Kavallerie-Division "Florian Geyer"[19]	(June 1942)	Florian Geyer
9.SS-Panzer-Division "Hohenstaufen"[20]	(January 1943)	Hohenstaufen
10.SS-Panzer-Division "Frundsberg"[21]	(January 1943)	Frundsberg
11.SS-Freiwilligen-Panzer-Grenadier-Division "Nordland"[22]	(March 1943)	Nordland
12.SS-Panzer-Division "Hitlerjugend"[23]	(June 1943)	Hitlerjugend
13.Waffen-Gebirgs-Division der SS "Handschar" (kroatische Nr.1)[24]	(March 1943)	
14.Waffen-Grenadier-Division der SS (galizische Nr.1)[25]	(June 1943)	
15.Waffen-Grenadier-Division der SS (lettische Nr.1)[26]	(February 1943)	
16.SS-Panzer-Grenadier-Division "Reichsführer-SS"[27]	(October 1943)	Reichsführer-SS
17.SS-Panzer-Grenadier-Division "Götz von Berlichingen"	(October 1943)	Götz von Berlichingen
18.SS-Freiwilligen-Panzer-Grenadier-Division "Horst Wessel"[28]	(January 1944)	Horst Wessel
19.Waffen-Grenadier-Division der SS (lettische Nr.2)	(January 1944)	

---

[7] Taken over from the Army, it was previously Generalkommando V.Armee-Korps.

[8] Originally numbered XIV. then changed to its final designation on December 27, 1944.

[9] Existed on paper only, it was to have controlled the two Hungarian SS divisions which were only ordered to be corps components in January, 1945.

[10] Developed from Hitler's personal bodyguard unit, some of its elements were larger and more lavishly equipped than a normal Waffen-SS division.

[11] Existed as a reinforced regiment then a brigade prior to attaining divisional status. It was, along with "Das Reich," "Totenkopf" and "Wiking" actually a Panzer Division before being officially designated as such, having been given a tank regiment.

[12] Created in October, 1939, from the existing pre-war units of the SS/Verfügungstruppe including Regimenter "Deutschland," "Germania" (which later went as cadre to "Wiking") and "Der Führer." The first division formed and deployed, it was awarded more Knight's Crosses (or its higher grades) than any other Waffen-SS unit. Although it only received tanks in 1942 and didn't use them in combat until 1943, it was the most successful German formation for the number of enemy tanks destroyed (4,800). In the opinion of the author, the best division in the Waffen-SS.

[13] Created in October, 1939, from existing concentration camp guard units, it attained a superlative reputation in defensive engagements.

[14] Formed from personnel of the Ordnungspolizei (Order Police) with three regiments. When reformed in 1943 it was reduced to two SS-Polizei-Grenadier-Regimenter.

[15] The earliest version cufftitle was the Polizei symbol (eagle and wreath).

[16] The first multi-national division, it was presented more awards of the German Cross in Gold than any other division. It was formed as "Germania" but had its name changed to avoid confusion with the existing regiment of the same name.

[17] Existed as Kampfgruppe "Nord" since March, 1941.

[18] Created for and primarily used in anti-partisan warfare in Yugoslavia from Rumanian Volksdeutsche.

[19] Formed from a cadre of the SS Cavalry Brigade and Hungarian ethnic Germans, it had four cavalry regiments (15, 16, 17, 18) until SS-Kavallerie-Regiment 17 was removed and eventually used as the for the 22.SS-Freiwilligen-Kavallerie-Division "Maria Theresia." It was destroyed in Budapest in February, 1945.

[20] "Hohenstaufen" and "Frundsberg" were both ordered created by Hitler in December, 1942, for combat in the West.

[21] Until November, 1943, titled "Karl der Grosse."

[22] Formed around the former "Nordland" Regiment of "Wiking."

[23] Formed from recruits of the Hitler Youth with "Leibstandarte" officer cadre.

[24] Formed from Croatian volunteers for partisan fighting in Yugoslavia.

[25] Composed of Ukrainian volunteers.

[26] Expanded from an existing Latvian Legion, it was, along with the other Latvian and Estonian units, possibly among the best foreign formations.

[27] Created by expanding the Sturmbrigade "Reichsführer-SS" which had been expanded from Himmler's personal escort battalion.

[28] Created by using the existing 1.SS-Infanterie-Brigade (mot) as cadre, it contained a large number of ethnic Germans though originally it was to be recruited from the SA.

[29] Expanded from an existing Estonian SS Legion.

20. Waffen-Grenadier-Division der SS (estnische Nr.1)[29]	(January 1944)	
21. Waffen-Gebirgs-Division der SS "Skanderbeg" (albanische Nr.1)[30]	(April 1944)	Skanderbeg
22. SS-Freiwilligen-Kavallerie-Division "Maria Theresia"[31]	(May 1944)	
23. Waffen-Gebirgs-Division der SS "Kama" (kroatische Nr.2)[32]	(June 1944)	
23. SS-Freiwilligen-Panzer-Grenadier-Division "Nederland"[33]	(February 1945)	Nederland
24. Waffen-Gebirgs-(Karstjäger)-Division der SS[34]	(July 1944)	
25. Waffen-Grenadier-Division der SS "Hunyadi" (ungarische Nr.1)[35]	(May 1944)	
26. Waffen-Grenadier-Division der SS "Hungaria" (ungarische Nr.2)[36]	(March 1945)	
27. SS-Freiwilligen-Grenadier-Division "Langemarck"[37]	(September 1944)	Langemarck
28. SS-Freiwilligen-Grenadier-Division "Wallonien"[38]	(September 1944)	Wallonien
29. Waffen-Grenadier-Division der SS (russische Nr.1)[39]	(August 1944)	
29. Waffen-Grenadier-Division der SS (italienische Nr.1)	(March 1945)	
30. Waffen-Grenadier-Division der SS (russische Nr.2)[40]	(August 1944)	
31. SS-Freiwilligen-Grenadier-Division[41]	(October 1944)	
32. SS-Freiwilligen-Grenadier-Division "30.Januar"	(January 1945)	
33. Waffen-Grenadier-Division der SS "Charlemagne"[42] (französische Nr.1)	(February 1945)	Charlemagne
34. SS-Freiwilligen-Grenadier-Division "Landstorm Nederland"[43]	(February 1945)	Landstorm Nederland
35. SS-Polizei-Grenadier-Division	(February 1945)	
36. Waffen-Grenadier-Division der SS[44]	(February 1945)	
37. SS-Freiwilligen-Kavallerie-Division "Lützow"[45]	(February 1945)	
38. SS-Grenadier-Division "Nibelungen"[46]	(March 1945)	

[30] Formed from Albanians and Moslems from Croatia. It was disbanded in January, 1945, and its elements given to "Prinz Eugen" and "30.Januar."

[31] Created around a regimental cadre of "Florian Geyer" (SS-Kavallerie-Regiment 17), it was destroyed in February, 1945, in Budapest.

[32] Disbanded in October, 1944, and numerical designation given to "Nederland."

[33] Expanded from an existing Brigade that had previously been a volunteer regiment.

[34] Redesignated as the Waffen-Gebirgs (Karstjäger) Brigade der SS in December, 1944.

[35] Along with "Hungaria" one of two nominal Hungarian divisions.

[36] Originally to have been a Panzer Division with SS-Panzer-Grenadier-Brigade 49 as its cadre. The Brigade went to "Götz von Berlichingen" instead.

[37] Expanded from the Flemish 6.SS-Sturmbrigade "Langemarck," not to be confused with the regiment of the same name assigned to "Das Reich" in 1942 after receiving its honor title for fighting on the Leningrad front.

[38] Created from an existing Sturmbrigade and composed primarily of Belgian volunteers.

[39] Was to have been formed from the Kaminski Brigade (number assigned in July, 1944) but those officers to be used were executed for their behavior during the suppression of the Warsaw ghetto.

[40] Formed from Ordnungspolizei units in White Russia, it was redesignated as a Brigade in March, 1945, with some elements transferring to "Hunyadi" and "Nibelungen."

[41] Created from the disbanded elements of "Kama," it included a significant number of Hungarian ethnic Germans.

[42] French unit that began in July, 1943, as a Grenadier Brigade.

[43] Expanded from a Brigade with the same title that existed since October, 1944.

[44] Expanded from the Dirlewanger Brigade with the addition of other units.

[45] Formed from the remnants of "Florian Geyer" and "Maria Theresia" after Budapest, including the engineer battalion of "Florian Geyer" that had been detached prior to the siege.

[46] Formed with the faculty and the last cadet class of SS-Junkerschule Bad Tölz as its cadre.

TACTICAL SYMBOLS AND ORDERS OF BATTLE

Two types of documentation can be used to ascertain the composition of a command. The first method is to use the charts incorporating symbols to designate each component. These were drawn up by the Kommandoamt der Waffen-SS within the SS-Führungshauptamt for corps and divisions, as well as numerous brigades, battle groups and the volunteer legions. The required sub-units were determined, to include necessary equipment and personnel, by the German Armed Forces structural system (Kriegs-stärkenachweisung). This system was constantly updated as technical advancements were incorporated and Waffen-SS units were generally formed along Army lines, though the quality of equipment allocated improved after the first campaign in Russia. Units expanding to a more powerful composition, such as an infantry division expanded to an armored unit, received the upgrade by the requisites laid out in the system. When a division was first created, the initial supervision was undertaken by a Formation Staff (Aufstellungsstab), most often led by the officer who became the commander when the unit formally activated. Higher echelons were not always in contact with the supply and manpower reality situations, so at times a chart indicating a particular composition was not always adhered to exactly. The most accurate time for this type of documentation is during initial formation or rebuilding in a non-combat area. The charts throughout the volume illustrate the composition of the unit on the date given and are within an individual biography for an officer who either led the entire component or one of its larger sub-elements.

The symbols that follow will allow the reader to interpret these Orders of Battle. All are generally representative as slight variations can be found, depending on who drew the chart. Within a component, units number from right to left. For example: an artillery regiment's first detachment is on the right within the artillery section while its fourth detachment is on the left. Arabic numbers indicate the number of weapons or vehicles of the type indicated by that particular symbol.

The second type of material is the use of Feldpost numbers (see Appendices). These were assigned to all military components using a numerical system that changed several times during the war with the result a specific number could be assigned to different units at different times.[1] While the system proves a unit existed (its mail was delivered to its location via the assigned number), it does not ascertain the strength of the unit. Often units were reduced to a fraction of the desired number of weapons and/or personnel. When used in combination with the unit war diaries, these two types of documentation allow an accurate determination of a given unit. While the war diaries allow insight into field changes, such as one unit absorbing another due to losses, these are not available in many cases.[2] With data being fed to Berlin followed by a time to add changes, the events in the field often out-paced the record keepers.[3]

---

[1] The system was throughout the Armed Forces with a Feldpost number assigned to Army units, ships of the Navy, Air Force units, etc.

[2] While some divisions have a good amount of surviving divisional war diaries, most do not have all available for all components. Also, many divisions of the latter half of the war, particularly those fighting in the East, have no surviving diaries. The most important for research are those compiled by the First Staff Officer (division) or Chief of Staff (corps).

[3] An example in the 1943 list is "Das Reich" and Regiment "Langemarck." The regiment is shown as composed of two Bataillone in 1943 when in actuality it ceased to be a Regiment in October, 1942, when its II.Bataillon was used to form the II.Abteilung of the new Panzer Regiment. I.Battalion continued in its former role: it had been the division's Kradschützen Bataillon (motorcycle battalion).

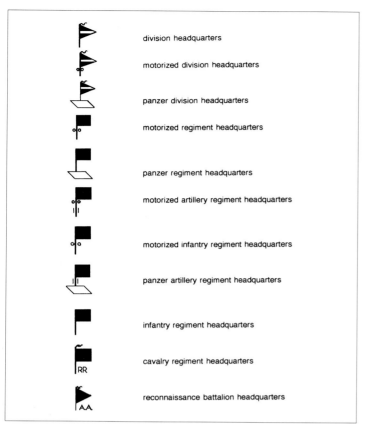

division headquarters

motorized division headquarters

panzer division headquarters

motorized regiment headquarters

panzer regiment headquarters

motorized artillery regiment headquarters

motorized infantry regiment headquarters

panzer artillery regiment headquarters

infantry regiment headquarters

cavalry regiment headquarters

reconnaissance battalion headquarters

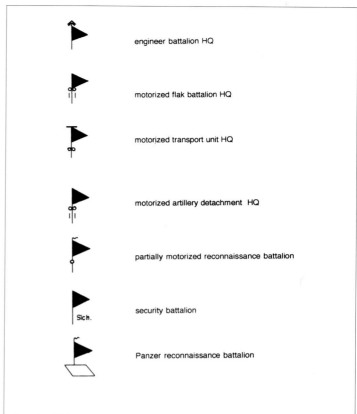

engineer battalion HQ

motorized flak battalion HQ

motorized transport unit HQ

motorized artillery detachment HQ

partially motorized reconnaissance battalion

security battalion

Panzer reconnaissance battalion

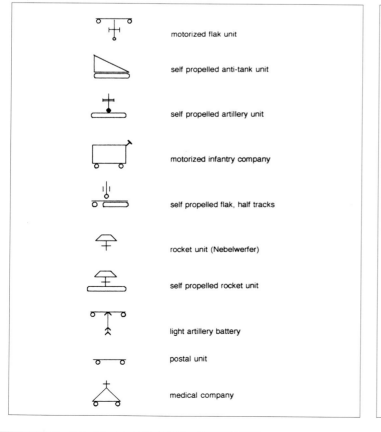

motorized flak unit

self propelled anti-tank unit

self propelled artillery unit

motorized infantry company

self propelled flak, half tracks

rocket unit (Nebelwerfer)

self propelled rocket unit

light artillery battery

postal unit

medical company

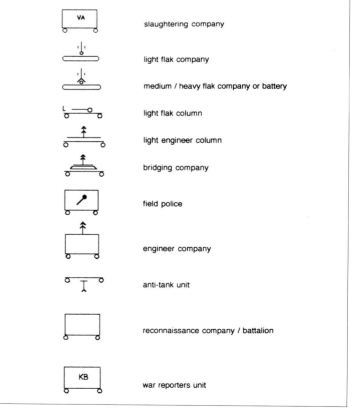

slaughtering company

light flak company

medium / heavy flak company or battery

light flak column

light engineer column

bridging company

field police

engineer company

anti-tank unit

reconnaissance company / battalion

war reporters unit

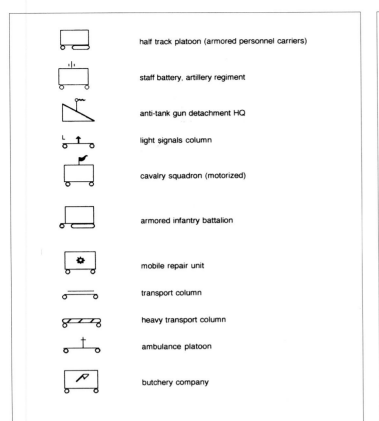

half track platoon (armored personnel carriers)

staff battery, artillery regiment

anti-tank gun detachment HQ

light signals column

cavalry squadron (motorized)

armored infantry battalion

mobile repair unit

transport column

heavy transport column

ambulance platoon

butchery company

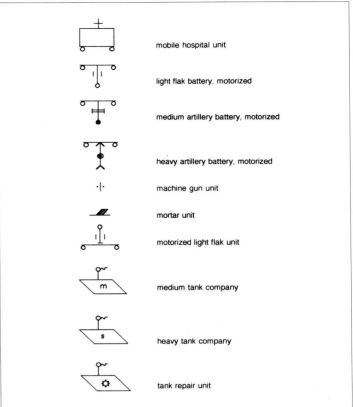

mobile hospital unit

light flak battery, motorized

medium artillery battery, motorized

heavy artillery battery, motorized

machine gun unit

mortar unit

motorized light flak unit

medium tank company

heavy tank company

tank repair unit

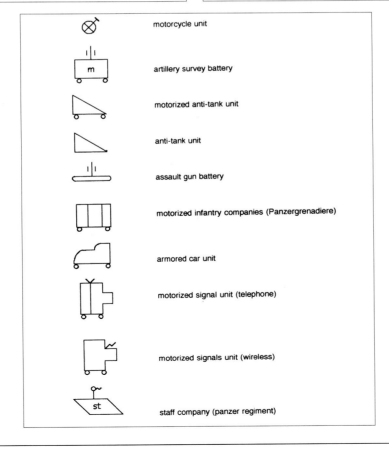

motorcycle unit

artillery survey battery

motorized anti-tank unit

anti-tank unit

assault gun battery

motorized infantry companies (Panzergrenadiere)

armored car unit

motorized signal unit (telephone)

motorized signals unit (wireless)

staff company (panzer regiment)

FRANZ AUGSBERGER

Franz Augsberger was the senior ranking SS officer school graduate and first cadet to reach full General officer standing. He was born in Vienna, Austria, on October 10, 1905, the son of a hotel landlord. Augsberger attended a military training institute for one year with the intention of a career as a soldier but the collapse of the Austro-Hungarian empire forbade his original occupation choice. He then attended a higher technical school, receiving a degree as a qualified engineer and architect.

From July, 1927 to October, 1930, he was a member of the Austrian Steirischer Heimatschutz but found their activities too slow and restricted.[1] Augsberger then served in the Sturmabteilung (SA) from October 30, 1930, to April 20, 1932, joining the NSDAP the day he entered service with the SA.

Following graduation, Augsberger set himself up as an independent architect in Vienna. He held that occupation until 1932 and also attended an academy for photographic art that same year. He learned fluent Norwegian while employed in Norway for one-and-a-half years as an engineer. Augsberger was in charge of Party propaganda in the Vienna area from the end of October, 1930, to June 19, 1933, when the NSDAP was declared illegal in Austria, prompting Augsberger to move to Germany. Joining the Allgemeine-SS on April 20, 1932, as an SS-Anwärter (probationary candidate), he was given SS membership number 139 528 when he became an SS-Mann in February, 1934. Augsberger served with the Austrian Legion from April, 1932, to October, 1933. After leaving the Austrian Legion in Lechfeld, he served with the Hilfswerk Schleissheim in the Prittbach training area near Dachau, being promoted to

SS-Unterscharführer on April 20, 1934, then to SS-Oberscharführer on June 1, 1934.[2]

Living in Germany after Austrian Chancellor Dollfuss made the NSDAP (and SS) illegal in that country, Augsberger transferred to the SS/Verfügungstruppe from the Allgemeine-SS as an SS-Oberscharführer on October 1, 1934. He served as a Zugführer (platoon leader) in the 5./SS-Standarte 1 (which later became Regiment "Deutschland") beginning October 1, 1934, until March 18, 1935.

Recommended to attend the first class at SS-Führerschule (SS Leaders School) "Braunschweig," he began classes in April, 1935.[3] Augsberger was promoted to SS-Hauptscharführer on April 1, 1935,[4] and, after examination at the end of January, 1936, also advanced in rank to SS-Standartenoberjunker.[5] He was commissioned as an SS-Untersturmführer with seniority effective from June 1, 1935.[6] As a cadet he did especially well in weapons training and communications.

Promoted to SS-Obersturmführer on July 1, 1936, he was the senior-ranked SS officer school graduate when promoted to SS-Hauptsturmführer on June 1, 1937. After graduation from Braunschweig, he went to the Rasse und Siedlungshauptamt (Race and Settlement Main Office or RuSHA) for additional training until the start of July, 1936. He then returned to Braunschweig as an instruc-

---

[1] "Lebenslaufbahn," the Steirischer Heimatschutz (Styrian Home Defense) was an Austrian Facist political movement that eventually lost its influence and members to the Austrian Nazi Party and later the NSDAP.

[2] The unit was absorbed by the SS/Verfügungstruppe and became the II/SS 1 (which in turn became Regiment "Deutschland"). Weidinger, "Division Das Reich," volume 1, pages 29-30.

[3] Both Bad Tölz and Braunschweig were redesignated as SS-Junkerschulen effective May 1, 1937. Schulze-Kossens, "Die Junkerschulen," page 166.

[4] SS-Stammrollen

[5] The two ranks are synonymous but the latter is specifically for cadets who, when starting their training, became SS-Junker.

[6] Most cadets of the first class had a commissioning date effective April 20, 1936.

Two photos of Franz Augsberger while with 5./SS-Standarte 1 prior to attending SS officer school.

tor, teaching weapons courses there for almost two years followed by a year of teaching at the SS officer school in Bad Tölz from mid-March, 1938 until March 1, 1939. In mid-February, 1937 he returned to the RuSHA for a further month of training. Augsberger married his wife, Ilse Peters, on April 8, 1936, and his only child, a daughter, Karin, was born that October. They met in Braunschweig while he attended officer school.

At the start of March, 1939, he moved to SS-Standarte "Der Führer" where he remained until the start of August that year. In June of 1939, he was the selection of Regiment "Der Führer" for a list of candidates to potentially become SS adjutant to the Reichsprotektor of Bohemia-Moravia, former Foreign Minister Constantin von Neurath. During August, 1939, he briefly was temporarily reassigned to an Allgemeine-SS command, leading II./ 90.SS-Standarte in Villach with the rank of Allgemeine-SS Sturmbannführer that he was promoted to on August 1, 1939. He then returned to his still permanent Regiment "Der Führer" assign-

ment. His Allgemeine-SS rank was changed to SS-Hauptsturmführer on March 21, 1940, to correspond with his Waffen-SS rank at that time.

From September 1, 1939, to the beginning of October, 1940, he led the 3./Ersatz Bataillon "Der Führer." Augsberger was also temporary commander of the entire SS-Ersatz-Bataillon "Der Führer" for a short period in the summer of 1940 until late June between assigned commanders, following which he returned to command of his Kompanie.

On October 1, 1940, he transferred from the "Der Führer" replacement unit to SS-Standarte "Westland" as a Kompanie Führer (company officer). With that unit he took further commander courses under Felix Steiner, who gave him excellent evaluations and recommended him for promotion to SS-Brigadeführer in April, 1944. Augsberger transferred again and took command of III./Nordland on December 12, 1940, and led that battalion until February 10, 1941.

Effective February 10, 1941, he was ordered to take command of the I./SS-Standarte 7, which was reorganized that month as a motorized infantry regiment.[7] Augsberger continued as commander until the start of December, 1941. On December 1, 1941, he was promoted to SS-Sturmbannführer.

Augsberger then led the entire SS-Infanterie-Regiment 7 (mot) until July, 1942, as a component of SS-Division "Nord."[8] These battalion and regimental commands resulted in the commander of SS-Division "Nord" (SS-Brigadeführer Carl-Maria Demelhuber) recommending him for promotion to SS-Obersturmbannführer. Augsberger won the Iron Cross II class on July 4, 1941, the Iron Cross I class on September 15, 1941, and the Infantry Assault Badge on January 15, 1942. On April 20, 1942, he was promoted to SS-Obersturmbannführer with seniority retroactive to the start of the same month. He also won the German Cross in Gold on May 30, 1942, for his Bataillon and Regiment commands with SS-Infanterie-Regiment 7(mot).

Hitler authorized the creation of a Legion composed of Estonians in August, 1942, which developed into the Estnische SS-Freiwilligen-Brigade which was ordered formed by the SS-Führungshauptamt in late September, 1942. Augsberger was selected as commander of the Estonian Legion effective October 20, 1942, though the date his command was finally announced to the Estonians appears to have been much later.[9] He was the first and

---

[7] The surviving former Totenkopfstandarten were again redesignated in the following months to become SS-Infanterie Regimenter.

[8] The end of the command per his personnel file is October. In June, 1942, the remaining battalions of the division were incorporated with newly formed elements to form the SS-Gebirgs-Jäger-Regiment 6 "Reinhard Heydrich." A new SS-Gebirgs-Jäger-Regiment 6 was formed under Franz Schreiber, the last commander of Division "Nord" (see volume 2). In the official divisional history, July seems to have been the actual end of Augsberger's assignment with "Nord," so his file indicates titular command post after that date. Schreiber, "Kampf unter dem Nordlicht," pages 196 and 201.

[9] "Stammkarte" and "Dienstlaufbahn." It appears the Estonians were unaware of his appointment as commander of the Legion until he was announced as Brigade commander in early July, 1943. Bender/Taylor, "Uniforms, Organization and History of the Waffen-SS," volume 5, page 153, infers he had no direct involvement with the formation staff and early recruiting of personnel since the Estonians wished confirmation of who the Legion commander would be during April, 1943. No doubt after a leave following his combat assignment he underwent additional larger unit

Augsberger (left) wearing the "B" collar tab after being commissioned as an SS-Untersturmführer at Braunschweig and (right) as an SS-Obersturmbannführer speaking with Knight's Cross holder Fritz Klingenberg.

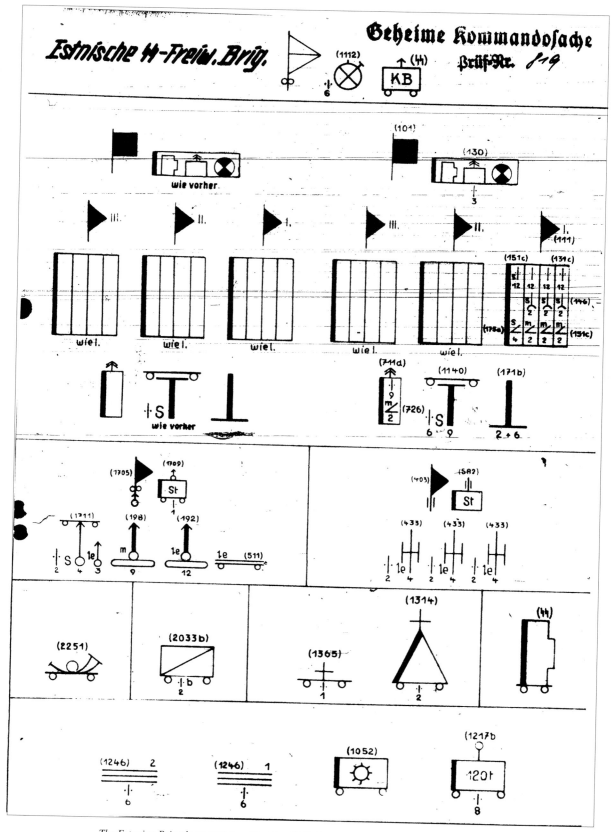

The Estonian Brigade as envisioned in May, 1943, by expanding the existing Estonian Legion.

only commander of the Estonian Brigade, officially being made commander on July 1, 1943, the date of his promotion to SS-Standartenführer.[10] As a Brigade commander he was positively evaluated as a tactician and leader by the commander of the 11.SS-Freiwilligen-Panzer-Grenadier-Division "Nordland," Swords holder Fritz von Scholz.[11] Augsberger led the Brigade and when it was expanded to a division in January, 1944, continued as divisional commander, being promoted to SS-Oberführer on January 30, 1944. Promoted to SS-Brigadeführer und Generalmajor der Waffen-SS on June 21, 1944, he was awarded the Knight's Cross from a recommendation by the commander of Army Group "Center," Generalfeldmarschall Ferdinand Schörner, on March 8, 1945. The text of that award recommendation reads as follows.

"As the division arrived in the area of Oppeln, the enemy had just crossed the Oder river in a wide front. To cover the northern flank of the armored fortress Oppeln, the divisional commander independently decided to take the villages of Birkenthal, Halbendorf and Preisdorf, which lay outside his own division's section. The above named villages were only taken after strong enemy resistance. The enemy was forced to the North, and the safety of the northern flank of the armored fortress Oppeln was thus secured with the building of a new defensive line.

On February 3, 1945, the strong enemy force, equipped with tanks, was successful in building a bridgehead over the Neisse river near Frohnau and was soon able to expand this bridgehead. SS-Brigadeführer Augsberger, located in Lossen, personally saw to it that the slowly arriving alarm troops and other miscellaneous combat factions were formed for an at-

tack which was conducted on the night of February 3/4. An enemy attack on the flank of his attack destroyed these troops, who proved incapable of defending themselves. This led to a new and very critical situation. SS-Brigadeführer Augsberger personally organized a new defense in the villages of Lossen, Johnsdorf and Jeschen. He attacked and re-established the situation by leading the fighting by his own personal example. The breakthrough of the enemy tanks to the south was therefore prevented and a much-needed new and secure Neisse-Front was established.

The difficulties under which the men of the 20.Waffen-Grenadier-Division of the SS (estnische Nr. 1), have fought, all the while being for the most part led by Estonian officers, earns, in consideration of the facts, the recognition that these men must fight far behind their lost homeland, and thus lack any tangible inspiration. Because of this situation, the difficulties in leading these men have only been overcome by the skillful leadership of the divisional commander and through his brave and personal example."[12]

Augsberger led the now-designated 20.Waffen-Grenadier-Division der SS (estnische Nr.1) until March 19, 1945, when he was killed along with his adjutant near Neustadt in Silesia leading portions of his surrounded command in one of three Kampfgruppen (battle groups) attempting to break out of the Oppeln pocket.[13]

Although initially distrusted by the Estonain commanders, who wished one of their own officers to lead the Brigade, he eventually gained their trust and respect with good insight into the Estonian's situation and problems. There is little doubt he would have become a corps commander, especially if a second Estonian division had been raised, having proven himself as both an able commander and administrator. He leadership in combat while assigned to "Nord" and the Estonian Division also attested to his personal bravery with his awards of the German Cross in Gold and Knight's Cross. In addition to his wartime decorations, he also received the SA Sports Badge in Bronze, the Reich's Sports Badge in Bronze and the German Horseman's Badge in Bronze.

---

command and administartive training. In February, 1943, he was at a class at the Panzertruppenschule Wündsdorf, "Personalverfügung," SS-FHA Kdo.d.WSS, 24/Sdr.Pf. dated January 30, 1943. Bender/Taylor's comment that he was involved with raising the Legion on page 204 of volume 5 is slightly misleading, as the unit was already a Brigade by that time. When given command of the Brigade, he was already stationed at the training area used for the Legion (and later the Brigade) and it is presumed he was the only assigned commander of the Legion. According to SS-Führungshauptamt document sources, he headed the Formation Staff of the new "Nordland" from March to the start of May, 1943, as a designated deputy until Fritz von Scholz assumed operational command.

[10] Communication sent to Augsberger by Himmler at Truppenübungsplatz "Heidelager" (where the Estonians were training) via the SS-Führungshauptamt dated July 2, 1943, giving him command of the Brigade and his promotion effective the previous day. Augsberger himself was not made aware of the promotion until at least July 6th.

[11] "Beurteilung," dated April 24, 1944.

---

[12] "Vorschlag für die Verleihung des Ritterkreuzes des Eisernen Kreuzes" dated February 16, 1945, and approved March 8, 1945.

[13] Bender/Taylor "Uniforms, Organization and History of the Waffen-SS," volume 5, pages 190-191.

ADOLF AX

The son of a textile worker, Adolf Ax was born in Mouscron, West Flanders, on June 23, 1906. After attending a German school in Brussels, then the State Realgymnasium in Wiesbaden, he studied law at the Universities in Freiburg and Vienna.

Ax joined the SS on October 29, 1930, and the NSDAP on December 1, 1930. On February 1, 1931, he became an SS Mann and was assigned to the 1./I./2.SS-Standarte, where he remained until April 24, 1934. He was promoted to SS-Truppführer on November 20, 1931, then commissioned as an SS-Sturmführer on January 27, 1932, at which time he took command of his Sturm. Here he was also promoted to SS-Obersturmführer on November 9, 1933.

Reassigned to Abschnitt XI as a Special Duties Officer and to continue training, Ax served there until May 17, 1935, when he joined the SS-Verfügungstruppe. He attended classes at the Higher Police School in Potsdam-Eiche (May 1 to June 15, 1934) and a Reich Leaders School during November/December, 1934, then the Abschnitt XI Leaders School in the first half of 1935. In early February, 1935, he started military training with the SS-Verfügungstruppe. In the pre-war years, Ax won the Reich and SA Sports Badges.

When he permanently transferred to the SS-Verfügungstruppe, he was assigned as a Zugführer in the 6./II./SS-Standarte 2 which later received the designation of Regiment "Germania." On July 1, 1936, Ax moved to SS-Bataillon "N" (Nürnberg) under the command of Ernst Deutsch. With this ceremonial unit, he led the 2.Sturm until June 10, 1939 and was promoted to SS-Hauptsturmführer on November 9, 1936. Felix Steiner, the commander of Regiment "Deutschland," commented on his abundant energy, wide knowledge of military matters and intelligence in an evaluation of Ax during August, 1937.

On June 10, 1939, the Panzerjäger Abteilung (anti-tank detachment) of the SS-Verfügungstruppe was formed and Ax took command of its 2.Kompanie until the unit dissolved in late August, 1939. His command was changed into the new Panzerabwehr-Ersatz-Kompanie until September, 1939, when Ax was given command of the reformed Panzerjäger Abteilung.[1] On October 20, 1939, (the day he married), the first division of the eventual Waffen-SS began forming under Paul Hausser. At that time, he was the first commander of the Panzerjäger Abteilung of the SS-V.T. Division (mot) which eventually received the honor title "Das Reich." He led the anti-tank unit until December, 1940. Promoted to SS-Sturmbannführer on May 25, 1940, Ax attended numerous classes while holding his command. At the Panzertruppenschule in Wünsdorf he took classes in mechanics and tactical leadership. An anti-tank course at the Panzerschule in Putlos was followed by a battalion commanders course while attached to the 29.Infanterie-Division. During the Western campaign Ax won both classes of the Iron Cross.

During December, 1940, the recently reorganized SS-Totenkopf-Standarte 11 was attached to the division as SS-Infantry Regiment 11, to replace Regiment "Germania," and Ax took command of the III.Bataillon.[2] He held this command into the first Russian campaign until the regiment was dissolved in late October, 1941, and its personnel divided between Regimenter "Deutschland" and "Der Führer" as replacements.[3] He became ill in December,

---

[1] Weidinger, "Division Das Reich," volume I, page 112.

[2] "Germania," portions of the division's artillery regiment and other elements were the cadre for forming the eventual "Wiking" Division beginning in December, 1940.

[3] Weidinger, "Division Das Reich," volume III, page 169. Ax's "Stammkarte" incorrectly lists him holding the command until April, 1942, an example of the unreliability of that particular document type for biographical research regarding assignments.

Adolf Ax (left) while assigned to Abschnitt IX of the Allgemeine-SS and later as an SS-Hauptsturmführer and company commander with SS-Bataillon "N" (note unique collar insignia for both assignments).

1941, with serious sinus problems and was sent to a hospital in Berlin until March 11, 1942. After being discharged, Ax was not yet fully recovered and took command of the SS-Panzerjäger Ausbildungs und Ersatz Abteilung (training and replacement detachment) in Hilversum until July 18, 1942, during which time he attended a battalion commanders course in Amsterdam during April.

Ax remained in Holland and was assigned as the Ia (First Staff Officer) of Carl-Maria Demelhuber, the Befehlshaber der Waffen-SS (Senior Waffen-SS Commander) "Niederlande," on July 18, 1942.[4] Promoted to SS-Obersturmbannführer on November 9, 1942, and to SS-Standartenführer on November 9, 1943, he was promoted to be Demelhuber's Chief of Staff on November 9, 1943. Demelhuber evaluated him as an excellent staff officer and recommended him for promotion to SS-Oberführer, which was granted

effective December 21, 1944. He was awarded the War Service Cross 2nd class with Swords in 1942, followed by award of the 1st class with Swords in 1944. In November, 1944, Demelhuber took command of Führungstab "Ostküste" and Ax was his Chief of Staff in Mecklenburg.[5]

On January 15, 1945, he was assigned as the Chief of Staff for the newly-formed XVI.SS-Armee-Korps commanded by Demehlhuber. When the commander of the 15.Waffen-Grenadier-Division der SS (lettische Nr.1), Herbert von Obwurzer, was captured by the Russians, Ax was sent by the corps as the temporary replacement commander from January 26 to February 15, 1945. During that brief command he was awarded the Knight's Cross on May 9, 1945, though the recommendation did not survive for study. He then replaced Joachim Richter on February 17, 1945, as commander of the 32.SS-Freiwilligen-Grenadier-Division "30 Januar"

---

[4] "Personal-Antrag" dated September 12, 1944, and signed by Demelhuber. A 1942 promotion recommendation gives July 10, 1942. The term abbreviation First Staff Officer post is given as both Ia and 1a in period documents.

[5] Krätschmer, "Die Ritterkreuzträger der Waffen-SS," page 883.

until March when he was sent to a higher troop formation training class in Bad Wiessee, being succeeded by Hans Kempin.[6] He was attending this class when the war ended.

In his excellent history "Latvian Legion," Artur Silgailis thought Ax "old" when he commanded the Latvian division, but at that time he was only 36 years of age, so his illness probably played a factor in his appearance. Tactically sound and intelligent, he was an experienced and fully qualified administrative staff officer but lacked the experience in larger formation leadership to be an effective divisional commander (his previous experience was as commander of a battalion). No doubt he was thought to be potentially more than capable since he was sent for divisional level command training. He died in Wiesbaden on February 6, 1983.

[6] "Personalverfügung," SS-Personalhauptamt, Amt VII-Hauptabt. I, Az: E./ My. dated March 6, 1945, with effect from February 17, 1945.

Ax (above right) as an SS-Obersturmbannführer with SS-Gruppenführer Carl-Maria Demelhuber while serving as Demelhuber's 1a in the Netherlands during a shooting competition in 1943. He is shown again (below left) during the same period with Demelhuber.

Adolf Ax (above center) with Demelhuber and below (right foreground) with his commander. In the lower photo at far right is SD officer SS-Standartenführer Dr. Fritz Rang with others of Demelhuber's staff. One officer wears his 1936 model SS dagger with knot as prescribed by regulations for Waffen-SS officers.

(Above) From left to right are Adolf Ax, Dr. Heinrich Lankenau, Hans-Albin Rauter (Higher SS and Police Leader Netherlands) and Carl-Maria Demelhuber in white summer uniform on June 21, 1943. (right) An autographed photo of SS-Standartenführer Adolf Ax.

In both these photos Ax is on the far right during maneuvers in Holland.

ERICH VON DEM BACH

Erich von dem Bach-Zelewski was born in Lauenburg, Pommerania, on March 1, 1899, the son of an estate owner. He spent his childhood with foster parents, joining the Army in 1914. The latter part of his name was legally removed at his request in November, 1940, due to its Polish sound.[1] He was commissioned as a Leutnant on March 1, 1916, and served in WWI with a Silesian unit as a machine gun company officer with the Grenadier Regiment "König Friedrich Wilhelm II" No. 10 during 1918-1919.[2] Awarded both classes of the Iron Cross, he was also given the Wound Badge in Black after being gassed.

After the war he served with border guard units in Silesia and then joined the Reichswehr as a Leutnant with Infantry Regiment 4. He only served from 1923 to February, 1924, when he was dismissed for suspected anti-establishment political views following the Munich Putsch of November, 1923. After working on an estate and as an appraiser, he ran an estate beginning in 1928. Married in 1921, he and his wife had six children between 1923 and 1940.[3]

Von dem Bach joined the NSDAP in February, 1930, and the SS on February 15, 1931, serving first with 1./III./27.SS-Standarte, later taking command of the III.Sturmbann on May 10, 1931. Commissioned as an SS-Sturmführer on July 20, 1931, he organized SS units on the Austrian frontier in early 1931. Promoted to SS-Sturmbannführer on December 6, 1931, he commanded the 27.SS-Standarte in Frankfurt/Oder from December 15, 1931 to July 12, 1932. He also held a seat in the Reichstag from the end of July, 1932, to the end of the war as a representative for Breslau. From June 16, 1932 to December 1, 1932, he led SS-Abschnitt VIII. In Liebenow he also served as the commander of SS-Abschnitt XII, leading that district from July 12, 1932, to January 31, 1934, during which time he was promoted to SS-Standartenführer on September 10, 1932, to SS-Oberführer on October 6, 1932, and to SS-Brigadeführer on December 15, 1933.[4] Bach then commanded SS-Abschnitt VII from February 12, 1934 to March 20, 1934. In the pre-war years, he was awarded the SA Sports Badge in Bronze, the Reich's Sports Badge in Silver, the Brunswick rally badge of 1931 and the Gold Party Badge.

Promoted to command SS-Oberabschnitt "Nordost," he commanded that main district from February 1, 1934 to February 15, 1936, during which time he was promoted to SS-Gruppenführer on July 11, 1934.[5] He also served as deputy head of the Gestapo in the Königsberg area during 1935 to February, 1936. Following a disagreement with Gauleiter Erich Koch, he moved to command SS-Oberabschnitt "Südost" from February 15, 1936, officially until June 26, 1941, but left the command at the start of May, 1941, for service in Russia. After serving several periods in training with the Army, he was commissioned a Hauptmann d.R. on December 1, 1936, with Infanterie Regiment 7. He also served as HSSPF "Südost" from June 28, 1938, until leaving for Russia in May, 1941. During October, 1939, von dem Bach was assigned as HSSPF for military area East/Upper Silesia, a former part of Poland that was later absorbed by his Oberabschnitt command. In addition, he was assigned by Himmler from October, 1939, to the Spring of 1940 as deputy

---

[1] "Genehmigungsurkunde" dated November 28, 1940, and signed by the Regierungspräsident for Breslau.
[2] "Stammkarte"
[3] "Lebenslaufbahn"

[4] Multiple and overlapping commands were commonplace in the Allgemeine-SS and a post could be held in that group while actually serving in the Waffen-SS, Polizei or a civil post. See Yerger, "Allgemeine-SS, The Commands, Units and Leaders of the General SS."
[5] He held his Oberabschnitt command and an Abschnitt simultaneously.

A gathering of pre-war SS officers in Allgemeine-SS uniform shows (from left to right): Fritz Weitzel, Erich von dem Bach, Wilhelm Rediess, Joachim von Ribbentrop (Foreign Minister and an honorary SS General), Paul Moder, Friedrich-Wilhelm Krüger and August Heissmeyer. Aside from Ribbentrop, all held a post as head of an SS-Oberabschnitt (Main District) or Higher SS and Police Leader during the careers. Heissmeyer became a Main Office head.

Reich Commissioner for the Consolidation of German Nationhood (RKFDV).[6]

At the start of the invasion of Russia he was HSSPF for the area of Army Group "C" which was redesignated as the HSSPF "Rußland-Mitte" (Central Russia) in February, 1942. His command expanded in April, 1943, to include White Russia and von dem Bach officially held permanent command until June, 1944, but his command duties were undertaken by deputies beginning in February 1942.[7]

Hospitalized in early 1942 with serious stomach problems, he was suffering the psychological effects of carrying out orders involving the extermination policies in the East within his HSSPF command. Given the rank of Generalleutnant der Polizei on April 10, 1941, he was promoted to SS-Obergruppenführer on November 9, 1941. He won the German Cross in Gold on February 23, 1943, for anti-partisan operations. Awarded bars to both his WWI

Iron Crosses (August 31, 1941 and May 20, 1942), he served as Himmler's special deputy for anti-partisan warfare from October 1942 until June 21, 1943, when he took command of all anti-partisan units. Holding that post until November, 1944, he was promoted to General der Waffen-SS on July 1, 1944, and also was awarded both classes of the War Service Cross and the Eastern Front Medal. He commanded Korpsgruppe "von dem Bach" from August to November, 1944, composed of units to suppress the Warsaw uprising for which command he won the Knight's Cross on September 30, 1944.[8] Both he and Dr. Oskar Dirlewanger (whose Brigade command was in von dem Bach's corps group) were awarded the Knight's Cross for the combat in Warsaw on the same day. Von dem Bach then led the XIV.SS-Armee-Korps from November, 1944 to February 4, 1945, and was awarded the Anti-Partisan Warfare Badge in Silver in November, 1944.[9] From February 4, 1945, to February 10, he commanded the X.SS-Armee-Korps, which was formed from portions of his anti-partisan command and available area troops. Von dem Bach then succeeded Oberst Fritz Fullriede on February 14, 1945, as commander the Oder Korps,

---

[6] Himmler's post had the authority of a Main Office and was involved with the maintenance of racial standards and the protection/enlargement of the German race. It eventually absorbed the Racial German Assistance Main Office (VOMI) concerned with actual resettlement of Volksdeutsche (ethnic Germans). Yerger, "The Allgemeine-SS," pages 19-20.

[7] His duties were performed by Georg Graf von Bassewitz-Behr, Gerrett Korsemann and Curt von Gottberg, the latter becoming his official permanent replacement on June 21, 1944. Yerger, "Allgemeine-SS, The Commands, Units and Leaders of the General SS."

[8] "Pressnotiz" (undated) and telex Knight's Cross recommendation dated September 12, 1944.

[9] "Feld-Kommandostelle," Verleihung des BDK.-Abs. I. Silber, dated November 13, 1944.

composed of straggling units found within his operational area. He ended the war with that command.

Ruthless and ambitious in performing his duties in Russia, he was admired by Hitler for his improvisational skills and strong military presence. However, he was a total failure as a corps commander, having no skills as a higher formation military leader, and never visited the front nor ensured the flow of supplies for his troops. He treated the surrendered survivors of the Warsaw uprising as prisoners-of-war, probably considering his own fate after the war. At Nuremberg he testified for the Allied prosecution regarding Himmler's goals in Russia, the Einsatzgruppen and anti-partisan operations.[10] His testimony denounced Himmler as well as incriminating himself. For that he was branded as a traitor by Hermann Göring and other defendants. After being released in 1951, following a suspended ten year sentence, he lived under domiciliary arrest until November, 1952, in Laffenau. He then worked as a night watchman. Arrested during December, 1958, in March, 1961, he was sentenced to four-and-a-half years in prison for deaths occurring in East Prussia before the war. Tried the following year for executing communists, he was sentenced to life in prison. Erich von dem Bach died in the prison hospital at Munich-Harlaching on March 8, 1972.

Above: SS-Obergruppenführer Erich von dem Bach wearing his German Cross in Gold.

Below: Erich von dem Bach (right) in Russia during 1941, while a Higher SS and Police Leader, listens to (from right) Reichsführer-SS Heinrich Himmler speak to the commander of the SS-Kavallerie Brigade, Herman Fegelein. Between them is Himmler's Chief of Staff, Karl Wolff. Fegelein was shot in 1945 for desertion and won the Swords to the Knight's Cross while Himmler committed suicide after being captured. Wolff ended the war as the Supreme SS and Police Leader for Italy.

---

[10] IMT, volume IV, page 475.

OTTO BAUM

The son of merchant and later mayor Emil Baum, Otto Baum was born in Hechingen-Stetten on November 15, 1911. He attended Volksschule for four years then Realgymnasium for nine years in his birthplace before passing his Abitur in 1930, excelling in his favorite subjects of mathematics and Latin. He also spent a decade learning the violin, creating a lifelong appreciation for classical music. Academically qualified for advanced education by passing his Abitur, he chose agriculture as a vocation and underwent practical training for two years until 1932 in Württemberg, Bavaria, and in Hohenheim near Stuttgart. In addition, he attended three semesters of advanced agriculture training in Hohenheim. His passion for plants continues to this day with gardening remaining a favorite hobby along with woodworking.

During his later educational period in Hohenheim he became a part-time member of the Allgemeine-SS on November 1, 1933, like all students of the period becoming interested and involved with the political situation and events in his country.[1] Assigned to the 3/I/13.SS-Standarte based in Stuttgart until early March, 1934, on March 6, 1934, Otto Baum enlisted in the Politische Bereitschaft (Political Readiness Detachment) in Ellwangen which would develop into several eventual SS-Verfügungstruppe units. He served first as an SS-Anwärter (candidate) until becoming an SS Mann on September 14, 1934. With opportunities and advancement were more available in the SS-Verfügungstruppe than the class-structured Army of that period, Baum decided on a military career that year and became a full-time SS member in December, 1934, with SS number 237 056.

Selected to attend the first classes at the new SS-Führerschule (Leader School) in Braunschweig, commanded by Paul Hausser,

Baum was designated as an SS-Junker on April 24, 1935. Active in sports since his youth, he especially enjoyed swimming and used the swim hall often at Braunschweig, being competitive in the 100 meter breaststroke since his school days. This first cadet group attended the facility and supplemental courses until February 10, 1936, followed by a platoon leaders course (Zugführer Lehrgang) at the Dachau training area until April of that year. Permanently influenced by his tactical instructor, Friedemann Goetze, and school commander Paul Hausser, he was promoted to SS-Standartenoberjunker on February 25, 1936, and commissioned as an SS-Untersturmführer on April 20, 1936.[2] Graduating fifth in his class from Braunschweig, he was posted to the 5./II./SS-Standarte "Germania" as a Zugführer. On September 13, 1936, he was formally awarded his SS officer sword.

The following year, Baum was sent to the Heeressportschule Wünsdorf for further training from May 5 to June 17, 1937. Also in 1937, Baum met his future wife while serving as adjutant during a platoon leaders course. Married in Arolsen, on November 13, 1937, Baum and his wife have five children. On September 12, 1937, he was promoted to SS-Obersturmführer, having since returned to Regiment "Germania", and was awarded the Austrian Annexation Medal on March 13, 1938.

In March, 1938, the new SS-Standarte 3 was created and Baum was reassigned to this unit, which became SS-Regiment "Der Führer", on May 1, 1938. He was posted to the Klagenfurt-based III.Bataillon of SS-Sturmbannführer Hilmar Wäckerle, serving as a Zugführer with 12.Kompanie. Baum and other junior officers were transferred to begin the training of the primarily Austrian cadets. In addition their own training, further instruction was given to the SS/

---

[1] Letter to the author from Herrn Baum dated October 29, 1995.

[2] Letter to the author from Herrn Baum dated August 4, 1986.

Otto Baum (left) as an enlisted man in 1934 wearing his dress bayonet with knot and (right) wearing the "B" collar tab worn by cadets and faculty at SS-Führerschule "Braunschweig" during 1935.

VT troops as the Regiment was one of the few fully motorized units of the Wehrmacht.

As part of the Army and SS-Verfügungstruppe training exchange programs initiated, Baum was temporarily assigned to the Ersatz Bataillon (replacement battalion) of Infanterie Regiment 56 from September 24 to December 24, 1938. He served there as a Zugführer in the 2.Kompanie and later led the 4.Kompanie until completion of the exchange training. His Army superiors were suitably impressed, stating in his evaluations the values of his "prudent and resolute leadership with a reliably steady and self-assured personality."[3] Aside from impressing his superiors with his energy and practical abilities, Baum proved a passionate and skilled horseman as well. The Army requested permission from Himmler to offer Baum a commission in the Army. He returned to Regiment "Der Führer" with the recommendation he be given command of a company.

"Der Führer" regimental commander Georg Keppler confirmed his own opinion of Baum's skill by giving him command of the 10.Kompanie effective November 15, 1938, and he held this com-

mand for the duration of his service with "Der Führer." The practical training with forming a motorized unit was of value for his next assignment. In the start of June, 1939, Baum received orders transferring him to the Infanterie Regiment (mot) "Leibstandarte SS Adolf Hitler."

Baum arrived at his new unit on June 1, 1939, and was assigned as 7.Kompanie commander in the II.Bataillon led by Carl von Oberkamp who also arrived in the same month.[4] Within a week Baum was leading his new command in exercises at the Glau drill grounds. He only trained with his new unit for two months before the start of the Second World War and his first campaign.

The "LSSAH," as a fully motorized unit, was heavily involved in the capture of Gola and areas along the Vistula. In the last week of the campaign Baum's Kompanie fought against the fortifications in the Modlin area. It was for these combats from September 21-25 that Baum was awarded the Iron Cross 2nd class on September 25, 1939, by Sepp Dietrich. The Regiment was relieved of their positions on September, 28 and Baum led his unit to the assembly area until they departed for Prague, where they served along with the

---

[3] "Beurteilung über Oberleutnant Otto Baum (SS-Obersturmführer)"

[4] Leibstandarte Tagesbefehl Nr. 114 v. 1.6.39

Baum's portrait after being commissioned as an SS-Untersturmführer wearing the SA Sports Badge.

Two at right: Two autographed photos of Baum, as a newly appointed SS-Untersturmfüher (top) and in an earlier portrait (right) with the early insignia used by Political Readiness Detachments. Note the number "2" on his collar tab, larger than those used when Regiment "Germania" was formed.

Poland 1939: Baum (above) reading a newspaper and below with his arm raised giving instructions to his men.

rest of the Regiment in securing the Protectorate of Bohemia/ Moravia. On November 9, 1939, Baum was promoted to SS-Hauptsturmführer.

Baum and his command participated in the capture of Rotterdam and the Hague during mid-May, 1940, then pursued the retreating British toward Dunkirk. While engaged with crossing the Marne, Baum was awarded the Iron Cross 1st class on June 15, 1940. On October 3, 1940, he was awarded the Infantry Assault Badge.

SS-Sturmbannführer Wilhelm Mohnke, the commander of II.Bataillon, recorded his impression of Baum in an evaluation.[5] In this, Mohnke described Baum as "a first-rate company leader whose abilities were especially made evident in the Polish and Western campaigns where his methodical leadership in all situations produced an exemplary attitude in his troops and proved his ability beyond the degree expected." In addition, notice was made of the short training time he had with his command before entering combat, a fact that made his successes even more noticed. His impression resulted in another transfer to a larger command.

On March 3, 1941, Baum was promoted to SS-Sturmbannführer and transferred to the "Totenkopf" Division as commander of III./ SS-Totenkopf-Infanterie-Regiment 3. Actually arriving in April,[6] he commanded this battalion until November 9, 1942. In April, Baum and his unit moved through East Prussia towards Russia by rail where they saw heavy combat in Latvia while fighting toward Demjansk.

Engaged in continuous combat from the early stages of the campaign, Baum was among the first "Totenkopf" men awarded the German Cross in Gold for his initial battalion command on December 26, 1941. That award, given for combat at Lake Ilmen and the Waldai hills areas, also allowed him a rare leave to return home during December.[7] Returning to the front, Baum was heavily engaged in the Demjansk pocket fighting, which he feels was one of the two most difficult combat periods of his service.[8] Baum's bravery and his skill denying the potential supply line for enemy troops around the Demjansk pocket resulted in his being recommended for the Knight's Cross by the commander of "Totenkopf," SS-Obergruppenführer Theodor Eicke, with the following report:

"SS-Sturmbannführer Baum defended his sector near Salutschje and has actively participated in the fighting against attacks by superior Soviet forces since February 23, 1942.

On February 7, 1942, at 0020 hours the Russians attacked after barraging the positions of Baum battalion with heavy artillery and grenade launchers after boxing in Baum's unit along the line connecting the villages of Schumilkino and Salutschje. The Russian infantry was also supported by tanks. The following enemy units were engaged in this attack:

> 20th Regiment of 7th Soviet Guard Division
> NCO class (battalion size) and platoon leaders class of the 7th Soviet Guards Division
> 42nd Soviet Brigade

Due to heavy casualties of the weakening battalion, the Russians were able to penetrate the northern sector of Schumilkino and the southern area of Salutschje. These penetrations only took place after bitter night fighting.

In response to the situation, SS-Sturmbannführer Baum gathered several of his men and part of a platoon sent up to reinforce his units. On his own initiative and without regard for his own life, he accompanied these men in a counter-attack and annihilated the enemy troops that had penetrated his positions in both Schumilkino and Salutschje.

At 0630 on the same day, the main fighting line was secured. All enemy attacks collapsed under heavy defensive fire along the main fighting line. After the conclusion of the fighting, Baum's units counted over 300 dead Russians lying in front of their positions.

The holding of the position of Baum's battalion was of decisive importance, since a Russian breakthrough would have put our positions in the North and East in danger of being overrun. In addition to that, it would have given the Russians the opportunity to take control of the highway between Kobylkino and Schubina. Control of this highway would have given the enemy the ability to supply materials as well as additional troops to their positions in the northern, western and southern fronts in Bicke. I request that SS-Standartenführer Baum be awarded the Knight's Cross of the Iron Cross in recognition of his heroic bravery and the resulting decisive success of his actions."[9]

Eicke personally presented Baum with the Knight's Cross in a brief ceremony less than a mile from the front. Following a brief celebration with cognac, Baum returned to his command and the fighting. Eicke, probably the most difficult Waffen-SS divisional commander to impress, was always a hard commander and cautious of new men under his command, preferring to make his own evaluations instead of accepting those of prior commanders. He considered Baum among his best commanders for his dash and instinctive bravery.[10]

---

[5] Evaluation dated November 30, 1940 and signed by Mohnke. Mohnke's biography will appear in volume 2 as he eventually commanded the 1.SS-Panzer-Division "Leibstandarte."

[6] "Lebenslaufbahn" dated August 21, 1946, written in captivity.

[7] "Wie sich SS Sturmbannführer Otto Baum des Deutsche Kreuz in Gold verdienste"

[8] Along with the Falaise combats in Normandy, letter to the author from Herrn Baum dated August 4, 1986.

---

[9] "Kurze Begründung und Stellungnahme der Zwischenvorgesetzten" dated April 21, 1942, and signed by Theodor Eicke.

[10] "Beförderungsvorschlag" to SS-Obersturmbannführer, commentary written by Eicke.

Baum (above, third from right) with other trainees of the SS/VT and (below) being decorated by Josef Dietrich after serving in the Western campaign with the "Leibstandarte."

A group photo of Waffen-SS officers after the Western campaign. Among those shown are (front row from left) Otto Baum, Wilhelm Mohnke, Georg Schönberger, Hans Weiser and Franz Augsberger. Mohnke later commanded the "Leibstandarte." Schönberger commanded the Tank Regiment of the "Leibstandarte" and along with Weiser was awarded the Knight's Cross. Augsberger is the first biography in the current volume. Below, another photo of the same time (Baum is 4th from left, front row) with Josef Dietrich (center).

Otto Baum (above) bids farewell to the men of 7./Leibstandarte after receiving orders transferring him to the "Totenkopf" Division and is also shown during the Western campaign at the center of the second photo.

On Eicke's recommendation, Baum was promoted to SS-Obersturmbannführer on November 9, 1942. One of Baum's regimental commanders with "Totenkopf," Matthias Kleinheisterkamp, had been a tactical instructor at Braunschweig and was one of the primary influences on Baum as a military officer, allowing him a free hand in shaping his battalion command and style.[11] It was also during his time with "Totenkopf" that Baum met and fought along side later Oakleaves to the Knight's Cross holder Karl Ullrich, the peer level officer he came to admire most during his military service.[12] They developed a close friendship during the time they served in Demjansk and remained in regular contact for decades after the war until Ullrich's death.

On November 9, 1942, during the latter stages of the "Totenkopf" Division expanding to become a Panzer-Grenadier Division, Baum moved to command the newly redesignated I./SS-Panzer-Grenadier-Regiment 5 "Totenkopf."[13] When divisional commander Eicke was killed, Baum took command of the regiment, replacing Max Simon who took command of the Division.[14] He

[11] Letter to the author dated January 6, 1996.

[12] Letter to the author dated January 6, 1996. Ullrich's career will be included within the series as he ended the war commanding the 5.SS-Panzer-Division "Wiking." When a commander in Demjansk, Ullrich commanded the "Totenkopf" Division's Pionier Bataillon (engineer battalion).

[13] Baum's previous regiment was renumbered "6" and received the honor title "Theodor Eicke" after the death of the first divisional commander in 1943.

[14] The biography for Max Simon (later commander of a Korps) will be in volume 2.

retained leadership of the regiment until officially leaving the "Totenkopf" Division on March 13, 1944.

Baum fought at the intense Kharkov battles, the major offensive north of Bjelgorod, and on the Mius river. Temporary divisional commander Hermann Priess recommended Baum for the Oakleaves to the Knight's Cross for his regimental command with the following report:

"In the night of February 23/24, 1943, SS-Panzer-Grenadier-Regiment 5 "Totenkopf," together with SS-Panzer-Grenadier-Regiment 6 to which I./Panzer Regiment "Totenkopf" was attached, were ordered to attack the enemy in the area north of Pavlograd. The town of Vjasowol was to be captured and the enemy pushed beyond the Malaja-Ternovka sector. At the same time a bridgehead was to be formed to permit the regiment to cross the Ternovka river.

During the early morning hours of February 24, SS-Obersturmbannführer Baum led the I./SS-Panzer-Grenadier-Regiment 5 in cooperation with SS-Panzer Regiment 3 in a daring assault past Vjasowol. He pursued the enemy beyond the Ternovka sector. Turning to the southeast, the commander used the attack momentum of his battalion to push to the edge of Werbki in spite of attacks by enemy tanks. The actions prior to the arrival of the Panzer Regiment served as a diversionary attack for the SS Division "Das Reich" which was advancing from the south. This allowed the two divisions to join early that same afternoon. This daring assault led by the commander, who constantly stayed at the very front of his battalion, prevented the escape of those enemy units which were still located west of the Ternovka sector.

On March 1, 1943, the SS-Panzer-Grenadier-Regiment 5 "Totenkopf" advanced to the north. As part of the "Totenkopf" Division attached to the SS-Panzer-Korps, its orders were to start out from Pavlovka and Nishnij Crel the next day. Then, turning to the northwest, it was to cross the Berestovaja river and press on past the hills near Berestovenka.

However, the I./SS-Panzer-Grenadier-Regiment 5 "Totenkopf," deployed together with the I./Panzer Regiment 3, encountered stubborn enemy resistance early the following night. The regimental commander decided to attack at all costs regardless of the very deep snow and difficult supply situation. This was decided on so as to join as quickly as possible the "Leibstandarte" which was advancing from the southwest and to cut the escape route to the west of the enemy units pushing east. This determined attack made it possible to join with the "Leibstandarte" by March 3rd and to pull the forces north. In this way the enemy escape route was closed. Meanwhile SS-Panzer-Regiment 3 pushed forward in the north as far as Kotjarovka and Medwedovka. These actions resulted in the encircling of large portions of the 3rd Russian Tank Army and

set the conditions for their destruction. SS-Panzer-Grenadier-Regiment 5 "Totenkopf" and the Panzer Regiment together captured the following: 21 T-34s, an armored reconnaissance car, 107 guns including anti-tank weapons, 95 anti-tank devices, 2 infantry guns, 44 machine guns, 29 mortars, approximately 1,000 rifles, 27 mobile field kitchens, 25 armored vehicles, 359 trucks, 300 wagons and carts as well as several hundred horses and oxen. This success was possible solely through the daring leadership of SS-Obersturmbannführer Baum.

On March 12, 1943, SS-Panzer-Grenadier-Regiment 5 "Totenkopf" was deployed to protect the flank during the action against Kharkov along the line from Ruskaja - Losovaja - Dergaci to Fesski - Mjakijmjaka. At that time the enemy was still strongly resisting in Kharkov. At 11:30 hours orders came from the division. The II./SS-Panzer-Grenadier-Regiment 5 "Totenkopf" was to be left behind to guard the old positions. The balance of the regiment was to push forward to the road from Kharkov to Cugujev through the eastern suburbs of Kharkov. Then Cugujev was to be captured along with the bridge across to the Donets river in order to prevent the escape of the enemy from the Smijev area.

The regiment started its attack at 1400 hours and reached Ssorokovka the same night despite catastrophic road conditions. The town was attacked and taken the next morning. While the enemy continued to resist, the regimental commander along with the I./Panzer Regiment 3 pushed on relentlessly. The regimental commander took his place at all times with the lead attacking battalion as an example of bravery for the entire regiment. Rogan on the Kharkov Cugujev road was taken by III.Bataillon along with a few tanks filled with the last drops of gas available. This action not only cut the enemy supply road but also established contact with the SS Division "Das Reich," completing the encirclement of Kharkov.

After being re-supplied with fuel by air, the regimental commander ordered an attack on Cugujev at 1500 hours the following day. This was done in spite of attacks on Rogan from the east. A short but very determined defensive effort near Kamenaja was overcome. The enemy was caught so much unaware by the rapid advance that it was possible to take Cugujev and capture all the Donets crossing points there the same evening. Again in this case, the foundation for a decisive success can be seen in the daring decisions, personal leadership and bravery of SS-Obersturmbannführer Baum.

SS-Obersturmbannführer Baum again demonstrated his personal bravery on June 5, 1943. While penetrating the heavy Russian positions near Beresoff under furious enemy fire by artillery and tanks, Baum broke into the enemy lines along with the advance element of his regiment. During the assault he was wounded but remained with his command.

Baum was also an exemplary model for his men on July 13/14. At the bridgehead in the Pssel sector he appeared in all the main areas of action, becoming the heart of the resistance against overwhelming enemy pressure. Inspired by his own personal bravery and prudent command leadership, all concentrated attacks by the enemy were repulsed with significant Russian losses."[15]

When the award was approved on August 22, 1943, Baum was the 277th soldier awarded the Oakleaves to the Knight's Cross. Baum was wounded again on August 19 and August 21, 1943, the latter time during a night combat at his command headquarters. He was awarded the Wound Badge in Silver on August 21, 1943.[16] That shoulder wound would require time in a Breslau hospital before returning to his command in early November, succeeding temporary commander Karl Ullrich.[17] He received the Oakleaves personally by Hitler at his headquarters along with Heinz Harmel, the

[15] Vorschlagliste für die Verleihung des Eichenlaubes zum Ritterkreuzes des Eisernen Kreuzes.

[16] Entry in Baum's Soldbuch.

[17] Ullrich, "Wie ein Fels im Meer," volume II, page 279, and Vopersal in "Soldaten, Kämpfer, Kameraden," volume IVa, page 71, say November 9, 1943. The exact date could not be confirmed by Herrn Baum and the source for Ullrich and Vopersal is unknown.

Baum (below) with Theodor Eicke and (above) Baum's command headquarters at that time in Russia.

Baum (without camouflage smock) speaks to some of his officers during the 1941 Russian campaign.

commander of Regiment "Deutschland." Following the award both men met privately with Hitler to discuss the situation at the front.

Divisional commander Hermann Priess bypassed the normal promotion recommendation forms and appealed directly to Reichsführer-SS Heinrich Himmler for Baum's promotion to SS-Standartenführer, requesting the advance in rank within a week of his inquiry letter.[18] With approval of the recommendation, Baum was formally promoted to full colonel effective January 30, 1944. During a week of leave by the divisional commander, Baum commanded "Totenkopf" in place of Hermann Priess during March, 1944, and was wounded again on March 13th.[19]

Placed in reserve until June, 1944, Baum visited SS officer, NCO and arms schools as a lecturer. Among the places he spoke were the SS officer school in Klagenfurt, the NCO school in Laibach, Yugoslavia and the schools incorporated into SS-Truppen-übungsplatz "Beneschau" near Prague. He also received a welcome leave to visit his family.

In the wake of the allied invasion he succeeded Otto Binge as commander of the 17.SS-Panzer-Grenadier-Division "Götz von Berlichingen" from June 18, 1944, until leaving on July 30th and being succeeded by Binge.[20] To the left of Baum's command was "Das Reich." When its temporary commander Christian Tychsen was killed, Baum assumed command of that division as well on July 28, 1944. Not knowing if Tychsen was captured or killed, Baum negotiated a truce and tried to exchange with the Americans to obtain his release but the former Panzer Regiment commander had been shot by an infantry patrol.

When commanding both "Das Reich" and "Götz von Berlichingen" divisions he was technically a corps commander, the only SS officer school graduate to hold a command of more than a single division at one time. Baum led "Das Reich" in the bitter combat at Falaise and his unit held the encirclement open allowing large numbers of German troops to escape. He was again decorated for his leadership in those battles. Baum's award of the Swords to the Knight's Cross followed a recommendation directly to Himmler from the Senior Commander "West," Feldmarschall Walter Model, for his leadership of "Das Reich" in the Normandy campaign and especially at Falaise. Those combats, along with his time at Demjansk, are still recalled by Baum as the most intense he experienced throughout the war. Granted on September 2, 1944, as the 95th soldier given the award, Baum was personally awarded the Swords to the Knight's Cross by Hitler at his headquarters followed by a personal meeting to discuss the war situation.[21] As commander of "Das Reich," Himmler personally promoted him to SS-Oberführer effective September 17, 1944.[22] Baum retained command of "Das Reich" until October 24, 1944.[23]

He was transferred to Italy and command of the 16.SS-Panzer-Grenadier-Division "Reichsführer-SS" as successor to Max Simon who went to command XIII.SS-Armee-Korps. Notified of the command on October 28, 1944, Baum arrived at divisional headquarters, a villa in Marzabotto south of Bologna, on November 1, 1944, and assumed command.[24] First subordinated to the I.Fallschirmkorps of General der Fallschirmtruppe Alfred Schlemm, Baum commanded this division until the end of the war.[25] After the fighting in Italy commanding the primary Waffen-SS unit in the country, and from late January, 1945, in Hungary, he surrendered with the remnants of his command to the British Army in St. Veith.

As with all Waffen-SS troops he was denied all civil and legal rights. Baum was not allowed to send a letter to his family until November 9, 1945, the first since May. His first letter from home was not given to him until early January, 1946. He was moved to England and in August 1946 was in the officers camp south of New Castle. During that time he worked as a volunteer gardener at the RAF base in Carlisle. In September, 1947, he was moved to Scotland but returned to England in mid-December where rationing and lack of heat in the barracks were normal. Moving to another camp on the mainland in Fallingbostel in August 1948, a hunger strike by the prisoners had little effect in improving their situation. Baum was finally released in mid-December, 1948, after three-and-a-half years unjustly imprisoned as a forced laborer.

Unquestionably one of the outstanding graduates of the SS officer school system, he was instinctively brave as well as being a natural strategist and tactician. His brilliance as a combat situation leader was certainly evident in both offensive and defensive engagements, gaining total devotion from his men. Fighting in most of the intense battles of the Eastern Front as a member of "Totenkopf" and in bitter Normandy combat, he was also among the most highly decorated Waffen-SS officers, as well as one of the few officer school graduates to reach full command rank. Holding three different combat divisional commands in the course of his career, he was the only SS officer school graduate to do so. He has assisted numerous researchers, both German and foreign, of his various commands, always maintaining a logical and highly intelligent perspective. Having worked in the textile industry as a supervisor after the war, Otto Baum lives today in retirement with his wife.

[18] Letter from Priess to Himmler's Field Command Headquarters dated November 23, 1943.

[19] Letter to the author dated January 6, 1996.

[20] Other sources, including a Stabsbefehl dated July 16, give him command effective June 20 but the 18th is confirmed by Herrn Baum. In field emergency conditions, the man often assumed a post before records or orders could be issued away from the action.

[21] Letter to the author dated April 9, 1989, "Pressenotitz" dated October 12, 1944, and "Fernschreiben" from Oberbefehlshaber "West" to Reichsführer SS dated August 23, 1944.

[22] Der Reichsführer-SS, Tgb. Nr. 4065/44 dated September 17, 1944, Himmler giving him command rank for his leadership of "Das Reich."

[23] Although the dates of his command are per Berlin, it is possible Lammerding did not return and take actual command until November 1 according to other period documentation sources.

[24] "Feld-Kommandstelle" dated November 6, 1944. It is interesting that the order mentions his Oakleaves but not his award of the Swords to the Knight's Cross.

[25] "Mein Einsatz in Italien" by Otto Baum. Schlemm was awarded the Knight's Cross on June 11, 1944, for his corps command.

The command pennant of Otto Baum shows the intensity of the Demjansk fighting and (below) he points to a target after being awarded the Knight's Cross.

SS-Sturmbannführer Otto Baum in his official portrait after being awarded the Knight's Cross and also showing his German Cross in Gold. On the right photograph he wears the rank of SS-Obersturmbannführer.

SS-Obersturmbannführer Otto Baum (left) with Heinrich Himmler in 1943 when the Reichsführer-SS paid a rare visit to the front.

A jubilant Otto Baum waves to much needed air support during the Demjansk fighting.

Karl Ullrich (above right) with Otto Baum and (below) Baum in Russia as an SS-Obersturmbannführer. Ullrich was commander of the "Totenkopf" Engineer Battalion at that time and will be in volume 2 for his command of the 5.SS-Panzer-Division "Wiking."

His battered command flag shows this to be Baum's command car (he is seated) and at that time was an SS-Sturmbannführer, prior to being awarded the Knight's Cross.

Max Seela (2nd from left) and Baum (2nd from right) after the encircled units at Demjansk were contacted by formations breaking the Russian lines. Seela ended the war as a Stopi (Corps Engineer Commander) and won the Knight's Cross.

SS-Sturmbannführer Otto Baum in the summer of 1942.

Two candid photos of Baum in Russia. On the left he wears the insignia of an SS-Sturmbannführer and on the right is an SS-Obersturmbannführer.

From left are Heinz Harmel, Otto Baum, Hitler and Himmler. Photo taken at Hitler's headquarters during the award of the Oakleaves to both Harmel and Baum.

Baum (center) with divisional commander Hermann Priess (right).

SS-Standartenführer Otto Baum (4th from left) as the commander of "Das Reich." Right of Baum is Heinz Werner ("Der Führer" Regiment battalion commander) who had just been awarded the Knight's Cross (he later won the Oakleaves). Beside Werner is "Der Führer" Regimental Commander Otto Weidinger who won the Knight's Cross with Oakleaves and Swords.

Hermann Priess (left) with Otto Baum (center) in Russia during the Mius fighting.

Formal portrait of SS-Obersturmbannführer Otto Baum after being awarded the Oakleaves to his Knight's Cross.

Two at left: (Top) Baum and Himmler during an inspection of "Totenkopf" and (left) the photo used in the SS newspaper "Das Schwarze Korps" announcing Baum's award of the Oakleaves. No portrait had as yet been taken so the award was added to an existing photo.

A formal portrait of SS-Standartenführer Otto Baum in September, 1944, with a personal dedication as commander of "Das Reich."

Baum (center) with Karl Kreutz (left) the commander of the "Das Reich" artillery regiment and Hans Schabschneider (artillery regiment) on the day Baum awarded both men the Knight's Cross.

Baum is awarded the Swords to the Knight's Cross by Hitler for his leadership of "Das Reich" during the Falaise battles. In the background is SS-Brigadeführer Hermann Fegelein.

SS-Oberführer Otto Baum (right) next to SS-Gruppenführer Max Simon as command of the 16.SS-Panzer-Grenadier-Division "Reichsführer-SS" is transferred. On the left is German Cross in Gold holder and divisional 1a, Ekkhard Albert.

Otto Baum, wearing his Swords, during an inspection of "Reichsführer-SS" in Italy, 1944.

SS-Oberführer
OTTO BAUM
Träger des Ritterkreuzes mit Eichenlaub und Schwertern

Kommandeur
17.SS-Panzer-Grenadier-Division "Götz von Berlichingen"
2.SS-Panzer-Division "Das Reich"
16.SS-Panzer-Grenadier-Division "Reichsführer SS"

Der Reichsführer-SS　　　Führerhauptquartier, den 2. August 1941

An den

SS-Hauptsturmführer

B a u m ,　Otto

(SS-Nr. 237 o56 - SS-T. Inf. Rgt.　3　　　)

Ich befördere Sie mit Wirkung vom 21. Juni 1941
zum SS-Sturmbannführer der Waffen-SS.

Der Reichsführer-SS

The formal promotion document signed by Himmler advancing Otto Baum in rank to SS-Sturmbannführer.

Vorläufiges Besitzeugnis

Im Namen des Führers und Obersten Befehlshabers der Wehrmacht

verleihe ich

dem

SS Sturmbannführer B a u m ,
Kdr. III./I.R.3/SS T.

das

Deutsche Kreuz in Gold

ħQu OħҺ, den 26.Dezember 19.41

Oberkommando des Heeres

~~Der Oberbefehlshaber des Heeres~~

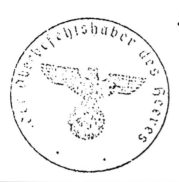

Generalfeldmarschall

The preliminary award document for Otto Baum's German Cross in Gold.

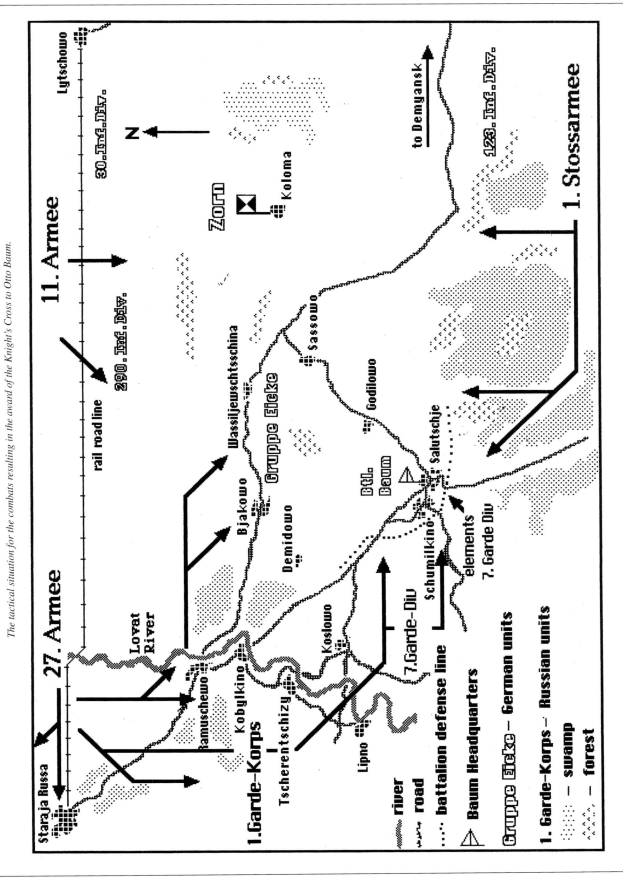

The tactical situation for the combats resulting in the award of the Knight's Cross to Otto Baum.

Vorläufiges Besitzeugnis

Der Führer
und Oberste Befehlshaber
der Wehrmacht

hat

dem SS-Sturmbannführer B a u m ,
Kdr.III./SS-T. I.R.3

das Ritterkreuz
des Eisernen Kreuzes

am 8.Mai 1942 verliehen.

HQu OKH, den 9. Mai 1942
Das Oberkommando des Heeres

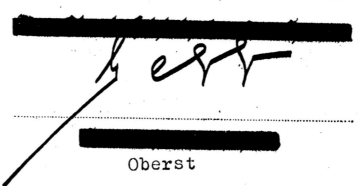

Oberst

The award certificate for the Knight's Cross given to Otto Baum and signed by a Colonel of the Army High Command.

VORLÄUFIGES BESITZZEUGNIS

DER FÜHRER

HAT DEM

SS-Obersturmbannführer B a u m
Kommandeur SS-Pz.Gr.Rgt. "Totenkopf"

DAS EICHENLAUB

ZUM RITTERKREUZ DES EISERNEN KREUZES

AM 22.8.1943 VERLIEHEN

HQu OKH, DEN 1.Oktober 1943.

OBERKOMMANDO DES HEERES

I.A.

Generalleutnant

Otto Baum's Oakleaves award document given to him as the commander of Regiment "Totenkopf."

Besitzzeugnis

Im Namen des Führers

wurde dem ᛋᛋ - Sturmbannführer

B a u m , Otto
Stab/SS-T.J.R.1 (mot.)

der Demjanskschild verliehen.

K.Gef.St.,den 31.12.1943

General der Infanterie

Für die Richtigkeit:

Oberleutnant

The Demjansk Shield award document given to Otto Baum at the end of 1943.

VORLÄUFIGES BESITZZEUGNIS

DER FÜHRER

HAT DEM

SS-Standartenführer B a u m
Kommandeur SS-Pz.Div."Das Reich"

DAS EICHENLAUB

MIT SCHWERTERN

ZUM RITTERKREUZ DES EISERNEN KREUZES

AM   2.9.1944   VERLIEHEN

HQu OKH, DEN   14.Oktober 1944.

OBERKOMMANDO DES HEERES
I.A.

The Swords to the Knight's Cross document given to Otto Baum for leadership of "Das Reich" at Falaise on the personal recommendation of Walter Model. Model appealed directly to Heinrich Himmler for the highest possible award to be given.

HELLMUTH BECKER

Hellmuth Becker was born the son of decorator Hermann Becker in Alt-Ruppin, Mark Brandenburg, on August 12, 1902. After primary schooling, he trained as an administrator with the local town council from 1917 to August, 1920. During 1919 he served with the Freikorps "von Grothe" and volunteered for the Army on August 1, 1920.[1] He served first with the 16th company and then the 5th company of Prussian Infantry Regiment No. 5 until moving to Artillery Regiment No. 2 in 1929. Becker served there as an NCO and was promoted to Wachtmeister on May 11, 1929. His final Army service was with the garrison headquarters in Stetten. During his Army service he passed his Abitur, while also studying economics and administration, and left the military on August 1, 1932. Becker married in April, 1930, and he and his wife eventually had five children between 1931 and 1943.[2]

Living in Stetten without a job after leaving the Army, he joined the SA on August 2, 1932, then also joined the NSDAP on April 1, 1933. On February 27, 1933, he joined the SS as a probationary candidate assigned to the III./9.SS-Standarte and left the SA the following day. He became an SS Mann on November 20, 1933, and served as adjutant of III./9.SS-Standarte from September 25, 1933, to the end of January, 1934. Promoted to SS-Scharführer on December 5, 1933, to SS-Oberscharführer on December 25, 1933, and to SS-Obertruppführer on March 28, 1934, Becker served as adjutant to the 74.SS-Standarte from February 1, 1934, to October 1 the same year.[3] Commissioned as an SS-Untersturmführer on June 17, 1934, he transferred to the SS-Verfügungstruppe on October 1, 1934, and was assigned to the Political Readiness Detachment in Hamburg. With that unit he took military training in Greifswald with Wilhelm Bittrich and Hermann Priess. Promoted to SS-Obersturmführer on March 10, 1935, he took command of the 2./I./SS-Standarte 2 (which later became Regiment "Germania") on the same day and led that company until transferring to the SS-Totenkopfverbänd in the beginning of July, 1935. In the pre-war years, Becker won both annexation medals (Austria and Czechoslovakia) and the Reich's Sports Badge in Silver.

From July 1, 1935 to July 1, 1937, he commanded the 9./SS-Wachsturmbann 1 "Oberbayern" (this became the 9./SS-Totenkopfsturmbann 1 "Oberbayern" in late March, 1936).[4] Promoted to SS-Hauptsturmführer on January 30, 1936, on July 1, 1937, he took command of the I./1.SS-Totenkopfsturmbann "Oberbayern" and held command until it was redesignated the I./SS-Totenkopf-Rekruten-Standarte on November 1, 1939.[5] During September, 1938, he also commanded the Sudetenland Freikorps. Promoted to

---

[1] For the most complete listing of Freikorps units, commanders and eventual fate of the units, see Jones, Nigel H., "Hitler's Heralds," pages 249-265. The operations, development and political situation that brought the Freikorps into existence is also covered. This volume, and Waite, Robert G. L., "Vanguard of Nazism, The Free Corps Movement in Postwar Germany 1918-1923," offer the best studies of these units. Many eventual leaders in the Third Reich served in a Freikorps, including Martin Bormann (Freikorps "Rossbach," later Hitler's powerful personal secretary), Rudolf Hess (Freikorps "von Epp," later Hitler's Deputy Führer), Kurt Daluege (Freikorps "Rossbach," later head of the Order Police), Hans Frank (Freikorps "von Epp," later Governor General of occupied Poland), Ernst Röhm (Freikorps "von Epp," later SA Chief of Staff) and Franz Felix Pfeffer von Salomon (leader of his own Freikorps and later became commander of the SA before Ernst Röhm). Almost all units were named for their commanders, normally junior ranked officers with combat commissions from the First World War. They generally did a better job at quelling unrest than the Army during their brief existence, especially in the Baltic states. Many units developned ties to early NSDAP groups.

[2] "Lebenslaufbahn," undated but ending with his award of the German Cross in Gold and "Antrag auf Bewilligung einer Notstandsbeihilfe."

[3] "SS-Stammrollen Auszug des Becker, Hellmuth." Wilhelm Bittrich, later commander of II.SS-Panzer-Korps, commanded the Standarte for most of the period Becker served as adjutant.

[4] The 1.SS-Totenkopfstandarte "Oberbayern" was formed on July 10, 1937. Information and research courtesy Ignacio Arrondo.

[5] When redesignated, command of the unit went to the former commander of SS-Bataillon "N" and later German Cross in Gold holder, Ernst Deutsch.

SS-Sturmbannführer on November 9, 1937, and to SS-Obersturm-bannführer on November 9, 1940, Becker took command of the I./SS-Totenkopf-Infanterie-Regiment 1 on November 1, 1939. During the Western Campaign of 1940 he won the Iron Cross 2nd class on May 24, and the Iron Cross 1st class on June 26. In 1941, he moved to command II.Bataillon of the same regiment until March 15, 1942, when he succeeded Heinrich Petersen as commander of SS-Totenkopf-Infanterie-Regiment 3.[6] Becker was awarded the Wound Badge in Black on July 11, 1941 (after being wounded the previous day), the Eastern Front Medal on July 13, 1942, and the German Cross in Gold on September 26, 1942.

Wounded seriously in the Demjansk pocket fighting in October, 1942, he remained regimental commander until November 9, 1943, when replaced by Karl Ullrich and was promoted to SS-Standartenführer on January 4, 1942. Divisional commander Hermann Priess recommended Becker for the Knight's Cross of the Iron Cross with the following report on August 25, 1943:

Hellmuth Becker (above) in Russia with the "Totenkopf" Division and (below) on the day he was awarded the Knight's Cross.

"On August 13, 1943, the Regiment, then the center of the Division, received the task to take the village of Nikotovka and the very important positions on the hill 199.8 and west of that the hill 197.4. After breaking strong enemy resistance (tanks and infantry), Nikotovka was in our hands during the early afternoon. During the following battles against the well-built and strongly fortified positions in the forested terrain and on the hills west of the village, the Russian front, which consisted of Russian tanks and anti-tank guns, threatened to bring the attack to a stand-still. SS-Standartenführer Becker, at his own decision, decided to take his strengthened reserve battalion to the north through the attack rows of the neighboring division (which had not taken part in the attack) and open the hills 197.1 and then attack further the strongly defended enemy positions on hill 199.8 and 197.4 from the north.

During determined attacks, which the commander personally took part in, hill 197.1 was taken. He continued on and attacked to the southwest and rolled up the enemy's flank situated between the hill positions on hills 199.8 and 197.4.

SS-Standartenführer Becker, by his own decision, and by the ruthlessness of his attacks which he led without regard for himself, was responsible for occupying the hills 199.8 and 197.4. With this success the requirements for the further attacks of the division on August 14, 1943 south of the Vertschik-pond in a westerly direction were met. These further attacks led to the annihilation of two Russian rifle divisions, two tank brigades and a motorized brigade.

I ask that SS-Standartenführer Becker, in recognition of his merit, be awarded the Knight's Cross to the Iron Cross."[7]

---

[6] Vopersal, "Soldaten, Kämpfer, Kameraden," volume IIa, page 383, gives October 25, 1941 as Becker's start of command. Therefore, Petersen may have been a substitute until the documented date in mid-March 1942. The regiment was redesignated as SS-Panzer-Grenadier-Regiment 6 in November, 1942, and received the honor title "Theodor Eicke" in March, 1943.
[7] "Vorschlagsliste Nr. 10 für die Verleihung des Ritterkreuzes des Eisernen Kreuzes," dated August 25, 1943 and signed by Hermann Priess.

Becker (2nd from left) stands next to divisional commander Theodor Eicke during the first Russian winter in 1941/42.

Following approval, Becker was awarded the Knight's Cross on September 7, 1943. On November 10, 1943, he was awarded the Wound Badge in Silver. After serving in reserve during the first months of 1944, Becker transferred to command SS-Panzer-Grenadier-Regiment 36 of the 16.SS-Panzer-Grenadier-Regiment "Reichsführer-SS" on March 13, 1944, and held command until July 13, 1944. During that time period he was promoted to SS-Oberführer on April 23, 1944.[8] He then left his new regimental command and returned to the 3.SS-Panzer-Division "Totenkopf" as divisional commander beginning on July 13, 1944, and remained there until the end of the war.[9]

Herbert Otto Gille, then commanding the IV.SS-Panzer-Korps, recommended Becker be decorated again. On September 4, 1944, he submitted the recommendation report requesting an award of the Oakleaves to the Knight's Cross for the "Totenkopf" commander with the following report:

"1. In October, 1943, the enemy had successfully widened the Dnjepr Bridgehead in the area of Misjurin Rog -

Dnjepropetrovsk to the West and had broken through with strong tank forces until reaching the area just short of Krivoi-Rog. In this threatening situation, the 3.SS-Panzer-Division "Totenkopf," under the leadership of SS-Oberführer Becker in the area of the XXXX.Panzer Korps, was assigned to penetrate the flank of the enemy. Despite the weakened battle strength of the division which was due to the previous difficult battles, SS-Oberführer Becker penetrated deep into the right flank of the opponent from the area south of Aleksandrija, leading his division with superior and decisive battle leadership. In the most difficult battles, which lasted three days, he had a decisive role in the annihilation of numerous Soviet tank forces and with that avoided the casualties of Krivoj Rog. The success is primarily the result of SS-Oberführer Becker's flexibility with respect to his enthusiastic decision-making and secondly his excellent personal action in the focal point of the battle.

2. During the battles in the area of Fauglia - St.Luze - Livorno - Pisa in the beginning of July, 1944, the Americans had succeeded in deeply penetrating and surrounding the left flank of the 16.SS-Panzer-Grenadier Division "Reichsführer-

---

[8] "Personalverfügung" dated March 18, 1944, and "Stammkarte."
[9] "Personalverfügung" dated July 20, 1944, and "Stammkarte."

SS." Through this arose the danger that the Division would be cut off from the rear. In this situation, SS-Oberführer Becker, situated with portions of SS-Panzer-Grenadier-Regiment 36 fighting in defense of the left wing, came to the independent decision to break out of his own position on his flank with the few remaining weak forces under his command and put an end to the threatening situation. He and his units were successful in destroying the strong forces of the enemy and to push his strongly burdened units through to freedom. Through his quick decision, energetic battle leadership and excellent personal bravery, SS-Oberführer Becker, at the front of his small group of men, avoided the encirclement and with that the threat to his division.

3. In the defensive battles in the area of Siedlce from July, 26 to August 11, 1944, the 3.SS-Panzer-Division "Totenkopf" was positioned on the flank of the 2nd Army to beat off massive enemy attacks. During very difficult battles which lasted for days, the divisional commander, SS-Oberführer Becker, again was located in the front lines in order to personally lead the defense or immediately engage in counterattacks. Through the decisive and - where necessary - the ruthless leadership of the divisional commander, the requirement for an orderly disengagement of the right wing of the army was accomplished. During the following disengagement movements in the beginning of August, 1944, SS-Oberführer Becker accomplished a completely orderly retreat of the division up to the Warsaw bridgehead through his hard leadership and the skillful coordination of his extremely weakened units. He personally led continuously, lightning counterattacks, which inflicted heavy casualties on the enemy. Enemy attacks which managed to penetrate his lines were, without exception, always repelled. These enemy attacks were answered with ruthlessness and for the most part the defense was personally led by SS-Oberführer Becker.

Two views of SS-Standartenführer Hellmuth Becker wearing both his Knight's Cross and German Cross in Gold. The right photo, originally showing a lower rank, had his new rank and Knight's Cross airbrushed in for publication in the German press.

Hellmuth Becker (left) as an SS-Oberführer and (right) as an SS-Brigadeführer.

4. After the strong attacks of the opponent in the area of Tlusza were blocked, new forces were brought up. On August 19, 1944, he tried to force a breakthrough over Volomin in a westerly direction towards Warsaw in the section of Grabie-Klembov. After an unusually strong and long lasting barrage of artillery fire, the enemy attacked the section of the deployed 3.SS-Panzer-Division "Totenkopf" with nine rifle divisions and parts of a tank corps. Up until August 21, 1944, the attacks against the positions of the SS men under the leadership of SS-Oberführer Becker continued uninterrupted for three days. Under the greatly hindered unification of all his available men, even the last typist and supply wagon driver, all attacks of the opponent, some even with bitterly led counterattacks, were destroyed. It was the service of the excellent leadership, tenacious energy and desire for action of SS-Oberführer Becker, that this great defensive success could be achieved. During the critical situations, SS-Oberführer Becker was always to be found at the focal point of the battle, during which he displayed his superior calmness, forcefulness and personal bravery and remained a shining example for his men.

In the time from August 19 to August 21, 1944, the following was destroyed in the section of the 3.SS-Panzer-Division "Totenkopf:'"

> 51 enemy tanks
> 4 heavy anti-tank guns
> 3 heavy machine guns
> 4 airplanes.

5. After the reorganization and quick freshening-up of his units, the enemy renewed its breakthrough attempts on Warsaw. The main thrust came again upon the 3.SS-Panzer-Divsion "Totenkopf," which was deployed in the section of Radzymin. After a five-hour barrage of fire, the enemy decisively attacked with eight rifle divisions, one motorized rifle brigade and parts of a tank corps with strong air force support into the division's positions.

The bitter struggle lasted for eight days, during which the fighting changed back and forth between enemy attacks and our counterattacks. The 3.SS-Panzer-Division "Totenkopf," under the leadership of SS-Oberführer Becker, destroyed all attempts of the bitterly fighting opponent to win land to the West. The divisional commander stood unshakable amongst his men during these difficult battle days, and he spurred them on to stand fast and hold out, and led them to decisive counterattacks with his example of bravery and calmness.

The division destroyed during these days 90 enemy tanks and five airplanes. The enemy breakthrough to Warsaw was beaten off and the opponent suffered a high and bloody number of casualties in personnel and a noticeable material loss."[10]

When approved on September 21, 1944, Becker was the 595th soldier of the German Armed Forces awarded the Oakleaves to the Knight's Cross with notice of the award and his photograph being published in the SS newspaper "Das Schwarze Korps," on November 30.[11] On October 1, 1944, Becker was promoted to SS-Brigadeführer und Generalmajor der Waffen-SS.

An aggressive and personally courageous commander, he was tireless in the field as well as inspirational to his subordinates. Trained in the camp system, he was close friends with Theodor Eicke who selected him as a regimental commander. Becker was investigated by Himmler on charges of misconduct in the field in which eight "Totenkopf" officers were willing to testify.[12] The official inquiry continued until the end of the war with no conclusions and did not prevent Becker's final promotion or advance to command a division.

On May 9, 1945, Becker surrendered to the Russians with the men of his command. Tried before a Soviet court, he was sentenced to twenty five years hard labor. Placed in charge of a reconstruction brigade, he was denounced by another prisoner for allegedly cementing a hand grenade in the wall of a house. Following a quick trial, Hellmuth Becker was executed by a firing squad on February 28, 1952.[13]

---

[10] "Vorschlag für die Verleihung des Eichenlaubes zum Ritterkreuz des Eisernen Kreuzes" dated September 4, 1944, and signed by Hermann Priess.

[11] It is interesting to note his photo in the official SS newspaper listed him as an SS-Oberführer while his portrait showed him at his newly promoted to rank of SS-Brigadeführer.

[12] Report written by SS-Obersturmführer d.R. Dr. Karl Bockhorn (regimental surgeon) on August 21, 1943.

[13] Krätschmer, "Die Ritterkreuztrager der Waffen-SS" and Vopersal, "Soldaten Kämpfer, Kameraden, Band Vb, give his death as February 28, 1953.

OTTO BINGE

Otto Binge was born on May 19, 1895, in Cottbus. Well educated, he passed his Abitur and was fluent in French. He joined the Army on August 21, 1914, with the Spandau-based replacement battalion of a Guard Foot Artillery Regiment until October. Transferring to the 3rd battery of Foot Artillery Regiment 26, Binge was promoted to Gefreiter on May 16, 1915, and to Unteroffizier on August 10, 1915. Moving to Foot Artillery Battery 114, Binge was advanced to Vizefeldwebel on January 27, 1917, and was commissioned as a Leutnant d.R. on July 3, 1917. Seeing combat in Russia, Serbia and Macedonia, Binge won both classes of the Iron Cross and the Bulgarian Eagle Order. While recovering from malaria he was posted to the replacement battalion of Foot Artillery Regiment 16 and went to a hospital in Strassburg. Following his recovery Binge went to the 3rd battery of the regiment and was sent to France where he was stationed at the end of the war, leaving the Army on January 26, 1919.

Binge joined a Freikorps in May, 1919, and fought in the Baltic. In September that year he moved to the Freikorps "Stever" and in March, 1920, joined the III.Marine Brigade. He saw action in Silesia and the Ruhr area until the end of September, 1920, and was awarded the Baltic Cross in 1919. Binge also won the Iron Cross 2nd class on March 1, 1917, and the 1st class on February 1, 1920.[1] He left the Freikorps on September 30, 1920.

Joining the Schutzpolizei as a Leutnant on March 1, 1922, his first assignment was in Mühlhausen until promoted to Oberleutnant on April 1, 1924. Binge then went to Eisleben until July 1, 1924, when he was posted to Essen. Promoted to Hauptmann der Schutzpolizei on April, 1, 1930, he served in Münster from the start of 1927 to May, 1929, when he moved to Potsdam. During these years he attended a large number of police schools including the Higher Police School in Eiche bei Potsdam. Stationed in Berlin from mid-May, 1930, to the start of 1938, he was promoted to Major der Schutzpolizei on April 20, 1937. After training with the Ordnungspolizei and a brief assignment in his home town during August to late-October, 1939, Binge was assigned to command Polizei Bataillon 22 of the Ordnungspolizei on October 30, 1939.[2] On May 6, 1940, he joined the artillery regiment of the Polizei Division as commander of its IV.Abteilung and trained with the Army from mid-February to mid-March 1941. Given the rank of SS-Sturmbannführer on November 1, 1941, he was promoted to SS-Obersturmbannführer on January 5, 1942, and to Oberstleutnant der Schutzpolizei on August 1, 1942.[3] He was awarded a clasp to his WWI Iron Cross 2nd class on September 15, 1942, and a clasp to the 1st class award on October 15, 1942. Binge remained with the Polizei Division and acted as commander from July 20, 1943, when Fritz Schmedes went to a commanders course, until August 25 when Fritz Freitag arrived as commander. Binge then went to the SS artillery training and replacement unit. After being placed in reserve on September 1, 1943, for three weeks he attended classes at the Army Artillery School in Berlin.

Binge took command of the artillery regiment of the 17.SS-Panzer-Grenadier-Division "Götz von Berlichingen" on December 18, 1943, and supervised the formation staff of the division from October, 1943, until Werner Ostendorff arrived in early January,

---

[1] "Beurteilung über Major Binge" for his training time with training section of Artillerie Regiment 171 during February and March, 1941.

[2] "Personalangaben" listing his Polizei career.

[3] "Stammkarte," and correspondence between Abschnitt XII and Oberabschnitt "Spree" listing him with the reserve formation of "Spree" dated October 14, 1942, and a later letter listing him with the 27.SS-Standarte of the Allgemeine-SS dated November 14, 1942.

1944. Promoted to SS-Standartenführer on April 20, 1944, Binge commanded the Division from June 15 to June 18, 1944, after Ostendorff was wounded again and until Otto Baum arrived. His official artillery regiment command lasted until August 7, 1944. However, Binge succeeded Baum as commander when the former went permanently to "Das Reich" and led the division from July 30, to August 29, when he suffered an accident and was replaced by Dr. Eduard Deisenhofer. He remained with the Division in reserve for more than a month until October 10.[4] He then spent the rest of the war assigned to the SS-Führungshauptamt and died on June 13, 1982. One of the overall unknown commanders, evaluations from Werner Ostendorff appear to indicate he was soft spoken and tactically somewhat ponderous in his regimental leadership during the Normandy campaign, since it was totally different combat from that he had encountered in Russia.[5] Ostendorff still considered him sufficiently effective a trainer and leader to recommend him on January 30, 1944, for promotion to SS-Standartenführer due to his honorable conduct and personality.

[4] Stöber, "Die Sturmflut und das Ende," volume I, page 441. He was officially listed in reserve effective October 10, 1944. SS-Führungshauptamt, "Stabsbefehl 25/44," dated October 24, 1944.

[5] "Beurteilung" dated August 8, 1944.

Otto Binge (right) with the commander of the 17.SS-Panzer-Grenadier-Division "Götz von Berlichingen," SS-Oberführer Werner Ostendorff.

WILHELM BITTRICH

Wilhelm Bittrich was born in Wernigerode, Harz, on February 26, 1894, the son of a later trade deputy. He trained as a gymnastics and sports instructor, joining the Army on July 30, 1914. Serving first with Jäger Bataillon No. 7 that was originally raised in the eastern German city-state Magdeburg, he transferred to the Flying Service on September 10, 1914, and remained there until May 1918. Commissioned a Leutnant, he was twice wounded, being awarded the Wound Badge in Black, both classes of the Iron Cross and the Pilot's Badge. As a pilot, he served with Flying Detachment A226 then Fighter Unit 37. From mid-March to July, 1919, he served with the Freikorps "Hülsen" and then the Freikorps "Ehrhardt" from January to June, 1920. Joining the Reichswehr in 1923, Bittrich trained German pilots in the Soviet Union and, from 1930 to 1932, was also a civilian employee with the Reichswehr.

Joining the NSDAP on December 1, 1932, Bittrich served in the SA from March to June, 1932. He then joined the SS on July 1, 1932, with Fliegerstaffel "Ost," and commanded that unit from the end of October 1932, to March 8, 1934. Commissioned as an SS-Sturmführer on October 31, 1932, he next commanded the 74.SS-Standarte from March 8, 1934, to August 25, 1934, when he transferred to the SS-Verfügungstruppe. As a trained officer in two services Bittrich could have chosen an Army or Luftwaffe career but chose the SS-Verfügungstruppe because of its wider scope for military experimentation as well as the less rigid organizational aspects and promotion procedures. He was promoted to SS-Obersturmführer on April 12, 1934, and then to SS-Hauptsturmführer on June 17, 1934.

Bittrich took command of the Politische Bereitschaft (Political Readiness Detachment) Hamburg until April 1, 1935. He then led the 2./I./SS-Standarte 1, which was actually a larger command, until September 29, 1936 (SS-Standarte 1 was bestowed the honor title "Deutschland" in mid-September 1935). Succeeding Carl-Maria Demelhuber as commander of II./SS-Standarte "Deutschland," he led that battalion until March 23, 1938, during which time he was promoted to SS-Sturmbannführer on October 1, 1936, and to SS-Obersturmbannführer on January 30, 1938.

Transferring to the new SS-Standarte 3 (later titled "Der Führer") then forming in Austria under Georg Keppler, he took command of its I.Sturmbann (later Bataillon) until promoted to SS-Standartenführer on June 1, 1939. Georg Keppler (then commanding the Regiment) gave him an exemplary evaluation in December, 1938. Transferring next to the "Leibstandarte," Bittrich served as Oberst im Stabe from his promotion date to SS-Standartenführer until replaced by Wilhelm Keilhaus on February 1, 1940. With the "Leibstandarte" he won the clasp to his WWI Iron Cross 2nd class on September 25, 1939.

Bittrich moved to Berlin and was assigned as a staff officer with the office for replacements for the SS-V.-Division within the Kommando der Waffen-SS in the SS-Hauptamt (after mid-August, 1940, in the SS-Führungshauptamt) from February 1, 1940, to December 1, 1940. After June, 1940, that post also included the replacement troops of the "Totenkopf" Division.[1] On June 7, 1940, he won a clasp to his Iron Cross 1st class for his time with the "Leibstandarte." Promoted to SS-Oberführer on September 1, 1940, he replaced Felix Steiner as commander of Regiment "Deutschland" at the start of December, 1940, when Steiner went to form the even-

---

[1] Kurt Knoblauch, who headed the replacements for the "Totenkopf" Division, became "Totenkopf" Division Ia and Bittrich absorbed his responsibilities as well. Knoblauch later headed the Kommandostab "Reichsführer-SS." See Yerger, "Riding East, The SS Cavalry Brigade in Poland and Russia" for photos and data on Knoblauch.

Wilhelm Bittrich (left) during the brief period when collar insignia was not worn by the numbered and named regiments as a security measure in 1940.

tual "Wiking" Division. Bittrich held command until October 14, 1941, when he was replaced by Jürgen Wagner. As commander of "Deutschland" he was recommended for the Knight's Cross by Paul Hausser with the following report:

"SS-Brigadeführer Bittrich has been awarded the clasp to the Iron Cross II and I Class. During action in Russia he commanded the SS-Regiment "Deutschland" until the divisional commander was wounded on October 14, 1941. He has led his regiment with personal cleverness, hardness, prudence and achieved great success.

In the battle for Jelnja he and his Regiment took hill 125.6 on July 22, 1941 and defended this until they were relieved on August 8, 1941, during continuous attacks by the Russians, who were superior in both numbers and material.

Further, he especially distinguished himself on October 13, 1941. The SS-Regiment "Deutschland," which was initially strengthened by a Panzer detachment of the 10.Panzer Division, had the task to reach the Moscow protection position along

the old road between Gshatsk and Moshaisk as the left column of the SS-Division "Reich" and dispatch reconnaissance patrols to the strongly defended Russian positions. The reinforced SS-Regiment "Der Führer," acting as the right column of the Division, had the same task along the highway.

At 1300 hours the commander of SS-Regiment "Deutschland" determined through reconnaissance that there was a weakly-occupied enemy position existed on a stretch of railroad tracks located between the highway and Mail Street. Recognizing that waiting any longer would give the enemy the chance to recognize his positions, which would result in the Russians calling in reserves to strengthen their weak position, the regimental commander decided to break into the Russian positions under protection of a quickly assembled artillery battery as well as a few Panzers. From then on the Regiment conducted a continuous attack for seven days, suffered heavy casualties and was without field kitchens (warm food) for the last four days due to the difficult weather conditions.

The break-in was successful; the opponent was completely

surprised. An anti-tank trench, which ran through the Russian positions and which was lined with barbed-wire obstacles, was quickly taken care of. During dusk a 500 meter deep and one km wide break-in position was established. Bittrich was successful in lengthening the break-in position to a length of 3 kilometer in conjunction with a neighboring regiment before dawn the next day. On October 14, 1941, during a hard battle conducted by both regiments, they were successful in turning the break-in into a break-through through the three km deep, cleverly and strongly built Russian positions. The strength of this position and the decisive meaning of the "quick power" of the commander of SS-Regiment "Deutschland" is confirmed by the extent of the booty. The following was captured by taking the Moscow protection position:

21	Cannons
14	Anti-Tank Guns
92	Heavy Machine Guns
10	Heavy Grenade Launchers
14	Tanks
65	Flame-throwers
2	Trucks
1	Personnel Carrier
1	Armored Patrol Car
1	Combat Engineer Equipment Dump
859	Prisoners were brought in

The breakthrough, which occurred within 24 hours, and the resulting quick taking and opening of the highway are to

A wounded Bittrich in without collar insignia but displaying his "Deutschland" cufftitle in an autographed photo and (right) he is with SS-Standartenführer Hermann Fegelein. The latter photo, taken in mid-1942, is during Bittrich's assuming command of the SS-Kavallerie Division that was formed with Fegelein's former SS-Kavallerie-Brigade command as its cadre.

be credited to the independent decision-making of the commander of SS-Regiment "Deutschland," SS-Brigadeführer Bittrich. The opponent has not been successful in beating off newly arriving troops during the following days following this battle. Moshaisk was occupied by SS-Divison "Reich" on October 18, 1941, and the Division, together with the 10.Panzer Division, used the line between the crossing 5 km south of the Moshaisk and the eastern edge of Moshaisk as the departure point for the continuation of the attack on Moscow."[2]

The award was approved on December 14, 1941. When "Reich" commander Paul Hausser was wounded, Bittrich, as senior regimental commander, took his place and led the division until officially leaving the command during the first week of January, 1942.[3] On October 19, 1941, he was promoted to SS-Brigadeführer und

---

[2] "Vorschlagliste Nr. 9 für die Verleihung des Ritterkreuzes des Eisernen Kreuzes," dated October 24, 1941, and written by Hausser.
[3] Weidinger, "Division Das Reich," volume III, page 305, gives the daily order in which he announces his departure. His "Personalverfügung" for his transfer gives a date of December 31, 1941.

Generalmajor der Waffen-SS, his "Reich" position being taken by Matthias Kleinheisterkamp when Bittrich became ill.

After four months with the SS-Führungshauptamt, Bittrich took command of the newly forming SS-Kavallerie-Division, which later became "Florian Geyer," on June 1, 1942. He had actually replaced Hermann Fegelein as commander of the SS-Kavallerie-Brigade for a month prior to that while the Brigade was being dissolved and used as cadre to form the division. Though officially titular commander of the SS-Kavallerie-Division until February 15, 1943, he left the division when called to Berlin in December, 1942. He was replaced in the field by senior regimental commander Gustav Lombard. For actions as commander of this division he was awarded the German Cross in Gold on March 6, 1943.

Bittrich arrived at Mailly-le-Camp in France on February 11, 1943, and four days later officially took command of the formation staff from Thomas Müller of what would develop into the 9.SS-Panzer-Division "Hohenstaufen." He officially commanded this division until July 10, 1944, when formally succeeded by Sylvester Stadler. His successes with the unit included bitter combat in Tarnopol.

Hermann Fegelein (left) with Bittrich during the activation of the SS-Kavallerie Division. Bittrich's rank insignia is of the pre-1942 design and is for an SS-Brigadeführer.

A formal portrait of SS-Gruppenführer Wilhelm Bittrich.

Promoted to SS-Gruppenführer und Generalleutnant der Waffen-SS on May 1, 1943, Bittrich replaced Paul Hausser as commander of the II.SS-Panzer-Korps on June 29, 1944.[4] Leading this corps until the end of the war (his command became permanent on July 10, 1944), he was awarded the Oakleaves to the Knight's Cross on August 28, 1944, for combat at Falaise and Caen.[5] Bittrich's defense of Arnheim was among the last great victories on the Western front. Sepp Dietrich personally awarded him the Swords to the Knight's Cross on May 6, 1945, for combat in Hungary while leading the II.SS-Panzer-Korps.

Naturally gifted and brave, he did not hesitate to criticize his superiors when he deemed it necessary. Bittrich often sided with senior Army commanders against ludicrous racial directives issued by Himmler, the latter protecting him when the Reichsführer-SS tried to have him replaced. In direct defiance to Himmler's standing order, he allowed church services for his command. Chivalrous to his armed enemy, this was especially shown at Arnheim. He was among the best Waffen-SS leaders, both as a commander, leader and tactician.

Captured by the US Army, he was handed over to the French who released him in 1954. He was active in HIAG, becoming senior officer of that organization after the death of Paul Hausser. Wilhelm Bittrich died in Wolfratshausen on April 19, 1979.

---

[4] Thomas Müller again took command of "Hohenstaufen," until the arrival of Sylvester Stadler.

[5] Telex from Model to Himmler and "Das Schwarze Korps" of January 11, 1945.

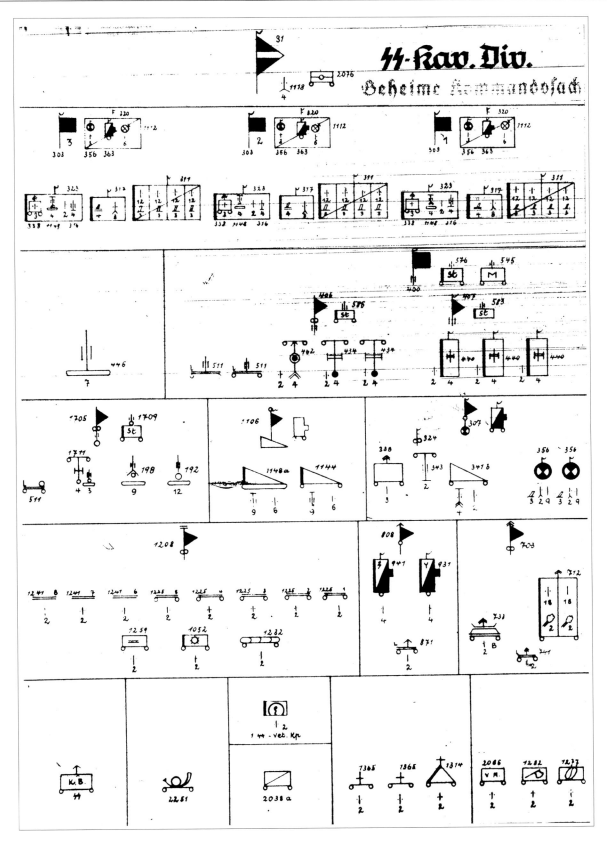

The SS-Kavallerie-Division in early September, 1942

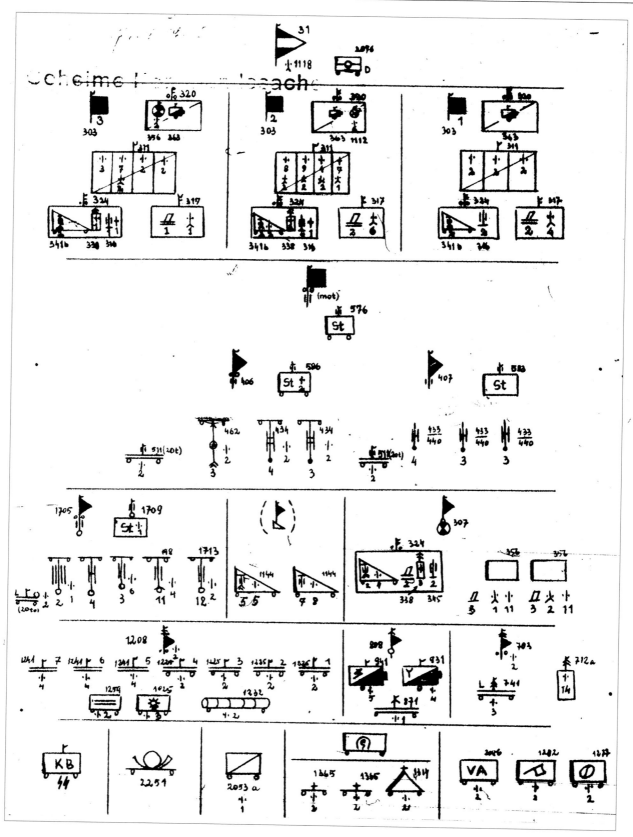

The SS-Kavallerie-Division on Christmas Eve 1942

GEORG BOCHMANN

One of the most highly decorated and skilled Waffen-SS commanders who spent his entire military career in the SS, Georg Bochmann was the son of textile factory worker Gustav Bochmann and was born in Albenau bei Aue in Saxony on September 18, 1913. He attended school in Schneeberg where he passed his Abitur. Bochmann then attended classes at the University of Leipzig and served in the Hitlerjugend from October 1, 1930 to May 2, 1933. He joined the NSDAP, as well as becoming an SS candidate, on March 14, 1933.

Bochmann was assigned to the 2./IV./7.SS-Standarte until May 24, 1934, when he moved to the 3.Hundertschaft (company) of the Political Readiness Detachment Sachsen. On November 1, 1934, he moved to the 2./III./SS-Totenkopsturmbann "Sachsen," being promoted to SS-Sturmann on November 9, 1934, to SS-Rottenführer on December 24, 1934, and to SS-Unterscharführer on January 25, 1934. He then moved to the 15.Hundertschaft of the same unit until April 20, 1936, when he took command of that unit until May 1, 1937.[1] Commissioned as an SS-Untersturmführer on April 20, 1936, then promoted to SS-Obersturmführer on April 20, 1937, Bochmann attended classes in the Dachau training area with 11./SS-Wachtruppe "Oberbayern" from August to December, 1935.

Beginning May, 1937, Bochmann became commander of the 3.Hundertschaft in Sturmbann I "Oberbayern" of the Totenkopfverbände until July 10, 1937, when he was given command of the 2.Hundertschaft of the I.Sturmbann in the new 1.SS-Totenkopfstandarte "Oberbayern."[2] Holding that post until November 1, 1939, he was promoted to SS-Hauptsturmführer on August 25, 1939, on the recommendation of Theodor Eicke.

Bochmann then moved to command the 14.(Panzer Jäger)/SS-Totenkopf-Infanterie-Regiment 1 when the "Totenkopf" Division began forming. Holding that command until March 27, 1941, he took additional training at the Army Infantry School in Döberitz (first half of November, 1939), with the 31.Infanterie-Division (late August to early September, 1940), then Armeeoberkommando 7 (late November, 1940), and finally a battalion and detachment leaders course in Königsbrück (mid-February to mid-March, 1941).[3] On June 20, 1940, he was awarded the Iron Cross 2nd class.

Transferred to the Panzerjäger Abteilung of the "Totenkopf" Division as commander of its 2.Kompanie on March 27, 1941, he was promoted to SS-Sturmbannführer on April 20, 1942. Bochmann was wounded three times in the first Russian campaign, on July 8, 1941, January 17, 1942, and April 20, 1942.[4] On July 8, 1941, he was awarded the Iron Cross 1st class. Bochmann held command of the 2./Panzerjäger Abteilung until mid-1941, when he took command of the entire Panzerjäger Abteilung.[5] During the fighting for the Demjansk pocket he led Kampfgruppe "Bochmann" for a week beginning in mid-April 1942, consisting of a Kompanie of SS-Totenkopf-Infanterie-Regiment 1, 3./Aufklärungsabteilung, the divisional Stürmkompanie, a Panzerjäger Kompanie, a Sturmgeschütz section and the divisional escort unit. Bochmann was approved for the award of the Knight's Cross on May 3, 1942, from the following recommendation submitted by Generaloberst Ernst Busch:

---

[1] "SS-Stammrollen"
[2] "Beurteilung," dated March 23, 1938, and signed by Max Simon.

---

[3] "Dienstlaufbahn"
[4] "Personal-Nachweis für Führer der Waffen-SS"
[5] He wrote the Knight's Cross recommendation for Fritz Christian with that command position and according to Krätschmer, "Die Ritterkreuzträger der Waffen-SS," page 295, he commanded the unit since the start of the Russian campaign. It is logical to assume he was given a command advance after his promotion to SS-Sturmbannführer.

"SS-Hauptsturmführer Bochmann, at the lead of his shock battalion, played a significant role in the successful attack of Gruppe "Eicke." Under strong leadership and brave personal action of the commander, The Bataillon Bochmann was successful in carrying out the taking of Nov-Ramuschevo in very hard battles which took place on the evening of April 21. SS-Hauptsturmführer Bochmann, under his own decision, pushed his battalion forward. In close combat with bayonets, 13 2.2cm cannons and 6 tractors were taken as booty.

From Nov-Ramuschevo came the first direct contact through signals (flags or signs or flashlights, not radio) from the leading attacking elements of the Gruppe "von Seydlitz" and also from elements on the west bank of the Lovat.

It is requested, that SS-Hauptsturmführer Bochmann, in recognition of his personal excellent action and the value of his success until taking up contact with Gruppe "von Seydlitz," be rewarded with Knight's Cross of the Iron Cross."[6]

Bochmann next led a motorcycle unit as official commander of the II./SS-Totenkopf-Kradschützen-Regiment "Thule" from October 21, 1942, to August 1, 1943. In the spring of 1943 Bochmann apparently turned his command over to a designated deputy (with his records keeping him listed as commander) and took command of the II./Panzer Regiment 3. Next replacing Eugen Kunstmann (killed on July 8, 1943) as commander of SS-Panzer-Regiment 3 on August 1, 1943, he commanded the armor unit of "Totenkopf" until November 1, 1943.[7] "Totenkopf" commander Max Simon recommended Bochmann for advanced command, as well as submitting the following recommendation on March 27, 1943, which resulted in his being awarded the 246th Oakleaves to the Knight's Cross in the German Armed Forces on May 17, 1943:

"On March 9, 1943, Bataillon Bochman occupied the security line in Schelstovo, as soon as aerial reconnaissance reported disengagement operations of the enemy. SS-Sturmbannführer Bochmann dispatched a battle-strong reconnaissance patrol to Katschalovka under his leadership. During this patrol, after he approached the enemy without being noticed, some 13 kilometers from his own lines, he was able to inflict high bloody casualties and claim four driveable trucks, one anti-tank gun (7.62mm) as booty and was able to destroy various cannons, vehicles and sleds. He returned to his point of departure having suffered no casualties.

The task of his battalion on March 10, 1943, was to take the village of Krassnokutsk as quickly as possible. This task was accomplished by SS-Sturmbannführer Bochmann by utilizing an especially clever action of his battalion. He led the lead platoon himself and was able to get a very clear picture of the enemy occupation of the village. Since evening had fallen, he decided to avoid a night street fight and attacked the village from three sides. The attack, which he personally led, was a great success. Many enemy dead, numerous cannons, anti-tank guns and much equipment was abandoned by the opponent.

The Bataillon Bochmann had the task, on March 17, 1943, to take the forested area located 3km southeast of Ssorokovka and with that the villages of Saroshnoje and Tetlega, in conjunction with the I.SS-Totenkopf-Kradschützen Regiment "Thule." During these attacks SS-Sturmbannführer Bochmann displayed excellent bravery. After the infantry rolled over the first field positions, he roared into the positions on an armored car and confused the enemy so much that they fled their positions. To take full advantage of this situation, he advanced immediately and with that gave his battalion the opportunity to quickly approach the village. In the village of Tetlega, which the enemy was bitterly defending, he pushed forward with his 5.Kompanie and immediately recognized the opportunity to run over the enemy positions in the village and in the shortest time was able to take the northern section of the village. He was also able to establish contact with the battlegroup approaching from the south."[8]

Promoted to SS-Obersturmbannführer on November 9, 1943, and to SS-Standartenführer on November 9, 1944, Bochmann succeeded Johannes Bauer as commandant of the SS Economic and Administrative Leaders School in Dachau from February 10, 1944, to November 15, 1944.[9] He turned command of the school over to Wilhelm Karius and returned to combat duty.[10] Oswald Pohl, head of the SS-WuVHA, was very impressed with Bochmann and recommended him for his promotion to full colonel.[11] Bochmann was also briefly assigned to command the Panzer Regiment of "Hohenstaufen" after the death of its commander Otto Meyer.[12] He was transferred to "Hohenstaufen" effective November 20, coming from a week with "Das Reich" where he may have been considered

---

[6] "Kurze Begründung und Stellungnahme der Zwischen-Vorgesetzten" also approved by the commander of Heeresgruppe "Nord," signed for him by Generaloberst, later Generalfeldmarschal, Georg von Küchler who himself won the Knight's Cross (September 30, 1939) with Oakleaves (August 21, 1943).

[7] It would appear he commanded on a temporary basis from the date of Kunstmann's death and then received the post officially on the date given. Vopersal, "Soldaten, Kämpfer, Kameraden," Band III, confirms Bochmann as commander of the II.Abteilung after Kunstmann became regimental commander (following the transfer of Kunstmann's predecessor, Karl Leiner).

[8] "Bericht über besondere Tapferkeitstaten des Ritterkreuzträgers SS-Sturmbannführer Bochmann, Georg, geb. 18.9.13, Kommandeur II./SS-T-Kradschützen-Regiment "Thule," dated March 27, 1943.

[9] "Personalverfügung" dated February 5, 1944, with effect from February 10, 1944. He was originally to have taken command in 1943 but did not leave his front line post at that time.

[10] According to two different "Dienstalterliste" he was to have been Panzer Regiment commander of the "Leibstandarte," possibly replacing Joachim Peiper during the Ardennes fighting, but the transfer never took place.

[11] "Beurteilung" dated September 30, 1944, and signed by Pohl.

[12] "Stammkarte," Personalverfügung" dated November 28, 1944, with effect from November 20, 1944, and Krätschmer, "Die Ritterkreuzträger der Waffen-SS," page 298.

Georg Bochmann (left) wearing double "Totenkopf" insignia and (right) as an SS-Sturmbannführer and holder of the Knight's Cross.

as a divisional commander replacement or to head the Panzer Regiment.[13]

On January 3, 1945, Bochmann replaced Wilhelm Trabandt as commander of the 18.SS-Panzer-Grenadier-Division "Horst Wessel." He led that division until relieved of his post on March 27, 1945.[14] For this command, Bochmann was recommended for the Swords to the Knight's Cross by General der Panzertruppe Walter Nehring, with the following report on March 25, 1945:

"At the order of the Supreme Commander of the Army Group "Center," the Panzer Armeeoberkommando 1 recommends SS-Standartenführer Bochmann, commander of the

18.SS-Freiwilligen-Panzer-Grenadier-Division "Horst Wessel" for the Swords to the Knight's Cross of the Iron Cross.

Standartenführer Bochmann rallied his men through his own personal action after heavy enemy fire had stalled his division's attack in the battle area north of Ratibor on the March 8, 1945.

On March 3, 1945, he personally led a night attack into the most forward lines during which time he took the objective under difficult conditions.

On March 14, 1945, near Langlieben, Bochmann personally initiated and skillfully led several counterattacks and took part in the action. Because the counterattacks served as the cornerstone of the defense against a storm of weapons and numerous units of the far superior enemy, the enemy was held. During these actions, Bochmann was located on the front lines and fought side by side with his men and stood in the midst of his troops that surrounded him, as the soul of the resistance.

---

[13] Christian Tychsen (commander Panzer Regiment "Das Reich") had been divisional commander for two days until he was killed. He was replaced temporarily by Otto Baum. Hans Weiss became commander of the Panzer Regiment and Heinz Lammerding returned to command "Das Reich."

[14] Tiecke and Rebstock,"im letzen Aufgebot," page 178. His personal records indicate earlier in March.

Leaders of "Totenkopf" Division are, from right, Georg Bochmann, Hermann Priess and Otto Baum. All three men were awarded the Knight's Cross with Oakleaves and Swords as well as commanded divisions during their careers. Priess led the I.SS-Panzer-Korps "Leibstandarte" at the end of the war.

In the especially difficult fighting which took place on March 16, 1945, Bochmann personally carried out several attacks in the front-most lines. It is Bochmann that must be recognized for Kreuzlinden (located southwest of Oberglogau) being held, and orders for mopping up the bridgehead in Coesl being carried out according to plan.

On March 19, 1945, it was again only his inspiring leadership personality in the Deutsch-Muehlen, that held this village against all enemy tank and infantry attacks. By holding the village, the order for the breakout of both divisions that night was successful.

During the breakthrough in the night of March 19/20, 1945, through Deutsch-Rasselwitz over Stubendorf on to Hotzenplotz, it was again the shining example of Bochmann's inspiring leadership. It should especially be noted, that, despite the serious wound he suffered on March 14, and despite all advice from doctors, he remained by the troops and held together their leadership."[15]

The award was approved on March 26, 1945, and Georg Bochmann was the 140th soldier awarded the Swords to the Knight's Cross. Hitler personally bestowed the award on Bochmann at his headquarters on March 30, 1945.

Bochmann's command was taken from him on March 27 by Feldmarschall Ferdinand Schoerner for refusing to lead a suicidal attack. However, Schoerner previously confirmed Bochmann's Swords recommendation with the comment "I approve the quick awarding of the Oakleaves with Swords on this battle-proven and crisis-breaking SS-Standartenführer. Bochmann is, because of his worthy personality and because of the performances he has displayed, worthy of this high award." Three days later Bochmann was given command of the 17.SS-Panzer-Grenadier-Division "Götz von Berlichingen" by Hitler when presented his award of the Swords, leading that unit until the war ended.

Fearless but discreet in combat, he was wounded five times during the war but always returned to his unit as soon as possible. For this, he was also awarded the Wound Badge in Gold. Max Simon described him as vigorous and hard-working in a 1940 evaluation and wrote numerous reports of his bravery and skills in Russia. Bochmann was also obviously well liked by both peers and subordinates, having a genuine concern for the troops under his command. In addition to his other decorations, he was awarded both pre-war occupation medals, the Infantry Assault Badge and the Eastern Front Medal. Married with one son, he surrendered with his last command to the U.S. Army at Rottach-Egern on May 9, 1945. He remained in command until the division was officially dissolved on June 11, 1945.

Well-educated, Georg Bochmann suffered poor health in the post-war years from recurring bouts of marsh fever contracted in Russia. Courteous and helpful to Waffen-SS researchers, he died in Offenbach am Main on June 8, 1973.

---

[15] Telex communication to Hermann Fegelein, Himmler's liason officer in Hitler's headquarters.

FRIEDRICH-WILHELM BOCK

A West Prussian born in Wreschen on May 6, 1897, Friedrich-Wilhelm Bock was the son of a minister. After passing his Abitur, he joined the Army on August 2, 1914. Posted to the artillery, he served with Field Artillery Regiment No. 38 until the start of October, 1914, then moved to Field Artillery Regiment No. 2. Commissioned as a Leutnant in February, 1918, he was wounded on September 11, 1918. Following his recovery, Bock served with Field Artillery Regiment No. 38 until leaving the service at the start of February, 1919. Awarded the Iron Cross 2nd class and the Wound Badge in Black, Bock served with a Freikorps in the Baltic during 1919.

After the war he worked with the agricultural ministry in the states of Mecklenburg and Pommerania until 1922. Bock then joined the Schutzpolizei in Hamburg on November 15, 1922, as a Wachmeister. He transferred to the Prussian Schutzpolizei in April, 1926, serving in Stettin, Trepkow and finally in Marienburg, where he was promoted to Major der Schutzpolizei. Assigned to the Schutzpolizei in Hannover at the start of September, 1939, he went to the General Government, where he commanded Polizei Bataillon 3 of the Ordnungspolizei from December, 1939, to April 1940.[1] Bock joined the NSDAP on May 1, 1933, and the SS as an SS-Sturmbannführer d.R. on November 1, 1941.

Moving to the Polizei Division, he took command of the II./ Polizei Artillerie Regiment during the first week of May, 1940. As commander of his unit in Russia, he won a clasp to his WWI Iron Cross 2nd class on August 21, 1941, and the Iron Cross 1st class on September 16, 1941. Bock was promoted to SS-Obersturmbannführer d.R. on January 5, 1942, then became a fully-active

Waffen-SS officer on April 1st and was awarded the Eastern Front Medal on August 2, 1942.

Artillery regiment commander Fritz Schmedes and Divisional Commander Alfred Wünnenberg recommended Bock for the Knight's Cross as commander of II.Abteilung with the following report:[2]

"SS-Obersturmbannführer Bock has excellently proven himself as a detachment commander of the SS-Polizei-Artillerie-Regiment since the beginning of the operations in the East during all attacks and defensive battles. During the difficult winter fighting of the previous year, he led a battle group on the Volchov and beat off many attacks by a superior enemy through quick accurate firing by his detachment. He was able to do the same at the end of January of this year on the Sinjavino Hills.

During the course of the local battles on the Neva, the Russians attacked at dawn on February 2, 1943, with forces far superior in number and materiel. The Russians came from the area of Kolpino on both sides of the "October Highway" and broke through during their first attacks on the positions of the 250th (Spanish) Infantry Division. Without encountering any notable resistance, the Russians pushed to the south, crossed over the October highway and carried out an attack against the hill street Stepanovk-Mischkino, the base of which was reached at 1100 hours. Before it was too late, Obersturmbannführer Bock recognized the danger , which would threaten the left flank of the SS-Polizei-Division should the Russians advance

---

[1] "Lebenslauf" dated February 25, 1941.

[2] "Vorschlagliste für die Verleihung" des Ritterkreuzes des Eisernen Kreuzes" dated February 20, 1943.

Friedrich-Wilhelm Bock (left) in Polizei uniform and (right) on the day he was awarded the Knight's Cross. The latter photo was issued during the period by Heinrich Hoffmann as a postcard.

further, and he gave his observation posts (which were located in Feklistovo and Mischkino) the order to engage in defensive close combat and also to defend the important hills and to hold at all costs. Under the leadership of the Battery Chiefs of the 4th, 6th, 12th batteries and the staff battery, as well as the arriving units of the Army Artillery observation posts, the artillery protection positions were occupied. From the beginning on these positions were defended with dash and determination. To secure the left flank, Obersturmbannführer Bock ordered his own defensive line near Feklistovo to bend around to the West, in order to check the advance of the enemy. Renewed enemy break-ins into Feklistovo were mopped up during immediate counter attacks. As the first reinforcements in the form of a cannon platoon arrived at 1400 hours, they were thrown immediately into battle in Feklistovo to protect the left flank at all costs. Obersturmbannführer Bock personally made sure that

the battle was taking place correctly by remaining on the front lines and along the defensive lines. Only his presence here made it possible for him to engage the arriving reinforcements correctly.

New reinforcements continued arriving until almost 1700 hours. An engineer and mounted company of the SS-Polizei-Division, which were brought up to plug a hole that was open in the positions of the neighboring units on the left, were put into action on the left flank. In the mean time, the Russians were advancing along the hilly streets in the direction of Mischkino with strong tank forces. The defensive front, the building of which Obersturmbannführer Bock had personally overseen, began to fall apart. Since no available tank-destroying weapons were available, Feklistovo could no longer be held. Obersturmbannführer Bock was also able to master this situation, since, during his own personally ruthless action during which he displayed decisiveness and calmness in the presence of enemy tanks, he saw to it that his weakening units remained organized and during which they built a new defensive line on the western edge of Mischkino and the northern edge of Porkusi. In the meantime, some tank-breaking weapons had arrived in Mischkino, and his men were able to smash two enemy tanks on the village's main street and hold the newly built defensive positions.

Through his independent decision-making, and also having barely any forces for future defensive actions which were important to hold the hilly road, Obersturmbannführer Bock was able to make sure that his division was able to complete their orders to build a new defensive position.

Because of his excellent performances in the defensive fighting around this important strong point and because of his ruthless personal action in the most difficult of situations, I recommend that Obersturmbannführer Bock be awarded the Knight's Cross to the Iron Cross."

signed Fritz Schmedes
SS-Standartenführer and Regimental Commander

"SS-Obersturmbannführer Bock, at his own decision, beat off the Russians with his weak artillery forces during their break-through of the open left flank south of Kolpino. His units also successfully defended the very important positions atop the hills between Miskino and Feklistovo in bitter close combat against masses of Russian soldiers. By always displaying bravery during these actions he enabled his troops to hold out. It is only his personal action that brought the Russian break-through on the left flank of the neighboring division to a standstill before they were able to complete their goal. Through this action, the goal of the Russians to break the surrounding front around Leningrad was reduced to nothing. SS-Obersturmbannführer Bock is worthy of being decorated with the Knight's Cross of the Iron Cross."

signed Alfred Wünnenberg
SS-Gruppenführer und Divisional Commander

The award was approved on March 28, 1943, as written on the recommendation.[3] Bock was also recommended for the German Cross in Gold during September, 1943, by commander Fritz Schmedes but the award was not approved at higher echelon. He retained his Abteilung command until August 1, 1943, when he succeeded Schmedes as regimental commander. He held command until the start of April, 1944, and was promoted to SS-Standarten-

Although of poor quality, this photo shows a significant event: the awarding of the Knight's Cross to Bock by Alfred Wünnenberg. The officer on the left holds the case for the decoration.

führer on November 9, 1943. Within the period of his regimental command, he led the remnants of the SS-Polizei-Division that remained in Russia until March 15, 1944, as Kampfgruppe "SS-Polizei-Division." He succeeded Fritz Freitag on October 24 when Freitag was transferred to a divisional command.[4] Bock's command was subordinated to Kampfgruppe "Schuldt," commanded by Hinrich Schuldt.[5] When Schuldt was killed on March 15, 1944, Bock took command of the 19.Lettische SS-Freiwilligen-Division until April 13, 1944, when he was succeeded by Bruno Streckenbach.

After briefly serving in reserve, Bock was the Arko (corps artillery commander) of II.SS-Panzer-Korps from the start of June, 1944, until promoted to SS-Oberführer on August 1, 1944. Succeeded at his Arko post by Hans Sander, Bock then took command

---

[3] It is interesting to note that incorrect dates are given in records of men, even one so important as the award of the Knight's Cross. In Bock's case, several documents incorrectly list April 1 as the award date.

[4] Husemann, "Die guten Glaubens waren," Band II, pages 206, 207 and 215.

[5] Schuldt was commanding the 2.Lettische SS-Freiwilligen Brigade that initially formed the center of the Kampfgruppe along with Bock's Kampfgruppe as well as Army elements. Bender/Taylor, "Uniforms, Organization and History of the Waffen-SS," volume 5, page 74. The Brigade was technically expanded while operational at the front to divisional size in January, 1944, but a Russian offensive temporarily halted the actual expansion. Schuldt's biography will be in volume 2.

of the 9.SS-Panzer-Division "Hohenstaufen" from Sylvester Stadler, who had been wounded.[6] His command consisted of part of the division with Walter Harzer leading the balance during the Arnheim battles. After Stadler returned on October 10th, Bock resumed his Arko post with the II.SS-Panzer-Korps until the end of the war. His award of the Oakleaves on September 2, 1944, was proposed personally by Feldmarschall Walter Model directly to Himmler for Bock's leadership in the difficult Normandy fighting.[7] He was the 570th soldier awarded the decoration, Model also recommended Otto Baum for the Swords at the same time, and both men were granted their decorations the same day.

Brave and honorable, Bock was among the best artillery commanders in the Waffen-SS. Physically strong, energetic and resilient, his energy and tactical skill as a difficult situation combat leader was acknowledged both by Fritz Freitag, while commanding the Polizei Division Kampfgruppe, as well as by Wilhelm Bittrich, the commander of the II.SS-Panzer-Korps. Married to the sister of SS-Brigadeführer und Generalmajor der Polizei Konrad Ritzer, Friedrich-Wilhelm Bock died in Hannover on March 11, 1978. Bock typified the excellent combat commanders who served with the SS-Polizei-Division, which remains one of the most historically overlooked divisions of the Waffen-SS by historians when compared to the better known armored units.

---

[6] Sander had served in the artillery regiment of the "Totenkopf" Division as commander of its III.Abteilung from 1939 to mid-May, 1941, then led the IV.Abteilung until January, 1943. He won the German Cross in Gold on October 31, 1942. As an SS-Obersturmbannführer he took command of the artillery regiment of the 10.SS-Panzer-Grenadier-Division (later titled "Frundsberg") in February, 1943. Promoted to SS-Oberführer on January 30, 1945, he was the Arko for the XIII.SS-Armee-Koprs in the autumn of 1944 and ended the war holding the same post for the III.(germ.)SS-Panzer-Korps. Stadler's biography will be in volume 2.

[7] "Frenschreiben" from Model to Himmler dated August 23, 1944.

ALFRED BORCHERT

Born in Barmstedt in Holstein on December 5, 1891, Alfred Borchert attended Volksschule in his birthplace until mid-April, 1907. From April 15, 1907, to April 1, 1909, he attended an NCO school in Neubreisach in Alsace. Transferred to Trepkow, he went to the officer candidate school there until the start of April, 1911, when he joined the infantry with the First Guard Regiment. Borchert served with that regiment until early August, 1914, when he transferred to Infantry Regiment No. 163, that originated in Schleswig-Holstein area of northern Germany, until mid-May, 1915. Promoted to Vizefeldwebel on August 1, 1915, and commissioned as a Leutnant on October 26, 1917, he served with Infantry Regiment No. 187 from mid-May, 1915, until receiving his commission. He then returned to his previous regiment where he served until taken prisoner by the British on September 27, 1918. Released on October 21, 1918, Borchert was awarded the Iron Cross 2nd class on October 31, 1914, and the Iron Cross 2nd class on August 19, 1916. In 1918 he was given the Hamburg Hanseatic Order (March 16) and the Mecklenburg Military Service Order 2nd class (May 29).[1]

After leaving the Army, Borchert joined the Schutzpolizei in Hamburg as a Leutnant on November 15, 1919. He moved to the barracked police company (Hundertschaft) there on October 23, 1923, and took command of the unit at the start of July, 1933. Promoted to Oberleutnant on October 1, 1920, to Hauptmann on February 1, 1923, and to Major on July 1, 1933, he joined the NSDAP on May 1, 1933. On December 10, 1937, he was promoted to Oberstleutnant and joined the Allgemeine-SS on July 1, 1939, with the rank of SS-Obersturmbannführer.[2] His initial SS assignment was as an officer in Administrative District 44 until April, 1941,

and he was promoted to SS-Standartenführer on November 9, 1941, though simultaneously undertaking continuing police duty assignments.[3] During early September, 1939, Borchert was a police training and replacement bataillon commander in Oranienburg and in mid-September, 1939, became a bataillon commander in Polizei-Schützen-Regiment 1 which was being incorporated as a component of the new Polizei-Division. From May to July, 1940, he was also deputy regimental commander. Borchert was awarded clasps to his WWI Iron Crosses on September 25, 1939 (2nd class) and June 23, 1940 (1st class).

In mid-September, 1941, he took command of the replacement units of the Polizei-Division and was promoted to Oberst der Schutzpolizei on November 9, 1941. From December, 1941, until wounded in the head on January 20, 1943, he commanded Polizei-Schützen-Regiment 3 (redesignated SS-Polizei-Infanterie-Regiment 3 in mid-October, 1942). During that time, Borchert commanded the SS-Polizei-Division from May 15, 1942 to July 18, 1942.[4] Divisional commander Alfred Wünnenberg recommended him for the German Cross in Gold for his regimental leadership with the following report:

> "Oberst Borchert, commander of the SS-Polizei-Schützen-Regiment 3 distinguished himself by displaying numerous acts of considerable bravery during the battles to surround Leningrad and break-through fighting to close the hole south of Tschudovo.
>
> On December 21 and 22, 1941, the Russians were successful in breaking in to our positions along a 400 meter wide

---

[1] "Lebenslauf" dated July 28, 1939, and "Personalangaben."
[2] "Dienstleistungszeugnis" dated May 22, 1941.
[3] It was typical that the Schupo officers admitted to the SS were shown on the roles with supplementary reserve formations until a proper post was found.
[4] Hausser, Paul, "Soldaten wie andere auch," page 370.

Two views of SS-Oberführer and Oberst der Schutzpolizei Alfred Borchert. In the right photo he is speaking with a trainee at one of the Waffen-SS NCO schools.

front near Novo Ssusi. The opponent had the idea of expanding this localized success by breaking through the depth of our main battlefield by bringing up strong infantry forces and engaging us with the strongest artillery fire.

After putting together all available troops and rearward elements, Oberst Borchert personally led the counterattack from the furthest forward positions on the front line. The enemy units which had broken in were surprised by this counterattack and he was able to beat them back to their original positions while inflicting heavy casualties on them. The enemy lost over 200 dead (counted) as well as large amounts of weapons, munitions and equipment.

During the continuing defensive battles, Oberst Borchert inflicted the heaviest casualties on the opponent again and again by executing various successful patrol troop operations. With that he had much to do with the collapse of the enemy's attempt to breakthrough the surrounding ring around Leningrad.

During the closing of the gap south of Tschudovo, Oberst

Borchert led the attack group "West." In a five day attack through waist deep snow, he was successful in ripping apart the enemy supply columns and holding off all enemy attacks.

After the SS-Polizei-Schützen-Regiment 3 was relieved by the southern attack group (58.Infanterie Division) on March 22, 1942, the Russians broke through the northern supply line and penetrated deep into the German positions. Although he had just been relieved in this section, Oberst Borchert attacked the enemy immediately with his relieved forces and did not rest before he was able to reestablish the old contact with the southern group and annihilate the enemy.

The attack group "West" has held its section despite strong attacks, a feat which must be attributed to the service of its proven commander. His personal, excellent bravery and the large success of the groups led by Oberst Borchert make him especially worth of being awarded the German Cross in Gold."[5]

[5] "Vorschlagliste für die Verleihung des Deutschen Kreuzes in Gold" dated April 11, 1942.

The recommendation was approved and Borchert was awarded the German Cross in Gold on May 19, 1942. He also transferred to the Waffen-SS active officer list as an SS-Standartenführer on April 1, 1942.

Following his recovery, he went to the SS-Führungshauptamt as Chef of Amt XII (Office for NCO Training) from September 1, 1943, until the end of the war.[6] Promoted to SS-Oberführer on February 1, 1943, he also attended a divisional commanders course during March and April, 1944, where the senior army course commander described him as reliable and conscientious.[7] In addition to

his combat awards, he won the War Merit Cross 2nd class on September 1, 1943, for his service in the SS-Führungshauptamt.[8] Married with two children, Alfred Borchert died in Hamburg on April 27, 1969.

[6] Final entry in both "Dienstlaufbahn" and "Stammkarte," his command is confirmed in the January, 1944, "Dienstalterliste." Schulze-Kossens, in a photo on page 250 of "Der Junkerschulen," incorrectly gave him as commander of the SS NCO school Posen-Treskau when he was in fact inspecting the facility while head of NCO training at that time.

[7] "Personalverfügung" dated March 10, 1944, and "Beurteilungsnotitz" dated April 14, 1944.

[8] SS-Führungshauptamt to SS-Personalhauptamt dated January 29, 1944.

KURT BRASACK

Kurt Brasack, the son of a businessman, was born in Schönebeck on the Elbe on April 6, 1892. After schooling he worked for the Karl Frasdorff Company until joining the Army on October 1, 1913, as a one-year volunteer. From his enlistment until January 11, 1916, he was assigned to Foot Artillery Regiment "Encke" No. 4, originally of recruits from Magdeburg, being promoted to Gefreiter on May 1, 1914, and to Unteroffizier on June 1, 1914. Promoted to Vizefeldwebel on January 27, 1915, and commissioned as a Leutnant d. R. on January 11, 1916, Brasack served as ordnance officer of Field Artillery Regiment No. 21 from January, 1916 into 1917. He then transferred to a unit originally from the former Nassau state area of western Germany, Field Artillery Regiment No. 27, and in 1918 was serving as a battery chief. When he left the Army on November 30, 1918, he was acting as adjutant to Pommeranian Foot Artillery Regiment "von Hindersin" Nr. 2, having won both classes of the Iron Cross and the Hungarian Bravery Medal.

After the war, he worked in his father's business as a salesman and was a member of the Stahlhelm from May, 1921, to 1930. Brasack married in 1921 and his family eventually contained a son and a daughter. On July 1, 1930, he joined the NSDAP and enlisted in the SS as an SS-Mann on March 1, 1931. Initially assigned to the II./21.SS-Standarte, he was promoted to SS-Truppführer on August 4, 1931, and was administrative officer to the II.Sturmbann from October 18, 1931, to March 3, 1932. Commissioned as an SS-Sturmführer on October 18, 1931, and to SS-Sturmhauptführer on March 3, 1932, he commanded II.Sturmbann from March 3, 1932, to April 20, 1934. In the pre-war years, Brasack won the Reich's Sports Badge in Gold and the SA Brunswick Rally badge of 1931.[1]

Promoted to SS-Sturmbannführer on April 20, 1933, and to

SS-Obersturmbannführer on November 9, 1933, he was to have been given command of the 4.SS-Standarte but the post went to another officer. Brasack led the Reservesturmbann of the 21.SS-Standarte from April 20, 1934, until taking command of the 91.SS-Standarte on May 7, 1934. He led that unit until January 1, 1937, and was promoted to SS-Standartenführer on September 9, 1934. Brasack then succeeded Richard Hildebrandt as leader of Abschnitt XI until September 22, 1937. Transferring to Abschnitt XXX, he led that district from September 22, 1937, officially until the end of the war, though he served with the Waffen-SS and the duties of his command were undertaken by substitutes.

Promoted to SS-Oberführer on January 30, 1938, he trained with the Army as a Leutnant d.R. during 1936 and 1938 with Artillerie Regimenter 14 and 51, as well as the Army artillery school in Jüterbog. Promoted to Oberleutnant d.R. on December 1, 1938, he joined the Waffen-SS as an SS-Obersturmbannführer d.R. on December 1, 1939. Assigned to the "Totenkopf" Division, Brasack was commander of the I./SS-Totenkopf-Artillerie-Regiment from December 1, 1939, to April 1, 1941. Following a detachment leaders course at Jüterbog, while still assigned to "Totenkopf," he went to the artillery regiment "Wiking" and took command of the I.Abteilung from April 1, 1941, to May 30, 1941, being succeeded by SS-Obersturmbannführer Ernst Fick. Moving to IV.Abteilung of the same division, he succeeded Constantin Heldmann as commander from May 30, 1941, to early January, 1942.

Brasack transferred to SS-Division "Reich" and took over command of the division's artillery regiment for Dr. Günther Merk on January 10, 1942, and was promoted to SS-Standartenführer d.R. on January 30.[2] Leading that regiment until March 18, 1943, he

---

[1] "Stammkarte" and "SS-Stammrollen."

[2] "Personalverfügung" dated January 20, 1942.

SS-Sturmbannführer Kurt Brasack (left) with his son while assigned to the artillery regiment of "Totenkopf."

also succeeded Herbert Otto Gille as Arko of SS-Panzer-Korps from the end of July, 1942, to October 7, 1942. His replacement at his Korps post by Karl Heinrich Brenner.

When divisional commander Herbert Vahl was wounded, Brasack took command of "Das Reich" from March 18, 1943, until Walter Krüger arrived to assume command on April 3, 1943. Brasack's artillery regiment command went to Karl Kreutz. From the time Krüger arrived until late June, 1943, Brasack was listed in reserve and was promoted to SS-Oberführer d.R. on April 20, 1943. He was then reassigned from June 29, 1943, to November 10, 1943, as Waffen-SS and Polizei supply transport commander for northern Russia, headquartered in Riga, Latvia. He succeeded SS-Oberführer Hans Scheider.[3]

Returning to a combat command, he led the artillery regiment of the 4.SS-Freiwilligen-Panzer-Grenadier-Brigade "Nederland" from November 10, 1943, to May 20, 1944.[4] Moving to the VII.SS-Panzer-Korps as Arko, he continued at that post when the corps was absorbed by the IV.SS-Panzer-Korps, succeeding Peter Hansen.[5] Promoted to SS-Brigadeführer und Generalmajor der Waffen-SS on January 30, 1945, he held the latter corps post until March 1, 1945. At his final command, he was awarded the German Cross in Gold on October 19, 1944. Brasack also won clasps to both his WWI Iron Crosses, the Eastern Front medal and was awarded the Wound Badge in Black.

An experienced, brave and resourceful artillery commander, he was well-appreciated and liked by the commander of IV.SS-Panzer-Korps, Herbert Otto Gille. Captured by the US Army, he was released in 1949 and later was active in HIAG. He died in Hamburg on September 28, 1978.

[5] "Personal-Antrag" from his promotion recommendation form to SS-Brigadeführer which also lists his decorations without award dates.

[3] For Scheider's biography see volume 2.
[4] "Personalverfügung" dated November 18, 1943. He was to have gone to the Ukranian Waffen-SS division as artillery regimental commander in November, 1943, but the transfer was cancelled and another officer received the command.

Kurt Brasack (left) with the commander of the "Totenkopf" artillery regiment (right)
SS-Standartenführer Fritz Allihn during 1940.

Below: Brasack (seated at left) with Heinrich Petersen (seated center) and other
artillery men from "Totenkopf."

Brasack (center) as an artillery detachment commander in 1940.

Kurt Brasack (left) and SS-Sturmbannführer Dr. Adolf Katz in 1940.

SS-Oberführer Kurt Brasack wearing his German Cross in Gold, WWII clasps to both of his WWI Iron Crosses and the General Assault Badge in 1944.

KARL BRENNER

Born in Mannheim on May 19, 1895, Karl Brenner graduated from a technical high school and volunteered for the Army on August 3, 1914. He served throughout the war until January 15, 1919, with Field Artillery Regiment "von Scharnhorst" No 10 from Hannover and was commissioned as a Leutnant in 1915. Wounded four times, he was highly-decorated, having been awarded both classes of the Iron Cross, the Wound Badge in Silver, the Prussian Military Service Cross in Gold 2nd class, both classes of the Oldenberg Service Cross, the Baden Knight's Cross 2nd class with Swords and the Baden Karl Friedrich Military Service Medal in Silver.[1]

Serving with the Baden Volunteer Battailon "East" from mid-January, 1919, until the start of April, 1920, Brenner took part in the Kapp Putsch.[2] He left the Army while assigned to Infantry Regiment 7.

After leaving the Army, he joined the Police in Baden, serving with the Sicherheitspolizei then the Landespolizei in that State until 1935, by which time he held the rank of Major der Landespolizei.[3] In 1935, he attended the Landespolizei Leaders School in Berlin and then served as adjutant to the Senior Commander of the Prussian Landespolizei during the same year.

Brenner also joined the Hitlerjugend in 1926, serving in Baden with the rank of Bannführer (the highest leader rank below the senior leadership of the organization) until March 1, 1935. He joined the NSDAP on May 1, 1933. During the summer of 1935, he trained with the Army at the Artillery School in Jüterbog and with Artillery Regiment 4 in Ulm.

From 1936 to the start of August, 1939, he headed an office in the Hauptamt Ordnungspolizei and in 1936 he was promoted to Oberstleutnant der Schutzpolizei. Brenner joined the SS on September 11, 1938, as an SS-Obersturmbannführer with seniority from July 1, 1938.[4] First assigned to the staff of the SS-Hauptamt, from January to August, 1939, he was responsible for Police Sports in the Hauptamt Ordnungspolizei and was promoted to Oberst der Schutzpolizei on April 20, 1939, then to SS-Standartenführer on August 15, 1939.

At the start of August, 1939, Brenner took command of the Police Sport School in Berlin-Spandau where he remained official commander until February, 1940. He went to Poland and by October, 1939, took command of the Polizeiregiment "Warsaw."[5] Brenner held that post until March 12, 1940, when he transferred to the "Totenkopf" Division as temporary commander of the artillery regiment.[6] Holding that command until May 4, 1940, he was succeeded by Fritz Allihn who had officially remained commander

---

[1] "Lebenslaufbahn" and "R.u.S.-Fragebogen"

[2] "Stammkarte" The Kapp Putsch was led by Wolfgang Kapp (1858-1922), a German right-wing politician. In 1920 he led the uprising named for him, an armed revolt in Berlin aimed at restoring the German monarchy. After seizing the Berlin government, a general strike broke his power. Kapp fled to Sweden and returned to Germany in 1922 where he died awaiting trial for treason.

[3] The Landespolizei (Land Police within each state) received military training for a number of years before that instruction was formalized by the Reichswehr in 1933 with Army officers assigned as training coordinators. In mid-March, 1935, discussions began to transfer the Landespolizei formally to the Army the following week, with the exception of the "Hermann Göring Regiment." Control then went from the Ministry of the Interior to the Commander in Chief of the Army. The actual police functions of the Landespolizei were taken over by the Schutzpolizei and Gendarmerie with former Landespolizei officers given equal rank in the Army at the start of August, 1935. The transfer was completed two months later. Only a few SS officers, including Georg Keppler, served with the Landespolizei, most seeing service with the Schutzpolizei.

[4] "Der Reichsführer-SS, SS-Personalkanzlei, dated August 12, 1938 and signed by the Chef der SS-Personalkanzlei.

[5] "Das Schwarze Korps," article of November 23, 1939, mentioning Brenner as commander of the regiment in that month. A substitute or deputy would have performed his Spandau school duties until he officially gave up command.

[6] "RFSS," SS-Personalhauptamt, Tgb.Nr. 83/40, dated March 7, 1940.

Two views of Karl Brenner in the uniform of a Polizei General. In both photos he displays his Wound Badge, WWII clasps to both of his WWI Iron Crosses and a Hitler Youth decoration.

during that time. Brenner next led the artillery regiment of the Polizei-Division until the start of November, 1941. With the Polizei Division he won a clasp to his WWI Iron Cross 1st class on August 17, 1941 having received a clasp to his 2nd class award thirteen days before.

Promoted to SS-Oberführer on November 9, 1941, and to SS-Brigadeführer und Generalmajor der Waffen-SS on January 30, 1942, he was Befehlshaber der Waffen-SS "Nordwest" from the start of November, 1941, to February 6, 1942. Promoted to Generalmajor der Polizei on January 30, 1942, Brenner was the Inspector of the Ordnungspolizei in Salzburg, undertaking anti-partisan operations from February 6 to July 1, 1942, when he left to assist with the forming of SS-Generalkommando.[7] With that command he served as Arko from October 7, 1942, to February 1, 1943. During his corps posting, he led one of four battle groups in the takeover of the French Navy port of Toulon during November and December, 1942. After five weeks with the Hauptamt Ordnungspolizei in Berlin as an office head, he next served as the Befehlshaber

der Ordnungspolizei Salzburg, heading anti-partisan military operations under Higher SS and Police Leader "Alpine Land" Erwin Rösener until late September 1943.[8] Promoted to SS-Gruppenführer und Generalleutnant der Waffen-SS on March 15, 1944, and to Generalleutnant der Polizei on January 1, 1944, Brenner next served as Befehlshaber der Ordnungspolizei for the Ukraine from mid-December, 1943, until June 6, 1944.[9] He was recommended for the German Cross in Gold on June 10, 1944, for actions while assigned to his Orpo post in the Ukraine with the following report by Reichsführer-SS Heinrich Himmler:[10]

"On March 2, 1944, SS-Gruppenführer und Generalleutnant der Polizei Brenner advanced with a small column of personnel carriers in the surrounded village of Borki. He personally led the defensive battles, by which Borki was able to be held for three days longer.

---

[7] Per his personnel records, this is probably the actual date of assuming his Salzburg post, versus being assigned. He is listed with that command in the January 31, 1942, issue of the SS "Dienstalterliste."

[8] For Rösener's career and photos see Yerger, "Allgemeine-SS," pages 74-75.
[9] "Abschrift von Abschrift" from the Chef der Ordnungspolizei dated March 16, 1944, confirms being assigned the position.
[10] "Begründung und Stellungnahmen der Zwischenvorgesetzten" from "Vorschlag für die Verleihung des Deutschen Kreuzes in Gold" dated June 10, 1944.

On March 15, 1944, the opponent pushed into the northern part of Kremianez; SS-Gruppenführer Brenner personally led the last reserves in a counterattack and threw back the superior enemy and out of this part of the village.

On March 21, 1944, our lines near Dytkoviecki were overrun by a Russian surprise tank advance. SS-Gruppenführer Brenner, through his personal action, was successful in heading off our retreating forces and building a new main fighting line.

On March 27, 1944, Russian tanks broke in near the position of the battlegroup command post in Suchovola. SS-Gruppenführer Brenner gathered the battlegroup staff and horses together then began to attack until the reserves arrived to conduct a counter-attack.

On April 2, 1944, our main fighting line was overrun by a superior forces, south of Brody. Under the leadership of SS-Gruppenführer Brenner, the scattered troops and the battlegroup staff were deployed for a counter-attack, which brought the enemy attack to a stand-still.

On April 5/6, 1944, Hill 261 southeast of Brody was taken by the opponent. Numerous counterattacks remained unsuccessful; renewed counterattacks under the leadership of SS-Gruppenführer Brenner resulted in the possession of the highway, important for supply traffic.

On April 13 and 14, 1944, the battle group was removed from the area between Brody and Hutniki, in the section of Stanislavzik according to orders. The retreating battle group was endangered by the strongly pursuing opponent. SS-Gruppenführer Brenner personally deployed the reserve troops and threw back the superior enemy. Through this action, the disengaging operations were able to be completed as planned."

Karl Brenner as an SS-Gruppenführer und Generalleutnant der Polizei.

The award was approved on June 16, 1944. During that period he was military advisor for Higher SS and Police Leader Hans-Adolf Prützmann's Kampfgruppe.[11] Succeeding Curt von Gottberg as commander of the Kampfgruppe named for him, after heading its military supervision, he led that battle group from July 23, 1944, to late September, 1944.[12] Brenner also substituted for Erich von dem Bach as head of anti-partisan operations from July to the start of September 1944.[13] Replacing Gustav Lombard as commander of the 6.SS-Gebirgs-Division "Nord" in early September, 1944, Brenner had been appointed the post on September 1.

Brenner was also awarded the Infantry Assault Badge on May 16, 1944, the Wound Badge in Gold on September 27, 1941, as a result of losing sight in his left eye in combat, the War Service Cross with Swords 2nd class in 1940 and the War Service Cross with Swords 1st class in 1944.[14] As commander of "Nord," his corps commander, Friedrich Hochbaum (XVIII.(Geb) Armeekorps), recommended him for the award of the Knight's Cross with the following recommendation on November 17, 1944:[15]

"In carrying out the disengagement operations of the XVIII.(Gebirgs)Armeekorps from the previous positions in the Karelien, the subordinated 6.SS-Gebirgs-Division "Nord" had the task to prevent an early pursuit of the Russians from Kistinki to Kuusamo, and, through defense of the shelter in Kuusamo, to enable the troops to gather the supply goods there.

On September 19, 1944, a regiment of Russians, engag-

---

[11] "Aktennotiz" dated April 5, 1944. For Prützmann's photograph and career see Yerger, "Allgemeine-SS," page 27.

[12] "Fernschreiben," Ch.vH/No, dated July 25, 1944, and sent by the Chief of the SS-Personalhauptamt, Maximillian von Herff.

[13] "Personalverfügung" dated October 6, 1944, officially transferring from his anti-partisan post to "Nord."

[14] Statistics sheet from Brenner's Knight's Cross recommendation.

[15] "Vorschlagliste Nr. 1 für die Verleihung des Ritterkreuzes des Eisernen Kreuzes" signed by Hochbaum on November 17, 1944, and approved December 31, 1944. Hochbaum himself won the Knight's Cross (August 22, 1943) with Oakleaves (June 4, 1944).

ing reserve troops of the division with two strengthened Jäger-Bataillonen and one Artillerie Abteilung in heavy frontal battles, was successful in shoving the retreat path near the Finnish-Russian border.

During a reconnaissance advance near one of the units, which was conducting an encircling movement from the West, the divisional Ia was killed on September 19. The majority of the division found itself some 70 kilometers west during these battles and in preparation for the retreat to the shelter of defensible positions in Kuusamo. Thanks to the insight and energy of SS-Gruppenführer Brenner, there were no clashes within the leadership of any sort due to the sudden loss of the Ia, even though he had taken over the command of the Division just fourteen days before. In ruthless action, he hurried immediately forward to his distressed reserve troops in order to lead in the breakout through the surrounding ring of their positions in the town."[16]

Brenner was approved to receive the Knight's Cross on December 31, 1944.[17] During the pre-war years, he also won the Hitler Youth Honor Badge in Gold number 12410 given to him by Reichsjugendführer Baldur von Schirach, the Olympic Games Decoration 2nd class, the German Horseman's Badge in Silver, and the Reich's Sports Badge in Gold, as well as receiving a personal letter of commendation from Himmler.

A professional artillery soldier and police officer who excelled in sports, especially running and skiing, his military skills were of much use to Higher SS and Police Leaders Curt von Gottberg and Erwin Rösener for anti-partisan operations, particularly in Carinthia and Upper Styria.[18] He married in 1935 and after he was divorced, his ex-wife Ursula married Josef "Sepp" Dietrich, with whom Sepp had a daughter prior to the divorce. Himmler feared a public scandal but the two officers remained friends. Brenner remarried in January, 1943, and from both marriages had a total of three daughters.

Karl Brenner surrendered to the US Army on April 2, 1945, and, after his release, moved to Karlsruhe, where he died on February 14, 1954. His personal recollections of combat operations as commander of "Nord" during January, 1945, are microfilmed in the National Archives.[19]

---

[16] "Kürze Begründung und Stellungnahme der Zwischenvorgesetzten"

[17] Date from his Vorschlag which confirms the error in Krätschmer, "Die Ritterkreuzträger der Waffen-SS" and other Knight's Cross holder texts.

[18] Detailed evaluation of Brenner from Rösener to Otto Winkelmann, head of the Ordnungspolizei, dated November 19, 1943.

[19] "The 6.SS-Mountain Division "North" and its part in Operation "Northwind," Northern Alsace, 1 January to 25 January 1945," written by Brenner in March, 1947.

KARL BURK

The son of a farmer, Karl Burk was born in Buchenau on March 14, 1898. He left school and worked in farming until joining the Army on April 15, 1913. Assigned to an NCO school in Sigmaringen until mid-February, 1915, he then moved to the NCO school in Weissenfels until the start of October, 1916. Leaving the school system, Burk was posted to the replacement battalion of Lower Sachsen Infantry Regiment No. 132 and quickly was reassigned to the regiment's 1st company, where he remained until November, 1918.[1]

From November, 1918, until mid-March, 1920, Burk served with the 2nd battery of Foot Artillery Regiment No. 10. He ended the war as a Sergeant and was awarded both classes of the Iron Cross. He remained in the post-war army and went to the 2nd battery of Artillery Regiment No. 5 where he stayed until leaving the service as an Oberwachtmeister on February 4, 1927. As a civilian, Burk studied labor management until 1934 and joined the NSDAP on May 7, 1933.

Burk joined the SS as an SS-Hauptscharführer on March 1, 1933, and was posted to the training command. From late February, 1934, to mid-March, 1935, he was a platoon leader at the SS Sports School in Korbach and was commissioned as an SS-Untersturmführer on April 20, 1935. Promoted to SS-Obersturmführer on November 9, 1935, he served as adjutant of Abschnitt XXX from April 20, 1935, until January 15, 1936. Burk then succeeded Friedrich Dernehl as Stabsführer of Abschnitt XXIV until the start of February, 1938. During that posting he was promoted to Allgemeine-SS Hauptsturmführer on September 13, 1936, then to SS-Sturmbannführer on September 12, 1937.

Burk next led the 70.SS-Standarte from the start of February, 1938 until January 9, 1939, when he took command of the 8.SS-Standarte. While leading 70.SS-Standarte he was promoted to SS-Obersturmbannführer on November 9, 1938. Leaving his command of 8.SS-Standarte, he was reassigned to Oberabschnitt "Südost" and was Stabsführer from September 1, 1940, to the start of March, 1941. During 1936, he trained with the Army's Artillery Regiment 64 as a reserve officer. Burk joined the Waffen-SS as an SS-Obersturmbannführer d.R. on March 1, 1940, having also been commander of the II./12.SS-Totenkopfstandarte since November 11, 1939. He gave up his command and Waffen-SS rank and returned to his Allgemeine-SS "Südost" staff duties at the start of October, 1940, but then rejoined the Waffen-SS as an SS-Obersturmbannführer d.R. on March 25, 1941.[2]

After training with the SS-Artillerie Ersatz Regiment until mid-April, 1941, and serving as a Special Duties Officer with the artillery regiment of Wiking, he was given command of SS-Flak Abteilung "Ost" on May 20, 1941.[3] His command supported and was attached to both Army and SS units as needed.[4] Promoted to SS-Standartenführer d.R. on March 6, 1942, he led the unit until August 1, 1942. Burk was also the first Waffen-SS officer to serve as a corps artillery commander with an Army unit, holding that

---

[1] "Lebenslaufbahn."

[2] The 12.SS-Totenkopf-Standarte was dissolved effective August 15, 1940.

[3] "Dienstlaufbahn" The unit consisted of three batteries (one each light, medium and heavy caliber) and a light flak column initially. Later a staff battery was added. Formed in Weimar, it was operationally subordinated to the 2.SS-Infanterie Brigade (mot) as a component of the Kommandostab "Reichsführer-SS." Burk's German Cross recommendation incorrectly gives June as the date he obtained command, the time the unit became operational versus his forming the detachment.

[4] Aside from being often attached to and supporting the 2.SS-Infanterie-Brigade (mot), the Abteilung was assigned to the XXVIII.Armeekorps and L.Armeekorps during 1941. Kriegstagebuch Nr. 1, SS-Flak-Abteilung "Ost."

Two photos showing Karl Burk as an SS-Oberführer and German Cross holder. The identity of the SS-Brigadeführer wearing a German Red Cross decoration is unknown.

post as well for the XXXVII.Armee-Korps during the summer of 1942. He won the German Cross in Gold for his "Ost" command on November 15, 1942, as a result of the following recommendation:

> "SS-Obersturmbannführer Burk was named Detachment Commander of the newly created SS-Flak-Abteilung (SS-Anti-Aircraft Detachment) "Ost" ("East") and is an especially passionate soldier, untiringly active, without any consideration for himself. He is a "go-getter," and at every time highly regarded by others. He has put the stamp of his personality on the young detachment which has distinguished itself by displaying bravery and good performances wherever it is put into action.
>
> On October 5 and 6, 1941, Burk's Anti-Aircraft Detachment "East" was subordinated to the 2.SS-Infanterie-Brigade (motorized) as it arrived at the front. Despite the fact that this young unit had no battle experience whatsoever, it was immediately thrown into battle when it arrived at the front. Since all of his officers and his NCOs lacked front-line experience, SS-Obersturmbannführer Burk took it upon himself to personally report the fire position for each and every anti-aircraft gun and personally gave all orders at each of his unit's positions. Because of this his detachment's first action was a complete success. This was of great importance for the young troops.
>
> On October 8, 1941, the furthermost line, located west of the point where the Trossna river entered into the Neva river, suffered from flank and rearward fire from Russian cannon boats; the Neva was not to be crossed. SS-Oberturmbannführer Burk, despite warning from the other Wehrmacht units, reconnoitered this position during the bright of day (since it would be pointless to do it at night). Under strong artillery fire, he located a suitable firing position on the bank of the Neva which was observable from the northern side. He then personally brought his guns, partly in the form of enlisted men platoons, to this position and was able to engage the Russian cannon boats with direct fire for the first time since their arrival. The closest boat received numerous direct hits and a fire started, the other boats saw this and pulled back. Since then no other Russian cannon boats have appeared on the Neva.
>
> In the same clever way, an enemy balloon and searchlight located in a forward position were destroyed. The battle and ensuing destruction were the result of an independent decision made by SS-Obersturmbannführer Burk as he had already conducted reconnoitering operations during the day. The reconnoitering operations had determined that it was impossible to bring his cannons forward, but that they could successfully open fire on the enemy positions from their current location. SS-Oberstrumbannführer Burk led these operations to their completion as well.

Karl Burk as an SS-Standartenführer wearing the German Cross in Gold awarded for his leadership of Flak Abteilung "Ost."

> In addition to the battle which took place on the ground, the detachment had to deal with 10-15 dive bomber attacks consisting of usually 8 to 10 bomber planes accompanied by a fighter protection of 6-8 "Ratas" (fighters bombers) on a daily basis. Through his personal example he taught his detachment to remain at one's cannon instead of seeking cover during attacks from dive-bombers. The result was a total of 15 downed planes in a short time, a success which can be attributed to the lessons taught by the detachment commander.
>
> The detachment, in close conjunction with Infanterie Regimenter 405 and 409, all of which were in transport to KRASNY-BOR, became the cornerstone of the defensive battles on the "October" highway and on the highway between LENINGRAD and TSCHUDOVO. The merit of these battles can be attributed again to SS-Obersturmbannführer Burk, who was able to engineer accomplishments far beyond his battle assignments and the expectations placed on him by offering his units to provide infantry-style support. His units were able to destroy enemy positions which included several infantry guns and platoons which were deployed in the enemy's forward-

most positions. The detachment was also able to destroy newly forming enemy positions and in one case they broke a successful Russian breakthrough at the last minute. On November 15, 1941, the commander of Infanterie Regiment 405 gave SS-Obersturmbannführer Burk his personal praise and recognition for the strong support he gave them by leading his detachment in battle. This praise and recognition was repeated later on November 29, 1941, by the commander of Infanterie Regiment 409, and still later by the commanders of 121. and 122.Infanterie Divisionen in written, as well as wire reports.

Besides the previously mentioned downing of 15 enemy aircraft, the detachment was able to destroy four 32-38 ton enemy tanks and force the retreat of two further 32 ton tanks. They were also successful in completely annihilating three heavily armored bunkers (with direct fire from their 8.8cm guns) and 15 lightly armored bunkers (with their 8.8 cm guns and 3.7cm guns). These successes were registered during the detachment's first actions from October 5 through October 15, 1941. The detachment commander always led by displaying and setting his own personal example, at times standing for 28 hours at his forward observation posts during which he personally led the offensive and defensive fire. This leadership gave his men the needed courage and rallied them to success.

On January 29, 1941, after a four-week break in Latvia, the detachment was sent out on the highway between NOVOGOROD and TSHUDOVO and defended it against continuous Russian attacks for six days straight. These attacks threatened to extend the Russian break-through to the south. The detachment had to defend itself to the east, north and west at the same time, often only with carbines and light machine guns. The leadership responsibilities of the detachment in these difficult situations required giving orders, choosing areas of deployment, making sure the detachment was adequately supplied with munitions and food supplies and that the wounded received proper care. These responsibilities required the detachment commander, SS-Obersturmbannführer Burk, to rely on his prudence, performance capability, decisiveness, and desire for action.

Since our own infantry were too weak and exhausted, SS-Obersturmbannführer Burk gathered his men together and formed a protection platoon with light machine guns and heavy grenade launchers. This platoon not only served to protect our units against enemy attacks, but over-and-above that, it dispatched several reconnaissance patrols which brought back valuable information for the higher officers. Also, during this action, the detachment was successful in downing 4 enemy bombers in two days. These bombers flew in only during the night and the men had to shoot them down by listening for their motors, since no spotlights were available, which added special importance to the success of the detachment.

Due to all of his personality traits, his continuously proven bravery and his constant close relationship to the successful infantry-style successes of his unit, SS-Obersturmbannführer Burk was recommended for the German Cross in Gold by the commander of Infanterie Regiment 424, Oberst Harry Hoppe. The 2.SS-Infanterie-Brigade (motorized) to which the Detachment has been up until this time subordinated to, is to be responsible for seeing to it that this recommendation passes through the necessary channels. They are to make sure that SS-Obersturmbannführer Burk receives this high recognition of which he is especially worthy."[5]

Burk also led Kampfgruppe "Burk" from March 31, 1942, to June 25, 1942, composed of mixed SS and Army units operating within the area of his "Ost" command.[6] Next serving as the commander of the SS-Flak-Ersatz-Abteilung, he was made an active Waffen-SS Standartenführer on July 15, 1943. Burk's unit defended the Ruhr dams during the historic raid by the RAF in May, 1943. His command expanded to become the SS-Flak-Ausbildungs und Ersatz-Regiment in March, 1943, and Burk remained commander until February 13, 1944.[7] He was promoted to SS-Oberführer on November 9, 1943. Transferred to the HSSPF "Ost," headquartered in Crakow, he was senior commander of border protection units until June 1, 1944.[8] Burk then was formation staff leader and senior infantry leader of the 5.SS-Freiwilligen-Sturmbrigade "Wallonien." He took official command of the Brigade from June 21 to September 18, 1944, and remained commander when it initially expanded into the SS-Freiwilligen-Grenadier-Division "Wallonien" until September 20, 1944.[9] At this command, he trained the unit while Leon Degrelle led the Battle Group. He remained titular commander until December 12, 1944, when officially succeeded by Nikolaus Heilmann.

---

[5] "Vorschlagliste Nr 1 zur Verleihung des Deutschen Kreuzes in Gold," dated March 14, 1942, and signed by Gottfried Klingemann, commander of the 2.SS-Infanterie-Brigade (mot).

[6] Subordinated as needed to both Army units and the 2.SS-Infanterie-Brigade (mot), the group contained a staff, Kampfgruppe Massel (Begleit Bataillon "Reichsführer-SS," 1., and 2./Schumannschaft Bataillon 232), Kampfgruppe Valentin (I./Infanterie Regiment "Barner," 3./Schumannschaft Bataillon 232), Schumannschaft Bataillon 636, 14./Infanterie Regiment 376, and 3./leight Reserve Flak Abteilung 743. Kriegstagebuch Gruppe "Burk," 31.März 1942 - 25 Juni 1942, page 1.

[7] The Flak replacement units of the SS began with the SS-Fla-MG-Ersatz-Kompanie formed in September, 1939. It became the SS-Flak Ersatz-Abteilung with three batteries and a staff battery in 1941. That unit expanded to the SS-Flak Ersatz-Regiment on January 1, 1943, and finally was redesignated as the SS-Flak Ausbildungs-und Ersatz Regiment in March, 1943. Stöber, "Die Flugabwehrverbande der Waffen-SS," pages 401-409, reproducing some of the related SS-Führungshauptamt orders.

[8] SS-Führungshauptamt, "Stabsbefehl Nr. 5/44, dated March 3, 1944.

[9] "Stammkarte" but his transfer as liaison to Vlassov shows him coming from the Brigade to the new post on October 6, 1944. His "Dienstlaufbahn" shows him in reserve after September 20. This is per the SS-FHA, he remained official or titular commander (on paper) after moving to his next assignment while day-to-day operations were undertaken by SS-Sturmbannführer Franz Hellebaut until Heilmann arrived on December 12, 1944. Mabire and Lefevre, "Leon Degrelle et la Legion Wallonie," page 219.

After spending two weeks in reserve, Burk was posted as the Waffen-SS military liaison officer to renegade Russian volunteer Colonel General Andrej Vlassov until February 12, 1945.[10] He then replaced Adolf Ax as commander of the 15.Waffen-Grenadier-Division der SS (lettische Nr. 1) until May 2, 1945, when the division's remnants retreated and Burk himself surrendered to the US Army. At his final command, he was promoted to SS-Brigadeführer und Generalmajor der Waffen-SS on April 20, 1945. In addition to his German Cross, Burk won a clasp to both of his WWI Iron Crosses (October 30 and December 8, 1941), both classes of the War Service Cross with Swords, the General Assault badge, the Infantry Assault Badge, the Army Anti-Aircraft Badge, the Eastern Front Medal, the SA Sports Badge in Gold and the Reich's Sports Badge in Silver.[11]

A well-trained and experienced artillery officer, he was among the more important anti-aircraft leaders of the Waffen-SS. Burk's actions as commander of Flak Abteilung "Ost" earned him praise from both Army and Waffen-SS commanders, including Lothar Debes.[12] Though not leading the "Wallonien" Division in combat, he was responsible for its formation and training. Burk was well-liked by Latvian Infanterieführer Arthur Silgailis and respected the Latvians. He ended the war commanding their respect, despite initial misgivings. To his credit, he refused to replace Latvian commanders with Germans, a problem for the morale of many foreign Waffen-SS volunteer units. Karl Burk died in Fritzlar on September 23, 1963.

---

[10] "Personalverfügung" dated October 6, 1944.
[11] "Stammkarte"

[12] "Abschrift" dated February 23, 1942, and written by Debes.

LOTHAR DEBES

The son of a Bavarian justice official, Lothar Debes was born in Eichstätt, in the district of Middle Franconia, Bavaria, on June 21, 1890. After passing his Abitur, he joined the Royal Bavarian Cadet Corps in Munich. Assigned to the 18th Bavarian Infantry Regiment "Prinz Ludwig Ferdinand" until January 10, 1911, he then transferred to the Prussian Army with Nassau Infantry Regiment No. 88 until the spring of 1913. In 1911-1912 he attended the War School in Danzig and was commissioned a Leutnant on January 27, 1912. During 1913 to early 1914 he was posted to the district command for Siegen and later in 1914 the command covering Hanau. In the summer of 1914, he transferred to Nassau Engineer Battalion No. 25 before returning to his original infantry regiment. There he served as a company officer from August, 1914, until promoted to Oberleutnant on September 18, 1915. He then took command of the 5th company until June 24, 1916. Debes was wounded by a grenade on June 24, 1916, and following his recovery was posted as a deputy adjutant and deputy Ia to the 18th Army Corps until September 27, 1916. He then went to the 223rd Infantry Division as second adjutant (until early October 1916) and ordnance officer (until 1918). Promoted to Hauptmann on October 18, 1918, during his final year in the military he was involved as a military transport officer, being stationed in Brussels and Berlin until May 1918. Wounded four times (twice in one day), Debes was awarded the Wound Badge in Black and both classes of the Iron Cross.[1] Evaluations by the Greater General Staff were extremly positive of his abilities and performance.[2]

Debes joined the NSDAP on May 1, 1930, and the SS as an SS-Sturmbannführer on March 1, 1937. He was an instructor at SS-Junkerschule Braunschweig until January 1, 1940. Promoted to SS-Obersturmbannführer on September 11, 1938, and to SS-Standartenführer on January 1, 1940, he then replaced Arno Altvater-Mackensen as commandant of SS-Junkerschule Braunschweig from January 1, 1940, to January 1, 1942. Promoted to SS-Oberführer on November 9, 1941, he was then assigned to 2.SS-Infanterie-Brigade leading an independent formation from January 1, 1942, until February 22, 1942. Debes than replaced Ernst Deutsch as commander of SS-Infanterie-Regiment 9 until August 1, 1942, when the regiment was transferred to the "Totenkopf" Division to become SS-Totenkopf-Kradschützen Regiment "Thule."[3]

Promoted to SS-Brigadeführer und Generalmajor der Waffen-SS on June 21, 1942, Debes succeeded SS-Standartenführer Werner Dörffler-Schuband as commander of SS-Junkerschule Bad Tölz from August 10, 1942 to February 15, 1943.[4] He was the only person to command both of the primary SS officer school facilities. During January, 1943, Debes took an armored commanders course at the Army armored school in Wünsdorf to prepare for his next command. On February 15, 1943, he was the first commander of the 10.SS-Panzer-Grenadier-Division "Karl der Grosse" (later retitled "Frundsberg"), establishing and leading the unit until November 12, 1943, when Karl von Treuenfeld took command. Debes then officially succeeded Matthias Kleinheisterkamp as commander of the 6.SS-Gebirgs-Division "Nord" from November 12, 1943, until succeeded by Friedrich-Wilhelm Krüger in May, 1944 (Debes actually arrived and assumed his command on December 15, 1943).

---

[1] "Lebenslaufbahn" dated September 21, 1936 and June 27, 1938.

[2] "Zeugnis für Hauptmann Debes," dated October 7, 1919, and signed by a Major of the General Staff, military transport command director, Brüssel.

[3] Appointed to SS-Infanterie-Regiment 9 on February 22, he arrived and assumed command four days later. Vopersal, "Soldaten Kämpfer Kameraden," volume III, page 25.

[4] "Personalverfügung" dated July 20, 1942, "Dienstlaufbahn," and "Stammkarte." His command was probably assigned the 1st but he did not return from Russia and assume the post until the 10th.

SS-Brigadeführer Lothar Debes, foreground, with members of his divisional staff. The Standarten-führer in the center wears the Blood Order ribbon. The name of the young Standartenführer and German Cross holder on the far left is unknown.

SS-Brigadeführer Lothar Debes, wearing his 1936 SS dagger with knot, is followed by his adjutant. Note the command pennant in the foreground.

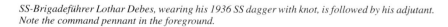

France 1943: Lothar Debes (2nd from left) tours his former command with Karl von Treuenfeld (3rd from left) who was succeeding him as divisional commander. On the far right is SS-Hauptsturmführer Alfons Benz, the commander of the Pionier Bataillon (engineer battalion) who led the engineer unit of the 16.SS-Panzer-Grenadier-Division "Reichsführer-SS" at the end of the war. The officer on the far left is an adjutant as seen by his shoulder cords.

On January 30, 1944, he was promoted to SS-Gruppenführer und Generalleutnant der Waffen-SS.

Lothar Debes spent the balance of the war in senior administrative posts. When the position of Befehlshaber der Waffen-SS "Ost" was recreated on June 15, 1944, he briefly assumed the command until June 21, 1944, but left for Italy before the post was dissolved again on July 21, 1944.[5] In Italy, Debes served as the Befehlshaber der Waffen-SS "Italien," under the Supreme SS and Police Leader for Italy (Karl Wolff), from June 21, 1944, to the end of the war. At his final post he was awarded the German Cross in Silver on February 7, 1945. He also won clasps to both of his WWI Iron Crosses, the War Service Cross 2nd class with Swords, and the Eastern Front Medal.

A professional, skilled and able commander in both administrative and field commands, Debes was well thought-of by his Army superiors. A fitness report by the commander of the 215.Infanterie-Division during May, 1942, described him as a man of upstanding and open character, clear in thought and secure in his own judgment, a brave commander with a wealth of military knowledge and understanding with excellent soldierly bearing.[6] Well-educated, he spoke French and English, while having a soft-spoken manner when speaking. Married on November 25, 1920, Debes and his wife had two daughters. One of the more historically overlooked professional military commanders, Lothar Debes died in Osnabrück on July 14, 1960.

---

[5] "Feld-Kommandostelle," dated August 1, 1944 with effect from June 15, 1944.

[6] "Beurteilungsnotizen," Kdo. Inf.Division 215, dated May 1, 1942.

LEON DEGRELLE

Leon Degrelle was probably the best known SS foreign volunteer. Born in Bouillon, Belgium, on June 15, 1906, he came from an upper middle class family. Intelligent and well educated, he attended ten semesters of university studies where he studied law. Degrelle left school in 1930 to run a publishing house and started his own newspaper. For the latter pursuit he visited Africa, Asia and the United States as a journalist. His national movement launched in 1935 developed into the Belgian Rexists. Degrelle's party swept the polls in May, 1936, winning numerous seats in both the Lower House and Senate. Arrested in May, 1940, he was released when Germany took the country and joined the German Army as a Private on August 8, 1941.

After three months with Infanterie Regiment 477, he was posted as the ordnance officer of Infanterie Bataillon 373, comprised of Belgian volunteers. Commissioned as a Leutnant on May 1, 1942, he was then promoted to Oberleutnant on May 15, 1943. Degrelle served there until June 1, 1943, when he transferred to the Waffen-SS as an SS-Obersturmführer d.R. Transferring to "Wiking" as a reserve officer, he was assigned as the ordnance officer of the expanded SS-Sturmbrigade "Wallonien" the same month. Degrelle won the Iron Cross 2nd class on March 3, 1942, the 1st class on May 21, 1942, the Eastern Front Medal on August 15, 1942, the Infantry Assault Badge on August 24, 1942, the Wound Badge Black on March 23, 1942 and the Silver Wound Badge on December 23, 1943.[1] On January 30, 1944, he was promoted to SS-Hauptsturmführer. When Brigade commander Lucien Lippert was killed, Degrelle took command and led the Brigade in combat from February 13, 1944 until succeeded by Karl Burk for incorporation of the command into the division. Degrelle would be the combat formation commander and Burk the formation and training officer. Awarded the Close Combat Clasp in Silver on March 19, 1944, for his brigade command Degrelle was awarded the Knight's Cross on February 20, 1944, from the following recommendation submitted by Herbert Otto Gille:

> "The Sturmbrigade "Wallonien" served with the units of the Army and the Waffen-SS that were left by themselves during the week-long battles in the area west of Tscherkassy and were able to repulse enemy attacks by themselves. After the brave commander of the Brigade, SS-Sturmbannführer Lucien Lippert, was killed on February 13 by a shot through the chest, Degrelle took over the leadership of the Brigade. Degrelle, who had already distinguished himself through numerous acts of bravery, proved himself during the decisive break-through battles in the last days of his excellent fighting leadership. In a loyal comradeship of arms he, along with his brave Walloonians who fought on his side and on the side of the men of the army and Germanic men of the Waffen-SS, was able to lead the breakout in an excellent fashion. I recommend the award of the Knight's Cross of the Iron Cross to this brave people's leader."[2]

Promoted to SS-Sturmbannführer effective April 20, 1944, Degrelle arrived in Estonia on August 8, 1944 and took command of Kampfgruppe "Wallonien" through the Narwa battles until September 18. On August 27, 1944, he won the Oakleaves for his leadership of the Battle Group from the following recommendation:

---

[1] "Personalangaben."

[2] "Vorschlag Nr. 2474 für die Verleihung des Ritterkreuzes des Eisernen Kreuzes" dated February 15, 1944, on the text pages. For reasons unknown, the cover page of the Vorschlag is dated May 31, 1944.

Leon Degrelle in a field portrait with his Knight's Cross wearing camouflage uniform and (right) prior to being awarded the decoration he stands at left. His sleeve insignia denotes mountain troops.

"An attack of the enemy on the August 23, 1944, with the main point against Estonian units resulted in the Estonians being completely routed. The entire southwestern and western flanks of Dorpats were open and only secured by alarm units of little fighting value.

At this time, SS-Sturmbannführer Degrelle was on the way to his heavy company which was engaged in battle further southwest from the enemy attack. During this morning trip, Degrelle recognized the situation and somehow managed to pull together the Estonian troops that were fleeing to Dorpat. At the strongpoint on the hills of Lemmatsi, he placed them together with weak German units to form a battle group which served to secure the line against attacking enemy units. This battle group held their positions the entire day.

His personal valor was recognized with these actions that motivated the few remaining Estonians to hold out. Degrelle

issued his orders standing above his men who were below in the trenches.

The fact that an enemy advance in the direction of the city of Dorpat, which would have served to cut off our units engaged still further south, was prevented can only be credited to SS-Sturmbannführer Degrelle's actions and independent decision-making."[3]

Returning from the front, Degrelle was presented the Oakleaves personally by Hitler and served as a lecturer, making speeches for the Propaganda Ministry until late January, 1945. On October 9, 1944, he was awarded the German Cross in Gold for combats in Pruskaja, Tcherjakov, and Kubano-Armianski during August-September, 1942, and for the fighting in the Tcherkassy area on De-

---

[3] Telex Eichenlaub Vorschlag dated August 24, 1944.

cember 23rd.[4] Degrelle also was awarded the Wound Badge in Gold on March 19, 1944. Promoted to SS-Obersturmbannführer on January 1, 1945, he commanded the 28.SS-Freiwilligen-Panzer-Grenadier-Division "Wallonien" from January 30, 1945, until the end of the war. On April 20, 1945, he was promoted to SS-Standartenführer.

Escaping from Germany to Denmark and Norway, he flew to Spain in Albert Speer's private plane and became a Spanish citizen in 1954. He lived there in exile under the legal name of León Jóse de Ramirez Reina until his death on April 1, 1994.[5] His memoirs were published and he remained radically political in his beliefs until his death. A post-war Belgian court sentenced him to death in absentia and he was even denied his last wish, which was to have his ashes buried on Belgian soil.

---

[4] "Vorschlag für die Verleihung des Deutschen Kreuzes in Gold" dated January 21, 1944, and written by Herbert Otto Gille.

[5] Degrelle's legal name change and nationality date courtesy research by Ignacio Arrondo.

Leon Degrelle (left) as an SS-Hauptsturmführer wearing his Knight's Cross poses for a portrait and (right) he salutes a review of troops after returning from combat in Russia.

From left (above) are Herbert Otto Gille, Heinrich Himmler and Degrelle. Degrelle congratulates troops (below). Behind him are Josef "Sepp" Dietrich and Hans Weiser.

Leon Degrelle (center) with Jürgen Wagner (left) whose biography will be in volume 2.

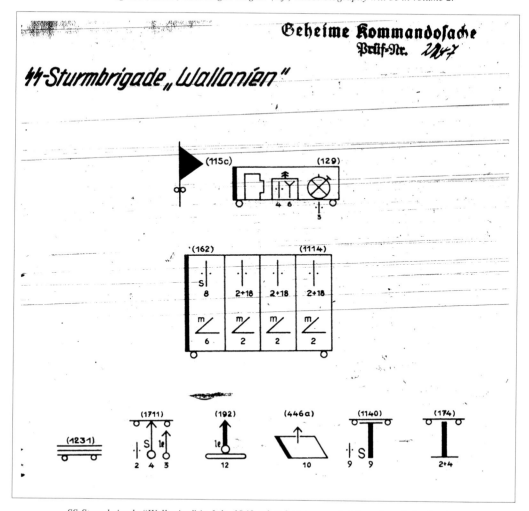

SS-Sturmbrigede "Wallonien" in July, 1943, when being expanded from the existing Legion.

DR. EDUARD DEISENHOFER

Eduard Deisenhofer was born in Freising, Upper Bavaria, on June 27, 1909. After passing his Abitur in 1928, he studied chemistry and then political economics at the Universities of Munich, Rostock and Würzburg where he passed his exams in February, 1934.[1] On May 25, 1930, he joined the NSDAP and the SA on June 1st the same year. He served with the SA in Würzburg until moving to the SS on October 1, 1930.[2] Promoted to SS-Scharführer on July 8, 1932, Deisenhofer served initially with the 8./57.SS-Standarte until the end of January, 1933.

Transferring to the 56.SS-Standarte, Deisenhofer served with its I.Sturmbann from the end of January, 1933, until November 9, 1933, when he was commissioned as an SS-Untersturmführer. During that posting he was promoted to SS-Truppführer on May 17, 1933, and to SS-Obertruppführer on August 21, 1933. Effective November 9, 1933, he was commissioned as an SS-Sturmführer and took command of the 2./I./56.SS-Standarte.[3] Deisenhofer held the post until transferred to Oberabschnitt "Süd" as Special Duties Officer on April 24, 1934.[4] Having been promoted to SS-Obersturmführer on April 20, 1934, Deisenhofer moved to the SS-Verfügungstruppe on June 15, 1934.

After commanding a Sturm with SS-Standarte 1 beginning on June 15, 1934, he moved to lead another platoon-size formation with II./SS-Standarte 2 until transferring, on February 27, 1935, to the SS-Totenkopfverbände. After training at Dachau until the start of April, 1935, Deisenhofer took command of a company-size formation with SS Wachtruppe "Oberbayern" for two years. Promoted to SS-Hauptsturmführer on September 15, 1935, he was posted to the III./SS-Totenkopfsturmbann "Sachsen" from April, 1936, until the start of July, 1937, where he served as a legal advisor. After only a few days holding a similar post with III./3SS-Totenkopfsturmbann "Thüringen," Deisenhofer was given command of II./1.SS-Totenkopfstandarte "Oberbayern" on July 10, 1937. Promoted to SS-Sturmbannführer on October 2, 1938, he held that command after it was incorporated into the "Totenkopf" Division as II./SS-Totenkopf-Infanterie-Regiment 1. Wounded in May, 1940, he received a doctorate in science from the University of Gottingen and was awarded both classes of the Iron Cross on June 26, 1940. Deisenhofer's first command after returning to duty was the III./SS-Freiwilligen-Standarte "Nordwest" which he led until taking command of Infanterie-Ersatz-Bataillon "Ost" on April 22, 1941.

Transferring again, Deisenhofer led the I./SS-Infanterie-Regiment 9 from mid-August, 1941, until severely wounded by a grenade on November 3, 1941. After his recovery Deisenhofer took command of I./SS-Totenkopf-Infanterie-Regiment 1 on February 18, 1942. At that command he was again wounded on April 30, 1943, and following another recovery was assigned to the SS-Kradschützen-Ersatz-Bataillon on July 1, 1942.[5] Promoted to SS-Obersturmbannführer on April 20, 1942, he commanded the SS-Kradschützen-Ersatz-Bataillon after his recovery until late September, 1942. Awarded the German Cross in Gold on April 29, 1942, for his leadership in the Demjansk pocket, Deisenhofer was also awarded the Knight's Cross on May 8, 1942.[6]

---

[1] "Lebenslauf"
[2] "Stammrollen"
[3] "SS-Personalbefehl" Nr.10, v. 24.November 1933.
[4] "SS-Personalbefehl" Nr.13 v. 4.Mai 1934.

[5] Vopersal, "Soldaten, Kämpfer, Kameraden," Band IIB, seite 684 and BDC file.
[6] "Das Schwarze Korps," August 20, 1942.

As an experienced front-line officer, he was a valuable Teaching Group Commander at SS-Junkerschule Bad Tölz from September 25, 1942, until the start of September, 1943. While at that post his own training continued, taking multiple classes with the Army in Wünsdorf and also serving with the replacement office of Oberabschnitt Fulda-Werra during February, 1943.

Next posted to the SS-Führungshauptamt, Deisenhofer served with the Inspectorate for infantry from the start of September, 1943, until November. He then moved to Amt XI (officer training) as head of that office until March 20, 1944. Returning to an operational unit, Deisenhofer took command of SS-Panzer-Grenadier-Regiment 21 of the "Frundsberg" Division, succeeding Martin Kohlroser. Promoted to SS-Standartenführer on April 20, 1944, he was ordered to command the 5.SS-Panzer-Division "Wiking" from July 20, 1944, until August 11, 1944, succeeding Herbert Otto Gille but never actually took command.[7] Hans Mühlenkamp succeeded

Gille, first as a temporary and then permanent commander. Deisenhofer was actually placed in reserve during August, 1944, while awaiting a new assignment. During that time he finished his thesis and passed his oral examination.

Succeeding Otto Binge, he took command of the 17.SS-Panzer-Grenadier-Divison "Götz von Berlichingen" for a month beginning on August 30. His command was taken by Thomas Müller and Deisenhofer went to Roumania to assist with Waffen-SS recruiting.[8] He then remained on reserve until the start of 1945.

Promoted to SS-Oberführer on January 1, 1945, Deisenhofer commanded a Kampfgruppe during the first three weeks of that year. His unit was composed of faculty and cadets available in SS-Truppenübungsplatz "Bad Saarow." When Herbert von Obwurzer was listed as missing, Deisenhofer was assigned command of the 15.Waffen-Grenadier-Division der SS (lettische Nr. 1) but he was killed in Arnswalde on January 31, 1945, while traveling to under-

---

[7] "Personalverfügung" dated July 20, 1944 and August 11, 1944.

[8] Krätschmer, "Die Ritterkreuzträger der Waffen-SS."

Two photos of Deisenhofer as a junior officer with the numbered insignia of a Totenkopfsturmbann. In one photo his SS lionhead pattern sword can be seen, possibly an SS honor pattern as the normal type was a "D" shaped degen pattern.

take the command. His post was instead taken by Adolf Ax who had already been in temporary command.

Intelligent, motivated, energetic and of upright character, he was among the best educated of the younger divisional commanders. Deisenhofer was naturally gifted and well-liked by all his commanders including Heinz Harmel and Gottfried Klingemann, both of whom gave him excellent evaluations.[9] In addition to his other decorations, he was awarded the Wound Badge in Black on June 20, 1940, the Eastern Front Medal on July 21, 1942, the Infantry Assault Badge, and after his second severe wound, the Wound Badge in Silver.

---

[9] Klingemann commanded Bad Tölz while Deisenhofer was a teaching group commander. Harmel led the 10.SS-Panzer-Division "Frundsberg" and his biography is in the current volume.

Right: Dr. Eduard Deisenhofer as an SS-Obersturmbannführer and Ritterkreuzträger.

SS-Sturmbannführer Dr. Eduard Deisenhofer (right) with the commandant of Gross-Rosen, Artur Rödl.

CARL-MARIA DEMELHUBER

Carl-Maria Demelhuber was born the son of a garrison administrator in Freising, Upper Bavaria, on May 27, 1896. He joined the Army as a war volunteer on August 2, 1914, and served with the Bavarian Field Artillery Regiment "Prinz Regent Luitpold" from the date of his enlistment until January 25, 1915. Moving to the anti-aircraft detachment of the same unit, he was commissioned a Leutnant in 1916. Awarded both classes of the Iron Cross, the Wound Badge in Black, the Bavarian Military Order 4th class, and the Bavarian Service Cross 3rd class with Swords in WWI, he fought as a member of the Freikorps "von Epp" from March, 1919, to May, 1920.

Remaining in the military after the war, he served with Bayerische Artillerieregiment Nr. 21 from May, 1919, to the start of February, 1920, and was promoted to Oberleutnant in 1919. After leaving the Army he attended a trade high school and then the University of Munich where he studied science and national economics. After passing his exams, Demelhuber received a commercial diploma in the Spring of 1921.

On January 1, 1921, he joined the Bavarian Landespolizei as an Oberleutnant and served as a platoon leader until September 1, 1927. He joined the NSDAP on February 20, 1922, and was given Party member number 4933. He left the NSDAP after the Munich Putsch of November, 1923, and never rejoined. Promoted to Hauptmann on June 1, 1933, he served as adjutant to the Police President of Munich from March 10, 1933, until leaving the Landespolizei on January 31, 1935. He had short-lived service in the SA as a Standartenführer with the SA training command from May 1, 1934, to March 15, 1935.

Moving to the SS, Demelhuber joined the SS-Verfügungstruppe as an SS-Obersturmbannführer on March 15, 1935. Given command of II./SS-Standarte 1, he attended classes at the Army school in Döberitz during May, 1935. He held that command until promoted to SS-Standartenführer on October 1, 1936. From October 1, 1936, to December 1, 1940, he commanded SS-Standarte 2 which became Regiment "Germania." "Germania" then went to form a cadre for the new Division "Germania" (later titled "Wiking") with SS-Obersturmbannführer Carl Ritter von Oberkamp as regimental commander.[1] In the pre-war years, Demelhuber had been awarded the German Horseman's Badge in Silver, the Nuremberg Party Day badge of 1929 and both occupation medals for Austria and Czechoslovakia. Himmler also presented him with a damascus SS honor sword. Demelhuber led Regiment "Germania" through formation of the initial SS division and during the Western campaign of 1940 until the unit transferred to become a cadre for the eventual "Wiking" Division. In 1939, he was awarded clasps to both his WWI Iron Crosses. On January 30, 1940, Demelhuber was promoted to SS-Oberführer, followed by a promotion to SS-Brigadeführer und Generalmajor der Waffen-SS on November 9, 1940.

Transferring to an administrative post in the General Government, he served as the Befehlshaber der Waffen-SS "Ost" headquartered in Krakau from December 1, 1940, until the post was dissolved on April 30, 1941.[2] Returning to a field command, he became the first commander of the 1.SS-Brigade (mot) from April 30, 1941, to June 17, 1941, in Russia, where his unit was attached to the Kommandostab "Reichsführer-SS."[3] Demelhuber then ex-

---

[1] For Oberkamp's biography see volume 2.

[2] He was given the appointment on November 9, before the post was actually established. It was later re-established in June, 1944.

[3] The Brigade formed from the dissolved Befehlshaber der Waffen-SS "Ost" post. The unit was organized in Poland as SS-Brigade 1 on April 24, 1941, with two Flak Kompanien and SS-Infanterie-Regimenter 8 and 10 as its primary combat com-

Carl-Maria Demelhuber in a Heinrich Hoffmann portrait wearing his Finnish Cross of Freedom 1st class with the rank of SS-Gruppenführer.

changed posts with Richard Herrmann and took command of Kampfgruppe "Nord" after Richard Herrmann failed in Himmler's view as a commander during the march to Northern Norway.[4] He arrived at the command in mid-June. Demelhuber also served as official commander of SS-Division "Nord" from June 17, 1941, to May 2, 1942. During that command, Georg Keppler was assigned as a substitute for him from September 21, 1941, while Demelhuber was reassigned as inspector of SS NCO schools in the SS-Führungshauptamt. When Keppler became ill, Demelhuber again assumed command. Hans Scheider took command of Division "Nord" (the existing elements of the new division) while Matthias Kleinheisterkamp was forming the new division elements starting on April 21, 1942. Kleinheisterkamp was assigned to command the new forming elements of the divisional command on April 1, 1942, while Demelhuber remained official commander until the date previously mentioned.[5] Demelhuber was also awarded the Finnish Cross of Freedom 1st class.

Promoted to SS-Gruppenführer und Generalleutnant der Waffen-SS on April 20, 1942, he served as Befehlshaber der Waffen-SS "Niederlanden" from June 11, 1942, to November 9, 1944, in Holland on the staff of HSSPF Hans-Albin Rauter. Promoted to SS-Obergruppenführer und General der Waffen-SS on June 21, 1944, Demelhuber was awarded the German Cross in Silver on November 9, 1943. He was then replaced in Holland by Martin Kohlroser in early November, 1944.[6] Demelhuber then commanded the Führungsstab "Ostküste" (Baltic Coast) from November, 1944, to mid-January, 1945.

Demelhuber led the XVI.SS-Armeekorps from January 15, 1945 to April, 1945, as well as being Himmler's standing deputy in the leadership staff "Ostseekürste" (Baltic Sea Coast) during March/April, 1945. He also was General Inspector of replacements in the SS-Führungshauptamt from March, 1945, to the end of the war.

An effective administrator, he was always smartly dressed and had the nickname "Tosca" for his favorite cologne. Well educated, intelligent and fluent in French, he married in May, 1921, and he and his wife had a son. Captured on May 16, 1945, he was interned in South Wales from 1946 to 1948. Having been widowed, after the war he married the widow of a junior SS officer. He was the last living former SS-Obergruppenführer when he died on March 18, 1988, in Seeshaupt, Prenzberg (Bavaria).

Demelhuber (above) explains a tactical situation to Paul Hausser, his divisional commander, during the Western campaign. (Below) Demelhuber speaks to Heinrich Himmler during his period commanding Regiment "Germania."

---

ponents, it was redesignated as the 1.SS-Infanterie-Brigade (mot) on September 1, 1941. The Brigade also included a motorcycle company, anti-tank detachment, and a heavy artillery detachment in 1942. In January, 1944, it was used as cadre to form the 18.SS-Panzer-Grenadier-Division "Horst Wessel." In the first Russian campaign the Brigade was a component of the Kommandostab "Reichsführer-SS" that had been formed as the Einsatz Stab "Reichsführer-SS" on April 7, 1941, and then re-designated on May 6, 1941, to control independant units under Himmler's direct control. See Yerger, "Riding East, The SS Cavalry Brigade in Poland and Russia 1939-1942," pages 85-88.

[4] Ordered to assume command of Kampfgruppe "Nord" on May 25, 1941, he did not take actual command until June 17. Schreiber, "Kampf unter dem Nordlicht," page 39.

[5] The new elements of the Division were forming at Truppenübungsplatz "Wildflecken" while the existing units fought as a battle group. Kleinheisterkamp would command the entire Division when the two parts combined.

[6] Kohlroser had previously been a regimental commander of SS-Panzer-Grenadier-Regiment 21 ("Frundsberg") after leading SS-Infanterie-Regiment 7 following the death of its commander on July 5, 1941. An officer in the "Leibstandarte" from 1933 to 1941, he was awarded the Blood Order on November 9, 1943, and the German Cross in Gold on April 20, 1942. From early May to the start of November, 1944, Kohlroser commanded the "Landstorm Nederland" and then held the Befehlshaber post until the end of the war. He died in Munich on November 14, 1967.

Demelhuber awards the Iron Cross I class to men of "Germania." The boxed awards can be seen in both photos and the ceremony is being filmed for the daily newsreels.

Congratulating his men on their awards of the Iron Cross, Demelhuber's troops wear the "2" collar patch number given to Regiment "Germania." Below, he addresses his men in front of his headquarters, flanked by the SS guard posts.

Demelhuber's residence during his posting as Senior Waffen-SS Commander Netherlands.

In Holland, SS-Gruppenführer Carl-Maria Demelhuber (right) confers with SS-Oberführer Victor Knapp.

From left to right are: Carl-Maria Demelhuber, Dr. Heinrich Lankenau, Kurt Caesar Hoffmann (awarded the Knight's Cross as Captain of the "Scharnhorst"), Dr. Wilhelm Harster and, in diplomatic uniform, SS-Brigadeführer Otto Bene. In both these photos of the same scene, note the Dutch SS officer in the background wearing their unique insignia on his peaked cap.

Demelhuber with the Captain of the "Scharnhorst" and beside them is Otto Bene.

Hans Jüttner (center), Carl-Maria Demelhuber and Luftwaffe General der Flieger Christiansen in Holland during 1944.

Demelhuber (2nd from right) with other senior officials in Holland, 1944. On the far right is SS-Brigadeführer Erich Naumann (Sipo/SD Inspector for Holland). To the left of Demelhuber are (front row): SS-Obergruppenführer Hans-Albin Rauter (Higher SS and Police Leader for Holland), Anton Mussert (head of the Dutch Nazi Party), Reichsführer-SS Heinrich Himmler, SS-Obergruppenführer Dr. Artur Seyss-Inquart (Reich Commissioner for Holland) and van Geelkeren (head of the Dutch Nazi Youth Storm). The scene is the SS/SD school in Avegoor during early 1944.

Opposite: Demelhuber examines the prize for a shooting competition among visiting senior officials and then participates in the event.

Demelhuber reviewing and talking with combat soldiers who are on leave in Holland.

At the dedication of a cemetery, from right are Anton Mussert (Dutch Nazi Party leader), Seyss-Inquart and Demelhuber. Below: Demelhuber and his adjutant inspect the new resting place for troops killed in action.

Hans Jüttner (right) with Demelhuber (center) in Holland during 1944.

Opposite: (Above) From left to right are Demelhuber, Hans-Albin Rauter, Luftwaffe General Karl Drum and Dr. Artur Seyss-Inquart. Below, Demelhuber watches Seyss-Inquart and Mussert.

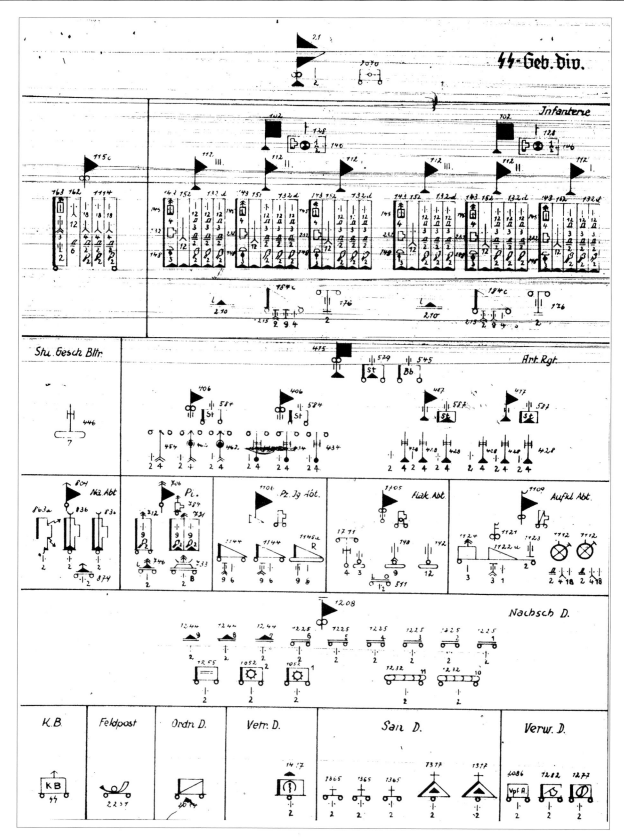

The SS-Gebirgs-Division "Nord" in February, 1942.

JOSEF "SEPP" DIETRICH

The most well-known commander of the Waffen-SS was a Swabian born on May 28, 1892, in Hawangen. Sepp Dietrich's family moved to Bavaria in 1900 and after his primary education he worked as a tractor driver. As an apprentice in the hotel industry after 1907, he visited Italy, Sweden, and Austria before joining the Royal Bavarian Army in mid-October, 1911.

Dietrich went to the 2nd battery of the 4th Bavarian Field Artillery Regiment "König" but was discharged from the service that November after a fall from a horse. After working as an errand boy, he rejoined the Army on August 6, 1914, with the 7th Bavarian Field Artillery Regiment. In October, 1914, Dietrich went to the 6th Bavarian Reserve Field Artillery Regiment with which unit he was wounded in action the following month. After his recovery and attending an artillery class at the Bavarian artillery school in Sonthofen in January, 1915, he was posted to the 7th Bavarian Field Artillery Regiment "Prinzregent Luitpold." Wounded again in the spring of 1915, he returned to duty with Infantry Gun Battery 10, serving with that unit with Assault Battalion 2 until February 19, 1918.

Transferring to one of the first armored units, Dietrich was posted to Assault Tank Detachment 13. He served in a vehicle with the nickname "Moritz" until the vehicle was destroyed on the last day of May, 1918. The crew then operated a captured British vehicle. Dietrich returned to the artillery on November 20, 1918, with his old unit, 7th Bavarian Field Artillery Regiment "Prinzregent Luitpold." He left the Army on March 26, 1919, with the rank of Vizewachtmeister. During WWI he was awarded both classes of the Iron Cross, the Wound Badge in Black, the Tank Battle Badge in Silver, the Bavarian Military Service Cross 3rd class, and the Austrian Bravery Medal.

After the war he moved to Munich at the beginning of April, 1919, and joined the Bavarian Landespolizei there on October 1, 1919. Posted to Landespolizei Gruppe I, he headed its reconnaissance platoon from late February, 1920, to 1927. Dietrich was commissioned as a Leutnant der Landespolizei in October, 1919, promoted to Oberleutnant in 1923, and to Hauptmann in 1924.

Taking a leave of absence from his police duties, he paid his own way to get to Silesia where he joined the 2nd company in the 1st battalion of the Freikorps "Oberland," where he fought Polish insurgents in Upper Silesia. Although not active with the NSDAP at the time, he took part in the November 9, 1923, Putsch in Munich. Dietrich then returned to his police assignment until leaving the Landespolizei in 1927.

After working as a clerk for a tobacco company and for the customs service, he was appointed manager of the Blue Buck Filling Station by its owner, Christian Weber. He remained there until 1928 and joined the NSDAP on May 1st that year. Four days later Sepp Dietrich joined the SS.

After two months leading the 1.SS Sturm in Munich, he retained command of it when its title expanded to the 1.SS-Standarte on August 1, 1928.[1] Commissioned as an SS-Sturmführer on June 1, 1928, he was promoted to SS-Sturmbannführer on August 1, 1928, and to SS-Standartenführer on September 18, 1929. Dietrich held command of the Munich Standarte until September 18, 1929, and then was SS Gauführer Oberbayern (Leader for Upper Bavaria) as well as the commander of Brigade "Bayern" (Bavaria) from September 19, 1929, until July 11, 1930. Sepp worked for the NSDAP

---

[1] Though titled as a Standarte, the unit was much smaller compared to full strength pre-war Allgemeine-SS regiments.

publisher Max Amanns, as the SS were unpaid at the time. He also began serving, along with Julius Schreck (Hitler's driver), as a personal bodyguard to Hitler and commanded the unofficial bodyguard unit beginning in 1929.

From July 11, 1930, when he was promoted to SS-Oberführer to October 10, 1930, he served as SS Oberführer for southern Germany.[2] Dietrich first held a seat in the Reichstag in late August, 1932, and continued to do so until the end of the war. At various times he represented Upper Bavaria/Swabia, Lower Bavaria and Frankfurt/Oder.

With the restructuring of the Allgemeine-SS, Dietrich was assigned as the leader of SS Abschnitte I and IV on July 11, 1930, and then succeeded Deputy Führer Rudolf Hess as commander of SS Gruppe "Süd" from the end of October, 1930, to the start of October, 1932.[3] Promoted to SS-Gruppenführer on December 18, 1931,

he was transferred to command SS Gruppe "Nord" from the start of October, 1932, to April 19, 1933. Moving to SS Gruppe "Ost" on April 19, 1933, he led this command until November 14, 1939.[4] Dietrich's command was then redesignated Oberabschnitt "Spree," and he officially commanded until the end of the war, but substitutes handled the duties while he saw service with the "Leibstandarte" and larger units of the Waffen-SS.

In addition to his other posts, Dietrich headed the SS Begleit-Kommando "Der Führer" entrusted with Hitler's personal safety from February 29, 1932, to March 17, 1933. This command expanded to the SS Stabswache "Berlin" and he remained commander until August 2, 1933. His next post, commanding the Gruppenstab SS Sonderkommando Berlin, combined the Sonderkommando Berlin, Sonderkommando Zossen and Sonderkommando Jüterbog and

---

[2] An SS Oberführer was a position by area of Germany, not just a rank.

[3] He may have retained his Abschnitt command during the period he led Gruppe "Süd" since the SS was still not actually large enough to require so many levels of command. He led Abschnitt IV until August 1, 1931. Yerger, "Allgemeine-SS," page 123.

[4] The Gruppen were redesignated as Oberabschnitte in mid-November, 1933. Several units had the same title at various times in the pre-war years. The dates of Dietrich's command disagree with "SS-Personalbefehl" of 1933 which are found to be less than accurate compared to actual events. For the various commands (Gruppen and Oberabschnitte) see Yerger, "Allgemeine-SS."

(Opposite Above) Josef Dietrich gives a speech wearing his dress SS sword. Behind him, from right to left, are Ernst Deutsch (commander of SS Bataillon "N," during the war a regimental commander and German Cross in Gold holder), Paul Moder (Abschnitt Leader, killed serving with "Totenkopf"), unknown, and Wilhelm Koppe (the last Higher SS and Police Leader of the General Government area of Poland). In the photo above, Dietrich sits next to Fritz Weitzel in an early photo wearing early SS style headgear.

Stadelheim prison during the June 30, 1934, purge of the SA leadership. During the initial stages of the purge, Dietrich accompanied Hitler from Berlin to Munich then returned to his command where one of his staff officers, Martin Kohlroser, had been commanding the firing squads. During the Polish campaign he was awarded a clasp to his WWI Iron Cross 2nd class on September 25, 1939, and two days later the clasp to his 1st class award.

Given the rank of General der Waffen-SS in March, 1940, (retroactive to July 1, 1934) Dietrich commanded the "Leibstandarte" through its expansion to a brigade. During the Western campaign he was awarded the Knight's Cross on July 5, 1940, and later for command of the regiment and its performance won the Oakleaves on December 31, 1941. On May 9, 1941, his command expanded into a division. Dietrich's command was redesignated as a Panzer Grenadier Division with a tank detachment on September 9, 1942.[6] Leading his newly strengthened command he won the Swords to the Knight's Cross on March 16, 1943, for the re-capture of Kharkov. He turned over command to Theodor Wisch on June 4, 1943. After a short leave he began forming what eventually became the I.SS-Panzer-Korps "Leibstandarte" on July 27, 1943. Dietrich held the post officially until succeeded by Hermann Priess on October 24, 1944, and was awarded the Diamonds to the Knight's Cross for his leadership in the Normandy fighting.[7] Substitutes ran operations with his corps command during August and early September, 1943, when Dietrich went to Italy and supervised the disarmament of the Italian Army. His Chief of Staff, Fritz Kraemer and then Georg Keppler, acted as commander when Dietrich undertook new duties beginning in early August, 1944. Dietrich was promoted to SS-Oberst-Gruppenführer und Generaloberst der Waffen-SS on August 1, 1944. For purposes of seniority, the promotion was effective April 20, 1942, the date Hitler had originally planned to have him obtain the rank. However, this was delayed as he would have out-ranked Paul Hausser, who in 1942 was forming the initial SS corps size formation. Dietrich also received the honorary rank of "Panzer Generaloberst der Waffen-SS," the only officer so designated.

On August 9, 1944, he took command of the 5.Panzer Armee, replacing Heinrich Eberbach who went to lead Gruppe "Eberbach" by order of Günther von Kluge to plan a counter-attack, until succeeded by Knight's Cross with Oakleaves, Swords and Diamonds winner Hasso von Manteuffel on September 11, 1944.[8]

Reporting to Hitler on September 14, 1944, he was ordered to form the 6.Panzer Armee which was retitled as the 6.SS-Panzer-Armee on the last day of January, 1945. Dietrich began forming the command in September and it was officially activated on October

he led the group staff from its creation on August 2, 1933, to September 3, 1933.

The elements of Sonderkommando Berlin and Zossen became the "Adolf Hitler Standarte" on September 3, 1933, and Dietrich took command of this unit which developed into the "Leibstandarte."[5] Promoted to SS-Gruppenführer on July 1, 1934, an order changed the title of Dietrich's command to the "Leibstandarte SS Adolf Hitler" on April 13, 1934. Expanded to a brigade starting in August 1940, it retained that older designation until April 17, 1940. Coming under the Ministry of the Interior in April, 1934, the unit could be financed with state funds. Two companies of the "Leibstandarte" performed the executions at

---

[5] Sonderkommando Jüterbog was dissolved and its personnel absorbed by the new unit in October, 1933.

[6] The division got a full Panzer Regiment in mid-October 1942 before leaving for the front in 1943, as did "Das Reich" and "Totenkopf." Though actually Panzer Divisions, they retained the older designation at that time.

[7] SS-Führungshauptamt, "Stabsbefehl Nr. 26/44," dated November 9, 1944.

[8] Eberbach was to have resumed his command in late August but became a prisoner-of-war on August 31.

Dietrich is nearest the camera taking a nap during the Western campaign. Below, he decorates men of the "Leibstandarte." Behind him is SS-Obersturmbannführer Martin Kohlroser.

(Above) Dietrich (left) with Max Wünsche and (below) he reviews the troops with Theodor Wisch and Albert Frey (far left).

A summer and a winter shot of Josef Dietrich wearing early SS-Obergruppenführer collar insignia and his Knight's Cross with Oakleaves.

24, 1944, initially comprising I. and II.SS-Panzer-Korps. He held this command, the largest Waffen-SS designated formation, until the end of the war.

In additions to his decorations for bravery and leadership, Dietrich was also the recipient of many civil and political awards. Göring awarded him the Gold Pilot Observers Badge with Diamonds and he received Blood Order No. 10 on November 9, 1933. Dietrich was awarded the Reich's Sports and SA Sports Badges in Gold, the Gold Party Badge, the NSDAP Long Service Award in Gold, and the 3rd class Army Long Service Award.

Married to the former wife of SS General Karl Brenner, he formally surrendered to U.S. General George Patton accompanied by his wife. Dietrich was held prisoner until tried in the Malmedy case in 1946. Found guilty, he was sentenced to 25 years in prison and paroled from Landsberg prison in October, 1955. A trial of superiors for the actions of a subordinate was unjust, nothing of the type occurring during the United States trial for a massacre similar to Malmedy in Vietnam. Dietrich was re-arrested and tried for com-

plicity in the June, 1934, purge of the SA leadership along with Michael Lippert.[9] After another prison sentence he was released in early February 1959, due to heart problems and bad circulation in his legs. He settled with his family in Ludwigsburg and enjoyed hunting in his final years. Active in HIAG, he died of a heart attack at home on April 21, 1966. The eulogy at his funeral, attended by hundreds of the men he had commanded, was given by Wilhelm Bittrich.

One of only two Waffen-SS men awarded the Diamonds to the Knight's Cross, he was an important early SS leader who gained Hitler's complete confidence and trust. His position as commander of the "Leibstandarte" allowed him direct access to the Führer and the power to ignore many directives and orders of Himmler. A superb combat leader in difficult situations, his honest concern for the men of his commands endeared them to him. That leadership

---

[9] Lippert and Theodor Eicke were the two persons responsible for shooting Ernst Röhm, Stabschef of the SA. At that time Lippert was chief of the guard unit at Dachau (his biography will be contained in volume 2).

ability, combined with the tactical skills of his senior staff officers, made him one of the best Waffen-SS commanders.[10] In the pre-war years he was a noted race car driver and was an excellent hunter until the end of his life. Personally courageous, he had a large degree of personal magnetism and got along well with those around him, showing compassion to those in need or trouble. He was not afraid to confront Hitler personally regarding the welfare of the men under his command, though he fell out with Hitler after the military failure in Hungary during 1945. His leadership skills were equal to Paul Hausser's, though of a different method. Dietrich's leadership training and influence on his "Leibstandarte" officers resulted in the other group of excellent war-time divisional and regimental commanders being produced, including Theodor Wisch, Kurt Meyer, Albert Frey, Joachim Peiper, Max Wünsche, Fritz Witt and Hugo Kraas.

---

[10] The most important of his staff primary officers were Rudolf Lehmann and Fritz Kraemer, both of whom eventually held senior commands and as such are examined in this series.

Left and below: In these two photos a serious looking Josef Dietrich is visited by Reichsführer-SS Heinrich Himmler.

Himmler visits I.SS-Panzer-Korps. In the upper photo, Himmler (center) is flanked by Dietrich and Georg Schönberger. Below Dietrich (center) is surrounded by Himmler and SS-Sturmbannführer Fritz Schuster, the command of Panzerjäger Abteilung 17.

Josef Dietrich contemplating the war and (right) walking with Erwin Rommel.

Two views of Dietrich wearing later style SS-Obergruppenführer insignia. At right he talks over breakfast with Hitler's personal photographer, Heinrich Hoffmann.

(Above) From left are Fritz Witt, Dietrich, Franz Staudinger and Theodor Wisch. Below, Dietrich decorates men of the "LSSAH." On the far right is Kurt Meyer and beside him is Max Wünsche.

(Above) Dietrich, in black Panzer uniform, takes a roadside rest with Himmler and Carl Oberg (Higher SS and Police Leader France) and in the lower photo he wears the same uniform.

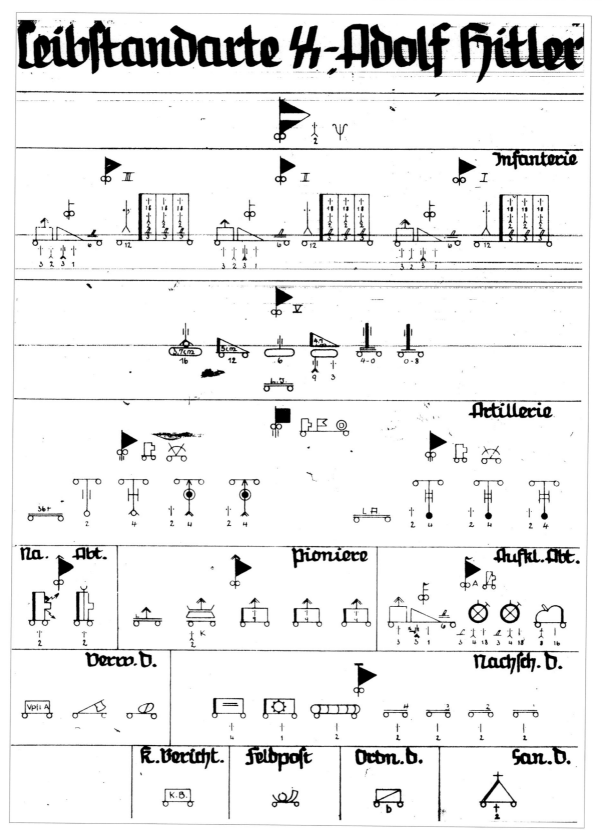

The "Leibstandarte SS-Adolf Hitler" in April, 1941.

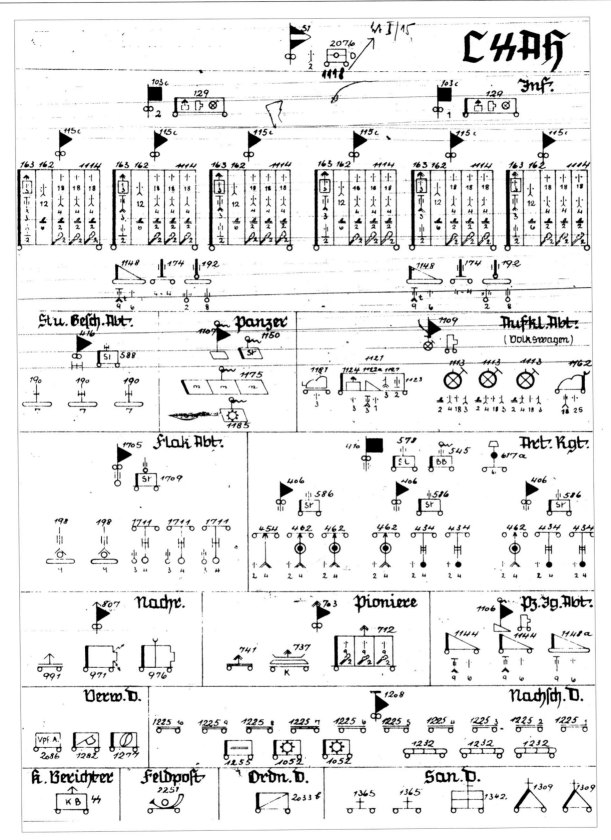

The "Leibstandarte" in mid-February, 1942.

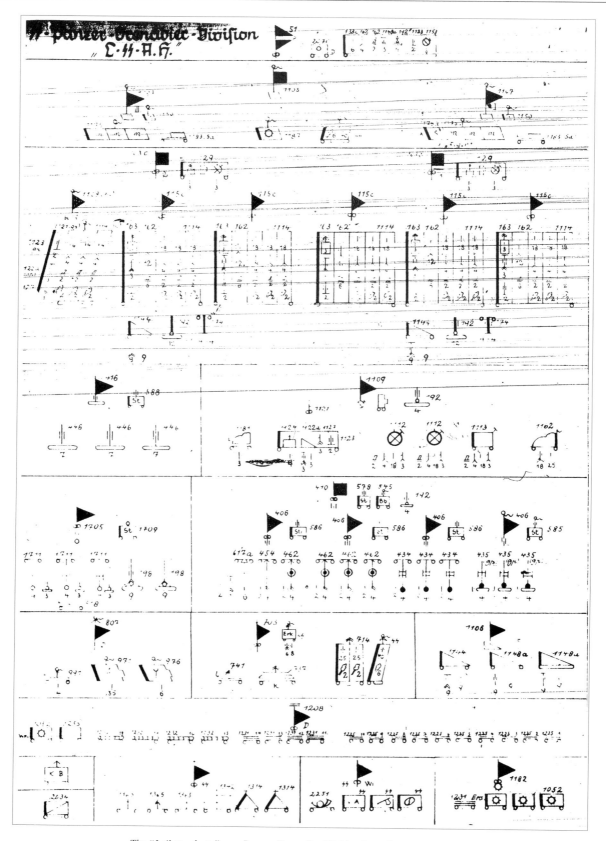

The "Leibstandarte" as a Panzer-Grenadier-Division in early December, 1942.

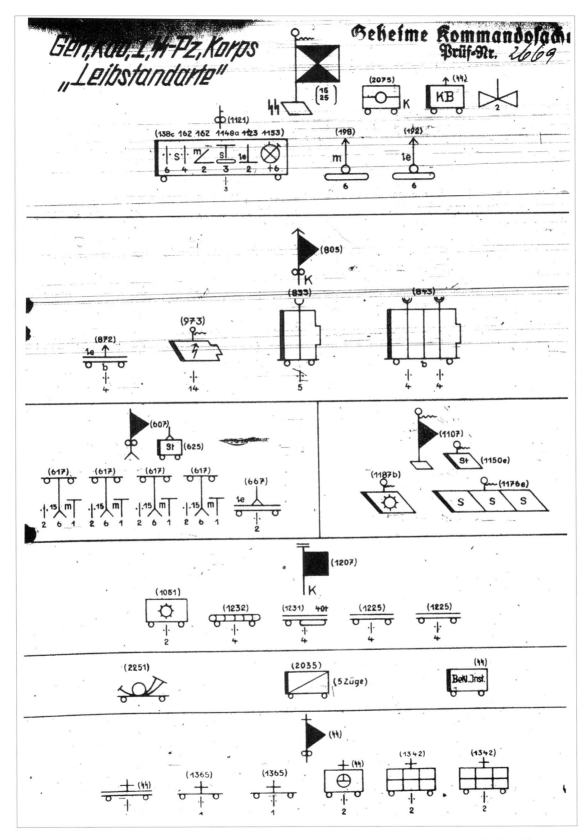

I.SS-Panzer-Korps "Leibstandarte" in July, 1943. Shown are the Korps units which does not indicate the divisions subordinated to it operationally.

HELMUT DÖRNER

Born on June 26, 1909, in München-Gladbach, Helmut Dörner was the son of a businessman. After completing his education, he joined the Schutzpolizei as an officer candidate on October 6, 1927. Posted in Düsseldorf until mid-March, 1933, he then transferred to Bonn as a reserve NCO with the Landespolizei detachment stationed there until the start of November, 1934. Continuing his studies. He was trilingual and passed his interpreters exams in 1931. Dörner was then reassigned to his home town area until May 1, 1937.

He took an officers course in Bonn from August 24, 1936, until March 24, 1937, and was commissioned as a Leutnant der Schutzpolizei on May 1, 1937. Promoted to Oberleutnant der Schutzpolizei on January 30, 1938, Dörner next served in Essen from the start of May, 1937, until late August, 1939, and joined the NSDAP on May 1, 1937. As adjutant to Schutzpolizei District Command I from late August to October 27, 1939, he was promoted to Hauptmann on September 11, 1939. As a company leader he went to the police training detachment in Essen until November 25, 1939, and joined the new Polizei-Division the next day.

Assigned to the Panzerjäger Abteilung, Dörner served as adjutant until the end of March, 1940, when he took command of a Kompanie. At that command, he was awarded the Iron Cross 2nd class on June 16, 1940, and the 1st class three days later. In August, 1940, he moved to Polizei-Schützen-Regiment 1 as commander of its supporting Panzerjäger Kompanie and joined the SS as an SS-Hauptsturmführer on January 1, 1940. Holding this command until the end of January, 1942, Dörner was wounded by a grenade during the fierce Luga river fighting on August 5, 1941, and was promoted to Major der Schutzpolizei on January 5, 1942. His award of the Wound Badge in Black came on August 15, 1941. On October 2, 1941, Dörner was also awarded the Infantry Assault Badge in Silver and, on December 24, 1941, the German Cross in Gold.

Dörner was then promoted to command the II./Polizei-Schützen-Regiment 2 from the end of January, 1942, to October, 1942, when the regiment was redesignated SS-Polizei-Infanterie-Regiment 2.[1] Promoted to SS-Sturmbannführer on April 1, 1942, his Bataillon was part of a Kampfgruppe composed of units assigned to the L.Armee Korps from February 10 to March 4, 1942.[2] Dörner also served as Fritz Freitag's deputy regimental commander from July 8 to September 2, 1942. For three separate actions he won the Knight's Cross on May 15, 1942, including the destruction of 58 enemy bunkers on January 27, 1942.[3]

After a leave and a detachment leaders course in Paris, he returned to the Division and led the eastern-most area troops of SS-Polizei-Infanterie-Regiment 2 during the Ladoga battles on the Northern Front. On February 15, 1943, he replaced Fritz Freitag as commander of the redesignated SS-Polizei-Grenadier-Regiment 2.[4] Promoted to SS-Obersturmbannführer on April 20, 1943, and to Oberstleutnant der Schutzpolizei on December 10, 1943, he held regimental command until December 2, 1944. Dörner was awarded the Close Combat Clasp in Silver on September 24, 1943. The award (the 650th) of the Oakleaves came on November 16, 1944, for his tactical leadership in the Szolnok area.

When Karl Schumers was killed, Dörner took command of the 4.SS-Polizei-Panzer-Grenadier-Division from August 18, 1944, until

---

[1] "Verordnungsblatt der Waffen-SS" dated October 15, 1942.
[2] The Division also supplied its 9./Artillerie Regiment. "Die guten Glabens Waren," volume 1, page 186, using information from the KTB for that period.
[3] "Das Schwarze Korps" dated July 2, 1942.
[4] "Verordnungsblatt der Waffen-SS" dated February 1, 1943.

Helmut Dörner (left) in Polizei uniform showing his German Cross in Gold and (right) as an SS-Standartenführer and Knight's Cross holder. The "SS" runes on his police tunic indicate full-time membership in the Waffen-SS.

succeeded by Fritz Schmedes on August 24, 1944.[5] After being in reserve briefly in December, he was assigned to command a Kampfgruppe of the IX.SS-Gebirgs-Korps and was killed leading that command in Budapest at the Bolnay Academy on February 11, 1945. Having been promoted to SS-Oberführer on January 15, 1945, Dörner was awarded the Swords to the Knight's Cross on February 4, 1945, for his leadership in Budapest but it is unknown if he ever received news of the award. In addition to his other decorations, he was given the Eastern Front Medal, the Police Long Service Award 3rd class and the German Life Saving Association Badge in Bronze.[6]

Seeing continuous service with the Polizei-Division since its formation, Dörner was not only brave but an excellent tactician.

The SS-Polizei Division, often overlooked compared to the more glamorous classic divisions, fought in some extremely hard battles on the Northern Front. Much of the success in many instances was due to Dörner's leadership and personal bravery which placed him constantly at the very front line in direct combat. As a company commander, his regimental (Hans Christian Schulze) and divisional (Arthur Mülverstedt and Karl-Pfeffer von Wildenbruch) commanders thought him among the very best in the entire division.[7] The commander of the 255.Infanterie Division, Generalleutnant Hans von Basse, gave him an official letter of commendation on March 5, 1942, for the assistance Dörner's battalion gave to Basse's command.

[5] "Die guten Glaubens waren," Band II, pages 340, 346 and 351. Other sources give the 17th.

[6] "Lebenslaufbahn" dated November 28, 1942.

[7] "Allgemeines Urteil" from a very lengthy overview of superiors opinions of Dörner between 1939 and 1942, dated March 20, 1942.

Dörner being awarded the Knight's Cross. Assigned to the Polizei Division, he wears a Polizei uniform but a Waffen-SS peaked hat while the divisional officer tying the ribbon wears Polizei headgear.

THEODOR EICKE

The son of a railway stationmaster, Theodor Eicke was born in Hamport bei Hudingen in Alsace on October 17, 1892. The youngest of eleven children, he left school and joined the Army as a volunteer in 1909. Posted to a Bavarian regiment, he served until 1913 with the 23rd Infantry Regiment "König Ferdinand der Bulgaren." Eicke then transferred to the 3rd Infantry Regiment "Prinz Karl von Bayern" until August, 1914. Moving to his third Bavarian unit, he served with the 22nd Infantry Regiment "Fürst Wilhelm von Hohenzollern" until transferring to the artillery branch in 1916. With the artillery he went to the Second Bavarian Foot Artillery Regiment until 1917. A paymaster throughout his service, Eicke's final unit assignment was with the replacement machine gun company of the 2nd Army Corps where he stayed until leaving the service with the rank of Unterzahlmeister on March 1, 1919.[1] He was awarded the Iron Cross 2nd class, the Brunswick War Service Cross 2nd class, the Bavarian Order of Merit 2nd class, and the Bavarian Military Service Badge 3rd class.

After leaving the Army, he attended a Technical College in Ilmenau in Thuringia until his radical political views and lack of funds forced him to leave in early September, 1919. Eicke then pursued a career in the Polizei, enlisting as a candidate with the police administration in Ilmenau during December, 1919. He was dismissed in early July, 1920, for engaging in political agitation against the Weimar republic. Eicke then passed his exams for the Schutzpolizei school in Cottbus during 1920, but was again not employed due to his political views. Those same views caused him to be dismissed in 1921 after only two weeks as an officer candidate with the police in Weimar. Eicke finally obtained a post with the police administration in Ludwigshafen am Rhein but was dismissed in January, 1923, again due to his political activities and radical views.

Employed by the I.G. Farben company from January, 1923, to March, 1932, he served first as a commercial agent and later as a security advisor. On December 1, 1928, Eicke joined the NSDAP and the SA. He served as a Truppführer in Frankenthal and later Ludwigshafen, transferring to the SS as an SS Mann on July 29, 1930.

In the pre-war years Eicke found an outlet for his radical views with the SS. Promoted to SS-Truppführer in August, 1930, he was commissioned as an SS-Sturmführer on November 27, 1930. Assigned to SS Sturm 147 in Ludwigshafen on August 30, he took command of the unit on November 27, 1930. Promoted to SS-Sturmbannführer on January 30, 1931, he then took over leadership of the II./10.SS-Brigade.[2] On November 7, 1931, he was promoted to be the administrative officer of the 10.SS-Standarte and then succeeded Fritz Berni as commander of the Standarte on December 21, 1931. Eicke was also promoted to SS-Standartenführer on November 15, 1931.

Arrested in early March, 1932, in connection with the procurement of explosives, Eicke received a two-year sentence in mid-July, 1932, after awaiting trial in solitary confinement. Given a leave of six weeks to recover his health, he instead returned to the 10.SS-Standarte. When his leave was canceled, he took refuge in Landau. Ordered to Munich by Himmler, Eicke was sent to Italy to take over the SS refugee camp in Malcesine. He held that post from mid-September, 1932, to mid-February, 1933, during which time

---

[1] Handwritten "Lebenslauf" dated March 22 and 29, 1933, and March 15, 1937.

[2] The SS copied the levels and command set-up of the SA with Brigaden being a short lived designation. The SS was too small in its early forms to incorporate so many command levels. Yerger, "Allgemeine-SS."

Theodor Eicke in two early photographs, on the left as the commander of the 10.SS-Standarte (note cufftitle of the unit).

he was promoted to SS-Oberführer on October 26, 1932. Leading an SS formation in celebration of the anniversary of the Fascists march on Rome, Eicke embarrassed the Reichsführer-SS when the parade enflamed the Austrian Press over control of South Tyrol. Austrian Party officials demanded the most severe punishment for Eicke, sending their requests directly to Hitler, Himmler and SA Stabschef Ernst Röhm.

Returning to Germany in mid-February, 1933, Eicke fled to Thuringia to avoid punishment for his actions. With the understanding his behavior was to change, he was allowed to return to his family in Ludwigshafen the following month. Assigned to the 46.SS-Standarte, Eicke had been plotted against by Gauleiter Josef Bürckel. This culminated in Eicke joining a mutiny against the local NSDAP leadership. Arrested on March 21, 1933, in the wake of that local insurrection, he was dismissed from the SS for failing to keep his promise to Himmler and improve his behavior.

While under arrest, Himmler had Eicke committed to a mental institution to keep him under wraps. Following his release on June

26, 1933, he re-entered to SS at his old rank and seniority. Assigned as a special duties officer to SS Gruppe "Süd" until June 20, 1934, when assigned a post on Himmler's staff. Eicke also took command of the concentration camp at Dachau on June 26, 1933, succeeding the disgraced Hilmar Wäckerle. Promoted to SS-Brigadeführer on January 30, 1934, he commanded the camp until July 4, 1934. The command was removed from control of Oberabschnitt "Süd" on March 9, 1934, and Eicke's command became independent.[3] During this posting, he developed the punishment system that set the standard in the camps. He also made the guard units into an elite and what almost developed into a separate entity within the SS. It was his intention the be an elite within the elite, as the guards of "criminal-prisoners" that were perceived as a threat to Germany.

When the purge of the SA leadership took place during the "Night of the Long Knives," Eicke and Michael Lippert, then chief

---

[3] "Pers.Akten" dated March 9, 1934, and initialed by Himmler.

of the guard unit at Dachau, were temporarily assigned to Stadlheim prison in Munich. It was Theodor Eicke who actually shot Ernst Röhm in his prison cell on July 1, 1934. Three days later he was made Inspector of all the concentration camps and guard units.[4] On July 11, 1934, he was promoted to SS-Gruppenführer. His willingness to obey all orders without question made him valuable to both Hitler and Himmler, though his own actions were often impulsive and irrational.

His Inspectorate post included the Totenkopfverbände in late-March, 1936, and he held this influential post until forming the "Totenkopf" Division.[5] Eicke also held a seat in the Reichstag from January 30, 1937, until his death. His position as head of the concentration camps and guard units made him among the most powerful SS leaders and provided him with immense resources that he continued to utilize, long after officially leaving that position on November 15, 1939. He was succeeded by August Heissmeyer as head of the SS-Totenkopfstandarten and by Richard Glücks as Inspector of Concentration Camps.

During the Polish campaign, Eicke served as the Higher SS and Police Leader assigned to the operational areas of Armee-oberkommando 8 and 10. That post developed into the HSSPF "Ost" in the General Government area of occupied Poland.[6] After the Polish campaign Eicke took command of the new "Totenkopf" Division, formed with camp guard units as its cadre, on November 14, 1939.

While leading his division, Eicke was severely wounded at Soaschino on July 6, 1941, when his command car hit a mine. Matthias Kleinheisterkamp and Georg Keppler took command until Eicke recovered from a shattered right foot and nerve damage. He returned to his command in September, 1941, and the same month was made a General der Waffen-SS. He was awarded the Knight's Cross on December 26, 1941, for his leadership at the Lowat and Pola rivers as well as for the intense fighting at Luschino.[7] Eicke led "Totenkopf" and the smaller elements in the Demjansk pocket and for that was awarded the Oakleaves and promoted to SS-Obergruppenführer und General der Waffen-SS on April 20, 1942. On June 26, 1942, Hitler personally presented Eicke his Oakleaves at Rastenburg. Eicke continued as commander through the division's expansion to a Panzer-Grenadier-Division in 1942, though poor health caused Himmler to order him to take a long leave following his award of the Oakleaves until October, instead of returning to Demjansk. Eicke took the leave as ordered, though

---

[4] Initialed order by Himmler gving him the command effective that date but the order is dated February 17, 1936.

[5] The camps and the guard units were divided into separate commands on November 15, 1939.

[6] Yerger, "Allgemeine-SS."

[7] "Das Schwarze Korps," January 22, 1942.

SS-Gruppenführer Theodor Eicke is the center of conversation among a group of officers.

Eicke (left) with fellow SS-Gruppenführer Karl Zech.

he attempted several times to be returned to his divisional command.

Returning to Russia with his division, Eicke was killed on February 26, 1943, when his observation plane was shot down near Michailowka. His body was recovered by a platoon of two assault guns, three armored personnel carriers, and two motorcycle groups led by SS-Untersturmführer Walter Becker and buried on March 1st.[8] Later, when forces retreated, his body was removed and buried again in Zhitomir. Both these recoveries were by voluntary units under heavy fire, with severe losses. Eicke was also awarded a clasp to his WWI Iron Cross 2nd class on May 26, 1940, the 1st class on May 31, 1940, the Gold Party Badge on January 30, 1940, and the Wound Badge in Silver. Married in December, 1914, he had two children. His 21 year old son was killed December 2, 1941.[9]

Eicke was both a famous and infamous personality. His involvement in the concentration camp system is documented and he was responsible for the strict punishment codes imposed during the

---

[8] Report of the Kampfgruppe Stabskompanie dated February 28, 1943.
[9] "Stammkarte."

pre-war years. His development of the guard units into an elite created an effective cadre for forming his divisional command. The resources available to him with the camps were continuously used in support of his division as well.

Totally devoted to Hitler and the Party, he was cruel and often short-sighted. Revered by the men of his divisional command, they accorded him the affectionate name "Papa Eicke." However, he was obsessively strict and forceful with his command. Not a military expert, he simply used all men and weapons to complete a combat assignment, regardless of the losses incurred. While this earned "Totenkopf" the reputation as possibly the best defensive unit of the Waffen-SS, it also brought personal problems for Eicke from the Army due to his lack of consideration for losses when undertaking an operation. He did whatever necessary to see to it that his men were well-supplied and seems to have had a split personality with regard to his pre-war and war-time commands. When losses ran so high it was feared the division would have no cadre for rebuilding, he appealed directly to Himmler to withdraw the division. He developed into a soldier and his own personal bravery, while over-zealous, was undoubtedly acknowledged.

In the foreground from left are Eicke, Karl Wolff and Heinrich Himmler.

A portrait and an autographed photo of Eicke with the early insignia of an SS-Gruppenführer.

Opposite top: From left are Matthias Kleinheisterkamp, Generaloberst Ernst Busch, unknown, Eicke and Richard Pauly.

Opposite bottom: From left are Hermann Priess, Eicke and Richard Pauly in Russia during the autumn of 1941.

Hitler awarding Eicke the Oakleaves to the Knight's Cross at the Führer's headquarters.

SS-Obergruppenführer Theodor Eicke

Below: Celebrating Eicke's award of the Oakleaves are, from left, Karl Wolff, Eicke, Richard Schulze, Wilhelm Keitel and Dr. Otto Schwab.

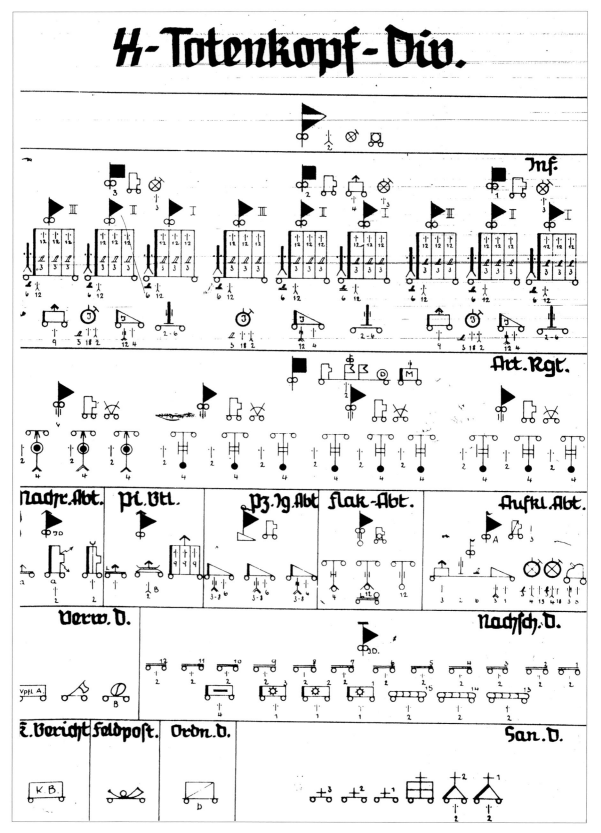

The SS-Totenkopf-Division in April, 1941.

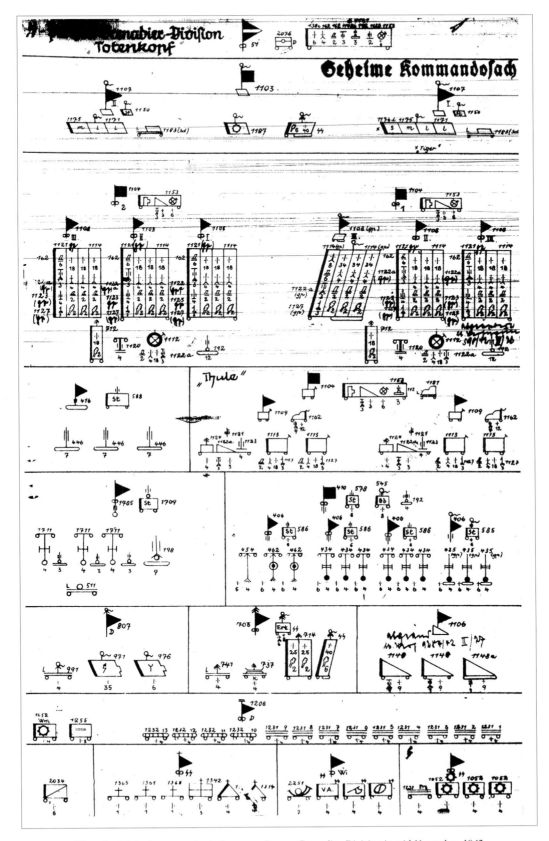

"Totenkopf," during expansion to become a Panzer-Grenadier-Division in mid-November, 1942.

HERMANN FEGELEIN

The oldest son of retired Oberleutnant Hans Fegelein, Otto Hermann Fegelein was born to a Catholic family in Ansbach on October 30, 1906. He inherited an early love of riding from his father that continued to grow following his family's move to Munich in 1912, where his father was assigned to a military riding school. Fegelein completed his primary education in 1917 followed by secondary education and two semesters of study at the University of Munich until 1926. It would appear that six months in the Army assigned to a machine gun unit with Cavalry Regiment 17 in 1925-1926 was his only formal military training. He may have also served briefly in a Freikorps unit.[1]

After enlisting in Munich with the Bavarian Land Police (Landespolizei) on April 20, 1927, he served as an NCO and later was a police officer candidate at which rank he left the police on August 16, 1929. With his family still living in Munich, access to his father's riding school on Albrechtstraße allowed him to indulge his passion for riding and equestrian competition that would eventually lead to his service career choice in the SS. Riding competitions also allowed him to travel extensively throughout Europe in the period between the wars.

Joining the Allgemeine-SS on May 15, 1933, he was commissioned an SS-Untersturmführer effective June 12, 1933. His first assignment was adjutant to the Reiterführer of SS-Gruppe Süd (later SS-Oberabschnitt Süd). Fegelein held this assignment and that of Special Duties Officer (Sonderführer) until July, 1934, when he assumed command of 15.Reiterstandarte in Munich until September that year. Having been promoted to SS-Obersturmführer effective April 20, 1934, he next assumed command of Reiterabschnitt

V and held that position until the command was dissolved at the end of October, 1936. In May, 1934, he advanced in position to be the Reiterführer of SS-Oberabschnitt Süd. After being promoted to SS-Hauptsturmführer on November 9, 1934, and SS-Sturmbannführer on January 30, 1936, Fegelein was among the fastest rising young Allgemeine-SS cavalry officers.

On June 16, 1936, Himmler selected Fegelein to be commander of the SS Main Riding School (SS-Hauptreitschule) to be constructed in Munich.[2] The school was a popular stop for numerous visiting senior SS officers and this, along with his reputation as a rider, made Fegelein one of the best known junior SS officers. He had competed well in numerous tournaments throughout the peacetime years and assisted in preparing the equestrian events for the 1936 Olympics in Berlin. Aside from being awarded the Riding Sports Badge (Reitersportabzeichen) in Gold during his time as commander of the school he was promoted to SS-Obersturmbannführer on January 30, 1937, and to SS-Standartenführer on July

---

[1] Fegelein's personal records indicate two years service in 1925-26 by which time the peak period of the Freikorps had passed.

[2] Letter from Himmler to SS-Oberabschnitt Süd appointing Fegelein commander of the school (besides his command of SS-Reiterabschnitte V). He was given until July 1, 1936, to establish the functional needs of the facility. The school was a component of SS-Oberabschnitt Süd, subordinate and reporting to the inspector of Allgemeine-SS cavalry (Inspekteur Allgemeine-SS Reiterei), SS-Obersturmbannführer von Wiokowski-Biedau who led that portion of the SS Main Office (SS-Hauptamt) and SS-Brigadeführer Weber, who was inspector of SS riding schools (Inspekteur der SS Reitschulen). Designed by architect Karl Meitinger and built by the firm of Otto Schiedermaier in Munich, work on the main structure began October 20, 1936, with a planned completion date of July, 1937. This school provided the SS riding instruction, permanent base for training and contestants for the numerous pre-war equestrian tournaments both in and outside Germany, with the first competition held in Munich from January 18-20, 1937. The school continued to supply competitors for tournaments as late as May, 1941, and in the pre-war years Hermann Fegelein was often a very successful competitor. Many men who competed while assigned to the school would later have positions among the SS-Totenkopf-Reiterstandarte, Kavallerie Brigade or later Kavallerie Division when they formed. Established as an Allgemeine-SS facility, the Waffen-SS later created other schools for mounted troop training.

Hermann Fegelein in a pre-war photo wearing the collar insignia for mounted units of the Allgemeine-SS and (right) in riding clothes during an equestrian meet.

25 the same year. Fegelein remained commander of the school, which he listed as his residence during the war years, until the first week of September, 1939.

As commander of the original SS-Totenkopf-Reiterstandarte, Fegelein was given the reserve rank of SS-Obersturmbannführer in the Waffen-SS in March, 1940, but was allowed to wear his higher ranking Allgemeine-SS insignia (he became a Waffen-SS Standartenführer on February 1, 1942). Awarded the Iron Cross 2nd class on December 15, 1940, and the Iron Cross 1st class on June 28, 1941, he was the only full commander of the SS-Kavallerie-Brigade during its existence.[3] On March 2, 1942, he was awarded the Knight's Cross based on an official recommendation which reads as follows:[4]

"Since January 25, 1942, the SS-Kavallerie-Brigade was located on the southeast front of 23.Armeekorps in the sector north of Nikulino-Polowinino-Saizewo-Dmitrowo-Sokolomo. The Brigade was assigned the task of preventing the advance of strong enemy forces that had breached the gap west of Rshev, towards the south against the rear of the 206.Division.

The Brigade foiled all attempts of the enemy with great dash accomplished in spite of heavy casualties. Not only did the SS-Kavallerie-Brigade defeat all efforts of the enemy, but they also led the main offensive attacks. In addition. they led the encircling and annihilation attacks which lasted for days.

During all the defensive and offensive fighting, the personal unshakability, exemplary bravery and constant desire to

---

[3] He returned to Debica for reformation with some Brigade elements and after mid-March, 1942, Gustav Lombard (see volume 2) commanded those Brigade elements still in Russia until April, prior to the formation of Kampfgruppe "Zehender." For the development and history of the SS-Totenkopf-Reiterstandarte and SS Cavalry Brigade, see Yerger, Mark: "Riding East, The SS Cavalry Brigade in Poland and Russia 1939-1945."

[4] The award was recommended on March 2, 1942, by the commanding general of XXIII.Armeekorps, General der Infanterie Albrecht Schubert. This is the earlier form of the recommendation and lacks the approval stamps of the final copy. This is not uncommon in personnel files, often several recommendations with slight variations in wording were submitted. It is odd that this took place for Fegelein's Knight's Cross as well as for his brother Waldemar's same decoration.

Two views of Fegelein at the SS Main Riding School in Munich while giving a tour to SS-Oberführer Günther Claussen.

Fegelein in the uniform of an SS-Standartenführer after being awarded the Knight's Cross for his leadership of the SS-Kavallerie Brigade.

attack was shown by the Brigade Commander. He was able to complete his assignments with constant attack operations, during which he rallied his men behind him.

On February 5, 1942, the Brigade attacked a strong enemy group northwest of Tschertolino on the personal decision of the Brigade Commander. The attack was carried out under his personal leadership with a tremendous swing in a bold advance, in spite of the most difficult terrain and weather conditions, against a vastly superior enemy in possession of strongly fortified positions.

Through the taking of the useful street emergency point and important train station in Tschertolino, accomplished only after heavy fighting against tough enemy resistance, the ring around the stronger enemy forces was closed. The encircled enemy was only annihilated after hours of continuous night attacks. These were led by the Brigade Commander who personally commanded the strongpoint group.

The enemy lost 1800 dead and tons of material while we suffered minimal casualties. The resulting shortening of the front freed stronger forces and the SS-Kavallerie-Brigade suc-

ceeded in tightening the ring around the encircled enemy southwest of Rshev in a bold attack. The route to the village of Jersowo, which was taken on February 14, 1942, after heavy fighting which teetered back and forth, completed the challenge for the destruction of the surrounded enemy group.

SS-Standartenführer Fegelein was able to completely defeat these strong enemy forces with his enthusiastic decision-making and full-tempered leadership. His personal bravery and readiness for action enabled the cleansing of the situation southwest of Rshev."[5]

When the Brigade began expansion to become the SS-Kavallerie-Division in the spring of 1942, Fegelein left at the start of May to assume a position in the SS-Führungshauptamt as head of the Inspectorate for cavalry and horse-drawn transportation (Inspekteur Reit-und Fahrwesen [Inspektion 3]).[6] He was promoted to SS-Oberführer on December 1, 1942.

---

[5] "Kurze Begründung und Stellungnahme der Zwischen Vorgesetzten."

[6] Within the SS-Führungshauptamt (which grew in complexity from its creation in 1940 until 1945). In 1940 Amt (office) II (Waffen Inspektion/weapon in-

Fegelein, in white uniform wearing his Knight's Cross with Oakleaves, is shown with SS-Obergruppenführer Werner Lorenz in Russia.

Hermann Fegelein (left) after being awarded the Knight's Cross in 1942 and (right) resting in mid-1943 while commanding the SS-Kavallerie-Division.

Returning to a field command, he was given command of SS-Kampfgruppe "Fegelein" on December 1, 1942, for which he was awarded the Oakleaves to the Knight's Cross on December 21, 1942.[7] Wounded while leading the Kampfgruppe on December 23rd, after his recovery he was assigned to take command of the SS-Kavallerie-Division on April 20, 1943, and was promoted SS-Brigadeführer on May 1st.[8] An award of the German Cross in Gold came on November 1, 1943, following a recommendation by temporary divisional commander Bruno Streckenbach, for Fegelein's leadership of the SS-Kavallerie-Division during the summer of 1943 which was then approved by the commander of LVII.Armeekorps.[9] The document attests to Fegelein's personal bravery in the field and reads as follows:[10]

---

spection) covered all weapon types. Later Inspektion 3 was cavalry and horse-drawn transportation. In addition, a separate Amtsgruppe A covered weapons, equipment and vehicles of all types. Under this separate Amtsgruppe, cavalry and horsed transportation was covered by Amt VI.

[7] The units composing this Kampfgruppe were already in combat when this battle group was ordered formed by the SS-Führungshauptamt: SS-FHA,Kdo. Amt. d. WSS, Org.Tgb.Nr. 8810/42 geh. "Aufstellung der SS-Kampfgruppe 'Fegelein,' dated December 21, 1942, with immediate effect. Not all units ordered for the Kampfgruppe were of the strength (or quality) envisioned by SS higher headquarters. The primary unit was the II./SS-Polizei-Regiment 3 from the 4.SS-Polizei-Division. In addition to a signals platoon, the Kampfgruppe contained a battery of foreign made artillery, an attached army artillery battery, an anti-aircraft detachment with light and heavy weapons and a small number of assault guns. Later Polizei Regiment 15 (provided by the Ordnungspolizei, having been formed as troops for a HSSPF command) arrived to become a component. having been ordered assigned when the Kampfgruppe was formed. Fegelein utilized several former members of the SS-Kavallerie Brigade in his staff that had reassigned to the SS-Führungshauptamt or other posts in Germany.

[8] In a message to the SS-Kavallerie-Division, Fegelein gives the date as April 23rd, but although given the command in April, he did not arrive and assume leadership until May, 1943. The divisional commander, Fritz Freitag, was ill and hospitalized so it was temporary commander August Zehender whom Fegelein relieved.

[9] Fegelein had already left command of the division, as Streckenbach signed the award recommendation as temporary divisional commander (Kommandeur SS-Kavallerie-Division i.V.) on October 7th. Bender/Taylor in "Uniforms, Organization and History of the Waffen-SS," volume 3, gives January 1, 1944, as the start of Streckenbach's command (his promotion date). As with all documents compiled away from the field, there are often inaccurate or misleading points, such as Fegelein's individual Berlin compiled records used by Bender/Taylor giving him actual command until November 1, when Streckenbach was already commanding the division as Fegelein's substitute. This points out the academic point of "full" versus "temporary" or "substitute" assignments.

[10] "Vorschlag für die Verleihung des Deutschen Kreuzes in Gold" dated October 7, 1943, and signed by SS-Standartenführer Bruno Streckenbach. The recommendation was approved the following day by General der Panzertruppen Friedrich Kirchner, the commander of LVII.Armeekorps.

(Above) Fegelein announces the last riding meet in Poland during May, 1941, and (below) he is shown in the center with officers of the SS-Kavallerie Brigade. On the right is Rudolf Maeker who served as senior staff officer during part of the unit's deployment in Russia and won the German Cross in Gold.

"December 23, 1942: Two Russian regiments supported by artillery attacked Golaja primarily from the east, but also from a northwesterly direction, with the intent of breaking through the wide front by attacking our forces there. Our troops were in need of rest and not yet organized, so it can only be attributed to the personal bravery and cold-bloodedness of the commander, SS-Brigadeführer Fegelein, that this attack was broken up against the unbending defense of our units. SS-Brigadeführer Fegelein rallied the battle groups through his display of energy, while staying with his troops on the front lines. Here he was wounded, but despite this, he fought on until mid-day, thus bringing the Russian attack to a standstill.

May 17, 1943: During the extremely intense fighting with the militarily-organized partisan groups under the leadership of Russian Lieutenant-General Kolpak, SS-Brigadeführer Fegelein was able to execute a severe blow to the main strength of the enemy during an attack that resulted in their defeat. During the fight, SS-Brigadeführer Fegelein set an example for his officers and men by personally destroying a strongly fortified bunker.

May 24, 1943: During the annihilation of a strong partisan battalion armed with heavy grenade launchers and machine guns, SS-Brigadeführer Fegelein led his men from the front of the attack which proceeded through very difficult swamp terrain. During the attack, Brigadeführer Fegelein stormed the strongly fortified partisan strongpoint with such enthusiasm that his men finished the task by completely destroying the enemy in a very short period of time. The results of this attack were cited in the Armed Forces report on June 12, 1943.

May 31, 1943: Based on statements from prisoners, SS-Brigadeführer Fegelein executed an attack with a patrol of his men against a partisan camp located in the swamps south of Poljaka. The opponent defended himself doggedly. The enemy, far superior in number, was able to fight for only 20 minutes. During that time, the partisan camp was taken through the cold-blooded action of the commander. The enemy lost a large number of dead and wounded, of which 11 dead and 22 wounded were left behind.

August 26, 1943: The Russians managed a breakout near Bespalowka with the newly arriving 353rd, 394th and 409th Divisions, along with the remaining portions of the 6th and 24th Security Divisions. The enemy was also supported by strong tank forces. Fegelein distinguished himself through his unequaled cold-bloodedness by always making appearances at the hot-spots on the front with his men. He displayed tenacious defense and rallied his men to the task.

August 28, 1943: After a very heavy artillery and grenade barrage on the thinly occupied lines of the 1st, 2nd and 3rd Squadrons of SS-Kavallerie Regiment 1, the Russians attacked with a 3:1 advantage in separate waves. The Russians were able to break through our lines deeply at four different points, and then sent strong forces through the openings. With that, the danger of an immediate attack on Werchine-Bischkin was obvious. With the Regiment's reserves of 60 men under the leadership of an SS-Untersturmführer, the Regiment was able to break through and reach point 168.4 and put up a shield against Bol-Gomolscha to the south. The surrounded elements of the Squadron were freed by a patrol, and a line connecting points 168.4 and 177.7 was established. During this 18-hour fight, SS-Brigadeführer Fegelein was found at the most important positions and, with his unshakability and his quick decisiveness, he was able to resolve even the most hopeless situations. With his influence, the tactical intention of the opponent, the advance through the forest, was hindered.

September 8, 1943: The enemy attacked hill 199.0 with an immensely superior force and couldn't be repelled from his position. In spite of this, SS-Brigadeführer Fegelein ordered the weakened 4th and 5th Squadrons of SS-Kavallerie Regiment 1 to counterattack. Through his personal leadership, the attack was successful despite extremely strong enemy defenses. Not only was the hill taken, but high casualties were inflicted on the Soviets.

September 13, 1943: The enemy opened a heavy artillery and grenade-launcher barrage south of and on hill 208.5. The left neighboring unit was gone and the 1st Squadron was attacked from the rear. Hill 157.1 had to be held until assault guns and tanks were brought up. The commander had been following the fighting from one of the hills and reported the diminishing strength of his troops, which had certainly tired due to the continuous fighting that lasted for several days and nights. SS-Brigadeführer Fegelein stormed the hill, and in spite of his heavily bleeding recent wound (the lower part of his arm had a bullet pass through it) positioned himself at the head of his right flank and held the hill until it was relieved. With his action the impending catastrophe was avoided."

Having been wounded again on September 9 and 13, 1943, Fegelein was transferred to recover and command of the division taken by Bruno Streckenbach. Fegelein began his final assignment following his recovery. On January 1, 1944, he was assigned as the liaison officer between Himmler and Hitler at the latter's headquarters. His September, 1943, wound also resulted in his award of the Wound Badge in Silver. Promoted to SS-Gruppenführer on June 21, 1944, Fegelein was awarded the 83rd Swords to the Knight's Cross of the Iron Cross given to a member of the German Armed Forces on July 30, 1944. The decoration was bestowed for the actions of his command during the late summer of the previous year following a recommendation by the commander of XLII.Armee-korps.[11] Along with the above decorations, he was awarded the Close Combat Clasp in Silver and numerous Rumanian awards for bravery and leadership.

He married Gretl Braun (sister of Hitler's mistress Eva Braun) in June of 1944, but the close ties by marriage to Hitler did not prevent Fegelein's eventual demise. With confusion and intrigue rampant during the final days of the Third Reich, Hitler searched for a scapegoat for Reichsführer-SS Heinrich Himmler's disloyal conduct and had Fegelein shot as a deserter on April 29th, 1945.

Fegelein was a career SS officer well-suited to the Allgemeine-SS period of his career, especially command of the Munich riding school. Although brave and highly decorated, some of his later

[11] "Aktenvermerk" dated August 6, 1944. The recommendation also was supported by the senior commanders of 8.Armee and 1.Panzer-Armee

awards (Oakleaves and Oakleaves with Swords) may reflect more the accomplishments of the men and units he commanded. Due to his lack of formal staff training, one can dispute Fegelein's abilities as a tactician or staff-qualified divisional level commander in comparison to some of the other SS cavalry leaders. In the field he was therefore more apt to depend, at least to some degree, on the skills of an able staff and experienced junior commanders when commanding at divisional level, though proof of his personal bravery under fire is documented. He fostered the careers of many of his subordinates and utilized numerous early cavalry officers within his later headquarters assignments. He appears to have been close with his most senior commanders and highly qualified staff while seeing to it that the bravery of his subordinates was acknowledged by awards or promotions.

(Left) Fegelein, with Knight's Cross, and Rudolf Maeker in Russia during 1942 and (right) Fegelein briefs members of the SS-Kavallerie-Division. On the left is his brother Waldemar, a regimental commander and holder of the Knight's Cross.

From left are Günther Temme, Fegelein and Gustav Lombard in Russia during the summer of 1943. Temme competed in the 1936 Olympics and was an important Brigade officer. Lombard ended the war as a divisional commander.

Fegelein, followed by Günther Temme, leaves the headquarters of the SS-Kavallerie-Division in Russia during mid-1943.

Fegelein meets a colt born during the transfer of his command from Poland to Russia in 1941. Below, he sits with the First Staff Officer of the SS-Kavallerie-Division, Knight's Cross holder Hans Diergarten.

SS-Brigadeführer Hermann Fegelein wearing both his Oakleaves and German Cross in Gold.

Two photos at left: Two portraits of Hermann Fegelein as an SS-Oberführer after being awarded the Knight's Cross with Oakleaves.

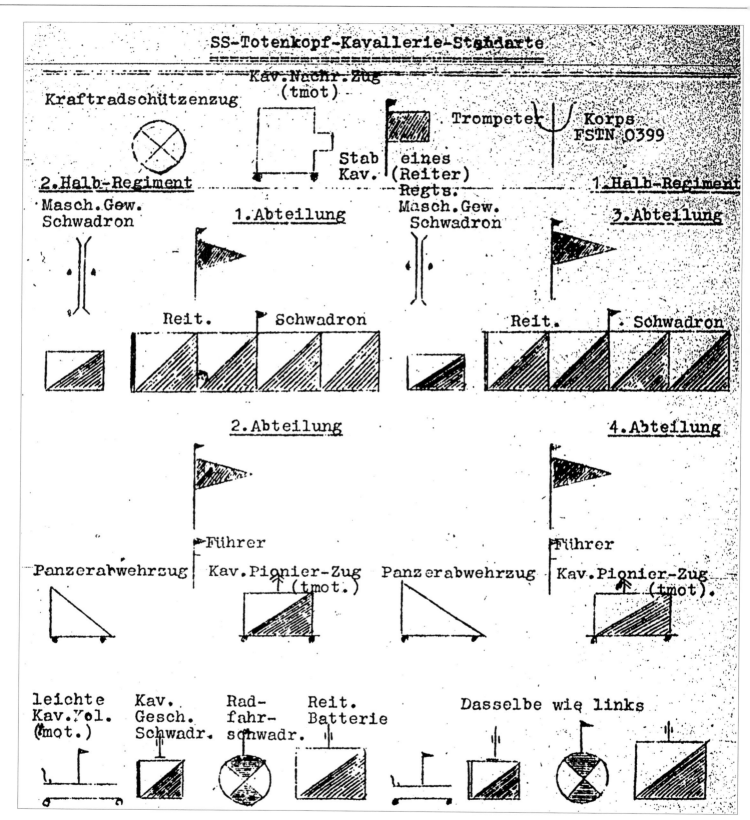

Fegelein's command of the SS-Totenkopf-Kavallerie-Standarte in 1939.

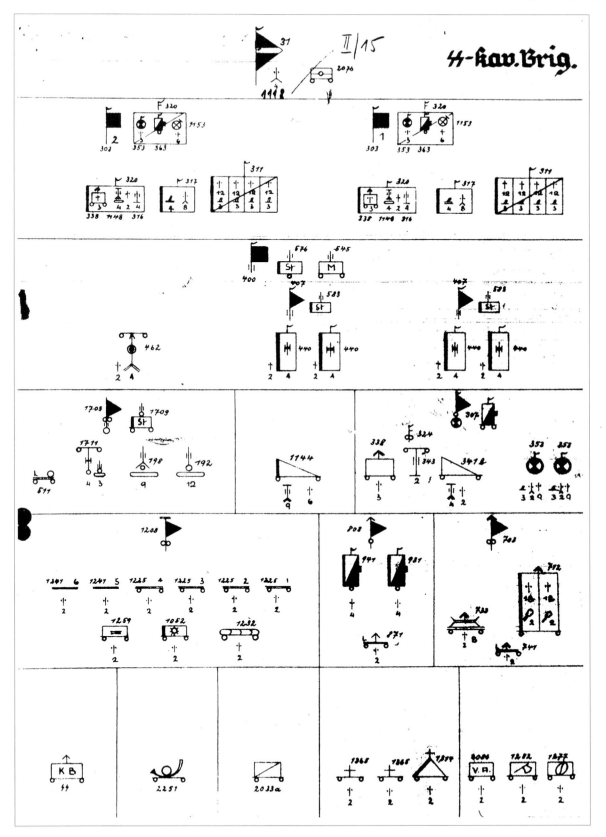

The SS-Kavallerie-Brigade in February, 1942, though the unit had suffered heavy losses in the Rshew area and was of lesser strength than shown.

FRITZ FREITAG

An East Prussian born in Allenstein on April 28, 1894, Fritz Freitag was the son of a railway official. He passed his Abitur on Easter, 1914, and joined the Army on April 14 the same year. Serving throughout WWI with East Prussian Grenadier Regiment "Kronprinz" No. 1, he saw combat on the Eastern and Western fronts. Commissioned as a Leutnant d.R. on November 6, 1915, he was a company commander from April, 1915, to December, 1918, with the same unit. Wounded four times in WWI, he was awarded the Wound Badge in Silver, both classes of the Iron Cross and the Hohenzollern House Order. From mid-January to mid-April 1919, he served with an East Prussian Freikorps.[1]

After leaving the Army, Freitag studied medicine and natural history. He gave up his studies on February 1, 1920, and joined the East Prussian Sicherheitspolizei, which later became the Schutzpolizei. Serving in Elbing as a platoon and company leader, he was promoted to Hauptmann der Schutzpolizei in 1923. Following brief service with the Landespolizei in 1933, he returned to the Schutzpolizei and was promoted to Major der Schutzpolizei in July, 1934. Freitag joined the NSDAP on May 1, 1933.

From July, 1934, to January, 1936, he commanded Schutzpolizei Abschnitt "Mitte." Transferring to the police officer school in Berlin-Köpenick, he served as chief of staff and a tactics instructor from January, 1936, until being promoted to Oberstleutnant der Schutzpolizei on April 20, 1939. Freitag then commanded the school until October 30, 1939, and served in police duties in the Polish campaign as Ia to Polizei Regiment 3 and chief of staff to the senior Ordnungspolizei commander attached to 14.Armee. After the campaign he commanded the police officer school Fürstenfeldbrück until December, 1940.

Joining the SS on September 1, 1940, as an SS-Obersturmbannführer, he initially was listed with the staff of Administrative District 6. From its formation in April, 1941, to August 9, 1941, Freitag served as Ia to the Kommandostab "Reichsführer-SS." He was then posted as Ia to the 1.SS-Infanterie-Brigade (mot) until mid-December, 1941, during which he was ordered to train in the field with the "Wiking" Division for a regimental command during August to October, 1941, but the assignment was cancelled.[2] Freitag was promoted to SS-Standartenführer on April 20, 1942, and to SS-Oberführer on August 6, 1943. He also was given the rank of Waffen-SS Standartenführer the same day as his Allgemeine-SS promotion to that rank (effective April 1) and was advanced to Oberst der Schutzpolizei on May 8, 1943.

From December 15, 1941, to January 4, 1943, he led Polizei-Schutzen-Regiment 2 (later the SS-Polizei-Infanterie-Regiment 2) of the SS-Polizei-Division. During the spring of 1942 Freitag led Kampfgruppe "Ost" in the Wolchow area composed of his command combined with other troops. These combats resulted in his award of the German Cross in Gold on April 30, 1943, from the following recommendation by Alfred Wünnenberg:

"During the attacks to close the Wolchow-Pocket from March 15-19, 1942, Freitag penetrated deep behind the Russian lines at the lead of his battalion, and led despite heavy enemy artillery fire in -30 degree C temperature. Through his personal bravery, and as champion of his battalion, he saw the battle through to its successful finish, including the taking of the Russian supply lines. Only through his personal and deci-

---

[1] "Stammkarte" and "Lebenslauf."

[2] "Dienstlaufbahn."

Fritz Freitag (left) in Polizei uniform and (right) as an SS-Standartenführer.

sive bravery was the attack objective of the division, the breaking of the enemy supply line, reached.

On April 14, 1942, the enemy attacked with strong tank support near Mosstiki with very strong forces in order to win back the old supply roads. SS-Standartenführer Freitag led the boxing-in movements of the enemy troops that had broken through and immediately led the deployed counterattack personally. Thanks to his excellent bravery during the evening of April 14, 1942, he was able to retake the old main fighting line and surround the enemy forces that had broken in.

On April 15, 1942, the opponent broke through with numerous tanks and very strong infantry forces. The situation on the defensive front appeared seriously endangered. At this time it was again SS-Standartenführer Freitag who was successful in bringing together men of all branches of service and of all ranks to inflict heavy casualties on the opponent. These actions made his plans for the next day needless. 1000 dead Russians was the result of this battle.

On April 23, 1942, the opponent renewed his attack with two-and-a-half infantry divisions and forty tanks after an hour long artillery barrage (statements of Ia of the 2nd Rifle Division who was taken prisoner). Through the personal bravery of SS-Standartenführer Freitag, who himself took over the leadership at the break-in point and admirably championed his men, the intent of the opponent to rupture out front was defeated.

During the operations on October 31, November 20, December 4, and December 28, 1942, in the area of Ivanovkoje, which consisted of 76 reconnaissance and patrol troop operations, all which were carefully and personally led by SS-Standartenführer Freitag, our troops inflicted heavy casualties on the enemy and captured numerous weapons and equipment. The successes of the patrol operations were read in the Wehrmacht report and were specially recognized in the divisional and corps daily order."[3]

---

[3] "Vorschlagliste für die Verleihung des Deutschen Kreuzes in Gold."

Assigned to replace Wilhelm Bittrich as full commander of the SS-Kavallerie-Division effective on February 15, 1943, he actually arrived at divisional headquarters on January 13th and assumed temporary command from temporary commander Gustav Lombard, as Bittrich had already left to form the eventual "Hohenstaufen" Division.[4] Freitag remained official commander until April 20, 1943, but was hospitalized in the final weeks, so it was another substitute commander, August Zehender, who actually turned over the unit over to its next leader in May, Hermann Fegelein.[5]

From April 20, 1943, to August 10, 1943, Freitag next commanded the remnants of the 2.SS-Infanterie-Brigade (mot), succeeding Fritz von Scholz who went to form the "Nordland" Division. Given new command and transfer orders on August 18, Freitag replaced Fritz Schmedes as commander of the SS-Polizei-Division Kampfgruppe from August 25, 1943, while Schmedes attended a divisional commanders course in Berlin. Freitag officially led the Kampfgruppe of that Division until October 20, 1943, (actually departing five days later) while Schmedes was with the "new" Polizei Division formation staff in Greece.[6] Freitag was then succeeded in Russia by Friedrich-Wilhelm Bock.

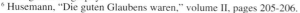

[4] His transfer to the temporary command was effective January 4, 1943.
[5] Fegelein was given the command effective April 20 but did not arrive until May. See Fegelein biography.
[6] Husemann, "Die guten Glaubens waren," volume II, pages 205-206.

(Below) From left are Otto Wächter, Freitag and Alfred Bizanz. Freitag's Heinrich Hoffmann postcard portrait is shown above after he was awarded the Knight's Cross.

Freitag's final command began effective October 20, 1943, and lasted until April 27, 1945.[7] He went to Truppenübungsplatz "Heidelager" and finished the forming and training of what became the 14.Waffen-Grenadier-Division der SS (ukrainische Nr. 1), succeeding Walter Schimana. Freitag also took training himself, taking a divisional commanders course in Hirschberg during February 1944. He then led the division of Ukranians at the front. His leadership of this command won him the Knight's Cross on September 30, 1944, from the following recommendation by Heinrich Himmler:[8]

"SS-Brigadeführer Freitag displayed admirable and personal preparedness for action while leading his division during a single battle in the Brody Pocket. Up until the last action, his division consisted not only of German soldiers, but also of Ukrainians from Galicia. These Ukrainians are soft inside and fickle, and they lack much in comparison to fighting German soldiers.

The holding together and leadership of such men who are not used to war and lack hardness, and over and above that the carrying out of the most difficult orders in battle, such as those of the Brody pocket, requires the most of a responsible leader.

The division, which stood in a decisive position in the pocket since July 12, 1944, got its first taste of battle as it witnessed the retreat of German troops. As the Grenadier Regiment 30 threatened to be dragged back with the retreating troops, it was the divisional commander who was there with the regiment's commander to ensure that threatening breakthrough did not occur.

During the further continuation of the battle, numerous volunteers of the division fled due to their inner cowardice, and in some cases used weapons to threaten their leaders and NCOs. During this crisis, it was again the decisive presence of the divisional commander, who was there in person to reestablish the situation by inflicting the required brutal measures against any whiners, that saved the situation.

The Division fulfilled its assigned objectives in the most difficult situation. This was achieved with Ukrainians, who, with very few exceptions, are not fighters and are only supported by the few German personnel.

Whenever the division was deployed in the focal point of the battle, and its success recognized and recorded, it can only be attributed to the service of the German leaders who were led by their divisional commander. He depended on every last bit of personal action during the focal point of the battle.

The tragedy in the action of the division lies with the fact that success in the battle could not be achieved, despite the exemplary behavior of its divisional commander.

After the annihilation of the division in the Brody pocket, he reported for duty to General Lindemann then departed, himself wounded, after the General's brave death as the last General to leave the pocket, and led all of the remaining fragments of units out of the encirclement. On July 22, 1944, late in the afternoon, he, unlike other battle groups, led his men out of another encirclement to the southwest at his own decision, during the massive enemy attack which resulted in many sacrifices."

In addition to the above detailed decorations, Freitag won clasps to both his WWI Iron Crosses (February 5 and March 6, 1942), the Wound Badge in Gold (wounded five times) on August 11, 1944, the Police Long Service Medal 1st class, the Olympic Games Decoration 2nd class, the War Service Cross with Swords and the Eastern Front Medal.

He surrendered to the British near Radstadt on May 8, 1945, and was imprisoned in an American camp in Graz, Austria, where he committed suicide on May 20, 1945, to avoid being handed over to the Russians.

A career police official with good education, Fritz Freitag was undoubtedly a brave and experienced troop commander with much combat time in Russia. However, he was a poor choice to command the Ukrainian SS Division, having no understanding or interest in their personal situation, political position, or the mentality of his foreign-born troops. Instead, he treated them as he would a German unit, including assigning German officers to all primary command positions, even junior posts, whenever possible. Freitag repeated his mistake when the division was rebuilt after being nearly destroyed in the Brody pocket battles, assigning inexperienced or young Germans to positions better filled by more experienced Ukrainians.

[7] "Personalverfügung" dated October 23, 1943, with effect from October 20, transferring him from the Kampfgruppe to command the "SS-Freiw. Division "Galizien."

[8] "Vorschlag Nr. 3692 für die Verleihung des Ritterkreuzes des Eisernen Kreuzes" without application date, marked approved September 30, 1944, and composed by Himmler. According to unconfirmed sources, he actually was given the decoration of October 25, 1944.

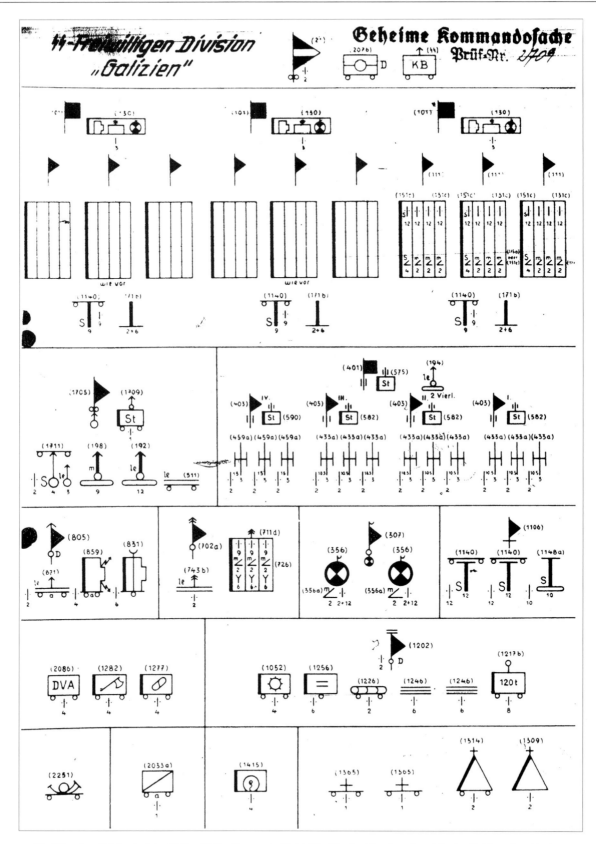

The Ukranian division in July, 1943, with its other semi-official title. No chart has been found for the division after this date.

KARL GESELE

Karl Gesele was born in Riedlingen on August 15, 1912. He joined the SS in August, 1931, with the 13.SS-Standarte. Two years later he moved to the Political Readiness Detachment "Württemberg," which later became part of Regiment "Deutschland," and was commissioned as an SS-Untersturmführer on March 25, 1934. Gesele served with the 9.(October, 1934 to May, 1935), 10. (May, 1935 to October, 1936), and 17.Kompanie of "Deutschland" as a platoon leader until early December, 1936. Posted next to the IV.Bataillon as adjutant, he was promoted to SS-Obersturmführer on January 30, 1937. Gesele was then given command of the 10./"Deutschland" from May, 1938, to August, 1940, during which time he was promoted to SS-Hauptsturmführer on June 30, 1939. During the Polish campaign he was awarded the Iron Cross 2nd class on September 20, 1939, and the 1st class on October 3.

Since he was an experienced field officer, he went to the SS-Junkerschule in Bad Tölz as a tactics instructor and in May, 1941, took command of a teaching group. Assigned to the recently formed SS-Kavallerie-Brigade in September, 1941, he served as Ia with the brigade until the last elements (Kampfgruppe "Zehender") were withdrawn in 1942 from the front to become cadre for the SS-Kavallerie-Division.[1] Promoted to SS-Sturmbannführer on January 30, 1942, he was awarded the German Cross in Gold on May 25, 1942. Gesele remained with the new SS-Kavallerie-Division as Ia under Wilhelm Bittrich until replaced due to illness in August, 1942.

Promoted to SS-Obersturmbannführer on June 21, 1943, after his recovery, Gesele was given command of the Begleit Bataillon "Reichsführer-SS" on October 5, 1942. This unit became the Sturmbrigade "Reichsführer-SS" in mid-February, 1943, with Gesele retaining command[2] He held command of the unit until October 18, 1943, and was awarded the Knight's Cross for his command on July 4, 1944, as a result of the following recommendation:

"The betrayal of the Italian monarchy brought about completely new military and political conditions overnight - for the Sturmbrigade Reichsführer-SS as well.

Already days before the Italian Generaloberst Magle had assigned accommodations for the Brigade in Aulene, in the middle of the Island of Corsica, along with every assurance of a supply base. However, the Commander of the Sturmbrigade "Reichsführer-SS" saw through these measures. Despite a clever maneuver, he had to follow the orders of Magli, under whose command he was then subordinated. He made sure that the Brigade would be positioned further south in the area around Sartene.

After the Brigade was informed by the Italian liaison officer that Italy had surrendered, SS-Obersturmbannführer Gesele quickly decided to depart to the South and relieve the 55th Black Shirt Legion from their positions in the port of Bonifacio. Their occupation of the port allowed the opportunity to build a bridgehead and allowed them to avert the invasion of English and American troops into Corsica at one of the

---

[1] Most of the Brigade had been taken from the front to be used as cadre for the SS-Kavallerie-Division, Gesele served as Ia to the Kampfgruppe. Yerger, "Riding East, The SS Cavalry Brigade in Poland and Russia 1939-1942," pages 201-206.

[2] Created by expanding Himmler's escort battalion (Begleit Bataillon) that had been a component of the Kommandostab "Reichsführer-SS" during operations in Russia, it was later incorporated as cadre into the 16.SS-Panzer-Grenadier-Division "Reichsführer-SS." Himmler's escort battalion was then reformed and again assigned to the Kommandostab. Additional documentation for Gesele's commands in 1944 and early 1945 updates the biographical synopsis in "Riding East," page 119, which was written before additional material was available.

most dangerous points. With that, they were able to avoid the difficulties for the German troops departing from Sardinia and also the encirclement of the Brigade by the Italian troops in Corsica belonging to Badoglio.

On September 11, 1943, the Brigade was relieved from the bridgehead by the Sardinian 90th Panzer Grenadier Division. The Brigade then received the task to take the city and port as well as the airport at Borgo. In the meantime, enemy positions in this city were strengthened with a Division of men, 15 artillery batteries and tanks. They received this task to assure a smooth departure of German units from Sardinia and Corsica.

SS-Obersturmbannführer Gesele attacked from the gathering area after destroying an enemy battalion on the coastal street heading east. Following the strong effects of the enemy's artillery, firing from position above the Brigade, the Brigade lost the drive of its motorized advance. Because of this, the commander decided to let his units withdraw. In spite of the strong enemy fire and the lack of artillery forces, he was successful in switching the unit over to the run and approaching

by evening the city and port of Bastia. Both were brought securely into German hands. With that, the blowing of two important bridges was avoided just in time. Still during the night, SS-Obersturmbannführer Gesele expanded the bridgehead and by morning he was successful personally leading the taking of the Teghime pass. With that, he also shielded the bridgehead to the west.

During the following days the Brigade held the bridgehead against the daily increasing pressure of the enemy. The Brigade commander was the soul of the resistance. He continuously appeared at the focal point of the battle and through his disregard of his own personal safety was able to accurately judge the situation. The calmness and confidence which streamed from his inner person always gave the men the feeling of superiority and the strength to hold out. Only with that

Below In the summer 1942 group photo taken during initial formation of the SS-Kavallerie-Division are (from right) Albert Faßbender, Karl Gesele (with German Cross in Gold), Franz Rehbein (backround, also a German Cross holder), Dr. Edwin Jung (divisional doctor) and in the left background is Hermann Fegelein. Opposite: Gesele is shown wearing the Knight's Cross awarded to him for his leadership of the Sturmbrigade "Reichsführer-SS."

was the possibility of a smooth departure for the German units assured.

On October 3, 1943, the last part of the bridgehead in Bastia was given up, only after the southern part of the airport in Borgo was evacuated according to plan during the night of October 2/3. At 2100 hours SS-Obersturmbannführer Gesele left the island by boat with the last security and bridge-blowing troops."[3]

As commander of SS-Panzer-Grenadier-Regiment 35 of the 16.SS-Panzer-Grenadier-Division "Reichsführer-SS," he served with that unit next from October 18, 1943, until January 5, 1945.[4]

Gesele then briefly became commander of the SS Cavalry School in Weede near Göttingen in the first week of January, 1945.[5] During the first week of March, 1945, he took command of the 37.SS-Freiwilligen-Kavallerie-Division "Lützow" and led the unit until it surrendered.[6] His promotion date to SS-Standartenführer, used in several sources, if granted is unknown. Karl Gesele died in Friedrichshafen on April 8, 1968.

---

[3] Unusual recommendation in his BDC file without a cover page or author indicated though marked officially as approved on the correct award date.

[4] Stammkarte entry (giving assignment dates) and data for an evaluation by the divisional commander, Max Simon, which indicates the regiment he commanded.

[5] Entry on his Stammkarte.

[6] Knight's Cross holder Waldemar Fegelein, brother of Hermann Fegelein, headed the formation staff and then took command of a regiment in the division when Gesele assumed command. Bayer, Hans: "Die Kavallerie der Waffen-SS," pages 390-391 and Krätschmer "Die Ritterkreuzträger der Waffen-SS," page 769 confirm the divisional command appointment although his Stammkarte entries cease in January, 1945. Bayer gives Fegelein the rank of SS-Oberführer which he did not attain.

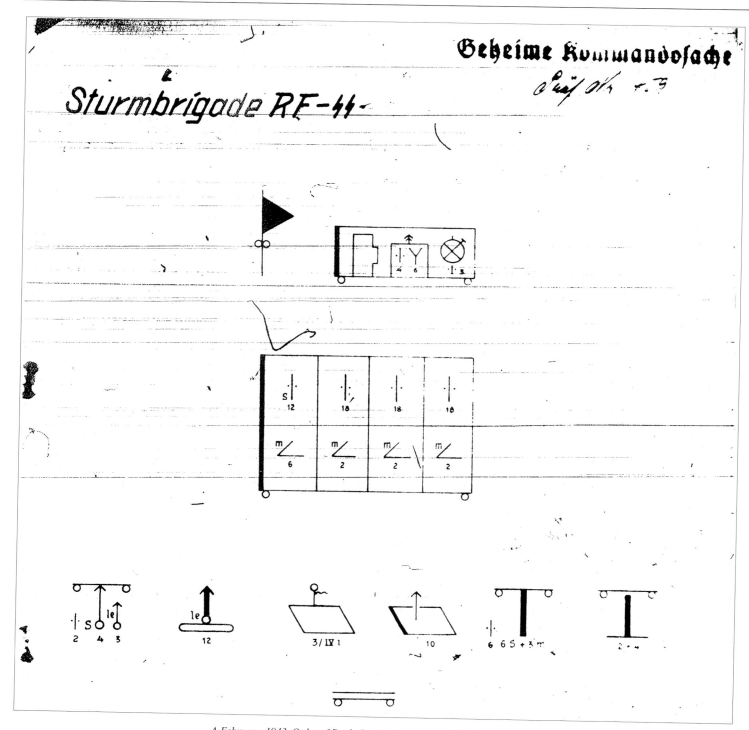

A February, 1943, Order of Battle for the Sturmbrigade "Reichsführer-SS."

HERBERT OTTO GILLE

T he most decorated soldier in the Waffen-SS was born on March 8, 1897, in Gandersheim-am-Harz. The son of a factory manager, Herbert Otto Gille joined the Army Cadet Corps on Easter, 1909 after completing his preliminary education. Attending the cadet school in Bensburg-am-Rhein until 1914, he then went to the senior cadet facility at Berlin-Lichterfelde in 1914. Appointed to a unit from Baden, he was assigned to Field Artillery Regiment No. 30 from September 1, 1914, until the start of November that year. After further training he transferred to Reserve Artillery Regiment 55 of the 75th Infantry Division and with this unit went to the front. He remained with his regiment until it was disbanded in January, 1919, serving as a platoon leader and battery officer. On January 27, 1915, Gille was commissioned as a Leutnant. Moving to another Baden originating unit, he served with Artillery Regiment No. 30 until April, 1919, and was promoted to Oberleutnant with seniority effective March 31, 1919. During WWI Gille won both classes of the Iron Cross, both classes of the Brunswick Service Cross and the Austrian War Service Cross 3rd class.

After leaving the Army in April, 1919, he studied agriculture while also working on an estate. The following year, he was the administrator of an estate in Bamberg. From 1923 to 1929 Gille was an Inspector of Public Farming Lands while continuing to administer private estates. During 1922 to 1926 he was also a member of the Stahlhelm. In 1929 Gille left the agricultural field and took a job in a Brunswick car factory until leaving in 1931 to start his own business, which he ran for two years. On May 1, 1931, he joined the NSDAP.[1]

Gille enlisted in the SS on October 10, 1931, and was assigned to lead the 5./I./49.SS-Standarte. On January 27, 1933, he assumed command of the Motorstaffel of the Standarte. Promoted to SS-Scharführer on September 25, 1932, to SS-Truppführer on January 27, 1933, and commissioned as an SS-Untersturmführer on April 20, 1933, he left the unit when he was commissioned as an officer. Gille was then promoted to become Stabsführer of Abschnitt IV, officially until April 9, 1934, but a substitute took over his duties after mid-October, 1933. He spent the balance of his Allgemeine-SS service, until May 20, 1934, as a special duties officer with the II./49.SS-Standarte. During the pre-war years he earned the SA Sports Badge in Silver.

Transferring to the SS-Verfügungstruppe, Gille led the 11./III./SS-Standarte 1 (later "Deutschland") until November 9, 1935. Promoted to SS-Obersturmführer on April 20, 1935, he moved to 12.Sturm and led it until the start of July, 1936. On November 9, 1935, he was promoted to SS-Hauptsturmführer. When the Standarte was expanded from three Sturmbanns to four, Gille's command became the 19./IV./SS-Standarte "Deutschland" and he retained his newly redesignated command until the start of October, 1936.[2]

Gille next moved to SS-Standarte "Germania" and replaced Werner Dörffler-Schuband as Stabsführer. He held that post until February 15, 1937, when he replaced Walter Krüger, who had become ill, as commander of II./SS-Standarte "Germania." Holding that command until succeeded by Werner Dörffler-Schuband on May 1, 1939, he took numerous additional training courses with the Army throughout 1937 and 1938. Promoted to SS-Sturmbannführer on April 20, 1937, he next returned to his WWI career field, the artillery.

---

[1] "SS-Stammrollen" and "Lebenslaufbahn."

[2] The unit later returned to a composition of three Sturmbanne and the IV.Sturmbann was used to form other units of the SS-Verfügungstruppe.

Herbert Gille (left) as an SS-Untersturmführer and (right) wearing the rank of SS-Hauptsturmführer.

When the artillery regiment of the SS/VT was formed under Peter Hansen, Gille was among the initial officers assigned to the formation staff at Truppenübungsplatz "Munsterlager" in May, 1939.[3] Actual training began on June 1, 1939. He was the first commander of the I.Abteilung and remained in command when the regiment was incorporated into the SS-V-Division, having been promoted to SS-Obersturmbannführer on October 19, 1939. Gille held that command in Poland and the Western campaign, continuing until the start of December, 1940. He won the clasp to his WWI Iron Cross 2nd class on October 26, 1939, and a clasp to his 1st class award on November 21, 1939. His unit was the artillery cadre for the new "Wiking" Division and Gille was the first artillery regiment commander, officially holding that post from December 1, 1940, until succeeded by Joachim Richter on May 1, 1943.[4] During that time, he was promoted to SS-Standartenführer on January

30, 1941, and to SS-Oberführer on October 1, 1941. On February 28, 1942, he was awarded the German Cross in Gold for his regimental leadership and personal bravery. In Russia he also won the General Assault Badge in May, 1941, and the Eastern Front Medal on September 15, 1942. Gille also was decorated with the Finnish Cross of Freedom 1st class.

He was the first Arko of SS-Generalkommando from June 20 to the end of July, 1942, when succeeded by Kurt Brasack.[5] Gille then again took command of Regiment "Westland" until the start of December, 1942. During the intense Rostov battles, he led SS-Panzergruppe "Gille" containing elements of "Wiking" and the Army 13.Panzer-Division. For his actions south of the city on the Don river he was awarded the Knight's Cross on October 8, 1942. All these other commands he held simultaneously in conjunction with his artillery regiment post. On November 9, 1942, he was pro-

---

[3] Yerger, "Knights of Steel," volume 1, page 195. Dörffler-Schuband became the commander of both SS-Junkerschule Bad Tölz. He ended the war with the rank of SS-Brigadeführer as an office chief in the SS-Führungshauptamt and died on September 27, 1959.

[4] "Aktenvermerk" dated November 9, 1940, and "Dienstlaufbahn."

[5] His personnel file (Dienstlaufbahn) gives Gille command of Regiment "Westland" from February to June, 1942, but this is not confirmed in post-war sources or elsewhere in his file, including the memoirs of divisional commander Felix Steiner. If this possible command took place, Gille would have been the replacement for Arthur Phleps who left the division to form "Prinz Eugen."

moted to SS-Brigadeführer und Generalmajor der Waffen-SS.

Gille succeeded Felix Steiner as commander of the "Wiking" Division on May 1, 1943, while Steiner went to form a corps.[6] From mid-July to mid-October, 1943, Gille's command destroyed more than 400 enemy tanks and hundreds of other heavy weapons. Promoted to SS-Gruppenführer und Generalleutnant der Waffen-SS on November 9, 1943, he held divisional command officially until the end of the first week of August, 1944, but actually left the division on July 20. He was succeeded by the commander of the division's Panzer Regiment, Johannes Mühlenkamp. As commander of "Wiking" Gille was awarded the Oakleaves on November 1, 1943, for the actions of his command defending a front line of over 30 miles. His Swords to the Knight's Cross were personally awarded by Hitler after having been approved on February 18, 1944. As overall commander of "Wiking" and Army divisional elements (131.Infanterie, 4. and 5.Panzer Divisions) surrounded in the Kowel pocket he was one of only 27 men awarded the Diamonds to the Knight's Cross on April 19, 1944, following a recommendation by the commander of LVI.Panzer-Korps. The only other Waffen-SS man awarded the decoration was Sepp Dietrich, both men being presented the award personally by Hitler.

Succeeding Matthias Kleinheisterkamp as commander of the IV.SS-Panzer-Korps, Gille arrived on July 20, 1944 (formally ap-

pointed August 6), and held that command until the end of the war.[7] On November 9, 1944, he was promoted to SS-Obergruppenführer und General der Waffen-SS.

Captured by American troops west of Vienna, he was held as a prisoner until May 21, 1948. After his release, he owned and operated a small book store in Stemmen and founded the Waffen-SS veterans magazine "Wiking Ruf," which later was titled "Der Freiwillige." Active in HIAG, Gille was married with one daughter and died of a heart attack on December 26, 1966.

An exceptionally gifted strategist and leader, he remained calm and humorous in the most difficult situations. Highly intelligent, militarily knowledgeable and personally brave, he was revered by the men of his commands who thought he could lead them safely from any dangerous combat situation. While some historians do not consider him among the top commanders because of losses suffered by his units, closer examination will see the intensity of many of the engagements Gille led, especially those in defense. His award of the Diamonds to the Knight's Cross and German Cross in Gold make him the most decorated man to serve in the Waffen-SS and he was undoubtedly among the very best commanders at both division and corps level.

---

[6] "Feld-Kommandostelle" dated May 28, 1943.

[7] The "Personalverfügung" for the appointment (dated July 20, 1944) has the arrival date crossed out and a handwritten addendum showing August 6, 1944, as the effective date of assuming command. Vopersal, "Soldaten, Kämpfer, Kameraden," Band Va, makes a good argument that Gille was ordered by Walter Model to take command of the Korps on July 28, 1944, and actually first met with its staff two days later.

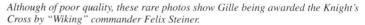

Although of poor quality, these rare photos show Gille being awarded the Knight's Cross by "Wiking" commander Felix Steiner.

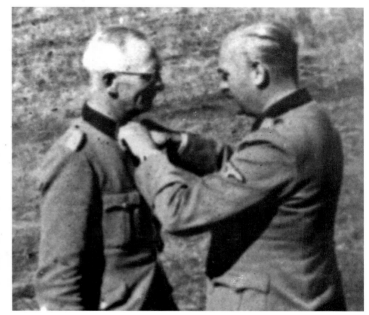

Herbert Otto Gille, an SS-Gruppenführer, wears his clasp to the WWI Iron Cross and Eastern Front Medal ribbon through his tunic button.

(Above) During the Western campaign, Gille (right) stops for some wild cherries with his adjutant, Ernst August Krag. Krag ended the war as an SS-Sturmbannführer in command of the "Das Reich" reconnaissance detachment. He was awarded the German Cross in Gold, Wound Badge in Gold and Knight's Cross with Oakleaves. (Below) Gille (right) as an SS-Brigadeführer escorts Himmler (center) during a visit to "Wiking." On the right is Swords holder August Dieckmann.

Two views of Gille as an SS-Gruppenführer in the field wearing his German Cross in Gold as well as his Knight's Cross with Oakleaves and Swords.

In these two photos, Gille (left) is about to be awarded the Swords. Hitler is shown decorating Hans Dorr, who was killed after being awarded the Knight's Cross with Oakleaves and Swords as well as the German Cross in Gold.

(Left) Gille as the "Wiking" artillery commander wearing his Knight's Cross and (right) he congratulates German Cross holder Günther Bernau who commanded Gille's regiment later in the war.

Gille (right) with "Wiking" regimental commander Hilmar Wäckerle.

On the left Gille wears the double "SS" collar insignia while an artillery commander. On the right he shows, in addition to his higher decorations, the General Assault Badge and clasps to his WWI Iron Crosses on the right breast pocket and tunic button hole.

(Left) The formal Oakleaves portrait and (right) Gille is awarded the Diamonds to the Knight's Cross by Hitler. Himmler stands at the far right and Hermann Fegelein is in the background.

SS-Brigadeführer Herbert Otto Gille awards the Knight's Cross to Albert Müller. In the upper photo, at left background, is Walter Schmidt. As an artillery detachment commander, Schmidt ended the war as an SS-Obersturmbannführer and was awarded the Knight's Cross with Oakleaves and the German Cross in Gold. In the lower photo, Manfred Schönfelder ("Wiking" 1a) assists with attaching the decoration. Both men wear white summer uniforms. Schönfelder was also awarded the Knight's Cross and the German Cross in Gold.

Gille during an inspection of IV.SS-Panzer-Korps units in 1944.

SS-Gruppenführer Gille talks with a wounded soldier. He carries his traditional walking stick, made in the field by the men of his command.

(Above) From left are August Dieckmann, Jürgen Wagner and Gille on the occasion of Wagner being awarded the Knight's Cross. The celebration continues below.

(Above) A jubilant Gille celebrates the award of the Knight's Cross to several of his men and (below) from left are Gille, Walter Nehring and Hans Dorr.

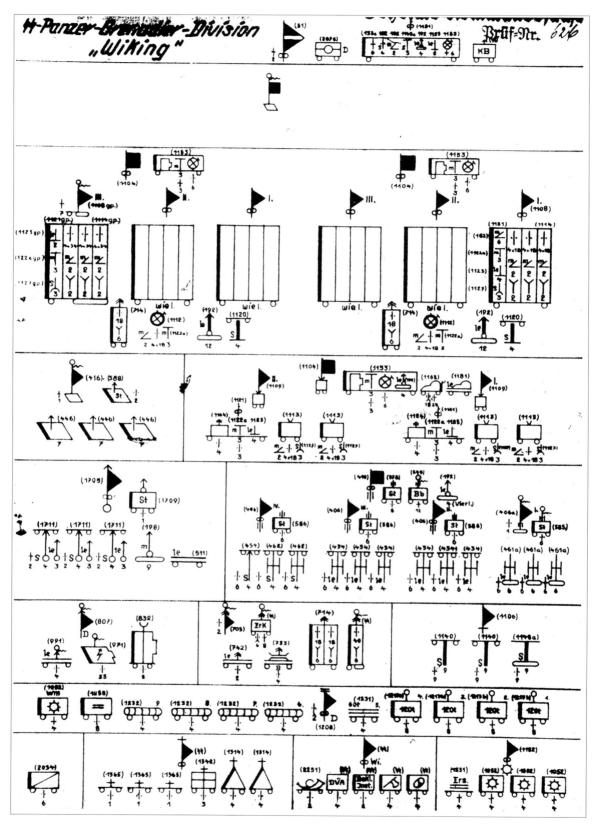

"Wiking" as a Panzer-Grenadier-Division including the first Waffen-SS tank unit to be operational. Gille commanded the artillery regiment at that time and soon took command of the division.

CURT VON GOTTBERG

Curt von Gottberg was born on February 11, 1896, in East Prussia, the son of an estate owner. He passed his Abitur after schooling in Königsberg and volunteered for the Army on August 2, 1914. Assigned to Kürassier (reconnaissance cavalry) Regiment "Graf Wrangel" No. 3 until September 20, 1914, he was commissioned as a Leutnant with seniority from February 18, 1914. Transferring to the 1st Guard Foot Regiment, he was promoted to Oberleutnant on April 20, 1919, the month he left the regiment. Wounded on the Western Front in 1917, he was awarded both classes of the Iron Cross and the Wound Badge in Black. Gottberg fought as a member of the Freikorps "Ehrhardt" and left the Army in 1924. After WWI he worked in agriculture, visiting Sweden and Italy.

He joinined the SA on November 15, 1931, and the NSDAP on February 1, 1932. On July 20, 1932, von Gottberg joined the SS and became an SS-Scharführer on April 1, 1933. Promoted to SS-Truppführer on April 20, 1933, and to SS-Obertruppführer on October 20, 1933, he was commissioned as an SS-Sturmführer on November 6, 1933. In the first half of November, 1933, he served as a Special Duties Officer with SS-Gruppe "West," then held the same posting with SS-Oberabschnitt "Südwest" until March 25, 1934. Promoted to SS-Sturmhauptführer on December 15, 1933, and to SS-Sturmbannführer on January 30, 1934, von Gottberg next headed the Political Readiness Detachment in Ellwangen until the start of October, 1934. He was promoted to SS-Obersturmbannführer on March 25, 1934, and when this unit was redesignated as the III./SS-Standarte 1 on October 1, 1934, he retained command. During this latter command period he was injured in a car accident, losing a leg, forcing him to give up his command.

Succeeding Erich Cassel as commander of the 49.SS-Standarte at the start of June, 1935, von Gottberg led the unit until mid-April, 1936. Moving to Oberabschnitt "Mitte," Gottberg then served as Inspector of auxiliary reserve formations until the beginning of October, 1937. In addition, he was the head of the Settlement Office in the Race and Settlement Main Office from July 1, 1937, to November 7, 1939. During that time he was promoted to SS-Standartenführer on November 9, 1937, and to SS-Oberführer on January 30, 1939.

Gottberg co-founded a German Association for Welfare and Settlement Assistance as well as heading an SS Bodenamt in Prague, used to buy property for the SS. His Prague post began in June, 1939.[1] During the September, 1939, Polish campaign he was in charge of Race and Settlement affairs connected to the Einsatzgruppen. Returning to Prague post after the campaign, he exceeded his authority for personal gain and was relieved, and was without an assignment until late July, 1940.

Gottberg moved to the SS-Hauptamt in October, 1940, and served as an Chief of Amt III (Schulungsamt/Indoctrination Office) from early January, 1941, to late July, 1942. On December 1, 1940, he was given the rank of SS-Obersturmbannführer d.R. in the Waffen-SS but gave up the rank on April 20, 1942, when he was promoted to SS-Brigadeführer und Generalmajor der Polizei. Going to Russia for police duties, Gottberg was the SS und Polizeiführer "Minsk" from July 27, 1942, to September 22, 1943. He was awarded the clasp to his Iron Cross 2nd class on December 6, 1942. Gottberg was awarded the German Cross in Gold on August 7, 1943, as a result of the following report:

"SS-Brigadeführer and Generalmajor of the Police von Gottberg was assigned to be the SS and Police Leader in White Russia. As commander of a mixed battle-group which included

---

[1] Koehl,"The Black Corps," page 120.

members of the SS and Police units, as well as units of the Army and Luftwaffe he was able to continuously lead actions in this area, and was especially successful in leading strong attacks and annihilating the enemy there. All of these actions displayed admirable planning and execution. Personally taking part in the actions, SS-Brigadeführer und Generalmajor der Polizei von Gottberg was able to prove his personal bravery. His admirable morale and reckless professionalism had been a model for his men and had stimulating effects on the units subordinated to him. The fact of his handicap (SS-Brigadeführer v. Gottberg had had a leg amputated) especially deserves to be emphasized.

von Gottberg proved his special leadership abilities and bravery during the execution of the larger operation "Kottbus," during which he often, even during the most difficult days, visited the surrounded troops personally, flying in with his reconnaissance Storch. By his personal example he overcame every crisis and completely carried out the operation successfully.

(Below) Hitler and Himmler during a parade review. Between them in the rear with dress sword drawn is Curt von Gottberg. Right, von Gottberg as an SS-Obergruppenführer

SS-Brigadeführer von Gottberg led during the following larger partisan operations:

Operation "Nürnberg" from November 19 - 25, 1942
Area: North of the Narodj Lake between Gleboki and Wilna
Our Forces: 1.SS-Infanterie-Brigade (motorized)
               SS-Polizei-Regiment 14
               two Schutzmannschafts-Bataillone and a town Gendarmerie

The successful completion of the assignment required incredible measures by the leadership and troops due to the difficulty of the terrain, the tenacious and cunning battle tactics of the opponent, but also the storms (snow and cold). The enemy had 2984 casualties during this operation. German prisoners, taken during earlier partisan attacks, were freed.

Operation "Hamburg" from December 10 - 21, 1942
Area: Forested area north of Slonim in the Njemen-Bogen
Our Forces: SS-Polizei-Regiment 2
               SS-Polizei-Bataillon I/23
               SS-Polizei-Bataillon I/24
               three Schutzmannschafts-Bataillone

The enemy was armed with 12cm and 7.5cm artillery pieces and in the possession of three tanks. During the battle 19 partisan camps were destroyed
Further, the following was taken as booty: three tanks, four cannons, three PAKs (anti-tank guns), five heavy machine guns, twelve light machine guns and 367 rifles. The enemy had 3186 casualties.

Operation "Altona" from December 22 - 25, 1942
Area: South of Slonim
Enemy Casualties: 1059 men
A large gun powder depot was also captured.

Operation "Franz" from January 5 - 14, 1943
Area: East of Ossipowitschi.
Enemy Casualties: 1349 men
Nine partisan camps were destroyed.
Captured: 280 rifles, one 7.62 cm cannon, two PAK, two heavy grenade launchers, a large ammunition depot.

Operation "Erntefest" from January 18 - February 5,1943
Area: both sides of the highway between Minsk and Slusk
Enemy Casualties: 3721 men
Captured: 433 rifles, nine heavy machine guns, 19 light machine guns, eight machine pistols, three grenade launchers, two polish PAKs (5cm) and other material.

Operation "Hornung" from February 8 - 26, 1943
Area: Pripec Marsches south of Sluzk
Our Forces: two SS-Polizei-Regimenter
               two SS-Polizei-Bataillone
               five Schutzmannschafts-Bataillone
Enemy Dead: 9662 men
Large amounts of captured material consisting of weapons and ammunition.

Operation "Kottbus" from April 28 - June 21, 1943
Area: on Lake Pelik north of Borissov
Our Forces: 16,662 men of the Wehrmacht and Polizei, until then the largest operation in central Russia.

The Partisan Republic "Lake Pelik," partly made up of Russian paratroopers, was completely annihilated.
Enemy Dead: 6042 men killed in battle, 3709 men suspected of being partisans were executed, 599 men were take prisoner
Our Casualties:127 dead (from which three were officers) and 535 wounded (from which ten were officers)
Booty taken, among other items: 19 cannons (7.62cm), nine PAKs, one anti-aircraft weapon, 18 grenade launchers, 30 heavy machine guns, 31 light machine guns, 16 hand held anti-tank weapons, 45 machine pistols, 903 rifles and extremely large amounts of ammunition and explosives.

I recommend SS-Brigadeführer and Generalmajor of the Police von Gottberg, for his uninterrupted action in the battles against partisans, his personal bravery and model composure, as well as for his successful execution of the operations assigned to him, be awarded the German Cross in Gold."[2]

He was placed in charge of the area encompassing White Russia, succeeding Gauleiter Wilhelm Kube when he was killed serving as Generalkommissar Weißruthenien. He held that post from September 22, 1943 to August 7, 1944, as well as being official permanent replacement for Erich von dem Bach as Higher SS and Police Leader for Central Russia and White Russia from June 21, 1944. Both posts were abolished in August, 1944. Gottberg was promoted to SS-Gruppenführer und Generalleutnant der Polizei on July 15, 1943, and was awarded the clasp to his WWI Iron Cross 1st class on February 20, 1943. For his anti-partisan operations he was recommended for the Knight's Cross by the commander of Army Group "Center." Awarded on June 30, 1944, that recommendation report reads as follows:

---

[2] German Cross recommendation submitted by the head of anti-partisan operations, Erich von dem Bach.

"SS-Gruppenführer and Generalleutnant der Polizei von Gottberg has successfully battled, in smaller and larger operations, the partisan units located in the area of White Russia since the beginning of his activities with the units subordinated to him. Through these continuous partisan battles he managed a wide curtailment of their strength, which allowed the execution of all military measures in Middle and White Russia. The excellent soldierly leadership abilities of the Gruppenführer and his personal preparations during the last two successful larger operations against the bands of partisans in the area of Uschatschi and against the Partisan Central Headquarters in the area of Lake Pelik are to be especially noted. At the lead of the SS- and Police forces and the numerous units of the Wehrmacht which formed the battle-group "von Gottberg," and which were subordinated to him for these operations, he was successful in the planning, action and execution of the operations. His notable judgment of the situation, his agile and last-but-not-least personal action in the focal points of the battle, and, over-and-above that, it must be attributed to the successful completion of these operation and the numerous amounts of booty captured, that the battles in this area were much easier than anticipated.

The success was underlined by the large number of prisoners taken and enemy dead as well as huge amounts of captured material, the results of which paralyzed the partisans in White Russia. Few casualties were suffered by our forces." [3]

On June 30, 1944, he was promoted to SS-Obergruppenführer und General der Waffen-SS und Polizei. Gottberg was also awarded the NSDAP Long Service Award in Bronze, both classes of the War Service Cross with Swords and the Anti-partisan Badge in Silver. Posted to France, he was placed in charge of anti-partisan operations there until October 18, 1944, but he never actually assumed the post.[4] On August 7, 1944, he was appointed commander of the XII.SS-Armee-Korps which had been formed from a cadre of Gottberg's Kampfgruppe, and held command until leaving due to illness on October 18, 1944. After his recovery in December he was assigned as deputy commander of the Replacement Army until the end of the war, as well as being employed with a staff rounding up straggling soldiers for replacements in the area of Army Group "Northwest." He committed suicide on May 31, 1945, in Leitzhäft.

Domineering, crude and greedy, his use of his Polizei posts for personal gain caused him problems throughout his career. His overbearing personality alienated those who would have supported him. Gottberg's operations with buying land and coordinating housing

Casual portrait of von Gottberg as an SS-Obergruppenführer wearing his Knight's Cross and German Cross in Gold.

projects brought him into conflict with other SS agencies and added to his list of competitive opponents. His arrogance and overreaching of his authority in Prague caused his recall and a severe reprimand.

The massive anti-partisan operations he conducted in the first half of 1943 in the Lake Pelik area were especially brutal. His command, composed of Ordnungspolizei formations, the Brigade "Dirlewanger," and auxiliary units from the Baltic states totaled almost 17,000 men and killed 15,000 partisans in combat or as prisoners. His lack of verbal reserve with his opinions of higher personalities also caused him reprimands and almost imprisonment in a concentration camp. Totally unqualified to command an operational front line corps, both tactically and with regard to personality, any success of his corps command was due to the input of his Army-supplied Chief of Staff, Oberst Ulrich Ulms. Widowed and remarried, he had three daughters and four sons.

---

[3] Recommendation submitted by Generalfeldmarschall Ernst Busch, commander of Army Group "Center."

[4] His Kampfgruppe was withdrawn on July 26, 1944, and von Gottberg was appointed to his Korps command in the SS-Führungshauptamt formation directive dated August 7, 1944, which formed the XII. and XIII. Korps, the latter under Hermann Priess.

JOSEF GRASSY

The senior Hungarian operational unit commander in the Waffen-SS, Josef Grassy was born in Szölös, Pressburg, on December 31, 1894. His family originally came from Italy with the name Grassi. Grassy attended a Catholic school before attending the Royal Hungarian Infantry Cadet School. After graduation, he attended the Royal Hungarian Military Academy "Ludowikia" in Budapest and was commissioned as a Leutnant on August 1, 1914.

After being commissioned he went to the Hungarian Infantry Regiment Nr 20 "Nagy-Kanisza" and served with that unit at the front throughout World War I. Promoted to Oberleutnant on May 1, 1915, he was wounded on August 28th the same year. In late March, 1916, he took command of the 1st company until wounded again on June 16, 1916. After his recovery he returned to his command in early November, 1916. In early 1917, he moved to command 2nd company, and by summer that year led the machine gun company. Holding that final combat post until 1919, he was awarded the Military Service Cross 3rd class with War Decoration and Swords as well as the Military Service Medal in Silver.

From March, 1920, to March, 1922, he was posted to the Royal Hungarian Military Academy and combated communists in Budapest. On March 1, 1922, he was promoted to Hauptmann on the General Staff. Transferred to the staff of Royal Hungarian Infantry Regiment "Maria Theresia" as a staff officer, he was promoted to Major in 1925. Grassy was assigned as the regimental commander in 1929 and was promoted to Oberstleutnant the same year.

In January, 1933, he was reassigned as the chief of staff of the 3rd Army Corps and was promoted to Oberst on August 28, 1934. As a tactics instructor, he returned to the Military Academy from January, 1935, to December, 1937, and then was chief of staff to 4th Army Corps until early July, 1939. From that time until August, 1940, he commanded Infantry Regiment 7.

Leaving his regiment, Grassy went to the Military Ministry until the end of 1940 as Chief of the General Staff for the aerial section. Taking command of the 15th Royal Hungarian Infantry Division at the start of January, 1941, he led the division until mid-October, 1943. Grassy led the division in Russia after March 1, 1942, and was promoted to Major General on April 1st. He then served as chief of the training detachment in the Hungarian Military Ministry until January 15, 1944.

Brought to trial in Hungary by the government for excesses committed when commander of his division in January 1942, he escaped to Austria and sought protection from the SD to escape serving a sentence. The Germans put him in prison. Released on March 1, 1944, Grassy was given the rank of Waffen-Brigadeführer und Generalmajor der Waffen-SS effective that date. He was assigned to the 9.SS-Panzer-Division "Hohenstaufen" until early October, 1944, during which time he attended a divisional commanders course in Hirschberg.

Grassy then took command of the formation staff on October 10, 1944, of what developed into the 25.Waffen-Grenadier-Division der SS "Hunyadi" (ungarische Nr. 1) in southwest Hungary, succeeding Michael Broser. The division was officially under the command of German Thomas Müller. Grassy held the post until the end of the war. On December 1, 1944, he was re-admitted to the Hungarian Army as a Feldmarschalleutnant by the German-imposed regime and was involved with the 1944 deportation of Hungarian Jews. He also succeeded Berthold Maack as commander of the 26.Waffen-Grenadier-Division der SS "Hungaria" (ungarische Nr. 2) from March 25, 1945, until the end of the war, becoming commander of all Hungarian Waffen-SS troops. The proposed Hungarian corps never went beyond the planning stage.

Injured in a car crash on May 6, 1945, Grassy was in a U.S. Army hospital until June 1, 1945. In November, 1945, he was moved to a hospital in Budapest. Tried in Budapest on January 8, 1946, he was found guilty and sentenced to death. Grassy was then extradited to Yugoslavia where he was retried. Sentenced to death, Josef Grassy was hanged in Zsablyla on November 5, 1946.

(Above) From left are Waffen-Hauptsturmführer Andras Szinay (1b), Josef Grassy, and Waffen-Sturmbannführer Adam Pohdradszky. Below: Josef Grassy seated nearest the camera in 1945 at Neuhammer.

WERNER HAHN

The son of Bernhard Hahn, Werner Hahn was born in Krischow on October 2, 1901. After his primary education he trained as a sales representative until joining the Army in October, 1918, as a twelve-year volunteer. On January 17, 1919, he joined the Freikorps "von Brandis" and saw combat in Poland, Lithuania and Latvia as a driver with the 1st Company. Hahn was awarded both the Baltic Cross and the Iron Cross 2nd class for his service. In December, 1919, he went to Infantry Regiment 24 and saw service during the Kapp Putsch, as well as in Pommerania, Mecklenburg and Mark-Brandenburg. Hahn then went to the 14th Company of Infantry Regiment 5 in 1920 before transferring to the 9th Company of Infantry Regiment 19, the mountain battalion of that regiment. He left the Army on October 9, 1931, having served beyond his original enlistment.

Hahn joined the NSDAP and SS on October 20, 1931, serving first with the 29.SS-Standarte. From 1932 to the end of 1933, he was posted to the auxiliary border protection police. Hahn served in Oberabschnitt "Süd" from January to March, 1934, helping to form SS-Verfügungstruppe units in that main district.[1] Commissioned as an SS-Untersturmführer on April 26, 1934, he was promoted to SS-Obersturmführer on April 20, 1935. After training in the Race and Settlement Main Office, he returned to Oberabschnitt "Süd" as RuSHA advisor until the end of 1936. Transferring to Berlin, he served as a detachment head in the RuSHA for two months. Hahn next transferred to the staff of III./72.SS-Standarte in December, 1937. He then took command of the III./72.SS-Standarte in Detmold/Lippe for the balance of the pre-war years

then into the war until February 27, 1943. Hahn was promoted to SS-Hauptsturmführer on September 12, 1937, then to SS-Sturmbannführer on September 10, 1939.

As a reservist with the Army beginning in 1936, he was an instructor at the Army Mountain School Hall in Tirol from the end of August, 1939, until mid-September, 1942. He was commissioned as a Leutnant d.R. on February 15, 1937, then promoted to Oberleutnant d.R. on June 3, 1939. During 1939 he saw combat assigned to an unknown front-line Army unit where he was awarded the clasp to his Iron Cross 2nd class. Hahn also was awarded the Wound Badge in Silver after being wounded three times: July 16, 1940 in France, in May, 1941, in Croatia and August 1, 1941, in the Kiev area. He was also awarded the Iron Cross 1st class (September 5, 1940), and the Infantry Assault Badge in Silver (October 1, 1941), during his Army combat service in which he became a Hauptmann d.R. He saw combat in the Western campaign, Yugoslavia and in Russia. After next serving with Gebirgs-Jäger-Regiment 100 and Gebirgs-Jäger-Ersatz-Bataillon 98 until February 21, 1943, he joined the Waffen-SS as an SS-Hauptsturmführer on that date. Hahn was assigned to the SS Mountain School as a training detachment leader until mid-April, 1943. He also served during part of that time as a deputy to the Inspector of SS mountain troops in the SS-Führungshauptamt.

Promoted to Waffen-SS Sturmbannführer on November 9, 1943, he took command of SS-Gebirgs-Jäger-Ausbildungs und Ersatz Bataillon 6 in Hallein from April 17, 1943, until August 15, 1944.[2] As commander of this training and replacement unit, Hahn took additional command courses with the SS for battalion and com-

---

[1] Date repeated throughout several compilations in his personnel file, the October, 1934, DAL still lists him in the post when the publication was issued (he is with the RuSHA in the July, 1935, issue). As with many entries in all issues, the events in the field were not always accurately portrayed by the time of publication, mistakes of six months or more not being uncommon.

[2] Dates from his evaluations and transfer orders. In Schreiber, "Kampf unter dem Nordlicht," page 399, the dates are slightly different, perhaps indicating the time he actually was there versus the period he held command.

pany command level instruction. All evaluations, by both Army and Waffen-SS superiors, indicate he was a very capable mountain troop instructor and leader.

Werner Hahn was given command of the formation staff of the eventual 24.Waffen-Gebirgs-(Karstjäger) Division der SS effective August 15, 1944, replacing Carl Marks.[3] He held the command and that of the unit through its brief upgrading to divisional status.

Hahn then retained command when the unit was reduced to being the Waffen-Gebirgs-(Karstjäger) Brigade der SS from December 5, 1944, until succeeded by Heinz Wagner in February, 1945.[4] As such, he was the only commander of the division. Married with five children, Hahn was also awarded the SA Sports Badge in Silver with the Allgemeine-SS. His later service is unknown but Werner Hahn survived the war and died on July 12, 1982.

---

[3] "Personalverfügung" dated August 18, 1944, with effect from August 15.

[4] Hausser, Paul, "Soldaten wie andere auch," page 418.

DESIDERIUS HAMPEL

Born in Sisek in Croatia on January 20, 1895, Desiderius Hampel was the son of a railway inspector for the Austrian rail system. He attended school in Lower Austria, Hungary and Croatia. His family's movements due to his father's work enabled him to become trilingual. In mid-October, 1914, he joined the Austro-Hungarian Army as a cadet.

Hampel served with the Royal and Imperial Infantry Regiment No. 16 (Croatian) throughout World War I. In April, 1915, he took command of a platoon until he was commissioned as a Leutnant on May 1, 1915. Hampel then led the 14th Company until autumn of that year when he was given command of the 4th (machine gun) Company. He held that post until mid-September, 1918, when he was promoted to deputy battalion commander. Promoted to Oberleutnant on May 1, 1917, Hampel was awarded the Austrian Bravery Medal 1st class, the Military Service Cross with War Decoration and Swords, and the Military Service Medal in Silver. After returning from front-line service, he and three fellow officers organized a security force to combat the Serbs. After spending a year under arrest, he fled via Vienna to Budapest. Following service in the Army he worked for an estate.

Hampel studied forestry at the University of Munich from 1925 to 1928 and then worked in that field until December, 1937. Rejoining the Hungarian Army, he served with the Honved Army in Budapest from December, 1937, to March, 1941, then commanded a Luftschutz unit in Csepel until leaving the Army in November, 1941. Hampel then enlisted in the Croatian Army on January 31, 1942, as a Major where he served as the Ic (intelligence officer) of the 4th Army Corps until mid-May 1942. He joined the Waffen-SS as an SS-Sturmbannführer on May 15, 1942, at the request of Arthur Phleps.

From May 25, 1942, to June 1, 1943, he commanded the III./SS-Gebirgs-Jäger-Regiment 1 in "Prinz Eugen." Hampel then led the division's training and replacement battalion from June 11, 1943, until the end of September, 1943.[1] Returning to a field command during October and November, 1942, he commanded a Kampfgruppe during the fighting in Kriva-Reka.

Promoted to SS-Obersturmbannführer on November 9, 1943, he commanded SS-Gebirgs-Jäger-Regiment 27 from September 28, 1943, officially until January 30, 1945.[2] In October and early November, 1943, he was assigned to the V.SS-Gebirgs-Korps during formation in Prague. For his regimental command, he won the Iron Cross 2nd class on January 30, 1943, and the 1st class on June 29, 1944. He was also awarded the War Merit Cross 2nd class with Swords on January 30, 1944.

Promoted to SS-Standartenführer on April 2, 1944, to SS-Oberführer on November 9, 1944, and to SS-Brigadeführer und Generalmajor der Waffen-SS on January 30, 1945, he was commander of the 13.Waffen-Gebirgs-Division der SS "Handschar" (kroatische Nr 1) from June 1, 1944, until the surrender in May, 1945.[3] On May 3, 1945, he was awarded the Knight's Cross for his divisional command.

A firm anti-communist, his final command was a questionable status as the division didn't attained full strength. He surrendered to the British in May, 1945. After the war Hampel lived in retirement in Graz, Austria, until his death on January 11, 1981.

---

[1] "Personalverfügung," dated July 1, 1943, with effect from June 11.

[2] SS-FHA directive dated October 14, 1943, assigning Hampel to his command and assigning the commander of the artillery regiment. His actual command in the field lasted until he took leadership of the entire Division.

[3] Biographical statistics compiled by the divisional Ia on January 11, 1945. As a dual divisional/regimental commander there is confusion as to his actual start of divisional command. The first commander, Karl Sauberzweig, was listed with the Division until November 15, 1944, in "Stabsbefehl Nr. 29/44," dated December 9, 1944. Sauberzweig was long since a corps commander by that date, showing the inherent inaccuracies of any type of documentation. While Hampel was "official commander" of the regiment, field leadership was taken by SS-Obersturmbannführer Karl Liecke (who is listed in the July, 1944, "Dienstalterliste" as regimental commander).

(Above) Desiderius Hampel (below) with "Handschar" divisional commander Karl Sauberzweig. Hampel wears the unique divisional collar insignia of the unit.

SS-Obersturmbannführer Desiderius Hampel

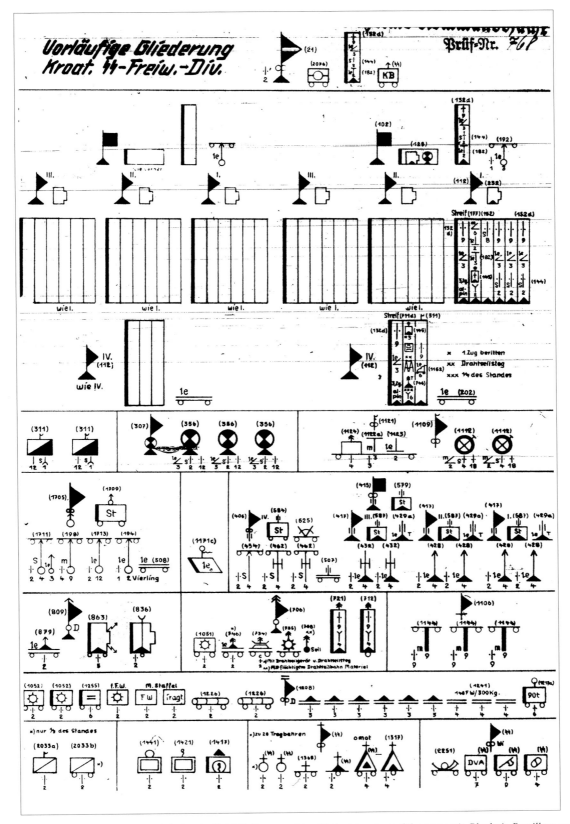

The Croatian SS division showing the form envisioned during April, 1943. Compare this with the later chart of the same unit. Blanks in Bataillone symbols indicate they were to be composed as per the one fully marked.

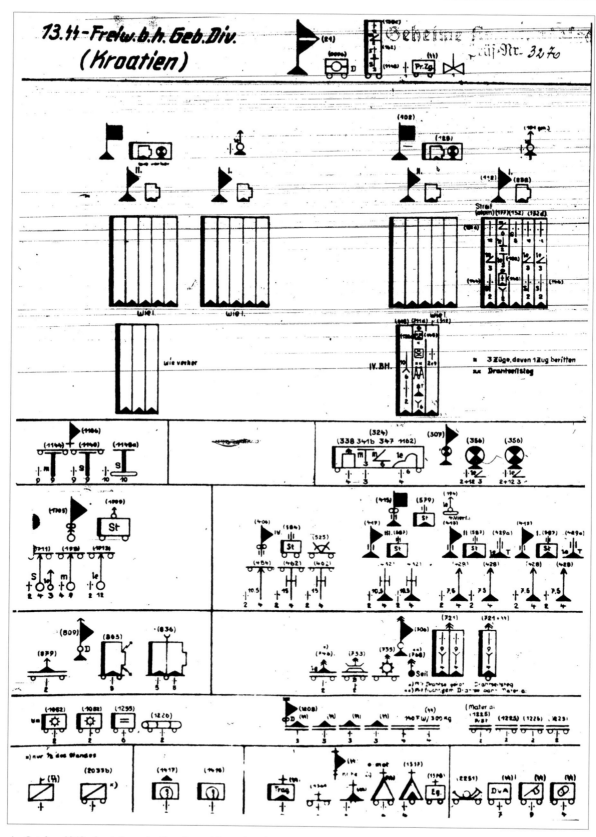

An October, 1943, chart shows the Croatian unit's combat elements to be far reduced from the earlier chart proposing its composition.

PETER HANSEN

The "Father" of Waffen-SS artillery, Peter Adolf Caesar Hansen, was born in Santiago, Chile, on November 30, 1896, the son of a munitions factory director. When his father died in 1901, Hansen's remaining family returned to Germany, where he attended his final schooling in Dresden. He joined the Army on September 1, 1914, and was posted to the Royal Saxon Field Artillery Regiment No. 48 until 1918. Commissioned as a Leutnant in the summer of 1916, he saw combat in France and Russia, serving as a battery officer, ordnance officer, signals officer, adjutant and battery commander. Hansen was wounded and suffered from typhus in WWI. He was awarded the Wound Badge in Black, both classes of the Iron Cross and the Saxon Service Order.

He remained in the Army after the "Great War," in 1918 serving with Area Command "North" as Ia to the staff officer for military transport. Hansen then served as 1c (intelligence officer) to Major Werner Freiherr von Fritsch and as an adjutant to the staff officer for mounted troops in 1920. After serving as a Quartermaster's adjutant, Hansen was assigned as liaison officer for a commission formed to control activities within the Baltic States. Promoted to Oberleutnant, he served as an adjutant in the Sachsen War Ministry. After leaving the military, he worked as a spinner and weaver in Chemnitz, then ran his own business in Gorlitz, Weimar and Erfurt.

Hansen joined the NSDAP and the SS in April, 1933. Assigned to Oberabschnitt "Mitte," he was promoted to SS-Scharführer on February 24, 1934, to SS-Oberscharführer on April 20, 1934, to SS-Obertruppführer on July 10, 1934, and was commissioned an SS-Untersturmführer on January 30, 1935.

Peter Hansen left the SS and joined the Army as an active Hauptmann on August 15, 1935. He served as a battery commander in Naumburg, Leipzig and Meissen until 1937, when he transferred to Artillerie Regiment 50 in Leipzig as commander of its schwere Abteilung until the start of 1939. Promoted to Major, he moved to command the II./Artillerie Regiment 50 until June 1, 1939, when he left the Army and joined the SS-Verfügungstruppe as an SS-Obersturmbannführer. Hansen formed and commanded the initial SS artillery regiment and led it in the Polish campaign. In October, 1939, his regiment was a component of the SS-Verfügungsdivision (later titled "Das Reich") and Hansen commanded the regiment until August 14, 1941, when replaced by Dr. Günther Merk. Promoted to SS-Standartenführer on October 19, 1939, and to SS-Oberführer on December 13, 1940, he moved to the SS-Führungshauptamt as chief of office IIb in Waffen-SS headquarters until the start of October, 1941. Hansen then was inspector of SS artillery and head of officer training until February 25, 1943, during which time he was promoted to SS-Brigadeführer und Generalmajor der Waffen-SS on January 30, 1942. His inspector post later developed into Inspektion 4 (Artillerie) within the arms inspectorates in April, 1942. In the inspectorate for NCO training, Hansen also headed the office supervising NCO schools from January to February 25, 1943.

Charged with the formation of the Lettische SS-Freiwilligen Legion (which developed into a division) on February 25, 1943, he held the post until May 1, 1943, when replaced by Carl Graf von Pückler-Burghauss. Hansen then returned to the SS-Führungshauptamt as head of officer training until the start of August, 1943.

Returning to an artillery post, Hansen served briefly as Arko to the IV.SS-Panzer-Korps beginning in September 1943. He was ill and hospitalized from October to December, 1943. In Italy, Hansen was commander of the Milizia Armata Polizei from December 1943, to the end of January, 1944, the precursor of the Italian SS Brigade and later the 29.Waffen-Grenadier-Division der SS (italienische Nr.1). Hansen then held the Arko post for the VII.SS-Panzer-Korps until mid-May, 1944, when succeeded by Kurt Brasack. After serving in reserve, he was assigned as Arko to the III.(germ) SS-Panzer-Korps from July 10, 1944, to August 22, 1944. In November, 1944, Hansen became Arko of the I.SS-Panzer-Korps, succeeding Walter Staudinger who assumed the senior artillery post in the 6.SS-Panzer-Armee.[1] He held that Arko post until early February, 1945. On February 5, 1945, he was transferred to the XVIII.SS-Armee-Korps as Chief of Staff and held that assignment until the end of the war.

Awarded clasps to both of his WWI Iron Crosses in 1939, both classes of the War Service Cross, the Infantry Assault Badge, the

German Horseman's Badge in Silver and the Finnish Cross of Freedom 1st class, he was the early driving force of SS artillery units. Well trained, conscientious, industrious, a good organizer and teacher, he was not a politically-indoctrinated officer. As a result, he was reprimanded several times by Himmler for failure to promote political indoctrination in his commands. Aside from his artillery knowledge contribution, he was influential in forming the Latvian and Italian SS units. His support of Latvian wishes for their units (and country), as well as complaining that his untrained Latvian unit would become "cannon fodder" if deployed without full training, brought about his recall. Hansen, by all reports, was simply a professional soldier. Captured by the French while in a hospital in May, 1945 (he had been ill during several periods of the war), he returned to the Rhineland after his release. Maintaining contact with former Latvian subordinates after the war, he died in Viersen on May 23, 1967.

---

[1] The July 1, 1944, "Dienstalterliste" copy in the National Archives (former personal copy of von Herff, head of the SS-Personalhauptamt) shows a handwritten notation confirming the I.SS-Panzer-Korps Arko post.

Peter Hansen (left) as an Army artillery officer and (right) in the uniform of an SS-Brigadeführer prior to 1942.

Hansen (foreground) with men of the Artillerie Regiment SS/VT. 2nd from right smoking is later Oakleaves winner Karl Kreutz, the last commander of "Das Reich" in 1945.

Inspection of the Artillerie Regiment SS/VT. With back to camera is Paul Hausser. Beside him watching the conversation is SS-Obersturmbannführer Peter Hansen. SS-Brigadeführer August Heissmeyer talks with the nearest two men: Herbert Gille (nearest the camera) and Hermann Priess beside him. Both were artillery detachment commanders at the time and both men ended the war as highly decorated Waffen-SS corps commanders.

Peter Hansen (seated far left) talks with detachment commander Karl Kreutz in Russia during 1941.

Opposite top: Regimental commander Peter Hansen (far left) and Paul Hausser (2nd from left) during artillery training in 1939.

Bottom: Leaders of SS-Division "Reich" in 1941 near Smolensk are, from left, Paul Hausser (divisional commander), Fritz Klingenberg (motorcycle battalion), Peter Hansen (artillery regiment), Otto Weiss (signals detachment), Otto Kumm (Regiment "Der Führer", Hans Mühlenkamp (reconnaissance detachment). Pointing to the map is Erwin Mix (intelligence officer) and beside him is Albert Landwehr (anti-tank detachment).

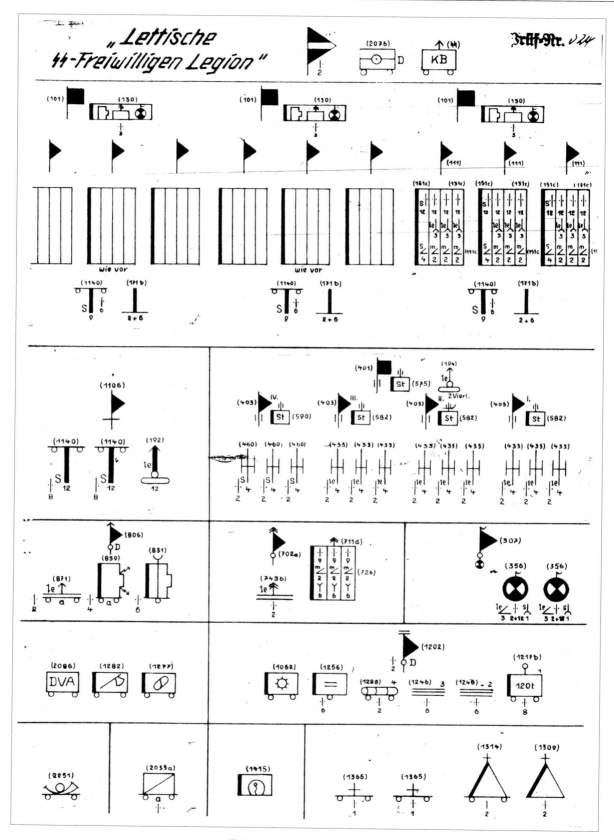

The Latvian Legion in March, 1943.

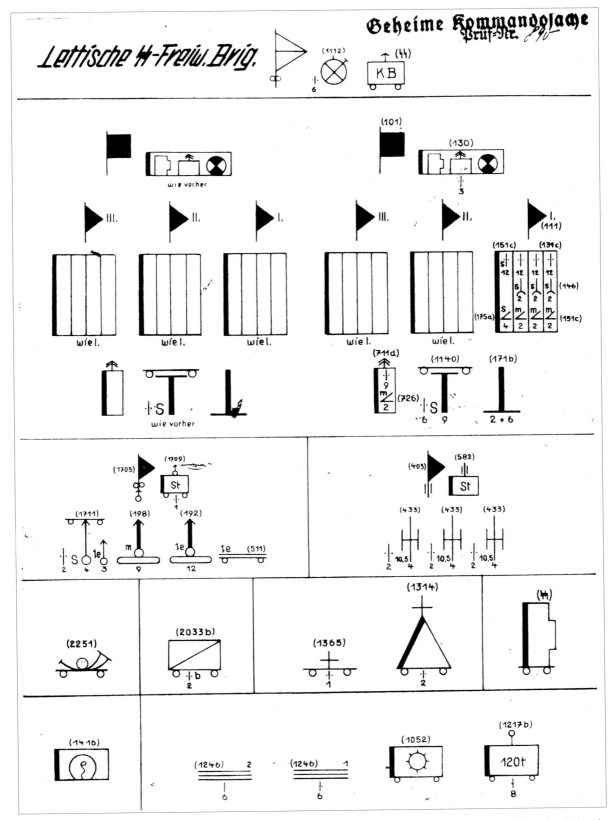

The Latvian Brigade in May, 1943, formed by adding support units to the existing Legion. As seen, some combats formations were initially reduced, though expanded again when it became a division.

HEINZ HARMEL

Heinz Harmel was born in Metz/Lothringen on June 29, 1906. In May, 1926, he joined the Army with the 15./Infanterie Regiment 6 in Ratzeburg. He left the service in late September after suffering an injury to his right eye, and pursued a career with the civil service in agriculture.

After two months service with the 10./Infantry Regiment "Lübeck" in the Army as a reserve sergeant, on October 2, 1935, Harmel joined the SS-Verfügungstruppe in Hamburg as an SS-Oberscharführer with 1./Regiment "Germania." He served as a platoon leader until moving to a similar post with the 7./"Deutschland" in Munich at the start of September, 1936. Commissioned as an SS-Untersturmführer on January 30, 1937, he stayed with 7./"Deutschland" until the end of March, 1938. On January 30, 1938, he was promoted to SS-Obersturmführer.

Transferring to the newly-forming Regiment "Der Führer" in Vienna at the end of March, 1938, Harmel became a platoon leader in 1./Der Führer" until the start of May, 1938. He then moved to the 9.Kompanie in Klagenfurt and became its commander on May 1, 1938. On January 30, 1939, he was promoted to SS-Hauptsturmführer. As commander of his company he won the Iron Cross 2nd class on May 30, 1940, and the 1st class almost immediately thereafter on June 1.

On November 14, 1940, he became commander of II./Der Führer and was promoted to SS-Sturmbannführer on April 20, 1941. He became full commander effective January 1, 1941.[1] With his battalion command he won the Infantry Assault Badge in Bronze on December 4, 1940, then was awarded the German Cross in Gold on November 29, 1941. Harmel held that post until moving to Regiment "Deutschland" as regimental commander on December 4, 1941, succeeding SS-Sturmbannführer d.R. Helmut Schulz.[2] He remained in Russia with elements of his regiment as a component of Kampfgruppe "SS-Reich" during the first half of 1942 before returning to the rest of the division which was being expanded to a Panzer Grenadier Division. On June 19, 1942, Harmel was promoted to SS-Obersturmbannführer.[3] He was awarded the Eastern Front Medal on August 15, 1942, and the Wound Badge in Black on March 21, 1943.

Approved for the award of the Knight's Cross and a single-handed tank destruction Badge on March 31, 1943, Harmel was promoted to SS-Standartenführer on April 20, 1943.[4] The two decorations were actually presented to him on April 2, 1943. He held command of "Deutschland" into the autumn of that year when he was wounded. Heinz Harmel was granted the 296th Oakleaves to the Knight's Cross on September 7, 1943, for his leadership of "Deutschland." The recommendation was written and submitted by "Das Reich" commander Walter Krüger and reads as follows:[5]

"The armored infantry units, including Regiment "Deutschland," were put into action on the left of the tank group of the Division for the attack on the enemy that had breached

---

[1] "Dienstlaufbahn," "Lebenslaufbahn," and information provided to the author by Herrn Harmel.

[2] Information courtesy Herrn Harmel, his "Dienstlaufbahn" gives December 11. Schulz was also an SS-Standartenführer in the Allgemeine-SS.

[3] "Stammkarte," Herrn Harmel gives the date as three days later, no doubt when he was actually informed of the promotion. In the majority of cases, the recipient of an award or promotion was actually informed several days after the official approval. This accounts for the time differences often encountered between personal veteran records or diaries retained by individuals and the documentation of the SS main offices.

[4] Oakleaves recommendation data sheet giving award data for other decorations and information kindly provided by Herrn Harmel.

[5] Undated text by Krüger approved on September 7, 1943.

(Above) Heinz Harmel (left) instructing SS-Sturmbannführer Otto Kumm (3rd from left). Between them is later Knight's Cross holder Friedrich Holzer. Below, at Himmler's headquarters in Hochwald in 1942 are, from right, Wilhelm Kment, Harmel, Rupert Dangl, and Gauleiter (also SS-Obergruppenführer) Ernst Wilhelm Bohle. Dangl and Kment won their German Crosses with "Reich."

A signed photo of Harmel as an SS-Sturmbannführer and (right) as an SS-Standartenführer he has lunch with Günther Wisliceny. Wisliceny was the last commander of Regiment "Deutschland" and won the Knight's Cross with Oakleaves and Swords, as well as the German Cross in Gold and Close Combat Clasp in Gold.

our line on the Mius river. The order was to capture hill 203.9, one kilometer north of the western part of Stepanowka. The town was to be taken and then protect the southerly directed main attack of the Division along its northeastern and northern flanks.

Several times the attack appeared to come to a standstill because of exceedingly tenacious enemy resistance from well-camouflaged, deep defensive positions. Also, a wide mine field was a barrier and concentrated artillery fire came from hill 213.9 which dominated the battle area. Here SS-Standartenführer Harmel, in the very front position, urged his battalions ahead again and again. During this phase of the battle, seven of the sixteen self-propelled guns supporting the regiment were disabled by mines.

Hill 203.9 was finally taken after a difficult struggle of several hours. Harmel was among his men constantly, either in his command vehicle or on foot. He quickly regrouped the first

battalion and decided to immediately attack Stepanowka without waiting to meet up with the tank unit and main body of "Deutschland." His intention was to take advantage of the confusion of the enemy and enter the town. However, soon after starting, it became evident the defenses of the town were still fully operational. The first battalion was stopped at the outermost row of houses. However, Harmel's decision allowed the outer fortifications to be breached. This served as the starting position for the next phase of the fight. That advantage prevented greater losses in taking the town, if it could have been done at all.

As he always did, Harmel rushed ahead in his command vehicle. The car hit a mine. He moved to another vehicle under heavy infantry and artillery fire. The second vehicle promptly hit a mine as well. Harmel then placed himself at the head of the first battalion and led it in the fighting into the town.

All the houses were defended and connected underground

so the attack progressed at a very slow rate. The underground defenses, as well as ravines and caves, made the support of our heavy weapons only slightly effective. Each soldier had to give his all against the numerically superior enemy who displayed remarkable fighting skills and spirit. The Russian counter-attack along the entire front engaged the rest of the division so no additional support to take the town was available. In the unusually hard battle the enemy fought to the death rather than surrender. SS-Standartenführer Harmel led his men from the very front of the fighting, urging them forward by his own example. He led them to victory despite the heavy losses and extreme hardship of the thirty hour battle.

Stepanowka was captured on the night of July 31 and August 1. The main part of the Russian 24th Guards Division was killed or captured. The enemy had been supported by super heavy mortars, artillery, 28cm mortars and even aerial bombardment with incendiaries which were dropped on the attacking troops. Among the material captured or destroyed during the battle were:

18 T-34 tanks	1 captured German self-propelled gun
2 reconnaissance cars	1 28cm mortar
3 15cm guns	8 75mm guns
1 multi-barrel gun	20 smaller caliber anti-tank guns
12 7.62 anti-tank guns	41 heavy mortars
8 super heavy mortars	33 light mortars.

Hundreds of machine guns and more than a thousand rifles were also captured. More than 800 of the enemy were killed and 400 were taken prisoner. Credit for this success is due principally to the leadership of SS-Standartenführer Harmel. He made possible the advance of the tank unit to hill 202 and eliminated the threat of a flanking move by destroying these heavy weapons. The taking of Stepanowka and its after effects were essential for regaining our former front line along the Mius river. When Harmel arrived on the battlefield, his fighting spirit and élan spreads to those he led.

During the present summer campaign, SS-Standartenführer Harmel distinguished himself while breaking through a deep system of enemy fortifications near Beresoff, north of Bjelgorod. His regiment was the first to attack the enemy positions. Here, as well as later during the attack on Teterewino and the tank defense battle near Kalinin. He excelled time-and-again as a living example of fighting spirit. At all times he was a decisive factor in the great success of his regiment."

Harmel was personally presented the award by Hitler and was also awarded the Close Combat Clasp in Silver on September 10,

1943. Suffering a head wound on October 2, 1943, he was evacuated to the SS hospital in Hohenlychen, but officially held command of the regiment until November 1, 1943, then was placed in reserve.[6] He took a divisional commanders course during March/April 1944 and was then reassigned. Promoted to SS-Oberführer on May 18, 1944, Harmel was commander of the 10.SS-Panzer-Division "Frundsberg" beginning April 27, 1944, and held command until April 27, 1945.[7] On September 7, 1944, he was promoted to SS-Brigadeführer und Generalmajor der Waffen-SS. As divisional commander, he was granted the 116th Swords to the Knight's Cross on December 15, 1944, as a result of the following recommendation:[8]

"On August 19, 1944, the 10.SS-Panzer Divison "Frundsberg," under the leadership of SS-Brigadeführer Harmel, had crossed the ORNE river in the area of PUTANGES during the course of the general withdrawal movements of the 7.Armee. "Frundsberg" had made this crossing together with the 2.Panzer Division, parts of various other infantry divisions as well as fragments of many Wehrmacht units. Due to their unshakable desire to resist, as well as the Division's hardness and bravery, they were successful in halting the strong enemy forces, which were supported with tanks, from advancing from the area of FALAISE to South to the line connecting the villages of MOTABARD, RONAL and HABLOVILLE. Thus "Frundsberg" held the way to the east open for the forces of the 7.Armee, as well as allowing parts of its own Division to disengage in the area of VILLEDIEU-BAILLEUL-LA LONDE until the morning of August 29, 1944.

In the meantime, additional strong enemy forces had broken through to the southeast from the area of TRUN. These had combined with American tank troops advancing to the north from MORTAGNE-ALENCON, thus concluding the encirclement of the 7.Armee. Due to very strong concentrated attacks, the ring grew tighter by the hour. Continuous heavy enemy artillery barrages, rolling air attacks, our lack of fuel and ammunition together with a failed attempt to try to supply the troops by air, and further, the recognition that the enemy's encirclement of our troops had concluded, had by this time noticeably broken down the will to resist of many troops who had just experienced the attack and many others who were in the process of being disbanded. This released a certain atmo-

---

[6] "Stammkarte" and SS-FHA notice from the hospital dated October 22, 1943. Helmut Schreiber took temporary regimental command. Weidinger, "Division Das Reich," volume IV, page 373.

[7] His "Personalverfügung" dated May 6, 1944, gives May 1 as the effective start date of the command. However, his greeting to the men of his new command and announcement to them of his appointment is dated April 28, 1944, and signed as "Divisionskommandeur."

[8] Award date on his Vorschlag per normal written approval procedures including the fact it is the 116th award. This is later than the November 28 date given by Schneider in "Their Honor was Loyalty," page 148. Herrn Harmel agreed with the date given.

During the first Russian winter, Harmel (3rd from right) watches Otto Kumm direct artillery support. Below, Harmel watches training maneuvers. On the left is Hans Bissinger who won the German Cross in Gold with Regiment "Deutschland."

(Above left) Harmel (right) with Walter Model in May, 1944, while in command of "Frundsberg" wearing his Knight's Cross with Oakleaves. On the right, an autographed photo as an SS-Obersturmbannführer in Russia prior to award of the Knight's Cross.

sphere of panic that bordered on despair. With this, no ordered leadership by superiors was possible within the pocket and, following the destruction of our communications positions, no contact with leaders outside of the pocket could be established. It appeared as if the collapse of the will to resist of those troops that were encircled stood before us.

In this situation (at the last minute), SS-Brigadeführer Harmel decided to attempt a break-through in a general north-northeast direction with the 10.SS-Panzer Division. "Frundsberg." At this time the remains of the Division were weak, but their confidence in their leaders was still secure. Under the personal leadership of the divisional commander, who always remained with the lead attack group of his battle group to reconnoiter the enemy situation and to uncover break-through possibilities, the Division was successful in advancing to the impeding section of ponds on the morning of August 20, 1944. Thanks to the untiring, enthusiastic effect Brigadeführer Harmel had on the leaders and men taking part in the attack, as well as his shining example, the Division was successful in taking the DIVES as well as the St.LAMBERT and MOISSY sections in a surprising advance against strong enemy resistance during the course of the day on August 20, 1944. With that, a substantial requirement was met for the success of further planned operations.

But, despite this success, SS-Brigadeführer Harmel was forced to determine that the enemy resistance in the northwest had increased so intensely, that a break-through in this direction was impossible. A break-through attempt could only be attempted in an east-northeasterly direction and only with the assistance of all encircled parts of the Division. Besides that, the situation had become incredibly more critical. The enemy had constricted the pocket further and in the south secure portions of an infantry division were overrun and wiped out. Through a unplanned convergence of the encircled portions of the Division at the crossings over the DIVES there were traffic jams of scathed troops, which were hammered by strong artillery fire. The result was a desperate, panicked retreat of thousands of leaderless soldiers of all branches of service. The restless collapse of the resistance forced its way through. With that, however, a break-out for the few portions of the troops that were determined to fight would be made impossible. The situation could only still be saved through a decisive and quick handling of the situation. An advising divisional staff of a Panzer division refused to hear the recommendations made by Brigadeführer Harmel for an immediate handling of the threatening situation and wants to make their further orders based on the results of a reconnaissance mission. The resulting day that this decision would have made, however, would have made the collapse inevitable.

Under the impression of the situation, Brigadeführer Harmel therefore decided to seize the collective leadership of all of the troops and soldiers that were located in the pocket. Harmel made this decision without regard for the other command posts.

He then became an enthusiastically recognized leader of all the entrapped soldiers as well as the soul of the resistance. In an electrifying address to the SS leaders and officers of all branches of the Wehrmacht present in the church in LAMBERT, a speech undoubtedly inspired by an unshakable desire to resist and by the trust in his own forces, he called to them to continue the battle and under his leadership they would indeed be able to force a break-through. Everyone followed him, only the previously mentioned divisional staff stayed back. In a small shack next to the church Harmel transformed the decisions he had made into orders. These decisions were determined based on his personal observations. The main points of his orders were the elimination of the traffic jam on the bridge, organizing battle groups, the unconditional holding of St. LAMBERT and MOISSY and finally the preparation for a violent break-through in the night of the 20th to the 21st of August, 1944, in an east-northeasterly direction to SOURDEVALS-COUDEHARD.

In a goal-conscious method and with extreme speed, the forces were ordered and prepared for a break-through. At all focal points Harmel personally appeared and spread his unbroken battle spirit to all the officers and men engaged in the battle. He forced retreating soldiers to again take up the battle with his iron hardness and continuously provided motivation to groups that had lost their courage. Only the exemplary shining soldierly spirit exhibited by the paramount personality of Harmel himself is to be thanked, that (among other things) the positions in St.LAMBERT could be held against strong pressure and the heaviest fire which enabled the last remains of the troops to cross the DIVES section of ponds to the east and arrive in the new preparations areas during the first hours of the night of August 20, 1944.

During the night the previously mentioned staff of a Panzer division tried again hold up the attack movements that had suc-

cessfully reached the river thanks to the energy of Brigadeführer Harmel and to then send out reconnaissance parties. SS-Brigadeführer Harmel carried out his intentions however, and placed himself immediately again at the lead of the battlegroups constructed from portions of the 10.SS-Panzer Division, Fallschirmjäger and Army troops. Together with his battle groups, and despite the absence of our Panzers, he led a night attack against built-up enemy resistance with unheard-of personal bravery. Harmel forced the break-through over SOURDEVALS and finally reached the remains of the II.SS-Panzer Korps (which had been fighting in the opposite direction) after difficult battle. With that, the choking enemy ring was blown open and the freeing of the trapped soldiers was successful. Besides the overrun remnants, the badly wounded supreme commander of the 7.Armee, SS-Oberstgruppenführer Hausser, as well as the seriously wounded commander of the 1.SS-Panzer Divison "Leibstandarte," SS-Brigadeführer Wisch, were led back and thus spared from being taken prisoner.

Besides saving the remainder of the 7.Armee, and his own division as well, with his excellent soldierly spirit, unheard-of and daring spirit of adventure and iron willpower, SS-Brigadeführer Harmel acquired such a battle spirit amongst his men that a few weeks later the units under his leadership were successfully able to beat off a strong enemy advance from the south in Nimwegen and thus prevent a union of that unit with the enemy units that landed in Arnheim. The enemy advance was held back for a long enough time that the enemy units in Arnheim could be annihilated.

In agreement with the then-supreme commander of the 5.Panzer-Armee and the present supreme commander of the 6.SS-Panzer-Armee, SS-Oberstgruppenführer Dietrich, I therefore recommend that SS-Brigadeführer Harmel be awarded the Swords to the Oakleaves of the Knight's Cross to the Iron Cross."[9]

As a divisional commander, he led "Frundsberg" in three of the most difficult combats of his career: Hill 112 during the Normandy fighting, at the Falaise pocket and during the September, 1944, Arnheim battles. Harmel spent the final weeks of the war attached to the SS officer school in Klagenfurt and ended the war commanding a Kampfgruppe attached to the rear area of Army Group "E" covering the southeast area of the front facing Italy.[10] After the war Harmel worked as a salesman and in 1996 celebrated his 90th birthday. When met by this author, his appearance was just as it was during the war with the exception of his now silver hair.

---

[9] "Vorschlag" dated November 25, 1944, written and submitted by Wilhelm Bittrich as commander of the II.SS-Panzer-Korps.
[10] It was an ad-hoc command organized by the local NSDAP Gauleiter, Friedrich Rainer. Research courtesy Phil A. Nix.

(Above) Harmel (note white summer uniform) tries to throw off the aim of a comrade during a shooting contest and (below) he practices with a P38.

In Russia Harmel (above) as an SS-Sturmbannführer and (below) he crosses a river as an SS-Obersturmbannführer.

This polite soldier's soldier still allowed himself several cigars each day.

An extremely respected and revered commander by both his subordinates and superiors, he held the additional respect of his men from having worked his way through the ranks. Numerous staff and attached officers have related that his first question after an engagement was the number of his men killed and wounded. This constant strong concern for the men of his many commands, his tactical skill and bravery throughout the war, made Heinz Harmel among the very best divisional commanders in the Waffen-SS. Especially important, in the opinion of this author, was his superior and exemplary leadership of Regiment "Deutschland" during the first Russian campaign. During that period he felt the battles in Jelnja-Bogen, at the outskirts of Moscow, Rshew, the armored battles around Orel and the intense Kharkov battles were the most intense of an almost continuous year of heavy combat. One of the most decorated commanders of the Waffen-SS, Heinz Harmel lives in retirement with his wife and has spent several years compiling the history of the 10.SS-Panzer-Division "Frundsberg."

An extremely modest man, he considers the men of his units more important than his own contribution. For that reason, I asked him which officers he commanded that impressed him the most

After recovery from a wound, Harmel is welcomed back by his men with the "key" to "Deutschland" Regiment. In the photo below are, from left, Hans Bissinger, Otto Reuter and Harmel. Reuter ended the war as a divisional 1a.

and the superiors who influenced him during the war as a commander. While with II./Der Führer, he was most impressed with Sylvester Stadler and Heinz Werner.[11] When commander of "Deutschland" Günther Wisliceny, Helmut Schreiber and Heinz Macher stood out with their leadership and bravery.[12] As a divisional commander, battalion commanders Hans Löffler and Friedrich Richter, as well as regimental leaders Heinz Laubscheer and Otto Paetsch, are recalled as outstanding.[13] He added that many, many men were outstanding and that selecting names to reply to my question was very difficult, but these were among the most memorable. Harmel's wartime superior officer influences were Paul Hausser, Georg Keppler and Otto Kumm. Harmel and his wife of more than 50 years have three children.

Below: Harmel (center) with Helmut Schreiber (left) and Günther Wisliceny. Schreiber won both the Knight's Cross and German Cross in Gold.

[11] Werner, then commander of 6.Kompanie, would win the Knight's Cross (August 23, 1944) with Oakleaves (May 6, 1945) and the German Cross in Gold (May 29, 1943). He ended the war as the commander of III./"Der Führer" with the rank of SS-Sturmbannführer.

[12] Wisliceny, then commander of III.Bataillon, was the last commander of Regiment "Deutschland." He won the Knight's Cross (July 30, 1943) with Oakleaves (December 27, 1944) and Swords (May 6, 1945) as well as the German Cross in Gold (April 25, 1943). He died on August 25, 1985, in Hannover. Schreiber, a Knight's Cross (July 30, 1943) and German Cross in Gold holder (April 9, 1943), commanded 10.Kompanie under Harmel. Heinz Macher, the commander of the regiment's 16.Kompanie (engineers) was the most decorated engineer of the Waffen-SS. He won the Knight's Cross (April 3, 1943) with Oakleaves (August 19, 1944), German Cross in Gold (August 7, 1944), Wound Badge in Gold (August 12, 1943) and the Close Combat Clasp in Gold (October 1, 1944).

[13] They respectivly commanded II./Panzer-Grenadier-Regiment 22, III./Panzer-Grenadier-Regiment 22, Panzer-Grenadier-Regiment 21, and Panzer Regiment 10 in the 10.SS-Panzer-Division "Frundsberg." Richter won the Knight's Cross (May, 1945) and the German Cross in Gold (November 14, 1944). He ended the war as an SS-Sturmbannführer and died on August 30, 1989. Paetsch was awarded the Knight's Cross (August 23, 1944) with Oakleaves (April 5, 1945) and the German Cross in Gold (April 24, 1943). He was killed on March 20, 1945, while commanding the Panzer Regiment of "Frundsberg" and was posthumously promoted to SS-Standartenführer.

(Above) Standing in his command vehicle, Harmel explains a situation to Otto Kumm (standing at left). Below, from left are Peter Sommer (First Staff Officer), Harmel, and (far right) Rolf Diercks (ordnance officer). Both Sommer and Diercks won the German Cross in Gold. The officer 2nd from right in the background with German Cross in Gold is Heinrich Schuster (adjutant).

Harmel, nearest the camera on horseback, looks at a newly dedicated cemetery in Russia. Below, he reviews newly decorated men of Regiment "Deutschland" of which eight display the German Cross in Gold. 3rd from left is Günther Wisliceny and 5th from left is Helmut Schreiber.

Two 1944 photos of SS-Oberführer Heinz Harmel in camo uniform as the commander of the 10.SS-Panzer-Division "Frundsberg."

(Left) Harmel (center) congratulates one of his men. He wears the single-handed tank destruction strip on his shoulder. On the right he proudly displays a field made congratulatory document given to him by the officers of "Deutschland."

Autographed portraits of Heinz Harmel (left) as an SS-Standartenführer and (right) as an SS-Oberführer.

An excellent studio autographed portrait of SS-Standartenführer Heinz Harmel showing his Knight's Cross.

WALTER HARZER

The son of a building inspector, Walter Harzer was born in Stuttgart-Feuerbach on September 29, 1912. After passing his Abitur in 1931, he attended a higher technical school to study construction engineering, during which time he visited England and France. Joining the NSDAP and SA in November, 1930, he left the SA to join the SS on November 1, 1931. In the Spring of 1933 he was assigned to the Political Readiness Detachment in Württemberg and from August, 1933, to March, 1934, he saw service in the Army with Infanterie Regiment 13 as a Gefreiter.

Harzer transferred to the SS-Verfügungstruppe in March, 1934, and was assigned to III./SS-Standarte 1 where he remained until attending the second class at SS-Junkerschule Bad Tölz during 1935-1936.[1] After graduation, he was commissioned as an SS-Untersturmführer on April 20, 1936. Harzer's first assignment after officer school was a posting with the Sicherheitshauptamt from the start of May, 1936, until November 9, 1936.

Next moving to SS-Standarte "Deutschland, he served as a Zugführer with 13.Sturm until September 20, 1937, then held the same position in 12.Sturm until December 15, 1937. From December 15, 1937, to the beginning of April, 1939, he held a similar position with 4.Sturm. During this latter command, he attended a machine gun platoon leaders course at the Army Infantry School in Döberitz in March, 1938, and was promoted to SS-Obersturmführer on January 30, 1939. From April 1, 1939, to the start of July, 1939, he led 14.Sturm and then commanded 9.Kompanie until November 1, 1939. On September 29, 1939, he was awarded the Iron Cross 2nd class.

Transferring to the SS Officer School in Braunschweig, he headed a teaching group from the start of November, 1939, to mid-November, 1940, then also added the duties of tactical instructor at the facility until March 12, 1941. On April 20, 1940, Harzer was promoted to SS-Hauptsturmführer. He then moved to the SS-Unterführerschule "Radolfzell" from March 12, 1941, to June 12, 1941, as a tactics instructor.

Returning to a field command, he replaced Josef Fitzhum as commander of II./SS-Infanterie-Regiment 4 until May 1, 1942.[2] He was awarded the Iron Cross 1st class on October 26, 1941, the Infantry Assault Badge on February 25, 1942, and the Eastern Front Medal on August 15, 1942. After two-and-a-half months of staff training with SS-Division "Reich," he went to the Army LVII Panzerkorps from July 11 to the end of November, 1942, for General Staff training under Chief of Staff (later General) Walter Wenck. He then attended a General Staff course at the Army War Academy. Following the course, he served as Ib on the staff of the 10.SS-Division from February 22, 1943, to April 10, 1943.

Promoted to SS-Sturmbannführer on April 20, 1943, he replaced SS-Sturmbannführer Baldur Keller as Ia of the SS-Panzer-Grenadier-Division "Hohenstaufen" in April, 1943, and stayed with that unit and assignment through its development into a Panzer-Division until October 24, 1944.[3] During that time he was promoted to

---

[1] This Bataillon was renumbered the IV.Bataillon on July 1, 1936, when a new III.Bataillon was formed. Weidinger, "Division "Das Reich," volume 1, pages 33-36. The expansion was brief as it was soon reduced to three Bataillone as other units of the SS-Verfügungstruppe were formed.

[2] Christian Tychsen took command of the unit in June and it was absorbed by the Panzer Regiment as its II.Abteilung in October with Tychsen retaining command. Yerger, "Knights of Steel," volume 2, page 24 and Panzer Regiment chapter covering covering the unit's development in volume 1.

[3] Harzer's start as Ia is given as April 10 in his Knight's Cross recommendation statistics page and "since formation of the division" in his German Cross recommendation. Baldur Keller was awarded the German Cross in Gold on January 16, 1944, as Ia of the "Totenkopf" Division. He ended the war assigned to the II.SS-Panzer-Korps as Ia with the rank of SS-Obersturmbannführer. After serving as a company commander with Regiment "Deutschland" during 1939-1941, he was Ia for "Prinz Eugen" and "Hohenstaufen" before going to "Totenkopf."

Below is the 4th wartime teaching class at SS-Junkerschule Braunschweig during 1940/41. Walter Harzer, commander of the class, is 4th from left in the front row. Right are (from left) Wilhelm Bittrich, Walter Harzer (1a) and Alexander Schwarz (adjutant) in 1943 while assigned to "Hohenstaufen."

SS-Obersturmbannführer on January 30, 1944. In the final months of his assignment with "Hohenstaufen" he led Kampfgruppe "Harzer," consisting of the remnants of the division awaiting transport to Germany from September 17 to September 27 per orders of Walter Model. The battle group was also known as Speerrverband "Harzer." Harzer's command consisted of Army and Luftwaffe battalions as well as the III./Landstorm Nederland in combating the Allied attempts to take Arnheim. During this time divisional commander Sylvester Stadler was wounded and his temporary successor, Friedrich-Wilhelm Bock, had moved with the other part of "Hohenstaufen" to Siegen.

On August 7, 1944, temporary divisional commander SS-Standartenführer Friedrich-Wilhelm Bock recommended Harzer for the award of the German Cross in Gold for actions in Russia and Normandy with the following report:

"Already on the first action day in the east, it was the service as well as clear and conscious leadership of SS-Obersturmbannführer Harzer that allowed him to take command of the first incoming units of the 9.SS-PanzerDivision "Hohenstaufen" arriving from the west. He led the men in the preparation for the building of a bridgehead over the Strypa section near Zlodniky southwest of Tarnopol on April 8, 1944. The further evacuation of the Castle Tarnopol was greatly influenced by this bridgehead.

During the course of the attacks during the time period from April 11 - 17, 1944, until the evacuation of Tarnopol from the west, SS-Obersturmbannführer Harzer supported the divisional commander in the leadership of the division in special measure. The battle leadership was conducted according to his plan. The success that the division had accomplished is to be credited to his service.

SS-Obersturmbannführer Harzer had taken a decisive role in the success of the first counterattack against the enemy that had broken through west of Caen on 29.6.44. Here especially he was the energetic and supportive leader, since the divisional commander had taken over another position.

SS-Obersturmbannführer Harzer recognized the weak positions of the enemy during this attack and set up his units for the further attacks on 30. 6 and 1. 7. 1944, so that the success that he had initially accomplished could be exploited to its fullest advantage. His energy brought, when all is said-and-done, the decisive success that the planned large attack of the enemy southwest of Caen was destroyed - despite the very great superiority of the enemy in men and material. The opponent had to retreat from his plan.

After the enemy was successful in taking Maltot during the night from 9. to 10. 7. 1944, the 9.SS-Panzer-Division. "Hohenstaufen" was put into action against the elements of the enemy that had broken through. The planning of the battle leadership led to success - despite the enemy's heaviest defense, the old main fighting line was reached. The enemy's intended breakthrough attempt west of the Orne to the South became a complete defensive success against the pressing superior enemy forces. Again it was the service of SS-Obersturmbannführer Harzer that his attack plan, prepared in detail, brought the decisive success.

On July 25, 1944, the enemy successfully broke through east of the Orne and south of Caen on both sides of the road between Ifs and Fontenay. Through the just earlier prepared measures of the Ia of the Division, SS-Obersturmbannführer Harzer was successful in carrying out the counterattack that was planned specifically for the possibility of this situation occurring - all in shortest time. He led it to a complete success. The division received the special recognition of the commanding general of the I.SS-Panzer-Korps for this success.

On August 2, 1944, still during the development of the defensive fighting east of the Orne, the division had to be relieved from its previous section in order to intercept enemy forces that had broken through in Beny-Bocage in the direction of Montchamp Dusert - Presles - Chênedolle in the direction of Condé - Vire with the further goal of reaching Condé - Falaise. SS-Obersturmbannführer Harzer displayed special service in the leading of his troops during this difficult assignment. The relief of the division was cleverly planned so that the enemy remained clueless of his intentions.

The armored battle group was brought up quickly and was thrown at the enemy so that the break-in was stopped. Up until August 5, 1944, 123 enemy tanks were put out of action."[4]

Harzer's award was approved and he was given the decoration on August 19, 1944. The battles on the Western Front, especially Arnheim, resulted in Harzer being further decorated. On September 25, 1944, SS-Obergruppenführer Wilhelm Bittrich, commander of II.SS-Panzer-Korps, recommended Harzer for the Knight's Cross of the Iron Cross in a report that reads as follows:

"SS-Obersturmbannführer Harzer, the first General Staff Officer (Ia) took over leadership of the remaining portions of the 9.SS-Panzer-Division "Hohenstaufen" to form a battle group. During the night of September 1/2, 1944, near St. Quentin, SS-Obersturmbannführer Harzer received the order to bring together all of the fighting troops south of St.Quentin and to secure all the streets leading to Cambrai from the south and the southwest against advancing enemy troops. After arriving in the ordered secured area, strong enemy tank forces had just crossed the planned securing line in the southwest and

---

[4] "Vorschlag für die Verleihung des Deutschen Kreuzes in Gold" signed by Bock, SS-Standartenführer u. Stellv.Divisions-Führer. Six awards of the German Cross in Gold went to "Hohenstaufen" that day.

A September, 1944, portrait of SS-Obersturmbannführer Walter Harzer showing both his Knight's Cross and German Cross in Gold.

had already pushed to the south towards Cambrai. Harzer therefore decided on a quick out-flanking maneuver to the east to surround the enemy further to the north and also to secure the streets leading to Cambrai from the south. The energetic and circumspect leadership of SS-Obersturmbannführer Harzer brought this undertaking to a full success despite a lack of fuel and battle vehicles requiring large quantities of fuel. Despite continuous tank attacks which lasted the whole day, Harzer held Cambrai and also successfully beat back the enemy which attempted an outflanking maneuver from a southerly direction to the east of the city. Just as suprisingly strong tank forces came from Arras (from the northwest) and advanced towards the city of Cambrai, Harzer no longer had any reserves from his weak battlegroup to throw against these forces and decided to lead his battlegroup out of the city in a northwesterly direction and form a new securing line while the enemy continued to try and hold them up.

Even though the enemy threatened his withdrawal path to the northeast from the south and northwest, SS-Obersturmbannführer Harzer was successful in leading his men from the city without noteworthy casualties and stayed to the last moment battling the enemy. He and the rest of the staff from the battlegroup remained there and were cut off from the rest of their troops. For two days and nights they had to avoid enemy columns and fight their way back to their troops.

Through his dogged steadfastness and his excellent bravery in an almost hopeless situation, SS-Obersturmbannführer Harzer managed to hold up the advancing tank forces of the enemy in Cambrai for over 24 hours and managed to pull the enemy to the northwest. These actions had the effect of holding open a path in the direction of Mons which allowed the still-fighting portions of the II.SS-Panzer-Korps to escape.

As English and American glider and parachute troops landed surprisingly in the area of Arnheim, SS-Obersturmbannführer Harzer received the order to attack and destroy the enemy with the few available troops of the 9.SS-Panzer-Division. Since his own battlegroup was not adequate to complete this task, Harzer collected all available soldiers of all branches of service together in Arnheim, and put them together with additional army, marine, air force and Waffen-SS troops which had been called up in the meantime. He formed battlegroups and immediately led them against enemy troops landing from the air, as well as the Dutch partisans, which were now in possession of a bridge. Through special circumspect and clever tactical leadership, Harzer was successful in bringing the enemy to defeat in heavy, rapidly changing battles conducted in a few city blocks surrounding the enemy. He also brought the important Arnheim bridge into our possession without damage. At the same time Harzer sent another battlegroup to conduct a surrounding attack against another enemy group which had landed directly west of Arnheim. His energy and personal bravery are to be thanked for the forced surrender of the enemy within 48 hours despite their dogged defense in very close quarters. The commander reported that over 10,000 prisoners as well as numerous amounts of war material was brought in."[5]

Moving to the V.SS-Gebirgs-Korps in October, he replaced Baldur Keller as Chief of Staff until November 20, 1944. After a week-long divisional commanders course in Hirschberg, he succeeded Fritz Schmedes as commander of the 4.SS-Polizei-Panzer-Grenadier-Division from November 28, 1944, to the end of the war.[6] On November 30, 1944, he was promoted to SS-Standartenführer. He was to have been promoted to SS-Oberführer in April, 1945, but chaos at the end of the war prevented approval of the promotion.

A tough, brave and experienced staff officer as well as divisional commander, he was a well-educated engineer, fluent in both English and French. Devoted to the men of his command, he was idolized by his subordinates and was an excellent example of a natural, professional leader produced by the pre-war SS officer school system. After the war he was involved in HIAG and served for many years as historian, gathering the groundwork and knowledge for numerous later official unit histories. Harzer was married in December, 1941, he and his wife having one child. As a research historian and scholar Harzer was both objective and extremely knowledgeable. A soldier's soldier, Walter Harzer died in a Stuttgart hospital of heart failure on May 29, 1982.

---

[5] "Vorschlag für die Verleihung des Ritterkreuzes des Eisernen Kreuzes" signed by Bittrich and dated September 25, 1944.

[6] The day before is given as the effective date in SS-Führungshauptamt, "Stabsbefehl Nr. 30/44," dated December 23, 1944.

PAUL HAUSSER

The "Father of the Waffen-SS" was born on October 7, 1880, in Brandenburg an der Havel. The son of Major Kurt Hausser, Paul Hausser joined the Prussian cadet corps in 1892. He first went to the cadet school in Köslin and later the main cadet school at Berlin-Lichterfelde. Hausser graduated and was commissioned as a Leutnant on March 18, 1899. He was first posted to a West Prussian unit and served as a battalion, then later regimental, adjutant with Infantry Regiment No. 155 until 1907. Continuing his military training, he then spent two years at the War Academy in Posen. From 1909 to 1912 he served as an aerial observer with the Imperial Navy and was promoted to Oberleutnant in 1912.

Appointed to the Army General Staff in 1912, Hausser served with the cartographic detachment and was promoted to Hauptmann in March, 1914. He remained with this posting until March, 1914, when he transferred to the staff of Crown Prince Rupprecht of Bavaria as a General Staff officer. During World War I, Hausser was posted to the 6th Army Corps and served as Ia to the 109th Infantry Division. Promoted to Major, in 1919 he was the Ia of the 1st Reserve Corps and then took command of Fusilier Regiment "Generalfeldmarschall Graf Moltke" No. 88 which was originally recruited in Silesia. Hausser then served briefly with special assignments General Command 59. During the war he was decorated with both classes of the Iron Cross, the Hohenzollern House Order with Swords, the Bavarian Military Service Order 4th class with Swords, the Knight's Cross of the Saxon Order of Albert 1st class, the Knight's Cross of the Württemberg Order of Friedrich 1st class with Swords, the Anhalt Friedrich Cross, the Austro-Hungarian Order of the Iron Cross 3rd class with War Decoration, and the Austro-Hungarian Military Service Cross 3rd class with War Decoration.[1]

In 1919, Hausser served with border protection units in the east. That same year he was posted as the liasion officer for the General Command in Glogau. From 1920 to 1922 he served as Ia to Reichswehr Brigade 5 then moved to the same assignment with District Area Command II until January, 1923. On November 15, 1922, Hausser was promoted to Oberstleutnant.

Hausser took command of the III./Infantry Regiment 4 from January, 1923, to April, 1925, and then returned to District Area II as Chief of Staff of 2.Division until the end of 1926. From January 1, 1927, to the start of July that year, he served as a staff officer with Infantry Regiment 10. Hausser then served as regimental commander until the beginning of November, 1930. During that command period he was promoted to Oberst on November 1, 1927, with seniority effective July 1, 1927. As commander of the Troop Training Area in Münsingen, Hausser served from November 1, 1930, to December the same year when he was reassigned as a temporary Infantry Leader IV (Infanterieführer). He held the post until the start of February, 1932. Promoted to Generalmajor on February 1, 1931, he left the Army on January 31, 1932, as a Generalleutnant.

In February, 1933, Hausser joined the Stahlhelm and was a leader in Berlin-Brandenburg for the War Veterans association from early February, 1933, to April 1934. He joined the SA Reserve as an SA-Standartenführer in March, 1934, and was posted to SA Reserve Brigade 25 until the start of November, 1934. During his SA service he met a former regimental comrade, Paul Scharfe, who introduced him to Himmler.[2] Himmler invited him to join the SS to

---

[1] Krätschmer, "Die Ritterkreuzträger der Waffen-SS," pages 159-160.
[2] Scharfe was a legal expert with the SS and became a Main Office head. For details and his photograph, see Yerger, "Allgemeine-SS," pages 3, 18 and 180.

Paul Hausser (left) in Army General uniform and (right) as an SS-Obergruppenführer.

study and solve the problems with training the SS-Verfügungstruppe. Hausser joined the SS on November 15, 1934, as an SS-Standartenführer with seniority effective the beginning of that month.

Hausser took command of the new SS-Führerschule in Braunschweig and served as commandant as well as developing the curriculum for both officer schools. He commanded the facility in Braunschweig until June 1, 1936, when he was succeeded by Friedemann Götze. Promoted to SS-Oberführer on July 1, 1935, and to SS-Brigadeführer on May 22, 1936, at the end of May he left command of Braunschweig and was appointed Chief of the Führungsamt. Hausser was also posted as the Inspector of both SS officer schools effective on August 1, 1935. When he gave up command of Braunschweig, Hausser also succeeded August Heissmeyer as head of the Leadership office in the SS Main Office until the start of October 1937.[3]

With his command responsibilities growing, Hausser assumed the posts of Inspector of the SS Verfügungstruppen (October 1, 1936

to August 10, 1939) and Inspector of the SS officer schools from August 1, 1935, to May 5, 1937.[4] He joined the NSDAP on May 1, 1937. Hausser's importance is evident in that during one period he simultaneously held three different commands in the SS-Hauptamt.[5] On June 1, 1939, he was promoted to SS-Gruppenführer and in late July, 1939, he went with the SS/VT units to be used in Panzer Division "Kempf" to East Prussia.[6] Hausser went with the attached units during the Polish campaign and was awarded a clasp to his Iron Cross 2nd class in September, then returned to Berlin in early October, 1939, where the division was disbanded.

---

[3] Koehl, "The Black Corps," pages 138 and 141.

[4] Some documents give his Inspector of the SS/VT post being officially held into 1940 but he was then actually commanding the first divison of the Waffen-SS (Hans Jüttner actually had the post) so the position was honorary.

[5] October 1, 1936 to May 5, 1937: Inspector of the SS/VT, Inspector of SS Officer Schools and Chief of the Leadership Office (Führungsamt).

[6] The SS units incorporated into Panzer Division "Kempf" were Regimenter "Deutschland," the SS artillery regiment, the signals detachment, reconnaissance detachment. Other SS/VT units, including the SS engineer battalion, the "Leibstandarte," and Regiment "Germania" served attached to other Army formations. Panzer Division "Kempf" was disbanded on October 9, 1939.

On October 9, 1939, Paul Hausser took command of the formation staff for the first division to be formed from SS troops. The division was officially ordered established on October 19, 1939, using the pre-war regiments "Deutschland." "Germania," and "Der Führer." All the units that fought in Poland were incorporated into the division which was given the designation SS-Verfügungstruppen Division (mot). Hausser's new command was officially operational in November, 1939, and he was promoted to Generalleutnant der Waffen-SS on November 19th.

In addition to his new divisional command, Hausser headed the Kommandoamt der Waffen-SS from June until mid-August, 1940. The office command post was then taken over by Hans Jüttner when the SS Main Operational Office was formed and absorbed Hausser's office. Leading his division in the Western campaign, in Yugoslavia and into Russia, Hausser was an extremely effective leader of one of the most successful divisions. He was awarded a clasp to his WWI Iron Cross 1st class on May 17, 1940, for his actions in the Western campaign. As a result of the following recommendation written during the campaign in Russia, Hausser was awarded the Knight's Cross on August 8, 1941:[7]

(Above) Hausser walks with an Army officer during an SS/VT inspection and (below) he is in profile as an SS-Brigadeführer at Braunschweig.

[7] "Vorschlagliste Nr. 411" submitted by Generalfeldmarschall von Brauchitsch on August 5, 1941.

Hausser's influence was felt in all ranks. In these two photos he personally observes and instructs enlisted trainees. At the time he was a corps commander.

In the same sequence as the previous two photos, Hausser adds advice to the regular training.

In these two photos, Hausser (center) enjoys a light-hearted moment with Wilhelm Kment (right) and Gerhard Hintze.

"SS-Gruppenführer Hausser proved himself as an excellent leader during the Western campaign. Outstanding tactical situational development, frank and personal action, taking command of the situation always at the most dangerous position, great confidence and calm, tenacious desire and mastering the most difficult situations - set him apart from others.

His battle leadership won decisive influence during the battles between Beresina and Dnjepr. - After the Beresina - Overcrossing, the SS-Divison "Reich" received the task, to relieve the strongly threatened 10.Panzer Division by conducting an attack on the left wing of the XXXXVI.Panzer Korps and afterwards to conduct an accelerating advance over Belynitschi to Schklov and further to the Dnjepr. In order to find the enemy's position and to annihilate the opponent which had skillfully retreated to the east, the divisional commander decided during the evening of July 7, 1941, to throw forward the strengthened Kradschützen Bataillon onto Esmon to push the opponent to the Oslik section. The Kradschützen Bataillon was also given the task of securing this area. The mass of the division was to frontally attack the opponent while the Kradschützen Bataillon successfully took care of the north flank. Near Somry, the opponent met SS Regiment "Der Führer" with tenacious resistance. The divisional commander rushed to the forward-most battalion in order to personally get a glance of the strength and equipment of the opponent. While passing through the village, he was wounded by a grenade fragment from a distance of just a few meters, but maintained the leadership of the Division. By bringing on the the masses of the available artillery, the divisional commander was able to push the attack into an unobservable forested area despite stubborn resistance of the enemy.

The opponent was the 100.Division(Moscow), one of the best Russian divisions. The skillful and energetic leadership of the divisional commander brought success in this extremely difficult terrain. He was able to throw back and, for the most part, to annihilate the enemy which was attacking from all sides. The quick advance from the Beresina to the Dnjepr during the destruction of the best Russian troops, ensured that the opponent would not be able to organize a defense behind the Dnjepr. These actions enabled the Corps to quickly cross over the Dnjepr and also the 10.Panzer Division to quickly and deeply follow up, which later proved to be a decisive event for the entire operation.

The SS Division"Reich" under the leadership of Gruppenführer Hausser took part in the following decisive battles during the Western campaign:

a) The Division independently took Walcheren Island in battle against Dutch and French troops in three days and insured the early capitulation of the fortress Antwerpen. This, combined with the taking of the flank near Vlissingen, made the port there unsuitable to the enemy.

b) The Division fought within Panzergruppe Kleist during the battles in Flanders in the Nieppe Forest against English troops who defended themselves bravely. They took the forest after a four-day battle and which was of decisive importance for the overall goal of encircling of the English-French troops in Flanders.

c) During the advance of the Panzer troops to the Plateau from Langes the Division had the task to secure the deep left flank of Gruppe Kleist. The Division advanced on the Seine where French troops from the Maginot-Line were

Hausser observing and instructing men of the SS/VT engineer battalion.

retreating to the southeast. They attacked them in the area around Chatillon s./Seine and annihilated them completely. The Division brought in 20,000 prisoners on one day as well as 14 batteries and numerous pieces of equipment."

Signed v. Vietinghoff
General der Panzertruppe und
Kommand.General d. XXXXVI.Panzer-Korps

"Gruppenführer Hausser displayed excellent personal preparedness for action during the heavy battles between Beresina and Dnjepr and then from Dnjepr to Jelnja. He always remained at the focal point of the battle and led his troops without regard for himself, despite the threat on the flank and from the rear. He led his superb troops to a decisive victory in difficult terrain which encompassed various rivers. The quick reaching of the Dnjepr in the area of the XXXXVI Armee Korps is a personal merit. The recommandation is approved."

Guderian
Generaloberst

Promoted to SS-Obergruppenführer und General der Waffen-SS on October 1, 1941, Hausser remained in command of his division through several title changes until October 14, 1941. While leading what was then designated SS-Division "Reich," Hausser was severly wounded on that date, losing the sight in his left eye and suffering damage to his jaw. He was succeeded as divisional commander by Wilhelm Bittrich, previously the commander of Regiment "Deutschland." For his severe wounds, Hausser was awarded the Wound Badge in Silver on May 9, 1942.

After his recovery, Hausser began forming the initial Waffen-SS corps in late May, 1942. After several designations, his command was titled II.SS-Panzer-Korps and Hausser remained in command until June 28, 1944. His corps was briefly retitled to become the 1.SS-Panzer Armee in the autumn of 1943 to confuse enemy intelligence but then reverted to its corps designation. Generaloberst Hermann Hoth recommended Hausser for the award of the Oakleaves for his corps leadership with the following report:

"On the first day of the offensive, July 5, 1943, the attack of the "Leibstandarte" faltered due to overwhelming enemy artillery fire from the hills at Schurawliny and south of Olchowka. The commanding general, being up at the front, recognized the crisis and immediately issued the highest measure of appropriate orders. Almost all the artillery of the corps was used for counterfire and the entire 8th Air Force Corps was directed on the enemy batteries. Realizing that an attack by the Division "Das Reich" would result in the necessary relief, Hausser hurried further towards the front and deployed the tanks of this division. He also ordered an immediate attack by "Totenkopf," which according to plan was to have been committed later to the rear of "Das Reich." The effect was telling. The attack of the "Leibstandarte" through the deeply-built enemy defensive line again gained momentum. The stronghold of Schurawliny was taken by assault in a pincer movement and by evening the second enemy defensive line was almost breached. The mopping up of the enemy on the right flank began.

On the second day of the offensive, the II.SS-Panzer-Korps had broken through the second enemy line when strong enemy armor forces were reported approaching from Prochorowka.

(Above) During a September, 1942, test drive of the amphibious schwimwagen are Hausser (standing) and in the rear SS-Standartenführer Werner Ostendorff (1a). The driver is the technical officer of the Motorcycle Battalion, Heinz Meiswinkel. Below, Hausser observes the SS/VT artillery regiment with regimental commander Peter Hansen (with binoculars). Hausser stands to the left of Hansen.

The commanding general, having hurried to the front, realized the favorable situation. He decided to turn the bulk of his corps toward Prochorowka to keep the enemy located there as far away from the battlefield as possible. He did this even though it was clearly visible that the XXXXVIII.Panzer-Korps was still engaged in hard fighting at the second enemy defensive line northwest of Olchowka from where the advance of II.SS-Panzer-Korps had been flanked. Leaving behind security forces at Pokrawa, *Hausser personally led* the tanks from "Das Reich" and "Leibstandarte" along the Lutschki/Prochorowka road. In heavy armored combat it was possible to throw the 2nd Soviet Armored Corps and the 5th Guards Mechanized Corps back to Prochorowka. Heavy losses were inflicted on the enemy and the heights at Teterewino were taken. Through these actions it was possible to turn the tanks again to the east and engage the 3rd Motorized Corps from the rear which was fighting opposite the XXXXVIII.Panzer-Korps.

On July 7, 1943, a crisis developed with the forces of "Das Reich" left behind to cover the right flank at Teterewino. They were attacked from the east by the newly-committed Russian 6th Armored Corps, 2nd Armored Corps, and 5th Guards Armored Corps. The enemy broke through in great depth through the infantry of "Das Reich" which had only itself to depend on. The commanding general, again in the appropriate location, decided to continue with the armored attack to the west despite the threat of a complete breakthrough. Thanks to the personal presence of Hausser, who aroused the tenacity of the armored infantry, they succeeded in finishing off the penetrated tanks in close combat and prevented a total breakthrough.

I hardly ever met Obergruppenführer Hausser during the operation at his advance headquarters, only up front with his divisions or returning from his troops. Despite his handicap from a previous serious wound, he untiringly led all day from the front. His presence, bravery and personal humor in even the most difficult situations, gave his troops buoyancy and enthusiasm while he held command of the corps tightly in his hand. As he had already shown during the offensive fighting at Kharkov, Obergruppenführer Hausser showed farsightedness in recognizing the operational situation and executed combat operations with bravery and energy. Again and again he has proven himself as an unusually qualified commanding general."[8]

The award was granted on July 28, 1943. During the Normandy campaign, Hausser replaced Generaloberst Friedrich Dollmann (who died of a heart attack) as commander of the 7.Armee from June 28, 1944, until wounded in the week of August 20. He was succeeded by General Erich Brandenberger at the start of September, 1944. The situation at the front caused a transfer originally ordered in July, 1944, to the SS-Führungshauptamt as head of the Kommandoamt, to be canceled. During his Armee command, Hausser also replaced Generalfeldmarschall Günther von Kluge for two days as commander of Heeresgruppe "B" after von Kluge committed suicide. He stayed until succeeded by Generalfeldmarschall Walter Model. At that point, Hausser was the only Waffen-SS officer to ever command a formation larger than an Armee.

On August 26, 1944, Hausser was approved to be awarded the 90th Swords to his Knight's Cross by Hitler as a result of the following report:

> "SS-Oberst-Gruppenführer und General der Waffen-SS Hausser, commander of the 7.Armee, has taken over command in a most difficult situation. He has continuously led from the front despite the heaviest possible enemy interference. A decisive resolve to attack Avranches with select armored formations was only denied success by enemy air superiority. Despite the threat of encirclement, Hausser stayed with his troops even though the possibility of his being evacuated was preferred by higher command echelons and offered. This way, the important influence of the commander was assured up to the day of the breakout from the pocket. Hausser experienced the breakout with the troops of the 2nd Paratroop Corps, fighting his way through with these troops under the heaviest artillery fire. In the course of the breakout he was severely wounded."[9] The award was presented to him personally by Hitler.

> After his recovery, Hausser replaced Heinrich Himmler as the commander of Heeresgruppe "Oberrhein" (Upper Rhine) on January 23, 1945, and held the command for five days until the command was disbanded. On January 28, 1945, Paul Hausser replaced Generaloberst Johannes Blaskowitz as commander of Heeresgruppe "G." This command contained the 1st and 9th Armies. After a heated argument with Hitler, Hausser was dismissed from his command on April 3, 1945. He spent the rest of the war on the staff of the Senior Commander "South West."

After the war, Hausser continued as a leader. He was a witness and defended the Waffen-SS at the Nuremberg trials. He also wrote the first post-war book on the Waffen-SS "Waffen-SS im Einsatz" (Waffen-SS in Action) in 1953 as well as a second volume "Soldaten wie andre auch" (Soldiers Like Any Other). Revered by all former members of the Truppe, he was the senior member of HIAG until his death in Ludwigsburg on December 21, 1972, at the age of 92. Hundreds of his former troops attended the funeral in Munich which

---

[8] Undated recommendation for the Oakleaves signed by Hoth and approved on July 28, 1943.

[9] "Vorschlag für die Verleihung des Eichenlaubes mit Schwertern zum Ritterkreuz des Eisernen Kreuzes" dated August 23, 1944.

resembled a state ceremony. The affectionate titles of "der Senior" and "Papa Hausser" were accorded him by all Waffen-SS veterans.

This tall, lean, Prussian-trained staff officer was undoubtedly responsible for the development and deployment of the Waffen-SS more than any other single individual. Hausser himself considered the SS officer schools his proudest achievement but his field commands may have been even more important. Few persons could reverse a tactical situation by physical presence alone such as did he. Hausser was definitely a lead-from-the-front commander, despite the fact that he was in his 60s during the Russian campaign. His dry, sarcastic sense of humor has been related to this author by many veterans telling hilarious comments he made in a variety of situations. That same dry humor made some enemies in the Army though his understanding of Army colleagues was to his advantage. Hausser was the first trained General-rank officer recruited for the SS-Verfügungstruppe and he combined the skill, training, and positive aspects of the Army with the progressive ideas of the Waffen-SS. He encouraged the exchange of Waffen-SS and Army officers for experience and training. Heinz Guderian called him one of *the* outstanding commanders and he was also acknowledged by Albert Kesselring, together possibly the best ground troop commanders in the Army and Luftwaffe. Naturally brave, he was not afraid to disobey ludicrous orders from either Himmler or Hitler and had remarkable physical stamina even after his severe wounds in 1941. Hausser and his wife Elizabeth were married on November 9, 1912, and together they had a daughter.

Hausser decorating Ludwig Kepplinger with the Knight's Cross as war reports record the event.

Opposite: Paul Hausser and Fritz Vogt during the parade honoring his 1940 award of the Knight's Cross, one of the first awarded to a man of the Division.

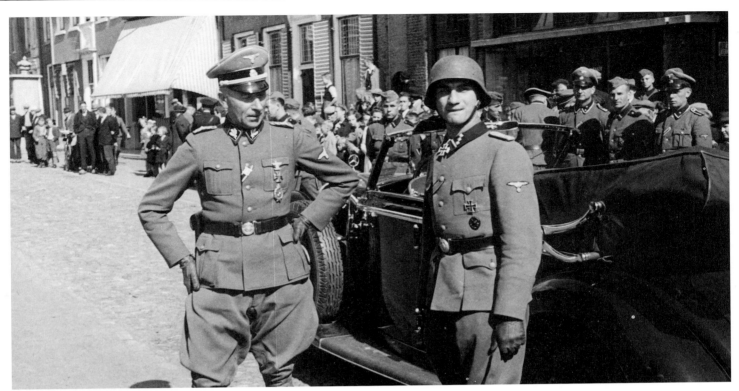

Two photos of the parade being reviewed by Hausser that especially honored Fritz Vogt's award of the Knight's Cross.

(Above) Hausser (with overseas cap) as a corps commander. On the left, his Chief of Staff Werner Ostendorff. On the far left is "Das Reich" commander Walter Krüger and behind him the commander of the "Das Reich" Panzer Regiment, Hans-Albin von Reitzenstein who was awarded the Knight's Cross. Below, an early war photo of Hausser (left) with an as yet unknown Oberführer. Hausser already wears clasps to both his WWI Iron Crosses.

Hausser in Russia wearing a white coat with (from left) Fritz Ehrath (commander I./Deutschland), Franz Grohmann (adjutant of I./Deutschland), Hausser, Heinz Harmel (Regiment "Deutschland" commander) and Heinz Macher (16./Deutschland). Photo taken on March 18, 1943, at the headquarters of I./Deutschland in Bjelgorod.

Hausser (center) with Heinz Harmel (left) and Werner Ostendorff in Russia.

A studio portrait of SS-Gruppenführer Paul Hausser.

At the completion of their training, men of the SS/VT artillery regiment are congratulated by Paul Hausser. Below, from right are Karl Wolff, Hausser, Heinrich Himmler and Werner Ostendorff during the 1940 period when collar insignia indicating units was temporarily banned for security reasons.

(Above) From right are Fritz Klingenberg, Werner Ostendorff, Paul Hausser, Helmut Schulz and Franz Grohmann in Russia during 1941. Grohmann later won the Knight's Cross and Helmut Schulz the German Cross in Gold. Below left, Hausser is awarded the Swords to his Knights Cross by Hitler.

Hausser (center) walks with an Army General and the head of the Leadership Main Office, Hans Jüttner (right) who was awarded the German Cross in Silver.

A humble Paul Hausser being awarded the Knight's Cross of the Iron Cross.

Two views of Hausser during a shooting competition with the officers of his corps command.

In conference with staff officers, Hausser (far right in both photos) listens to Otto Weidinger (far left) in the upper photo. Weidinger ended the war as commander of Regiment "Der Führer" and won the Knight's Cross with Oakleaves and Swords as well as the German Cross. For a time he was Hausser's divisional adjutant. In the lower photo Hausser sits with SS-Hauptsturmführer Walter Barnet and SS-Obersturmführer Albert Stahlmann.

(Above) From right are Jakob Fick, Hausser, Heinrich Himmler and Walter Krüger ("Das Reich" commander) during the summer of 1943. Fick, then leading the reconnaissance detachment, was awarded the Knight's Cross and ended the war a regimental commander with "Götz von Berlichingen." Right, Hausser speaks to Himmler as Krüger watches.

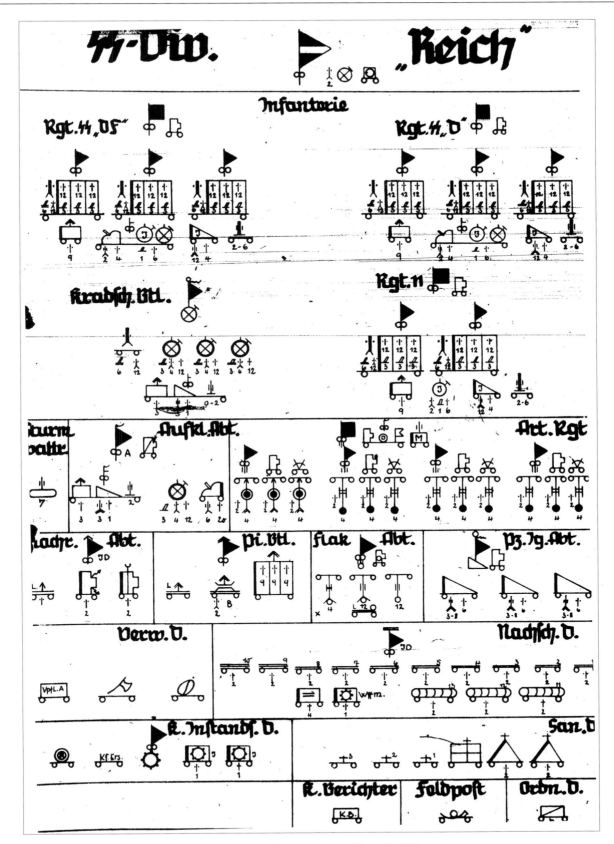

Paul Hausser's divisional command in April, 1941.

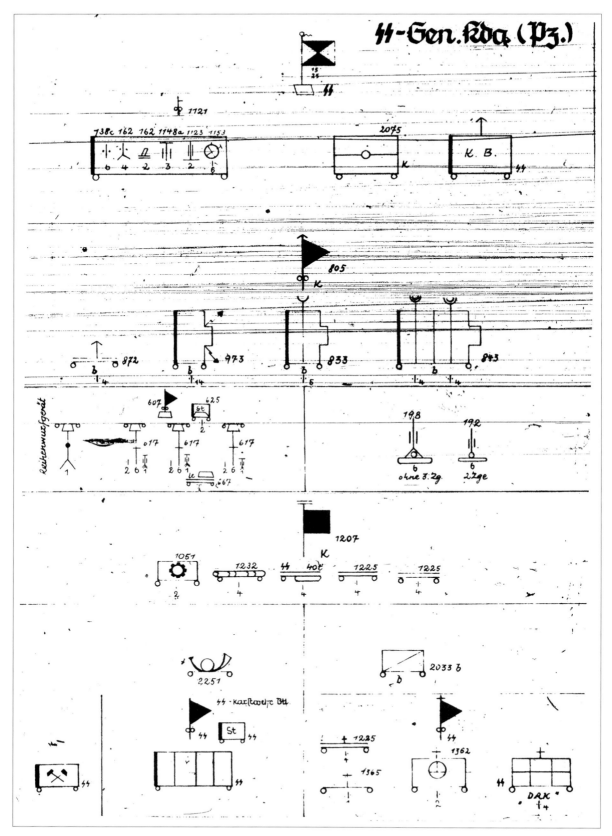

Components of the initial SS corps (SS-Generalkommando) which became II.SS-Panzer-Korps

NIKOLAUS HEILMANN

Born in Gundhelm on April 20, 1903, Nikolaus Heilmann was well educated and passed his exams to become a teacher. He joined the Schutzpolizei on April 1, 1925. Following an officer candidate course, he was commissioned as a Leutnant on April 1, 1929, then promoted to Oberleutnant on April 1, 1932.[1] In the Schutzpolizei he served as a platoon leader, adjutant and finally as a tactical instructor at the police officer school in Berlin-Köpenick.

During 1938, Heilmann served with the Army in Austria during March in the liaison staff of the Ordnungspolizei commander assigned to 2.Armeeoberkommando (Karl Pfeffer-Wildenbruch) and with Infanterie Regiment 94 in September/October.[2] On May 1, 1939, he joined the SS as an SS-Hauptsturmführer assigned to the auxiliary reserve unit of Oberabschnitt "Ost" located in the operational area of the 75.SS-Standarte.

Promoted to SS-Sturmbannführer on April 20, 1941, and to SS-Obersturmbannführer on January 5, 1942, (both being Allgemeine-SS rank), he joined Polizei-Schützen-Regiment 3 when it formed in October, 1939, eventually becoming regimental adjutant. Heilmann was the Ia of the Polizei Division from April 11, 1940, to the start of September, 1942. He won both Iron Crosses with this division, the 2nd class on June 27, 1940, and the 1st class on September 9, 1941. Promoted to Major der Polizei on April 20, 1941, and to Oberstleutnant der Polizei on January 5, 1942, he returned to the now-designated SS-Polizei Division, after recovery from illness, as Ia from January 30, 1943, to April 4, 1943.[3] While Ia, he also served as a temporary regimental commander for four weeks.[4]

Heilmann gave up his Polizei rank and took the rank of SS-Obersturmbannführer d.R. in the Waffen-SS on April 1, 1942, and was promoted to SS-Standartenführer on June 21, 1943. For brav-ery during his long service with the SS-Polizei Division, Heilmann was recommended for the German Cross in Gold by Alfred Wünnenberg. The award was granted on August 3, 1942, after approval of the following written endorsement:

"On September 9, 1941, the Polizei-Schützen-Regiment 1 had the assignment to attack from the area around Wyrise to the north and to take Ssussanino. Following strong enemy resistance, especially on the forest northeast of the Suida river, the attack, which began at 1600 hours, was stalled on the Suida river near Krasnizy and near Wikine. The situation was especially difficult because of this, because besides the strong pressure from enemy forces coming from the North and Northeast, there were still strong remnants of 3-4 divisions from the area around Lugi advancing to the north toward Vyriza. In front of these troops stood only weak security forces of the 8.Panzer-Division. Oberstleutnant Heilmann, therefore, personally advanced to the left of the deployed III./Polizei-Schützen-Regiment 1 near Virkono and called for the battalion to immediate attack. Under his brave leadership, a crossing over the Suide was successful and the strong positions on the edge of the forest north of the river were broken and the enemy was thrown from these positions. With that, Ssussanino was in our hands before nightfall at 1915 hours. Also with that the strongly-threat-

---

[1] "Lebenslaufbahn" dated July 12, 1939.
[2] "Bescheinigung" dated January 14, 1939.
[3] The text of his Knight's Cross recommendation only refers to the second period of his posting as Ia when he actually held the post twice.
[4] "Berförderung in der Waffen-SS" dated February 27, 1943, and signed by Alfred Wünnenberg.

ened right flank of the 269.Infanterie-Divison, which lay on the southern edge of Krasnogvrdeissk, was secured and the enemy was forced to retreat into an almost impassable swampy forested area.

During the successful battles to close the gap around Volchov, the enemy had interrupted the supply route to Gruppe "Kolberg," situated east of Wegeknick. Attacks to free the supply route were unsuccessful due to the numerically superior enemy forces. During the night of February 25/26, 1942, the enemy brought up strong forces and positioned them at their point of penetration with the intent to expand it to the East and West.

In conjunction with continuing enemy pressure near Trogubovo, the enemy's intentions were recognized. They intended on advancing over Frijatino to Trogubovo in order to close off our forces in the area of Olschevka and Spasskaja Polistj from their supply base. Statements by prisoners confirmed these intentions.

The Division, therefore, decided to have Gruppe "Kolberg" take the line extending from hill 37.0 to the northern edge of Boloto Nishuee to hill 36.1 and to advance it's right flank and take back Arning. At 1515 hours Kolberg received the order to reconnoiter hill 37.0. At 1730 hours the situation had developed such that the enemy, in the form of some 800 men equipped with twenty light machine guns, one hundred machine pistols and one light infantry gun (confirmed by statements made by prisoners) stood 1.7 km southwest of Prijutino. The possibility that Gruppe "Kolberg" could take back the objective became questionable !

The decision of the Ia, Oberstleutnant Heilmann, in absence of the divisional commander: find and contain the enemy in its flanks during its advance to the North with night patrol troop operations departing from General Haenicke's camp from the east with accompanying action from a combat engineer and construction company. At the same time a put-together company of construction engineers (made up of construction engineers from remnants of two construction companies and the divisional staff's construction company) south of Prijutino to hold up a further enemy advance on Frijutino, and in recognition of the new situation there, to secure the village of Frijutino itself.

During forceful action in the most difficult terrain (hip-high snow) the operation was successful. The enemy was tied up by the heavy attacks and its intentions spoiled. Also, the retaking of Frijutino over hill 37.0 by Gruppe "Kolberg," which began on February 27, 1942, at 1830 hours, was successful and was not influenced by the enemy.

Oberstleutnant Heilmann displayed the highest bravery during the hard battles for the closing of the Volchov Front from May 15, 1942, and afterwards. Many times he had crept

SS-Standartenführer Nikolaus Heilmann wearing both the Knight's Cross and German Cross in Gold.

to the front-most lines under heavy enemy pressure and reconnoitered the terrain from where he formulated his recommendations for the following day's attack plans.

Heilmann's spirited behavior and his resulting good relations with the fighting troops were essential requirements for the success of the Division. On March 23, 1942, the enemy was along the Erika-Vista and had broken through to the South. During the days thereafter the enemy attempted to spread out to the North and reopen supply lines. During these operations they employed their newest tanks (T-34s). Oberstleutnant Heilmann reconnoitered the situation in the presence of heavy weapons which were engaging the Russian tanks. After actions of an 8.8 cm gun and three light field howitzers in the battle area north of the Friedrich-Vista, they were successful in stopping the advancing enemy tank attack. They were also successful in disrupting enemy supply lines with the help of their forward artillery observers, which gave the Division a favorable starting point for a renewed advance on these supply lines. The reconnaissance operations were accomplished by Heilmann under strong and effective enemy pressure. It was here again that he distinguished himself by displaying special bravery."

From June to August, 1943, his personal records show he was assigned to "Das Reich," probably for staff training. In August, 1943, he was assigned as Chief of Staff of the new IV.SS-Panzer-Korps until October 8, 1943, when the entire Korps staff was incorporated into the VI.SS-Freiwilligen-Armee-Korps (lettische). Heilmann continued as Chief of Staff and did so until succeeded by German Cross in Gold holder Peter Sommer. Promoted to SS-Oberführer on February 11, 1944, he next succeeded Carl Graf von Pückler-Burghauss as commander of the 15.Waffen-Grenadier-Division der SS (lettische Nr. 1) from February 17, 1944, until relieved by Herbert von Obwurzer on July 21, 1944. From July 21, 1944, until August 12, 1944, he served as Chief of Staff in Herbert Otto Gille's reformed IV.SS-Panzer-Korps staff until succeeded by Manfred Schönfelder.[5]

Heilmann was awarded the Knight's Cross on August 23, 1944, for his command of this division from the following recommendation:

---

[5] Schönfelder won the Knight's Cross on February 23, 1944, as Ia of "Wiking." Awarded the German Cross in Gold on June 11, 1942, he ended the war as an SS-Obersturmbannführer and died on March 3, 1983.

"The 15.Waffen-Grenadier-Division der SS (lettische Nr. 1) had reached the planned positions on July 11, 1944, after long and difficult battles which required frequent changes in positions. The battles were fought against superior enemy infantry and tank forces. The result was strong enemy casualties. The Latvian infantry was, however, shaken by the continuing fighting of this type, and it could not be anticipated that a strong enemy attack would be met with any serious resistance.

Near the right neighbor (23.Infanterie-Division) the condition was OK, even though the division had suffered considerable casualties. Near the left neighbor (19.Waffen-Grenadier-Division der SS) there was panic due to a surprise enemy tank attack and a great part of the Latvian infantry was fleeing. The result of this was that the southern wing of the division no longer could be considered a secure front. Because of this fact, it had to be considered that continuing pressure on the 15.Waffen-Grenadier-Division der SS would result in it not being able to hold out. With that there was the danger that shortly the gap in the front would be ripped open. This would

The 14th Divisional Commanders Course held by the Army in the summer of 1944. Heilmann is in the back row, 2nd from right. The SS-Brigadeführer in the front may be Josef Grassy but this is unconfirmed.

enable the Russians to penetrate through to the important street intersection and the bridge in Opotschka would be free.

In this dangerous situation, SS-Oberführer Heilmann decided to force his division to hold the Oden forest position under all circumstances, to go to his companies and personally stop any retreat. That the 15.Waffen-Grenadier-Division der SS was able to put up a renewed resistance and did not lose contact with the neighboring divisions is due to the service of the few SS officers, NCOs and men under the leadership of the continually-proven SS-Oberführer Heilmann, commander of the Division. SS-Oberführer Heilmann pressed on from company to company in this difficult situation without consideration for himself; day and night during heavy artillery and infantry fire, in completely unobservable terrain and sometimes right through the center of the battles, where he forced the fleeing Latvian grenadiers and their leaders back to the front, partly by threatening them with violence, partly by words. His heroic action and his unbendable desire to resist is to be appreciated, that the wavering Latvian units held the fire and that the threatening Russian break-through to Opotschka in the section of the strongly hit 15.Waffen-Grenadier-Divisionder SS could be foiled, a breakthrough which could have produced disastrous results.

I consider SS-Oberführer Heilmann especially worthy of the Knight's Cross of the Iron Cross due to his proven excellent bravery and the timely-warded-off danger for the northern wing of the 16.Armee."[6]

Heilmann served in reserve for four months beginning August 12, 1944, during which he attended a divisional commanders course in Hirschberg, Silesia.

He took command of the formation staff of the 28.SS-Freiwilligen-Panzer-Grenadier-Division "Wallonien" on December 12, 1944.[7] Succeeding Karl Burk, he trained and led the division while Leon Degrelle led a separate Kampfgruppe in action. As commander of the division, Heilmann was killed in action at Mittwalde west of Schweibus on January 30, 1945.

Somewhat short-sighted politically, he was a well-trained and experienced staff officer with the Polizei Division, obviously brave in combat. Indifferent to the situation of the Latvian troops, he was a less-than-perfect-choice to command that division, although corps evaluations seemed satisfied with his performance. Nervous in intense command situations, he was often short-tempered and impatient. In addition to his other decorations, he was awarded the Eastern Front Medal (August 18, 1942), the Police Long Service Award in Bronze, and the medal of the German Lifesaving Association. He was married with two children.

---

[6] "Vorschlag für die Verleihung des Ritterkreuzes des Eisernen Kreuzes" dated July 24, 1944, signed by the commander of the VI.SS-Armee-Korps.
[7] "Personalverfügung" dated December 12, 1944, and "Stabsbefehl Nr. 1/45," dated January 14, 1945.

CONSTANTIN HELDMANN

The son of a government councellor, Constantin Heldmann was born in Detmold on March 7, 1893. He joined the Imperial Navy as a sea cadet in February, 1912, then transferred to the Army in June of 1913. After attending the War School at Anklam he was commissioned as a Leutnant. Throughout WWI he was posted to a Westfalian Infantry Regiment, No. 51. Achieving the rank of Oberleutnant, he was captured by the French and released in Switzerland in August, 1918, but it was another year before he returned to Germany. Heldmann won both classes of the Iron Cross, the Wound Badge in Black and the Lippe Service Cross 2nd class. From October, 1919, until leaving the Army in March, 1920, he served with the Freikorps "Gabcke."

As a civilian, he worked for an export company in Hamburg, visiting Africa and South America before working for an Ilgau-based company from 1925 to 1932. He joined the NSDAP on April 1, 1931, then the SS in March, 1933. Commissioned as an SS-Sturmführer on December 24, 1933, he was assigned to the staff of Abschnitt XIII and was posted as its Stabsführer on January 15, 1934. Promoted to SS-Obersturmführer on March 12, 1934, and to SS-Hauptsturmführer on June 17, 1934, he left his Stabsführer post on September 19, 1934, and took command of the 22.SS-Standarte from October 1, 1934, until October 1, 1935. Promoted to SS-Sturmbannführer on April 20, 1935, he served as special duties officer for Abschnitt XV during October, 1935, and then was Stabsführer of Abschnitt IX from November 1, 1935, until March 15, 1937. Heldmann also served in the Army for artillery training during various periods beginning in 1935 with the rank of Leutnant d.R. As a reserve officer he was assigned to Artillerie Regimenter 1 (Güstow) and 2 (Schwerin), as well as taking courses at the artillery school in Jüterbog in early 1939.

After promotion to SS-Obersturmbannführer on January 30, 1937, Heldmann served as a leader of a National Socialist camp in Tutzing from mid-March until the start of August, 1937. Heldmann then was promoted to Stabsführer of Oberabschnitt "Main" until July 1, 1939, when he took command of Abschnitt IX. He held that post until September 1, 1939, when he transferred as Stabsführer of Oberabschnitt "Mitte." He officially held that assignment until the start of February, 1943, but served with the Waffen-SS after November, 1939. In a similar manner, he was the official commander of Abschnitt IV from the start of February, 1943, until the end of the war. On September 11, 1938, he was promoted to Allgemeine-SS Standartenführer.

Heldmann joined the Waffen-SS as an SS-Hauptsturmführer d.R. on November 20, 1939, as a Batterie Chef with the SS-Artillerie-Ersatz-Abteilung. Promoted to SS-Sturmbannführer d.R. on December 13, 1939, he took command on that date of the SS-Totenkopf-Ersatz-Artillerie-Abteilung I and held command until the start of January, 1941. He then transferred to "Wiking" as the first commanding officer of its IV./Artillerie Regiment until the start of June, 1941, when he was succeeded by Kurt Brasack.

Moving to command an Abteilung, he went to the SS-Artillerie-Ersatz-Regiment from the start of June, 1941, to September 26, 1941. Heldmann then went north and commanded the I./Artillerie Regiment of Kampfgruppe "Nord" from late September, 1941, to July 15, 1942.[1] The battle group and the recently established division being separate, Heldmann also deputised for German Cross in Gold holder Friedrich Gutberlet, as commander of the new artillery

---

[1] Confirmed as such by the January 30, 1942 and April 20, 1942, issues of the SS "Dienstalterliste."

component formed for the division, from October, 1941, to March, 1942.[2] Returning to Germany, Heldmann commanded the SS-Artillerie-Ersatz-Regiment from July 15 to August 25, 1942.

Returning to Finland, Heldmann served with the Germanische Leitstelle of the SS-Hauptamt and was responsible for the replacements for and welfare of men in the SS Finnish Battalion. He held that assignment from August 25, 1942, until March 9, 1944, and was promoted to SS-Obersturmbannführer d.R. on April 20, 1943.

---

[2] He is listed as "Kdr. I/Art Rgt "Nord" in the January, 1942 and April, 1942, "Dienstalterliste." It is unknown who was in command of the new Gebirgs Artillerie Regiment ordered formed in Germany in the first week of December, 1941. Gutberlet's German Cross is not in Scheibert, Horst: "Die Träger des Deutschen Kreuzes in Gold." This book also does not include numerous German Crosses in Silver, indicated by symbol as awarded, shown in various issues of "Dienstalterliste." Additionally, personnel files were not consulted which add other names to the list of Gold awards.

[3] Unconfirmed sources list Heldmann as commander of the Brigade from August 20, 1944, to "the end of the war" but this discounts the assignment of a divisional designation to the unit.

In his final operational area Heldmann served in Italy. From early March, 1944, to the end of the war he was Inspektor of heavy weapons attached to the Supreme SS and Police Leader for Italy, Karl Wolff. He also was Ia of the Waffen-Grenadier-Brigade der SS (italienische Nr. 1) from early September, 1944, until January, 1945.[3] Heldmann also served as deputy commander to Otto Jungkunz from November, 1944. He took command of the 29.Waffen-Grenadier-Division der SS (italienische Nr. 1) from February 15, 1945, until the end of the war. Heldmann was awarded both classes of the Iron Cross, the War Service Cross 2nd class, the Knight's Cross with Swords of the Order of the Finnish Lion, the Finnish Freedom Cross 3rd class and the Finnish Frontfighters Service Cross. He was described by Otto Jungkunz as a man of exemplary temperment and character, solving a rumored alcohol problem he had in Finland. Heldmann married the daughter of one of his employers in January, 1927. His eventual fate is unknown at the time of this writing.

RICHARD HERMANN

Richard Herrmann, the first Waffen-SS General killed in action, was born in Gruenberg on December 20, 1895. He joined the Army on August 18, 1914, with Infantry Regiment No. 143, a unit originally from Lower Silesia. Later serving with a Pommeranian unit, he was posted to Infantry Regiment "von der Marwitz," being awarded both classes of the Iron Cross, the Wound Badge in Silver, the Hessen Bravery Medal and the Hessen Iron Cross in World War I. Remaining in the Army after the war, he served from the end of 1918 to May 20, 1920, on the eastern border with the 35th Infantry Division. Herrmann than moved to a machine gun company in Eutin until leaving the Army on October 1, 1920.

He joined the Landespolizei as a Leutnant in Hessen after leaving the Army and eventually became a Hauptmann der Landespolizei, attended the higher police school in Berlin during 1926. Leaving the Landespolizei at the beginning of February, 1929, Herrmann joined the NSDAP on September 1, 1930. He served the NSDAP in Swabia as an area leader and district speaker until the start of July, 1931.

On July 1, 1931, Richard Herrmann joined the SA and was working as a merchant. He served as Stabsführer to SA-Gruppe "Hochland" until 1934, then led the 86.SA Brigade until January 27, 1937. He transferred to the SS on January 27, 1937, with the rank of SS-Brigadeführer with seniority from January 15, 1934. As head of the German national basketball and handball associations until 1938, he also headed the sports office in the SS-Hauptamt from late January, 1937 to early September, 1939. Herrmann was similarly involved with Sipo and SD sports from March, 1937, to June, 1940. Recalled to the available Army officer list in 1939 as a Hauptmann d.R., he led the 7.SS-Totenkopfstandarte from September 6, 1939, to June 8, 1940, when succeeded by Hans Scheider.[1] Herrman next served as the Befehlshaber der Waffen-SS "Nord" from June 12, 1940, until May 25, 1941.

Given the rank of SS-Brigadeführer und Generalmajor der Waffen-SS on June 21, 1940, Richard Herrmann was also the first commander of an SS mountain formation when he took command of SS-Kampfgruppe "Nord" after it formed on February 28, 1941.[2] Leading the group until May 25, 1941, he was dismissed from his command as a result of the unit's poor unit performance during the march from Norway to Finland. Transferred to command a component assigned to the Kommandostab "Reichsführer-SS," he was given leadership of the 1.SS-Brigade which was later designated as the 1.SS-Infanterie-Brigade (mot). Herrman led this unit in combat during the first Russian campaign from June 25, 1941, until killed in action in Russia on December 27, 1941.[3]

A professional soldier in the infantry without a background or training in mountain troops, his failure with the "Nord" battle group was understandable. In the pre-war years he was obviously an athlete and sportsman. He seems to have been far more effective with his motorized infantry command which followed. Herrmann was awarded the bar to his WWI Iron Cross 2nd class in 1940, the War Service Cross with Swords in 1939 and the Olympic Games Decoration 1st class.

---

[1] For Scheider's biography see volume 2 ("Nord").

[2] Bender/Taylor, volume 2, page 148 and Mollo, Andrew: "Uniforms of the SS" volume 7, page 61.

[3] His Brigade command was effective May 25, 1941, but it is logical to assume he did remain in Finland until his successor, Carl-Maria Demelhuber, arrived in mid-June. Schreiber, Franz: "Kampf unter dem Nordlicht," pages 35 and 39. Published sources state Walter Krüger briefly led the Brigade while the two men exchanged posts. "Unsere Ehre heisst Treue," page 21, a heavily-edited copy of the Kommandostab "Reichsführer-SS" war diaries.

The commander and staff of Kampfgruppe "Nord." SS-Brigadeführer Richard Herrmann is in the front row, center.

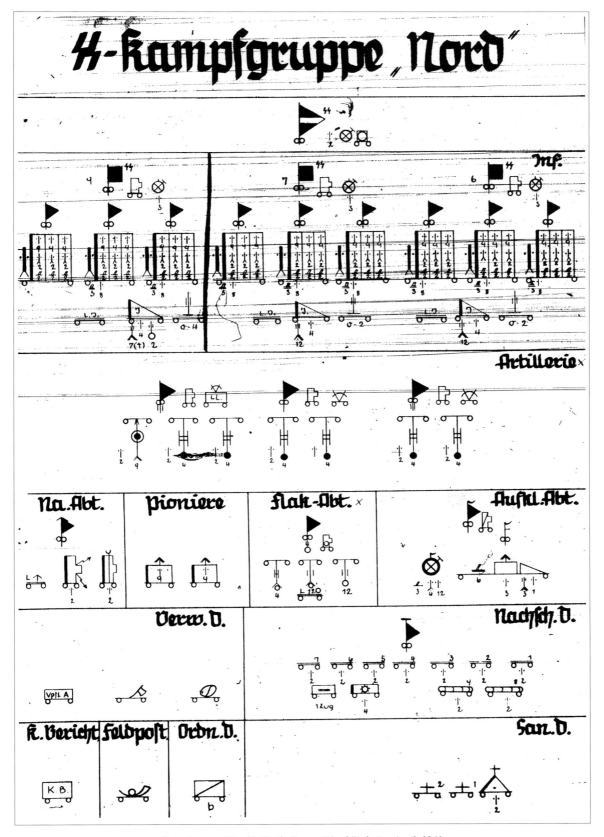

Kampfgruppe "Nord" (Battle Group "North") during April, 1941.

FRIEDRICH JECKELN

Friedrich Jeckeln was born the son of a factory worker on February 2, 1895. He studied engineering before joining the Army in August, 1914. During World War I he served with Baden Field Artillery Regiment 76 and Fusilier Regiment "Fürst Karl Anton von Hohenzollern" No. 40. Jeckeln also trained as a pilot. He left the military in 1920 as a Leutnant having won the Iron Cross 2nd class, the Wound Badge in Black, the Baden Service Medal and had been placed on the Army Honor Roll.

After serving with eastern border protection troops during 1920, Jeckeln worked for his grandfather. He was involved with the Young German Order from 1922 to 1924.[1] Marrying for the second time in July, 1929, he lived off his new wife's income beginning in 1928. Jeckeln never fulfilled his financial obligations to the three children he had in his first marriage, prompting his ex-wife to complain directly to Hitler in February, 1932. Jeckeln's response blamed his former father-in-law, claiming he was a Jew (obviously of no relevance). In total he fathered nine children.

On October 1, 1929, Jeckeln joined the NSDAP and held a seat in the Reichstag representing South Hannover from July, 1932, to November, 1933. His seat then represented East Hannover until the end of the war. He also joined the Allgemeine-SS as an SS-Sturmbannführer on March 15, 1930. Jeckeln first led the I./12.SS-Standarte from March 15, 1930, to June 22, 1931. Promoted to SS-Standartenführer on June 22, 1931, he was entrusted with the ad-ministrative formation of the 17.SS-Standarte, while also commanding the 12.SS-Standarte from June 22, 1931, to September 20, 1931.

Promoted to SS-Oberführer on September 20, 1931, he was given command of Abschnitt IV from that day until January 30, 1933, when succeeded by Berthold Maack so he could assume command of SS Gruppe "Süd."[2] He was promoted to SS-Gruppenführer on February 4, 1933, then to SS-Obergruppenführer on September 13, 1936. After leaving his "Süd" post on July 15, 1933, Jeckeln was without an SS assignment for three weeks. In June, 1933, he also was a regional advisor and head of the Landespolizei for the state of Braunschweig. Given the rank of Oberstleutnant der Schutzpolizei on October 1, 1933, Jeckeln led SS Gruppe "Nordwest" from August 10, 1933, until July 9, 1940, when succeeded by Günther Pancke.[3] On January 30, 1939, he was given the Gold Party Badge. Jeckeln also held the post of Higher SS and Police Leader "Center" from June 28, 1938 to July 11, 1940. Moving to Oberabschnitt "West," he was commander from July 12, 1940, officially until June 29, 1941, as well as being the Higher SS and Police Leader for the same area. Jeckeln actually left these posts in the hands of substitutes after May 1, 1941, as he prepared for police duties in Russia.

During the Western Campaign of 1940, he saw combat commanding the I./SS-Totenkopf-Infanterie-Regiment 2 with the "Totenkopf" Division. In May, 1941, he was with Himmler's personal staff and the head of the Sipo and SD to plan operations in Russia. Jeckeln then took up his first command post in the East. On April 1, 1941, he was promoted to General der Polizei.

---

[1] Almost every political and religious organization of the period had a youth group. Among the largest was the Catholic school-aged New Germany ("Neudeutschland") and the Steel Helmet Youth ("Stahlhelmjugend") of the WWI veterans group, the Stahlhelm. The Pathfinders ("Pfadfinder") were the German equivalent of the Boy Scouts. When the Hitler Youth became the only legal youth group in Germany in 1936, all the existing groups were assimilated, dissolved or went underground.

[2] Maack's biography will be in volume 2, as he was the last commander of the 20.Waffen-Grenadier-Division der SS (estnische Nr. 2).

[3] The command was redesignated as Oberabschnitt "Nordwest" in mid-November, 1933, and was retitled Oberabschnitt "Mitte" on April 1, 1936. Yerger, "Allgemeine-SS," page 91.

Heinrich Himmler (foreground in both photos) gives a speech to the first class of SS-Führerschule Braunschweig. In the top photo Jeckeln is to the right of Himmler and beside him is Karl Wolff. Below, Jeckeln is 3rd from right while Wolff is 2nd from right.

A formal and an informal portrait of Friedrich Jeckeln. On the left he wears the earlier style SS-Obergruppenführer insignia and on the right displays the post-1941 collar insignia of the same rank.

On June 23, 1941, he was transferred as the Higher SS and Police Leader for South Russia and held that post until switching commands with Hans-Adolf Prützmann.[4] Jeckeln then assumed his new post as Higher SS and Police Leader for North Russia on November 1, 1941, until mid-January, 1945. His commands in Russia were especially brutal. Under his leadership, mass executions took place on numerous occasions, especially with his command in South Russia which included units of the Ordnungspolizei and foreign volunteer battalions. At Kamenets-Podolsky, Jeckeln's units killed 23,600 people in August, 1941.[5] In a ravine in Kiev on September 29/30, 1941, another 33,000 people were executed, one of the most infamous (but not the largest) killings undertaken by a Higher SS and Police Leader in Russia.[6] In Dnepropetrovsk, 15,000 were killed during October, 1941, and a further 15,000 were executed in Rovno

on November 7/8, immediately after Jeckeln took over Prützmann's command.[7] Jeckeln was awarded a clasp to his WWI Iron Cross 2nd class in October, 1941, the Iron Cross 1st class on May 12, 1942, the Wound Badge in Silver on June 27, 1942, and the Eastern Front Medal on July 29, 1942. He was also given both classes of the War Merit Cross with Swords.

Becoming more involved with anti-partisan operations, Jeckeln commanded an anti-partisan Kampfgruppe named for himself from February 17, 1942 to August 13, 1942, in the area south of Leningrad where he was wounded in June.[8] Wishing to be a successful "com-

---

[4] His Oberabschnitt "West" command overlapped his new post in Russia on paper though a substitute obviously performed the duties in Germany, no doubt his Ia.

[5] Operational Situation Report Number 80 dated September 11, 1941. Jeckeln's total killings in the month of August were more than 44,000 according to the report.

[6] Jeckeln's command was assisted by Einsatzkommando 4a from Einsatzgruppe C. Operational Report USSR Number 101 dated October 2, 1941.

[7] Operational Report USSR Number 135 dated November 19, 1941, reports that Jeckeln killed 10,000 in Dnepropetrovsk on October 13th according to Sonderkommando 4a. The Rovno incident is in Operational Report USSR Number 143 dated December 8, 1941.

[8] The battle group was ordered formed on February 17, 1942, with Jeckeln as commander and began operations on March 4. It consisted of a mixture of SS, Army and Ordnungspolizei units: Infanterie Regiment 320 (three Bataillone and two support Kompanien), Ordnungspolizei Bataillone 56, 121, 305, 306, 310, V./Leibstandarte, Aufklärungsabteilung 158, Freiwilligen-Legion "Norwegen," Panzerjäger Abteilung 158, seven infantry gun platoons from the 58.Infanterie-Division, four infantry gun platoons from the SS-Polizei-Division, two Batterien of Artillerie Regiment 158, and the Artillerie Regiment of the SS-Polizei-Division. Kriegstabebuch Nr. 1, Kampfgruppe "Jeckeln," 4.3.1942-13.8.1942.

Waffen-Gruppenführer Rudolf Bangerskis (Inspector General, Latvian Legion) and SS-Obergruppenführer Friedrich Jeckeln listen to Waffen-Oberführer Arthur Silgailis.
Dated September 19, 1944, the photo was taken at the headquarters of Kampfgruppe "Jeckeln" near the Latvian border. A biography for Silgailis will be in volume 2.

bat" commander, he formed another Kampfgruppe in November, 1943, but it never saw action. He was awarded the German Cross in Gold on December 19, 1943, for anti-partisan operations in Staraja Russa, during Operation "Heinrich"(anti-partisan attacks), and leadership of the Orpo units under his command in the Newel. The award was made even though the formal recommendation was not submitted by Army Group "North" until May, 1944.[9]

Jeckeln also served as head of the Replacements Inspection for Russia from January, 1944, to January, 1945. A third Kampfgruppe "Jeckeln" was formed in early July, 1944, to assist the 11.Armee in Latvia combating partisans, with Jeckeln himself leading it until the final weeks before it dissolved at the end of August, 1944. For that command, he was awarded the Knight's Cross on September 5, 1944, which had been approved on August 27th as a result of the following recommendation by the commanders of Army Group "North" ("Nord") and 18th Army (18.Armee):[10]

"On August 16, 1944, SS-Obergruppenführer and General of the Police Jeckeln immediately and independently decided to switch over from the defense and to counter-attack the enemy. Enemy forces had engaged in a heavy attack, succeeding in breaking into the positions of the battle group's Latvian units. He exposed his left flank and left several other positions weak without regard so that the counter-attack could proceed. As a shining example of personal bravery while at the lead of his men, he successfully threw back broken-in enemy forces and the front was once again firm in his hands. Through his energy and lack of regard for his own person, this clever counterattack, which he personally led, prevented the Russians from advancing into the positions of the 122.Jäger Division which would have ripped open the front in the area of the Romanian 38.Armee Korps. Due to this decisive action and his continuous service as a leader, as well as his personal preparedness for battle, I hold SS-Obergruppenführer Jeckeln as worthy to be awarded the Knight's Cross."

The preliminary recommendation submitted by the commander of the 18.Armee was also seconded by the commander of Heeresgruppe "Nord" as follows:

"I hold SS-Obergruppenführer Jeckeln to be exceptionally worthy of the award of the Knight's Cross. The action he displayed within the 18.Armee was of wide-reaching significance - for the Army Group as well. Only his continuous presence and personal action at the front lines enabled this important success to be achieved. SS-Obergruppenführer Jeckeln had already distinguished himself through excellent, clever and dashing leadership, most recently in the area of Mitau-Schaulen. He is to be recognized as the reason that the strong and surprise enemy tank advances during the last weeks of July, the goal of which was to cross the Mitau and advance into Riga, could be stopped."

Although appointed as the Higher SS and Police Leader for Belgium and France, Jeckeln remained in Russia and the post was run by substitutes. On July 1, 1944, he was given the rank of General der Waffen-SS. On October 15, 1944, his house and all his family's possessions were destroyed in an air raid. Returning from Russia in mid-January, 1945, Jeckeln oversaw the replacement units within the area of the Higher SS and Police Leader Southeast until mid-February, 1945. On February 15, 1945, Himmler gave Jeckeln command of the V.SS-Freiwilligen-Gebirgs-Korps which he led until the end of the war.[11] The commander of Army Group "Center" recommended him for the Oakleaves on February 14, 1945, for his leadership on the Oder Front and in the Breslau area where his command included Alarm Units, Hitler Youth and Volkssturm.[12] He was the 802nd person awarded the Oakleaves on March 8, 1945. Having no formal military training and even less actual tactical skills, the award can be assumed to represent the efforts of the troops under his command.

Never a professional military officer, he was an example of the pre-1933 SS street fighters of the Allgemeine-SS, being fully involved in early political infighting in Brunswick. A radical and brutal supporter of Himmler's policies in Russia, his actions there were among the most destructive in terms of human life. Crude, short-tempered and cruel, he was close friends with Theodor Eicke and supplied Eicke's command with supplies captured as a result of his operations in Russia. His irrational, spur-of-the-moment decisions were regularly made without considering the long-term effect. Jeckeln's arrogance also brought an order from Himmler to take several weeks leave in July, 1944, after arguing with Walter Krüger, his more knowledgable superior in military matters. The conflict was over the formation of the VI.Waffen-Armee-Korps der SS (lettische) which was supposed to see operations in his area.

Jeckeln was captured by the Russians at the end of the war. Extensively interrogated, he was tried in Riga, Latvia, on February 3, 1946. He was hanged the same day.

---

[9] "Nachträglicher-Vorschlag Nr. (Blank) für die Verleihung des Deutschen Kreuzes in Gold" approved on December 19, 1943, but formally submitted on May 23, 1944.

[10] Telex recommendation by the commander of Army Group "North" dated August 17, 1944.

[11] The text of his Oakleaves recommendation gives February 8, 1945, as the start of his command period.

[12] "Vorschlag" for the Oakleaves submitted on February 14, 1945, and approved on March 8, 1945.

OTTO JUNGKUNZ

The son of a businessman, Otto Jungkunz was born in Würzburg on July 23, 1892. After training as a technical engineer he joined the Army on October 1, 1913, with Bavarian Infantry Regiment "Wrede." Promoted to Unteroffizier in July, 1914, he served with the machine gun company of the unit and then transferred to a reserve infantry regiment. Promoted to Vize-Feldwebel d.R., he ended his service with the 23rd Bavarian Infantry Regiment "Konig Ferdinand der Bulgaren" and left the Army on March 1, 1919. Awarded both classes of the Iron Cross and the Bavarian Service Cross 2nd class, he was also wounded twice and received the Wound Badge in Black.

From April 15, 1919 to July 5, 1919, Jungkunz served with a Freikorps unit in Würzburg and then worked there as an engineer. He joined the SS as a candidate on October 1, 1931, and the NSDAP on January 1, 1932. Promoted to SS-Scharführer on July 8, 1932, to SS-Truppführer on October 9, 1932, to SS-Obertruppführer on October 15, 1933, Jungkunz was commissioned as an SS-Sturmführer on November 9, 1933.

From mid-October, 1933, to the end of February, 1934, he led the 5./I./56.SS-Standarte. On March 1, 1934, he took command of the 51.SS-Standarte and led the unit until April 1, 1936.[1] Promoted to SS-Obersturmführer on April 5, 1934, to SS-Hauptsturmführer on June 18, 1934, to SS-Sturmbannführer on November 9, 1934, to SS-Obersturmbannführer on November 9, 1935, and to SS-Standartenführer on April 1, 1936, he commanded SS Abschnitt VI from April 1, 1936, to March 21, 1938. During that time Jungkunz also served in the Army reserve with the cavalry school in Hannover

and eventually was promoted to Leutnant d.R. On April 20, 1937, he received his final Allgemeine-SS promotion to SS-Oberführer.

From March 21, 1938, until the end of the war he was the official commander of Abschnitt VIII but served with the Waffen-SS beginning on February 15, 1940. He left the Army reserve on that date and joined the Waffen-SS as an SS-Hauptsturmführer d. R. in command of the SS Kraftfahr-Ersatz-Abteilung. Commanding that detachment until mid-August 1942, Jungkunz was promoted to SS-Sturmbannführer d.R. on August 1, 1940, to SS-Obersturmbannführer d.R. on April 20, 1941, and to SS-Standartenführer d.R. on August 10, 1942, he was held in reserve in the latter half of August, 1942, and then was garrison and headquarters commander at Himmler's eastern headquarters in Hegewald in the Ukraine until January 12, 1944.

Promoted to SS-Oberführer d.R. on April 20, 1943, he went to the SS-Personalhauptamt in January, 1944, as a reserve officer with the staff detachment. After being added to the paper "Stabsabteilung im SS-Personalhauptamt" composed of Waffen-SS men assigned to the Allgemeine-SS, he was assigned to Karl Wolff's Supreme SS and Police Leader command. In Italy, Jungkunz took command of the 1.Sturmbrigade italienische Freiwilligen Legion in late January, 1944, succeeding Peter Hansen.[2] This developed into the Waffen-Grenadier-Brigade der SS on September 7, 1944, and he remained commander when it was further expanded become the 29.Waffen-Grenadier-Division der SS (italienische Nr. 1). Jungkunz held command until February 15, 1945. He officially turned over command to his previous brigade Ia and designated deputy,

---

[1] "SS-Personalbefehl" Nr. 12 dated April 6, 1934, effective March 1.

[2] According to Hausser, "Soldaten Wie Andere auch," page 428, its designation in February, 1944, was the 1.Italienische Frei.-Sturm-Brigade Milizia Armata (Pol).

Constantin Heldmann. For the remainder of the war he served in the Führungshauptamt as the chief technical advisor in Amt VIII (Arms Office).

Awarded a clasp to his WWI Iron Cross 2nd class on February 15, 1945, both classes of the War Service Cross with Swords (January 30, 1941 and January 30, 1943), Jungkunz also was awarded the NSDAP Long Service Award in Bronze and the Reich's Sports Badge in Gold. Married, with no children, he died on June 9, 1945.

HANS KEMPIN

The son of merchant Willi Kempin, Hans Kempin was born in Berlin-Lichtenberg on June 7, 1913. Following his education he obtained a position in the banking business in 1928 where he remained until assuming a full-time paid SS career beginning in March, 1935. He joined the SA in September, 1930, and the NSDAP on December 1, 1930. Kempin left the SA in July, 1932, and joined the SS.[1]

Assigned to the 1.Motorsturm of the 44.SS-Standarte in Eberswalde, he stayed with this Allgemeine-SS unit through basic training and officially was an SS-Mann in November, 1932. Kempin transferred to the Sonderkommando "Jüteborg" when it formed on July 8, 1933. The unit was dissolved on October 7, 1933, and incorporated into the "Adolf-Hitler-Standarte." Kempin thus became one of the earliest members of what developed into the "Leibstandarte." He was promoted to SS-Rottenführer on December 1, 1933, then remained with the elite Leibstandarte SS "Adolf Hitler" until the end of March, 1934.

Kempin was selected to attend the first class at SS-Führerschule Bad Tölz, with courses beginning on April 1, 1934. In the latter stages of the course, Paul Hausser visited the school for a tour prior to establishment of the initial class at SS-Führerschule Braunschweig. It was during that period that Kempin met his most influential superior for the first time. The basic classes ended on December 22, 1934, followed by a platoon leaders class in Munich with members of I./SS-Standarte "Deutschland" until the end of February, 1935. On March 1, 1935, he was assigned to 13./SS-Standarte "Deutschland" as a platoon leader and was formally commissioned as an SS-Untersturmführer in Berlin on April 20, 1935.

Returning to "Deutschland," he served under the commander of I.Bataillon, Ritter von Hengl, until early November, 1935, as a platoon leader in 1.Kompanie. His own command style was developed from the example of von Hengl.[2]

Transferring to SS-Führerschule Braunschweig on November 4, 1935, Kempin served as a machine gun tactics and weapons instructor at the facility until the end of January, 1938. On April 20, 1936, he was promoted to SS-Obersturmführer. This period also allowed Kempin the advantage of more personal command instruction by Paul Hausser. On February 1, 1938, he moved to Regiment "Germania" and was commander of the 1.Kompanie soon after his arrival. Kempin remained there until after the Polish campaign and was promoted to SS-Hauptsturmführer on June 30, 1939.

When the initial SS division began forming in October, 1939, Kempin transferred back to SS-Regiment "Der Führer" as commander of 1.Kompanie. He led this unit in the Western Campaign of 1940 and was awarded the Iron Cross 2nd class on May 30, 1940, for combat in the Arras area. During the mid-June fighting in the Plateau von Langres area, he took command of the 13.Kompanie and was awarded the Iron Cross 1st class as its commander on July 20, 1940. Kempin retained the command until the initial stages of the first Russian campaign. For combat in 1940, he was also awarded the Infantry Assault Badge and the Wound Badge in Black.

In Russia, Kempin briefly led II./"Deutschland" during July, 1941, then took command of III./"Der Führer." Promoted to SS-Sturmbannführer on September 1, 1941, he was wounded in the left leg two days later and recovered in Stralsund. With his brother

---

[1] "Lebenslaufbahn," "Stammrollen" and letter to the author dated October 8, 1986.

[2] Letters to the author from Herrn Kempin dated April 2 and October 18, 1987. Transferring to the Army, von Hengl won the Knight's Cross on August 25, 1941, as an Oberstleutnant in command of Gebirgsjäger Regiment 137 and ended the war as a General der Gebirgsjäger.

Hans Kempin (left) as an SS-Obersturmführer while an instructor at SS-Junkerschule Braunschweig wearing "B" collar insignia and (right) as an SS-Hauptsturmführer explaining a tactical situation to Army officers in Russia while a battalion commander in Regiment "Der Führer." The "SS3" collar insignia denotes that regiment.

having been killed in Greece with the "Leibstandarte," Kempin was a last surviving son and so according to then current regulations was assigned as an instructor after his recovery.[3] At SS-Junkerschule Bad Tölz he was assigned as a Lehrgruppenkommandeur from February 20, 1942, until April 15, 1942.[4] During that time his primary class was a police officer course attended by former cadets to teach them motorized tactics for replacing their horse-drawn operational experience with the Polizei Division. Kempin then transferred to Braunschweig and assumed a similar teaching post there until the end of 1942.

On January 1, 1943, Kempin replaced Ernst Schützeck as commander of the SS-Unterführerschule "Posen-Treskau," despite his relatively junior rank.[5] He actually received his orders to assume the command via telephone. Immediatly travelling to Paris for a

three week detachment leaders course for fast mobile troops, he only held command of the school for four months until being given a larger assignment. His first NCO class, all volunteers from the Reich Labor Service, had created an excellent impression. Succeeded by Erich Schimmelpfennig, Kempin transferred to the SS-Truppenübungsplatz "Beneschau" and took command of the SS-Panzer-Grenadier-Schule effective May 1, 1943.[6]

Assigned to what would be his most challenging command, Kempin was posted as the commander of the newly established SS-Panzer-Grenadier-Schule "Kleinschlag" in Prossnitz. Kempin created and developed the training facility, units and programs. He also oversaw the completion of building the actual school and himself taught classes. Among the units and training created were those for armored infantry units (both ground troops as well as vehicle

---

[3] Letter to the author from Herrn Kempin dated April 2, 1987.
[4] "Personalverfügung" dated February 19, 1942.
[5] "Personalverfügung" dated January 12, 1943.

[6] "Personalverfügung" dated April 27, 1943. Posen-Treskau became an officer training school after Braunschweig was destroyed in an air raid, the NCO school moving to Laibach in Yugoslavia.

(Above) Kempin awarding Iron Crosses to the men of his command during August, 1941, and (below) the temporary headquarters of his command at the same time. Kempin sits at right.

(Left) The headquarters at the SS-Panzer-Grenadier school Kleinschlag and (right) the SS NCO school Posen-Treskau with its first class on parade.

commanders), sharpshooting and sniper training and instruction of foreign personnel, both officers and officer candidates. The school maintained operational examples of all tank types for training including T-34s sent to the school by Paul Hausser after Kharkow. Kempin and his staff also evaluated the MP-43/44 assault guns and hosted numerous senior commanders or officials who toured the facility, the largest of its type. The school also was used for the development of tactics such as a counter to the allied use of flame-thrower tanks in Normandy. With 220 officers and an average of 22,000 trainees at a given time, the command numerically equalled that of a division. On December 1, 1943, Kempin was promoted to SS-Obersturmbannführer.

In 1944, Kempin began submitting requests to the senior Waffen-SS commander of the area, Carl Graf von Pückler-Burghauss, requesting transfer to a front-line unit. Those requests were repeatedly denied by Pückler-Burghauss due to a replacement of Kempin's ability being unavailable, as well as Kempin's last surviving son status.[7] On April 20, 1944, Kempin was awarded the War Merit Cross I class with Swords but it would be more than ten months before his requests for a front-line command were finally approved. On February 17, 1945, after the bombing of Dresden, he handed command of the school to Wilhelm Trabandt, who led it until the facility dissolved into several late-war Kampfgruppen.

Kempin immediatly went to the front, assigned to quickly establish and lead the Army's 547.Volksgrenadier Division composed of remnants of units from the Kurland battles. At that time he was promoted to SS-Standartenführer by Hasso von Manteuffel by order of Heinrich Himmler as Heeresgruppe commander.[8] Sent to the Oder Front to assist and relieve the forces of Otto Skorzeny, his command lasted only a month before Kempin came into personal

conflict with the NSDAP Gauleiter for the area. He was replaced and ordered into Fortress Frankfurt/Oder without a command as an individual soldier. The political official's order was ignored by Hasso von Manteuffel (3.Armee) and Theodor Busse (Heeresgruppe "Süd") who wished him to remain a divisional commander. Kempin was ordered to Fortress Frankfurt/Oder as commander of the 32.SS-Freiwilligen-Grenadier-Division "30 Januar" as a replacement for Adolf Ax in mid-March, 1945.

Kempin's small and often-divided command spent some of the final weeks of the war in the area of the XI.SS-Panzer-Korps as flank protection, often unable to contact or locate corps commander Matthias Kleinheisterkamp's headquarters. Kempin's unit covered the withdrawal of 9.Armee towards the west in pursuit by massive Russian forces. After his few surviving troops escaped encirclement towards Halbe and the area of 12.Armee, he released the 148 men remaining in his command of their obligation to fight south of Tangermünde at Jerichow and surrendered to the US Army on May 7, 1945.[9]

Kempin was interrogated and badly treated in several camps, eventually ending up at the prisoner-of-war camp in Hannover-Buchholz. When he was to be handed over to the Russians he escaped and had to remain in hiding for two years until exonerated from any possible guilt or extradition to Russia.[10] Kempin became a farmer, eventually owning one of the most technically advanced farms in West Germany, and was often visited by foreign agricultural experts. Married on July 25, 1938, Hans Kempin died in Evessen on November 30, 1992.

Among the most influential training officers and arms school commanders, he has been recognized as one of the best battalion commanders of Regiment "Der Führer," both with regard to lead-

---

[7] "Beurteilungsnotiz" dated November 6, 1944, and written by Pückler-Burghauss.

[8] Letters to the author dated September 15, 1985, October 18, 1987 and September 16, 1989.

[9] Letters to the author from Herrn Kempin dated July 9, 1986 and April 2, 1987.

[10] Letter to the author from Herrn Kempin dated August 10, 1987.

A formal portrait of SS-Sturmbannführer Hans Kempin.

ership as well as bravery, especially at Jelnja. He was deserving of higher decorations for his leadership in Russia during the first Russian campaign according to subordinates of all ranks and higher officers were impressed with both his school assignments and commands.[11] Kempin held more senior commands, with two schools and two divisions, then any other SS officer school graduate. Physically impressive, he presented a gentleman's military bearing and remained in contact with the men of his Regiment "Der Führer" commands until his death.

---

[11] "Beförderung in der Waffen-SS" submitted by the SS-Führungshauptamt and dated July 26, 1943. "Beurteilung" dated September 22, 1942, by the commander's office of SS-Junkerschule Braunschweig. Also testimony of drivers, platoon leaders and junior officers of his command in the possession of the author, all of whom had been under Kempin's command from the Western Campaign into Russia.

(Below) Kempin (2nd from left) greets Carl Graf von Pückler-Burghauss during a visit to Kleinschlag. Note the command car pennants and license plate. Pückler-Burghauss will have a biography in volume 2. Right, Kempin reviews the honor platoon of the 4th Company at Posen-Treskau in mid-1943.

(Above) Kempin shows a captured U.S. Grant tank to Paul Hausser during an inspection of the SS-Panzer Grenadier School. Below, earlier in the Western campaign he sits (center) with men of 5./Deutschland.

Kempin gives at lecture at Kleinschlag, acting as both a teacher and the administrator at the facility.

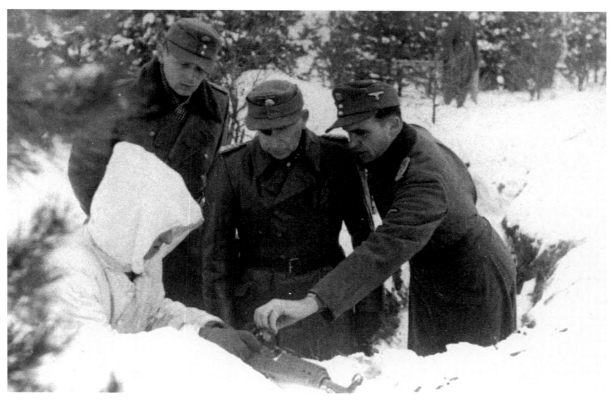

(Above) Kempin (left) with Paul Hausser (center) and Josef Leitner at Kleinschlag during a winter visit by Hausser. Below, Kempin (tallest) gives a tour of Kleinschlag to SS-Obergruppenführer Karl-Hermann Frank (beside Kempin with overseas cap) and Carl Oberg (foreground).

Kempin takes a break following a lecture and (right) he walks with Paul Hausser, the most personally influential officer he met during his career.

A portrait of Kempin as an SS-Sturmbannführer. On the right, he is with SS-Obergruppenführer Arthur Phleps and SS-Standartenführer Otto Kumm during a visit to the school. Phleps and Kumm will have a biography in volume 2. At the time of the photo they respectively were the commander and chief of staff of the V.SS-Gebirgs-Korps.

An autographed photo of SS-Sturmbannführer Hans Kempin.

GEORG KEPPLER

Georg Keppler, the son of Army officer Oberst Otto Keppler, was born in Mainz on May 7, 1884. After passing his Abitur, he joined the Army as a Fahnenjunker on February 28, 1913. Assigned to a unit originally from Hannover, he served with Fusilier Regiment "Generalfeldmarschall Prinz Albrecht von Preussen" No. 73 until wounded on August 29, 1914. He ended his posting with that unit as regimental adjutant. After attending the War School in Glogau during October, 1913, to May, 1914, he was commissioned as a Leutnant on June 19, 1914.

Following recovery from the wounds he received at St. Quentin, he was reassigned to the 39th Infantry Brigade and then the 19th Reserve Division from 1915 to November, 1918. Promoted to Oberleutnant in 1917, he was twice-again wounded and was present at the signing of the surrender on November 11, 1918. Keppler left the Army in August, 1919, while assigned to Infantry Regiment "von Courbière" Nr. 19 (a unit from the city of Posen) where he had been posted since November the previous year. He was awarded both classes of the Iron Cross, the Wound Badge in Silver, the Hanseatic Cross and the Brunswick War Service Cross.

After serving with security troops in Hannover, Keppler left the military on January 31, 1920, and joined the Schutzpolizei in Hannover. He remained in Hannover until the end of June, 1926, and after October 10, 1924, commanded a company. Moving to Thuringia, he was promoted to Hauptmann der Schutzpolizei on June 21, 1920, and transferred to the Landespolizei on July 1, 1926. Keppler was a company officer in Hildburghausen from January, 1927, to mid-February, 1928, then acted as a consultant to the head of the Landespolizei in Thuringia until 1929. He then commanded the Landespolizei detachment in Jena until November 20, 1933. Promoted to Major der Schutzpolizei on July 1, 1931, he joined the NSDAP on October 1, 1930. From November 20, 1933, to May 24, 1935, Keppler commanded the Schutzpolizei in Gotha and also was commander of the Munich Landespolizei Regiment from October, 1933, to late June, 1934.

He left the Polizei and again served with the Army in Infanterie Regiment 32 until October 10, 1935. Keppler left the Army, joining the SS-Verfügungstruppe as an SS-Sturmbannführer on October 10, 1935. His first post was commander of I./SS-Standarte 1 (replacing later Army General Georg Ritter von Hengl) until succeeded by Heinz Bertling on March 23, 1938.[1] In July 1936 the Standarte was given the honor title "Deutschland." In the pre-war years he was awarded the German Horseman's Badge in Silver and the Silesian Eagle.

Keppler then was the first commander of what developed into one of the most successful Waffen-SS regiments. Based in Vienna, Austria, he formed, trained and then led the new SS-Standarte 3 beginning March 23, 1938. Promoted to SS-Standartenführer on April 20, 1938, his regiment received the honor title "Der Führer" in early September that same year. In June of 1939, Keppler's regiment served as the Wachregiment for the Reichsprotektor of Bohemia and Moravia, Constantin von Neurath. Promoted to SS-Oberführer on May 13, 1940, and to SS-Brigadeführer und Generalmajor der Waffen-SS on November 9, 1940, Keppler led Regiment "Der Führer" during the Western campaign. He was awarded clasps to both his Iron Crosses on May 13, 1940. On Au-

---

[1] After later commanding a SS-Totenkopf-Infanterie-Regiment 2, Bertling went to the staff of the "Leibstandarte" in January, 1942, and in 1943 commanded the 1.SS-Infanterie-Brigade (mot). Promoted to SS-Oberführer on November 9, 1943, he was assigned as commander of the Indian Legion in August, 1943, and ended the war on the staff of SS-Brigadeführer Werner Ballauf. During WWI he served as an officer and with the Freikorps, joining the SS in April, 1931.

(Above) In the summer of 1939, Keppler (with peaked cap) talks to Peter Hansen, the commander of the SS/VT artillery regiment. Below, Keppler (center), listens to new Knight's Cross holder Ludwig Kepplinger. Paul Hausser is on the right.

Keppler stands off to the right with men of "Der Führer." On the far left is Heinz Harmel and beside him wearing a helmet is Otto Reuter, later awarded the German Cross in Gold.

gust 15, 1940, he was among the first men awarded the Knight's Cross in the Waffen-SS as a result of the following recommendation submitted by Paul Hausser:

"The Regiment "Der Führer" was the only infantry regiment in the area of the corps to successfully break through the Grebbe Line. The abilities of SS-Oberführer Keppler had wide-reaching operational effects. The capitulation of the armored fortress "Holland" and the Dutch Army are to be attributed to these effects. Whether during reconnaissance, action or while leading his regiment, SS-Oberführer Keppler especially proved himself by displaying personal action and bravery. He personally deployed the III.Bataillon during the violent crossing over the Issl and the storming of the Grebbe Mountain under strong enemy machine gun and artillery fire. With the conviction that the breakthrough at this key position would result in a decisive engagement for further movements, SS-Oberführer Keppler and his regiment were able to see through these difficult battles, which naturally cost many bloody casualties, through his personal action. Only after the battles were concluded was it determined that the brave action of the commander and his regiment had such far-reaching results for the defense of the armored fortress 'Holland.'"

Keppler commanded "Der Führer" until succeeded by Otto Kumm on July 11, 1941.[2] All his subsequent commands involved divisional or larger units. When "Totenkopf" commander Theodor Eicke was wounded, he recommended Matthias Kleinheisterkamp as his own temporary replacement. Keppler was sent by Himmler to take Kleinheisterkamp's place who then returned to his regimental command. Georg Keppler led "Totenkopf" in extreme combat from July 15 to September 21, 1941, when he briefed and turned over his command to a recovered Theodor Eicke.

Keppler was assigned briefly to command SS-Division "Nord" as a replacement for Carl-Maria Demelhuber. He suddenly fell ill with a brain tumor and was unable to assume the command. Keppler was hospitalized and under medical care until April 1, 1942, with Demehlhuber reassuming command of SS-Division "Nord." On January 30, 1942, he was promoted to SS-Gruppenführer und Generalleutnant der Waffen-SS.

Georg Keppler took command of SS-Division "Reich" on April 1, 1942, as it began its largest expansion. At completion of this, it had been redesignated the 2.SS-Panzer-Grenadier-Division "Das Reich" and had added a tank regiment. In early 1943, Keppler re-

---

[2] Yerger, "Otto Kumm," page 26 and Weidinger, "Division Das Reich," volume II, page 414.

(Above) Keppler watches a march of Regiment "Der Führer" and (below) he is in the photo center beside SS-Oberführer Carl Zenner.

(Left) Keppler with his regiment in 1940 and (right) as an SS-Gruppenführer wearing the Knight's Cross.

turned to Russia with the Division as a component of SS-Generalkommando (later II.SS-Panzer-Korps). Taken ill in February, 1943, with a recurrence of his prior illness, he handed command of "Das Reich" to the commander of its Panzer Regiment, Herbert Vahl, on February 10, 1943. Keppler was then under medical care until August 30, 1943.

Transferred to Prague, he succeeded Alfred Karrasch as the Befehlshaber der Waffen-SS "Böhmen und Mähren" from August 31, 1943, until his post was officially assumed by Carl Graf von Pückler-Burghauss on March 20, 1944 (Karl Herrmann had taken Keppler's place beginning on January 15, 1944, until March 20, 1944, as his designated deputy). With his headquarters in Budapest, Keppler served as Befehlshaber der Waffen-SS "Ungarn" (Hungary) from April 6, 1944, to September 1, 1944, during which time he was promoted to SS-Obergruppenführer und General der Waffen-SS on June 21, 1944.

When Josef Dietrich took command of the 5.Panzer-Armee, Keppler was assigned as commander of the I.SS-Panzer-Korps and arrived at his command the morning of August 16, 1944.[3] He held command until Hermann Priess assumed command on October 24,

1944, when the command was pulled from the front and transported to Westphalia for rest and refit.

He then was posted to his previous Befehlshaber der Waffen-SS assignment from November 1, 1944, until the post was abolished on February 2, 1945, after the fall of Budapest. He was, however, given another combat command as his priority duty. While Felix Steiner was ill, Keppler next commanded the III.(germanisches) SS-Panzer-Korps from October 30, 1944, until succeeded by Generalleutnant Martin Unrein on February 4, 1945.[4] For the remainder of the war, Keppler commanded the XVIII.SS-Armee-Korps, having replaced Heinz Reinefarth on February 12, 1945. Surrendering with his command to US troops on May 22, 1945, he was released in late April, 1948, and moved to Upper Bavaria until 1952. Keppler then ran a chemist's shop in Hamburg until he retired in 1961. He died in Hamburg on June 16, 1966.

A brilliant divisional and corps commander, his contributions in numerous difficult replacement command positions were deserv-

---

[3] National Archives, Microfiche Publication M1035, Fiche 0598, B-0623, page 1, written by Keppler.

[4] Other sources give February 1 or February 9.

In September, 1939, Heinz Harmel salutes General Dollmann, the commander of the XVII.Armee-Korps. Keppler stands at left.

ing of an award beyond the Knight's Cross. Paul Hausser thought him trustworthy as well as clearheaded and vigorous as a commander. He held more senior commands than any other Waffen-SS commander, ample testimony to his skills as a strategist and leadership ability. Adored by those he commanded, he defended their reputation in any instance, such as when he demanded and received a formal apology for alleged insults to the "Totenkopf" Division by the staff of XXVIII.Armee-Korps after personally confronting corps commander General Mauritz von Wiktorin. In an objective retrospective analysis of field leaders, Georg Keppler must be considered as among the very best Waffen-SS commanding generals.

Two portraits of SS-Oberführer Georg Keppler.

From left are Otto Kumm and Georg Keppler during a briefing session following the invasion of Russia in 1941.

Keppler (right) with Heinz Harmel in Russia and (above) the artist portrait done of him by Wolfgang Willrich.

(Above) *During training, Keppler (right) walks with Paul Hausser. Between them in the rear is Karl Ullrich and over Hausser's other shoulder is the 1a of "Reich,"*
Siegfried Max Schulz. Below, Keppler (right) and Paul Hausser (left) talk with Ludwig Kepplinger, among the first junior officers awarded the Knight's Cross.

SS-Oberführer Georg Keppler wearing the Knight's Cross awarded him for leadership in the 1940 Western campaign. A brilliant commander, he was no doubt deserving of higher awards beyond the Knight's Cross for military skill and leadership, but his career was plagued by illness. He held more senior field combat commands than any other SS officer.

Right: SS-Obergruppenführer Georg Keppler in an informal portrait. Below he sits (wearing peaked cap) with the men of his command during 1941.

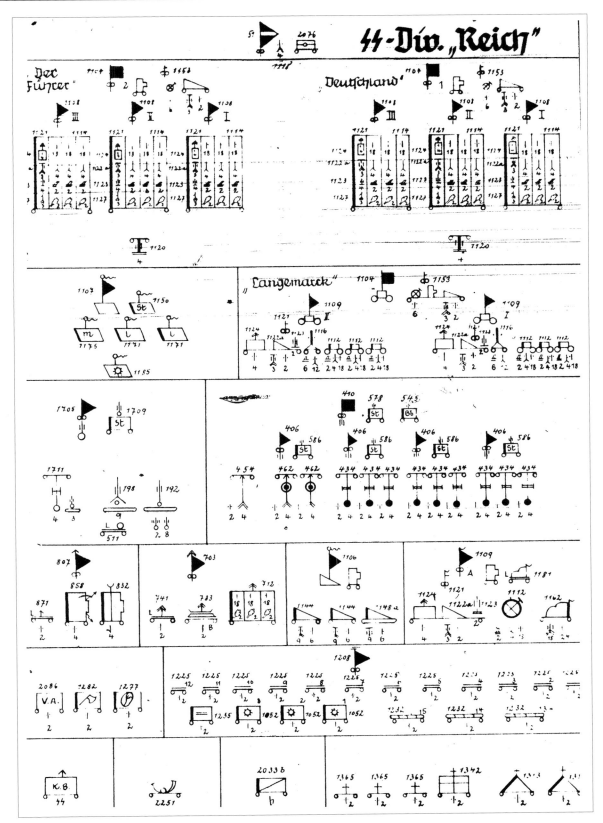

"Reich" during the late April, 1942, phase of Keppler's command expanding it to Panzer-Grenadier-Division status. "Langemarck" is added but only one detachment of armor is supplied (it was expanded to a regiment in October).

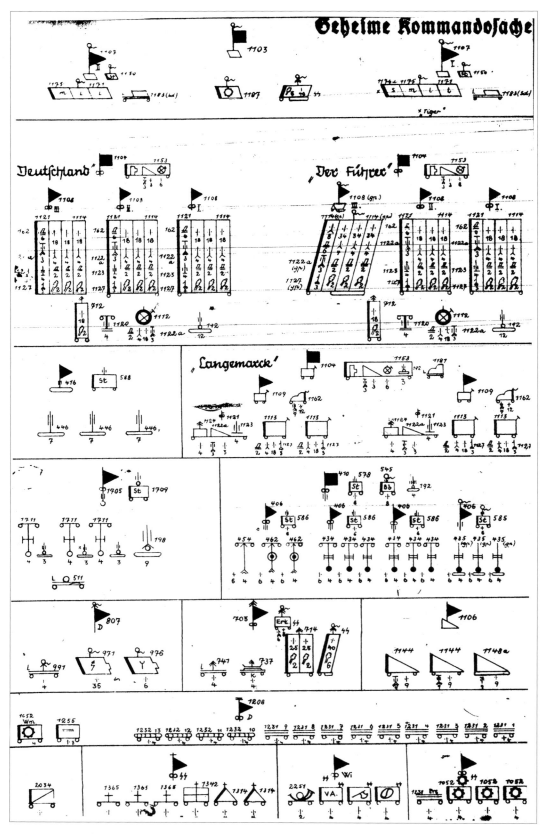

"Das Reich" as an SS-Panzer-Grenadier-Division in November, 1942, during the final stages of expansion.

MATTHIAS KLEINHEISTERKAMP

The son of a railway official of the same name, Matthias Kleinheisterkamp was born in Wuppertal/Elberfeld on June 22, 1893. After passing his Abitur, he joined the Army on August 1, 1914 as a Fahenjunker. During his first two months of service he was assigned to Engineer Battalion 7, a unit originally recruited from Westfalia. In October, 1914, he briefly transferred to Infantry Regiment No. 130, a unit originally from the former province of Lorraine, before moving the same month to Reserve Infantry Regiment No. 219. There, Kleinheisterkamp served as a platoon leader, battalion then regimental adjutant, and finally as a company officer until January, 1919. In the period of demobilizing the Imperial Army, he served in early 1919 with 7th Army Corps, Infantry Regiment No. 605 and Reserve Infantry Regiment No. 55 until March, 1919. Commissioned as a Leutnant, he was awarded both classes of the Iron Cross and received the Wound Badge in Black for a head wound inflicted by a grenade.

From March, 1919, to October that year, Kleinheisterkamp served with the Freikorps "Lichtschlag" within the Guard Land Protection Corps (Garde Landesschützenkorps). He then moved to the III./Regiment 7 of the same parent unit until the end of 1920. On January 1, 1921, Kleinheisterkamp transferred to the Reichswehr as a Leutnant with I./Infantry Regiment 17. Serving as a platoon leader, machine gun officer and finally as mobilization officer in 2nd Battalion, he was promoted to Oberleutnant on February 1, 1928. He took command of 5th company on April 1, 1929, and was promoted to Hauptmann on October 1, 1929. Remaining with the regiment until the start of October, 1933, he was commanding 17th company when he transferred to his next assignment.

From the start of October, 1933, until leaving the Army at the beginning of February, 1934, Kleinheisterkamp served as the regi-

mental adjutant of Infantry Regiment 6. He joined the SS as a candidate on November 1, 1933, and became an SS Mann on January 24, 1934. Serving first as 1a advisor with Abschnitt XIII until early March, 1934, he was promoted to SS-Scharführer on February 10, 1934, to SS-Oberscharfüher two days later, to SS-Truppführer on February 14, 1934 and to SS-Obertruppführer on March 19, 1934. He then held a similar post with Oberabschnitt "Nord" until mid-April 1934, and was commissioned as an SS-Untersturmführer on April 12, 1934. Kleinheisterkamp remained with Oberabschnitt "Nord" until the end of March, 1935, as a training advisor and was promoted to SS-Obersturmführer on June 17, 1934.[1] Transferring to the SS/VT at the end of March 1935, Kleinheisterkamp was an infantry tactics instructor at SS-Führerschule Braunschweig until the start of April, 1936. Promoted to SS-Hauptsturmführer on April 20, 1935, and to SS-Sturmbannführer on June 1, 1935, he was promoted to Chief of Staff to the Inspector of the SS/VT (Paul Hausser) from April, 1936, to the beginning of August, 1938. Promoted to SS-Obersturmbannführer on April 20, 1937, he was given a strong formal reprimand and reassigned after a verbal confrontation with Sepp Dietrich.

On August 4, 1938, Kleinheisterkamp was next posted to SS-Regiment "Deutschland." After a month of familiarization, he was assigned to the regimental staff until December 1, 1938, when he formally succeeded Werner Ballauf (who left in November) as the commander of III./"Deutschland." Leading a mixed formation with his command as a basis, he served in the Polish campaign and led the escape column that evacuated all foreign diplomats from Warsaw with their families. He was awarded clasps to both his Iron

---

[1] "SS-Stammrollen."

Matthias Kleinheisterkamp (above) is in the center of a group of recruits and instructors at SS-Führerschule Braunschweig in 1935. Below, in the same period he stands in the left foreground with school commander Paul Hausser, on the right wearing SS-Oberführer insignia.

Kleinheisterkamp in two photos while teaching at Braunschweig. In one photo he can be seen wearing his 1933 model dress dagger.

Crosses for combat in Poland, the 2nd class on September 13 and the 1st class on October 2. Kleinheisterkamp then led his battalion when the first SS division was formed. He would be recommended for the Knight's Cross three times before higher echelons finally approved the award. Paul Hausser wrote the first recommendation for the award for actions in the Western campaign of 1940 and reads as follows:

"After the violent crossing of the Beveland Canal on Zeeland on May 18, 1940, for which his battalion had to fight very hard, the III./SS-Regiment "Deutschland" took the area between the dam of Beveland to Walcheren in a fast advance. Some of the men were on bicycles.

About 900 Frenchmen were captured by the battalion during the day. On the following day, the battalion was able to take the dam which crossed over the 1.5 kilometer long swamp on both sides from Beveland to Walcheren under the most difficult conditions. The battle lasted over eight hours and the men fought against an eastern front of new French forces with a size of two regiments that displayed a well-planned-out and tough defense.

At 2000 hours, the enemy resistance was broken. In a night pursuit, Vlissingen was also taken. Here, some 4000 French prisoners were captured by the Regiment.

The passionate energy, the toughness and the bravery of SS-Obersturmbannführer Kleinheisterkamp and his troops must be appreciated in that the French division in Zeeland could be destroyed and Vlissingen taken.

Besides this, he performed excellently in the war area with his battalion during the breakthrough over the mine-infested areas in Holland and the dams in the eastern part of the Beveland Island, which was swarming with French soldiers."[2]

Promoted to SS-Standartenführer on May 18, 1940, he was transferred to the "Totenkopf" Division and replaced Friedemann

---

[2] "Vorschlagliste Nr. 4 für die Verleihung des Ritterkreuzes des Eisernen Kreuzes" dated July 18, 1940, written by Felix Steiner then approved by Paul Hausser.

Goetze who had been killed in action as commander of SS-Totenkopf-Infanterie-Regiment 3. He held command from June 3, 1940 to October 27, 1941, and briefly acted as divisional commander in the second week of July, 1941, when Theodor Eicke was wounded. Relations between Eicke and Kleinheisterkamp were not friendly during his period with "Totenkopf." Eicke's reputation for transferring those he did not like or blocking promotions made it very unusual that he would still recommend Kleinheisterkamp for the Knight's Cross. This second time, he was also refused at higher level, but the document text indicates his abilities as a regimental commander:

"SS "Totenkopf" Division reached Rosenov and the south perimeter as ordered, in two columns. The assignment was to cover the flank of the LVI.Armee Korps. Through a cleverly-put-together attack plan, SS-Oberführer Kleinheisterkamp successfully took Rosenov at 1030 hours on July 4, 1941, in close combat despite strong enemy occupying forces. He also managed to take the bridges there intact.

A new assignment was received on July 6, 1941, from LVI.Armee Korps. SS 'Totenkopf' Division was to attack early on the morning of July 6, 1941, on both sides of the enemy positions and surround the enemy in the hills eastwards and southeastwards of Rosenov. There he is to smash him and advance onto Sebesh. After reaching the street Sebesh-Opotschka, the division is to continue under security to the south and southeast along the street to Opotschka.

Under the firm leadership of its regimental commander, SS-Totenkopf-Infanterie 3 performed the unimaginable during these and the following days. The break through the Stalin Line, through its numerous concrete bunkers, the opponent being in possession of all the terrain points which ruled this landscape, was only possible due to the masterful leadership of SS-Oberführer Kleinheisterkamp. Kleinheisterkamp was always at the most forward line and followed the continually changing situation of this difficult battle and his fast and sure decisions were always the motivation of the attacks. What made it difficult for him during this battle was the fact that it had to be conducted without anti-aircraft or fighter plane support.

In the night from July 6/7, 1941, the divisional commander was badly wounded and SS-Oberführer Kleinheisterkamp, on order of the divisional commander, assumed the leadership of the division and lead it from this point until the arrival of a new divisional commander. He led during the difficult battles of the division, especially around Sevesh and hill 202, as well as near Opotschka and Porchov. On the night of July 7/8, 1941, there was a lack of ammunition and the hill 202 was again lost after a strong Russian counterattack. That same night the 290.Infanterie Division received the order to relieve the SS "Totenkopf" Division, but SS-Oberführer Kleinheisterkamp,

upon his own decision, decided again to attack in order to hand over a secure situation to the 290.Infanterie Division Only after taking the strongly defended city of Sevesh and re-conquering hill 202 did Kleinheisterkamp allow his units to be relieved.

Only through his strongest personal action and his calm, as well as secure leadership in the heaviest battles, did SS-Oberführer Kleinheisterkamp lead not only his regiment, but also the division, to a large victory.

SS-Oberführer Kleinheisterkamp, who had already proved himself excellently during the Polish and Western campaigns, was previously recommended for the award of the Knight's Cross to the Iron Cross by the commander of the SS-V.Division. In recognition of his accomplishments and decisive successes, I request that SS-Oberführer Kleinheisterkamp be awarded the Knight's Cross to the Iron Cross."[3]

Promoted to SS-Oberführer on July 19, 1941, and to SS-Brigadeführer und Generalmajor der Waffen-SS on November 9, 1941, he was sent on leave by Eicke and was in reserve until the end of December, 1941. Originally to have been assigned commander of SS-Division "Nord," he instead replaced Wilhelm Bittrich as commander of SS-Division "Reich."[4] General der Panzertruppen Heinrich-Gottfried von Vietinghoff-Scheel recommended him for the Knight's Cross for the actions of his division during January 10 to March 15, 1942, some of the most bitter defensive engagements of the war.[5] The award was finally approved with this third recommendation and Kleinheisterkamp received the decoration on March 31, 1942. Kleinheisterkamp held command until the division was withdrawn, except for a Kampfgruppe under Werner Ostendorff, for rebuilding as a Panzer-Grenadier-Division and was replaced by Georg Keppler on April 1, 1942.

Moving to the mountain division command he was to have assumed in early 1942, he led the newly forming divisional elements of "Nord" in Germany from the start of April, 1942, until these newly formed portions were transferred to Finland. His new command was combined with Kampfgruppe "Nord" in June, 1942, and Kleinheisterkamp succeeded Hans Scheider. He remained commander of the completed division until succeeded by Lothar Debes on December 15, 1943. During his Finland posting he had an excellent relationship with Eduard Dietl, probably because Kleinheisterkamp remained a professional soldier void of political interests as well as his ability as a commander. While commanding "Nord" he was awarded the Finnish Cross of Freedom 1st class and promoted to SS-Gruppenführer und Generalleutnant der Waffen-

---

[3] "Vorschlagliste Nr. 4 für die Verleihung des Ritterkreuzes zum Eisernen Kreuz" written by Theodor Eicke.

[4] "Personalverfügung" dated December 31, 1941.

[5] Short recommendation submitted by von Vietinghoff on March 17, 1942. Von Vietinghoff himself won the Knight's Cross on June 24, 1940, as a General der Panzertruppen commanding the XIII.Armee-Korps and the Oakleaves as a Generaloberst commanding the 10.Armee on April 16, 1944.

(Above) Himmler reviews men of "Nord" while Kleinheisterkamp in on the left. In the bottom photo, taken later as an SS-Gruppenführer, he signs directives for his command.

SS on May 1, 1943. He was also awarded both classes of the War Merit Cross with Swords, the 2nd class on April 20, 1942, and the 1st class on September 1, 1942.

The balance of his career assignments were to lead higher formations. After serving briefly in the operational reserve begining in mid-December, 1943, Kleinheisterkamp took command of the III. (Germ.) SS-Panzer-Korps from Felix Steiner from February 25, 1944, until April 16, 1944. He next formed and led the VII.SS-Panzer-Korps during May/June, 1944, until the corps was absorbed by the IV.SS-Panzer-Korps.[6] He then led that corps officially until succeeded by Herbert Otto Gille on July 20, 1944, (Gille formally was assigned to take the command on August 6). Kleinheisterkamp next led the XI.SS-Armee-Korps, after February 1, 1945, designated a Panzer-Korps, from August 1, 1944, until the end of the war.[7] While commanding this unit, he received excellent evaluation comments from Generaloberst Gotthard Heinrici, the commander of Kleinheisterkamp's superior Army Group and one of the best defensive combat Generals.[8] While leading this corps based on the remnants of the Army's V.Armee-Korps, he was promoted to SS-Obergruppenführer und General der Waffen-SS on August 1, 1944. He was the only commander of this corps.

Kleinheisterkamp then resumed command of the XI.SS-Panzer-Korps until he was captured in late April, 1945. Awarded the Oakleaves on May 9, 1945, as the 871st soldier of the armed forces for defensive leadership in the Küstrin area, Kleinheisterkamp's award was recommended by General der Infanterie Theodor Busse, the commander of the 9.Armee. However, while leading a rear guard action in Fortress Halbe, Kleinheisterkamp was captured during combat the night of April 29/30, 1945, and committed suicide as a prisoner the following week.[9]

A professional Army soldier for two decades, he was respected and honorable, ignoring the political nature of the civil elements of the SS which almost caused him to be dismissed in the pre-war years. His SS officer school teaching period influenced many later regimental and divisional commanders per comments given by them to the author. Kleinheisterkamp led "Reich" in some of the most bitter fighting of the first Russian campaign and his excellent leadership of "Nord" has been generally overlooked by historians. From all accounts, he was an excellent tactician and leader, well liked by Paul Hausser who acknowledged his ability as well as personal bravery.

---

[6] "Personalverfügung" dated May 19, 1944. Other sources give him command in early January, 1944, and then placed again in reserve. The period given is his confirmed uninterrupted command before absorbtion by the IV.SS-Panzer-Korps. See Preradovich, "Die Generale der Waffen-SS," page 42 and Vopersal, "Soldaten, Kämpfer, Kamaraden," Band Va, page 116.

[7] He did not lead the XII.SS-Armee-Korps as stated in some sources (Bender and Taylor, "Uniforms, Organization and History of the Waffen-SS," volume 2, page 45) as the XI.SS-Korps formation directives give him as the commander effective August 1. Spiwoks and Stöber, "Endkampf zwischen Mosel und Inn," pages 360-362 and other text research courtesy of Ignacio Arrondo.

[8] Heinrici was awarded the Knight's Cross on September 18, 1941, as a General der Infanterie commanding the XXXXIII.Armee Korps. On November 24, 1943, he won the Oakleaves and on March 3, 1945, was decorated with the Swords to the Knight's Cross for his command of 1.Panzer Armee with the rank of Generaloberst.

[9] Sources vary as to the actual date of his death, either May 2nd (also given as date he was listed as missing) or May 8th.

Kleinheisterkamp is on the right during 1935 at Braunschweig.

Kleinheisterkamp wears the later style SS-Brigadeführer insignia and his Knight's Cross.

Above and left: Two portraits, one signed, of Matthias Kleinheisterkamp wearing the pre-1942 collar insignia for an SS-Brigadeführer.

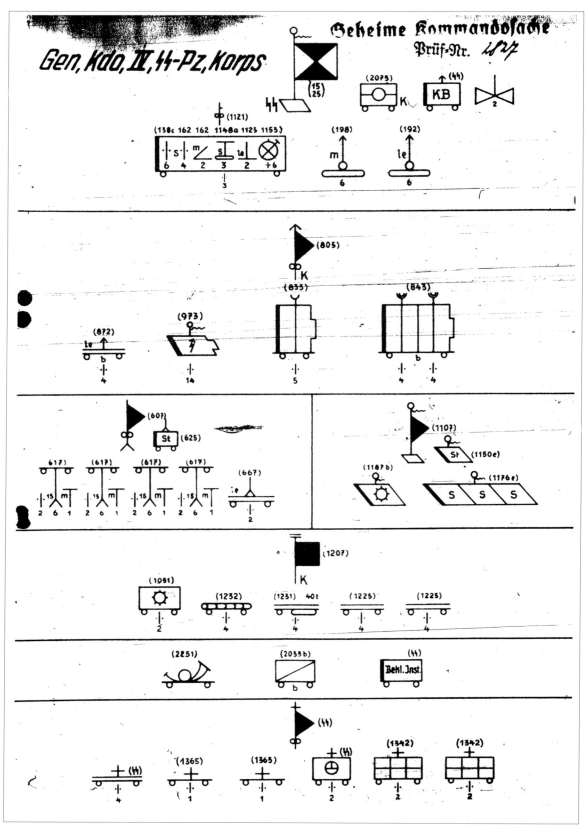

IV.SS-Panzer-Korps during August, 1943.

FRITZ KLINGENBERG

One of the most famous and militarily successful graduates of the SS Officer Schools was Fritz Klingenberg. Born on December 17, 1912, in Röwershagen, he left studies in science and history at the University of Rostock in 1931 and joined the SA. In November, 1932, he joined the SS and was assigned to the 3./IV./22.SS-Standarte.

The following year he became an officer candidate with the "Leibstandarte" and attended the first class (beginning in April 1934) at the newly opened SS-Führerschule Bad Tölz. Commissioned as an SS-Untersturmführer on April 20, 1935, he helped to form the SS NCO school "Merkers" during March, 1935, after taking additional training in weapons with men from Regiment "Deutschland." Following more training with SS Standarte "Deutschland," he was assigned to the 7./SS-Standarte 2 (which later became Regiment "Germania") as a platoon leader until October, 1935. Klingenberg then moved to 5.Kompanie with a similar assignment until the end of 1935.

From the start of 1936 until December that year he served as adjutant to II./"Germania."[1] Promoted to SS-Obersturmführer on December 12, 1937, he went to the SS/VT Inspectorate staff on December 10, 1936, and then became adjutant to Paul Hausser in the spring of 1939.[2] Promoted to SS-Hauptsturmführer on June 30, 1939, when Panzer Division "Kempf" was formed from Army and SS/VT troops for the Polish campaign, Klingenberg acted as its adjutant during the campaign. After Poland, he continued in that post under Hausser when the initial Waffen-SS division formed in October, 1939. He held that position until the start of August, 1940. On June 23, 1940, he won the Iron Cross 2nd class and the 1st class award the following day.

On August 1, 1940, Klingenberg was given his first command, leading the 15./"Der Führer." The motorcycle support company of the regiment, he retained command when the company became a component of the Division's new Kradschützen (motorcycle) Bataillon in February, 1941.[3] As commander of this company, Klingenberg was a major participant in the swift and successful Yugoslavian campaign. His unit was primarily responsible for the capture of Belgrade, which resulted in Klingenberg being the first Waffen-SS officer mentioned in the daily Wehrmachtsbericht (Armed Forces Report) on April 13, 1941.[4] The success of his unit also resulted in the award of the Knight's Cross on May, 15, 1941. The decoration, later personally bestowed on Klingenberg by Hitler, was granted as a result of the following recommendation:

"On April 4, 1941, SS-Hauptsturmführer Klingenberg, then leader of a small vanguard of the motorcycle battalion, had the mission assignment to take the bridge across the Danube river near Belgrade in a surprise attack. At 0800 hours Klingenberg reached Pancevo and found that the bridge spanning the Tamis river had been blown. He crossed the river in fishing boats, taking some motorcycles with sidecars with him. On those motorcycles he reached the bridge across the Danube with a small group at 11:30. The bridge had been blown at 06:00.

Klingenberg succeeded in getting a motorboat in running order, crossing the river with ten men, two machine guns, and five sub-machine guns. On the way, the boat hit a sandbar but

---

[1] "Bestätigung" dated January 15, 1936, with effect from January 1.
[2] "Bestätigung" dated December 7, 1936.

[3] SS-FHA, Org.Tgb.Nr.45/41, "Aufstellung eines Kradsch.Btl. bei "Reich," dated February 22, 1941. His company became 2./Kradschützen Bataillon. For the history of the unit see Yerger, "Knights of Steel" volume 2, pages 12-73.
[4] Report dated April 12, 1941. It mentioned Klingenberg by name, a rare instance for so junior an officer. See Krätschmer, "Die Ritterkreuzträger der Waffen-SS," page 968.

Fritz Klingenberg (left) on the rifle range at Bad Tölz and (right) decorating a soldier of the motorcycle battalion of SS-Division "Reich."

after much work was refloated. Then the motor stopped working and the men almost hit a pier. After restarting the engine, Klingenberg and his men reached the southern end of the bridge.

He formed a small bridgehead and sent the boat back to get more men from his unit. Klingenberg himself advanced towards Belgrade on foot and penetrated into the city. Meeting a group of Serbian soldiers, he fired on them and made them lay down their arms. In vehicles taken from the Serbs, Klingenberg advanced on the Ministry of War. The building was destroyed and emptied. Klingenberg placed outposts and sent a Serb messenger to the mayor of Belgrade with the order to appear at once and hand over the city. The mayor appeared at 18:30 and formally handed over the city, being under the impression that stronger German units occupied Belgrade. In order to feign a stronger force, Klingenberg, with his now reinforced combat patrol, drove through the city and fired on any Serbian soldiers encountered. Small and large groups were encountered with about 1,000 prisoners being taken.

Klingenberg then occupied the city until further troops arrived during the night."[5]

When the commander of the Kradschützen Bataillon, August Zehender, was wounded on June 29, 1941, Klingenberg assumed command and his Kompanie command was taken by Heinz Wagner.[6] He led the Kradschützen Bataillon (having been wounded on October 19) until forced by superiors into a hospital to recover from illness which had plagued him since the autumn of 1941. Christian Tychsen succeeded him as commander of the Kradschützen Bataillon on January 4, 1942.[7] In the time of his command he also

---

[5] "Vorschlagsliste Nr. 8 für die Verleihung des Ritterkreuzes des Eisernen Kreuzes," written and dated April 18, 1941, by Paul Hausser.

[6] "Geschichte des SS-Kradschützen-Bataillon SS-Division "Reich." Zehender's biography, later the commander of the 22.SS-Freiwilligen-Kavallerie-Division "Florian Geyer," will be in volume 2.

[7] Yerger, "Knights of Steel," volume 2, page 18. Tychsen, who was later the commander of Panzer Regiment "Das Reich" and won the Knight's Cross with Oakleaves, is included in volume 2 for his command of the 2.SS-Panzer-Division "Das Reich" during the Normandy campaign.

Taken while adjutant to Paul Hausser, Klingenberg wears the formal adjutant's cords in this studio portrait.

won the Infantry Assault Badge in Bronze on July 3, 1941, and was promoted to SS-Sturmbannführer on September 1, 1941.

Portions of the Bataillon returned with the majority of the Division in early 1942 for expansion to Panzer-Grenadier-Division status. After his recovery, Klingenberg began the task of rebuilding his command while the balance of its troops (along with other divisional elements) fought in Russia as a component of Kampfgruppe "SS-Reich" under the divisional Ia, Werner Ostendorff.[8]

In March, 1942, Klingenberg was ordered to SS-Junkerschule Bad Tölz where he served as an instructor and later teaching group commander. In July, 1943, he briefly rejoined "Das Reich" to gather data for instruction at the school and then returned to Bad Tölz. During that brief posting he was wounded on July 6, 1943. While assigned to Bad Tölz, he was promoted to SS-Obersturmbannführer on December 21, 1943. Paul Hausser, at the time the commander of the II.SS-Panzer-Korps, recommended Klingenberg for the award of the German Cross in Gold on March 26, 1944.[9] Hausser's serious wound, received in October, 1941, and other events had delayed the award being recommended. Hausser's effort in pursuing the recommendation is testimony to the high regard he had for Klingenberg. The award, granted on April 28, 1944, and presented in May, resulted from the following text recommendation covering earlier period combat engagements:

"On June 30, 1941, 1.Kompanie succeeded in taking the enemy by surprise and breaking into his positions south of Losca, forming a bridgehead on the opposite side. With the battalion commander wounded, Klingenberg took advantage of the surprise and stormed past 1.Kompanie with his 2.Kompanie. They took Losca and broke through a regimental-sized enemy unit which had assembled in the woods behind them. They then took a second village six kilometers away and created the conditions for continued pursuit of the enemy. The Russians suffered heavy losses in men as well as tanks, anti-tank guns and large numbers of small arms.

On July 3, 1941, the motorcycle battalion, led by Klingenberg, pursued the enemy and encountered tough resistance near Perewos west of the Beresina river. The enemy unit, with the help of engineers, tried to ferry their units across the Beresina. Leading with his 2.Kompanie, Klingenberg attacked this strong force and took Perewos in house-to-house fighting. The enemy had to leave an engineer unit behind with all their equipment, due to heavy losses, and retreated.

From July 22 to August 3 the motorcycle battalion was heavily engaged in the hard fighting at the Jelnja river. The

unit had a six kilometer sector to defend against constant enemy attacks and closed all breaches of the line. The unit held its ground against two enemy divisions and inflicted heavy losses. Klingenberg lead the combat at the most difficult points of the line.

On October 6, 1941, the unit was ordered to relieve the reconnaissance detachment north and west of Mashina, then repel the enemy that was attacking in force. A short time before the relief, the Russians attacked with rocket launchers for the first time. The men of the reconnaissance unit, already ordered to get out, were confused by the fire from the new weapon and headed for rear-area positions. SS-Hauptsturmführer Klingenberg was at the front at the time and deployed his unit. He got his men into position so a large-scale enemy attack was completely repelled. The following counterattack captured two villages. Two days later, Klingenberg and his motorcyclists fought along the road from Gjsatsk, made contact with the 10.Panzer-Division, and fought hard in Nikolskoje. The enemy lost numerous tanks, trucks and other vehicles while the battalion captured many prisoners.

On October 19, 1941, the battalion had the order to attack the main road crossing south of Moshaisk from an easterly direction. The heavily fortified positions were taken after a difficult fight. Several dug-in tanks and other vehicles were abandoned in the face of the battalion attack while the enemy suffered very heavy losses.

On December 12, 1941, the Russians attacked the motorcycle battalion northeast of Roshdestweno with two regiments. Klingenberg, who was at divisional headquarters at the time, immediately returned to his unit where the enemy had broken through the lines. Taking his place at the lead of the front-most unit, they threw back the enemy, repelling the rest of the attack and inflicting heavy losses.

During a fact-finding mission to "Das Reich" on July 5, 1943, Klingenberg acted as a substitute II./Panzer Regiment commander to gather data for teaching classes at Bad Tölz. He attacked with great courage near Lutschki where the enemy lost 12 tanks and 14 artillery pieces while Klingenberg's men took 100 prisoners."

Klingenberg became commandant of Bad Tölz on March 15, 1944, the only graduate of the school to become its commander, when he succeeded Werner Dörffler-Schuband.[10] While there he was promoted to SS-Standartenführer on December 21, 1944. He held that post until he was ordered to take command of the 17.SS-Panzer-Grenadier-Division "Götz von Berlichingen" effective January 12, 1945. He actually assumed command nine days later.[11]

---

[8] The Kampfgruppe elements returned in June, 1942, and were incorporated into the division. Ostendorff, one of the best tacticians in the Waffen-SS, will have a biography included in volume 2 for his leadership of the 17.SS-Panzer-Grenadier-Division "Götz von Berlichingen."

[9] "Vorschlag Nr. 1 für die Verleihung des Deutschen Kreuzes in Gold" dated March 26, 1944, and hand signed by Hausser with approval date of April 28, 1944.

[10] Telex from Knoblauch (SS-FHA) to Klingenberg dated March 9.

[11] Date of his transfer order ("Personalverfügung") dated January 13, 1945, effective the previous day and divisional Order of the Day in Stöber, "Die Sturmflut

Klingenberg with Hitler the day he was presented with the Knight's Cross and a portrait wearing the award as well as double "SS" collar insignia.

Two portraits of Klingenberg, on the left as an SS-Sturmbannführer and an autographed Heinrich Hoffmann postcard portrait taken while an SS-Hauptsturmführer.

Klingenberg was killed commanding the Division on March 22, 1945, and full leadership was then given to Georg Bochmann.[12]

One of the brightest and best graduates of the SS officer school system, Klingenberg was both daring and successful.[13] Some de-

gree of this probably came from the lengthy personal contact and tutelage obtained from Paul Hausser. His capture of Belgrade was one of the classic actions of the Second World War. Kligenberg's greatest contribution was with his teaching and command assignments with Bad Tölz. He was primarily responsible for the successful implementation of training programs for the numerous foreign volunteers that passed through the facility who eventually formed a large portion of the Waffen-SS leadership cadre.

---

und das Ende," volume 2, page 468. Between the dates of his assignment and actual assumption of command, leadership of the unit was given to Oberst Gerhard Lindner from the OKH reserve pool.

[12] For the four days before Bochmann's arrival, daily running of the unit was performed by Oakleaves winner Vinzenz Kaiser and then Knight's Cross holder Jakob Fick.

[13] He received excellent evaluations from Hausser as well as Werner Dörffler-Schuband.

(Above) Klingenberg (2nd from left) during an informal lunch with Hitler after the Knight's Cross was presented. The decoration for the award in on the table. Below, from left are Heinz Lammerding, Klingenberg, Jakob Fick, Wilhelm Kment and Oswald Pohl.

(Left) Klingenberg, wearing his Knight's Cross, speaks with Franz Augsberger and (right) during a visit to "Das Reich" in 1943.

During 1941 are, from left, reconnaissance detachment commander Hans Mühlenkamp (Oakleaves winner and later a divisional commander), Erich May (engineer battalion), Klingenberg, Werner Poetschke (Knight's Cross) and Ludwig Wolf (adjutant of the reconnaissance detachment).

HUGO KRAAS

The oldest of seven sons born to the family of schoolmaster Franz Kraas, Hugo Gottlieb Kraas was born in Witten an der Ruhr on January 25, 1911. Hugo Kraas passed his Abitur and began schooling in Kiel as a teacher, attending two semesters before the death of his father forced him to leave school and help look after his family in 1933.

He joined the RAD (National Socialist Labor Corps) on April 19, 1933, and served for four months, joining the NSDAP on May 1, 1933.[1] Joining the SA on October 1, 1933, he was a platoon leader in the SA training command until leaving the SA on April 19, 1935. Kraas then volunteered for the Army and served with 10./ Infanterie Regiment 6 "Ratzeburger Jäger" at the start of July, 1935. His company commander was later Waffen-SS corps commander Matthias Kleinheisterkamp. Promoted to Gefreiter on September 30, 1935, he left Army service the same day.

Kraas next joined the SS/VT on October 15, 1935, as an SS-Rottenführer in 1./I./SS Standarte 2. He stayed with this unit through its being titled "Germania" until the start of April 1937. Promoted to SS-Unterscharführer on January 30, 1936, he was selected to attend the third cadet group at SS-Junkerschule Braunschweig. Classes began the start of April, 1937, and Kraas became an SS-Standartenjunker on October 1, 1937. Promoted to SS-Standartenoberjunker on March 1, 1938, and commissioned as an SS-Untersturmführer on March 12, 1938, he graduated second in his class then attended a platoon leaders course at the Dachau training area.

Assigned to the "Leibstandarte," he was posted as a platoon leader to 7.Kompanie on April 1, 1938, for one month. Kraas then transferred to the 14.(Panzerjäger) Kompanie until November 2,

1939, and was promoted to SS-Obersturmführer on April 20, 1939. He won the Iron Cross 2nd class on October 16, 1939, for actions in Poland. Kraas transferred to Kurt Meyer's 15. (Kradschützen) Kompanie in early November, 1939, and served as a platoon leader until August 15, 1940.[2] On May 25, 1940, he was the first man in his regiment awarded the Iron Cross 1st class and was personally awarded the decoration by Generalmajor Friedrich Zickwolff, the commander of the 227.Infanterie Division.[3] When the 15.Kompanie became the reconnaissance detachment of the "Leibstandarte," Kraas' platoon was expanded to become the 2.Kradschützen Kompanie of the Aufklärungsabteilung and he was made company commander. Promoted to SS-Hauptsturmführer on September 1, 1940, he held this command until February 21, 1942, and on December 25, 1941, was awarded one of the first German Crosses in Gold given to the "Leibstandarte" for combats in Rostow.

During a reorganization, a new V.Bataillon was formed from the "Leibstandarte" Wachbataillon and Kraas was assigned as commander on February 21, 1942.[4] Promoted to SS-Sturmbannführer on April 20, 1942, Kraas took his unit to the Leningrad front. His command was redesignated the I./SS-Panzer-Grenadier Regiment 2 on July 5, 1942, when the "LAH" reorganized its infantry regiments and he continued as commander until May 13, 1943.[5] On June 21, 1943, he was promoted to SS-Obersturmbannführer. The bitter fighting in Kharkov resulted in Kraas being awarded the

---

[1] Most men served six months in the RAD prior to military service.

[2] Lehmann, Rudolf: "Die Leibstandarte," volume 1, page 210.
[3] Zickwolff was awarded the Knight's Cross as a Generalleutnant and commander of the 113.Infanterie Division on June 2, 1942. He was killed on September 17, 1944, commanding the 343.Infanterie Division.
[4] The old V./Leibstandarte became the schwere (heavy) Bataillon.
[5] A new VII.Bataillon was formed as the unit Wachbataillon on January 15, 1942.

SS-Standartenführer Hugo Kraas during a tour following his award of the Knight's Cross.

Knight's Cross on March 28, 1943, as a result of the following report submitted by regimental commander Theodor Wisch:

"Kraas, who was in action on the Donez river south of Tschugujev with his battalion during the defensive battles, stood at the focal point of the defensive battles experienced by the regiment between February 6 - 9, 1943. Kraas personally saw to it that the last reserves of his regiment were gathered in battalion strength on the 8th and 9th of February, 1943, and after hard fighting, the enemy forces that had penetrated our lines were thrown back or annihilated. With that, Kraas had avoided a roll-over of our front by two Russian regiments which were positioned in Gliniza.

During the night of February 9, 1943, Kraas recognized the difficult situation as the Russians had gathered their units (in the strength of two battalions) in front of our positions. While fighting at the lead of his companies, he attacked and annihilated them. The success of the attack avoided a situation in which the Russians would have penetrated our retreat, and therefore saved the Regiment from suffering severe casualties.

In the attack on the northern section of Kharkov during the night of March 11-12, 1943, it was Kraas' unit which was sent to Alexejevka as the Regiment's forward battalion. He and his men had the task of penetrating through the unusually strong built-up enemy positions located at the city's edge, and to free the way along the street Dorgoatschi-Charkov for the planned action of the III.(armored)Battalion. Kraas fought in spite of unusually hard resistance until reaching a position 100 meters from the edge of the village of Alexejewka. He laid there during the whole day in the heaviest fighting and could not advance further due to the climbing terrain, which was littered with high buildings.

Despite the action of the heavy weapons which were personally led by Kraas, or the attack troops which he had sent in, a break-in could not be accomplished. The battle was unusually hard.

Kraas, who was fighting along with his troops in the very front lines, rallied his companies again and again to attack. After the 2nd company was successful in advancing to his positions from the west, Kraas forced the frontal break-in of the mass of the battalion into the village. Kraas fully took advantage of this situation and at 1100 hours on March 12th, he stormed the strong enemy positions on the northern edge of the city and completed the breakthrough. This enabled the Regiment to continue the attack into the inner city.

I recommend that SS-Sturmbannführer Kraas is worthy of the award of the Knight's Cross to the Iron Cross because of his excellent leadership capabilities, his high sense of responsibility and his unusual personal bravery."

In the summer of 1943, Sepp Dietrich was transferring divisional command to Theodor Wisch in order to form I.SS-Panzer-Korps. Command was transferred to Wisch on June 4, 1943, and from that date Hugo Kraas officially replaced Wisch as the commander of SS-Panzer-Grenadier-Regiment 2. He held the regimental command until wounded on January 5, 1944. Command of the unit was transferred to Rudolf Sandig and it later became a Kampfgruppe.[6] Kraas was recommended for the Oakleaves to the Knight's Cross with the following report, again written by Theodor Wisch:[7]

"On July 5, 1943, during the operation 'Zitadelle,' the SS-Panzer-Grenadier-Regiment 2 had the task of breaking open the bunkers in the Russian positions south of Bykovka and to take the hill 234.8, located north of Bykovka. The bunkers were tenaciously defended and well built up, enjoying an approach saturated with mines.

During the night of July 4-5, 1943, the unit attacked, after which the Regiment's command posts were pushed forward to the former Russian outposts on hill 228.8. After the new command post had been situated, the Regiment prepared to attack the forward lines at 0400 hours in the strength of two battalions. The enemy's defensive fire was extremely strong. The Grenadiers fought against the tenaciously defending Russians, and in spite of the enemy's performance were able to slowly gain more ground meter-by-meter. The enemy's resistance could only be broken with attack groups which annihilated his machine guns, heavy grenade launchers and his anti-tank gun positions in the tank ditches.

---

[6] Sandig won the Knight's Cross on May 5, 1943, as an SS-Sturmbannführer and commander of the II./SS-Panzer-Grenadier-Regiment 2. He also won the German Cross in Gold on January 25, 1942, and ended the war as an SS-Obersturmbannführer. Lehmann, "Die Leibstandarte," volumes III and IV/1 indicate Sandig had led the unit in Russia and it is assumed he took command when Kraas was wounded. Kraas' official command lasted until April according to his personnel file, so Sandig was initially a substitute or temporary commander.

[7] "Vorschlagliste Nr. 5 für die Verleihung des Eichenlaubs zum Ritterkreuz des Eisernen Kreuzes" dated January 3, 1944.

Josef Goebbels congratulates newly decorated officers at a reception. From right are Heinz Macher, Hermann Buchner, Hugo Kraas, Max Wünsche and Kurt Meyer.

Portraits of Kraas as (left) an SS-Sturmbannführer with Knight's Cross and (right) as an SS-Standartenführer after his award of the Oakleaves was presented.

During the extremely difficult battle there were heavy casualties. During the reorganization of the units there was a pause in the battle, which enabled the Russians to strengthen their resistance. This crisis was resolved by the decisive personal action of the Regimental Commander, SS-Obersturmbannführer Kraas. Kraas, located in the furthermost lines in the tank ditches, organized all remaining forces so the attack could be continued, and, since the combat engineers that had been subordinated to his battle group were all casualties, personally blew the tank and assault gun crossing over the tank ditches. Kraas, himself a member of one of the attack groups, equipped mostly only with shovels and hand-grenades, then attacked the tanks on hill 220.5 with his attack groups and broke them in the shortest time. Only by his heroic and personal example could the advance of the attack be continued.

After hill 220.5 was taken, SS-Obersturmbannführer Kraas immediately ordered the continuance of the attack onto Bykovka and hill 234.8 north of there. Rallied on by the exemplary bravery of their commander, the Grenadiers reached their day's goal despite dogged defense by the Russians. SS-Obersturmbannführer Kraas was the driving force during these attacks. Continuously rushing to the hot spots of the battle with a handful of men he had gathered together, he rallied his Grenadiers to continue on, and, together with them managed to take Bykovka and hill 234.8 at about 1600 hours.

The exemplary bravery of SS-Obersturmbannführer Kraas and his decisive action is to be acknowledged, that the Grenadiers accomplished the very important attack goals of the first day of the battle. These goals were necessary for the continuance of the attack along the entire southern front of the Division.

On December 27, 1943, SS-Panzer-Grenadier-Regiment 2, under the leadership of SS-Obersturmbannführer Kraas, was positioned on the left open flank of the Division in defense of the wide front from north to east. The Russians were deployed and ready for action with their strong tank and infantry forces near the eastern edge of Starosselje to the eastern edge of Kotelnja and up to the north to the railway. After the Russians

(Above) In an earlier photo SS-Sturmbannführer Hugo Kraas is seated next to Knight's Cross holder Heinz Macher. The "Totenkopf" German Cross holder also at the table is Hermann Buchner. Below, Knight's Cross holders Kraas (right) and Heinz Macher listen to questions from the home front during a promotional tour in March, 1943.

advanced from north to east and back with tanks and lively reconnaissance forces, they attacked at about 1300 hours in regimental strength, supported by thirteen T-34s used as assault guns. The attack became mired in the defensive fire of the Grenadiers of the SS-Panzer-Grenadier-Regiment 2, and three T-34s were knocked out.

Because of this strong defense, the enemy prepared their infantry and tank forces to advance on December 27, 1943. These forces, which were positioned before the section of left open flank of SS-Panzer-Grenadier-Regiment 2, had the strength of about a corps. They were obviously positioned there to advance in a general southwesterly direction, to break through the defensive front of the SS-Panzer-Grenadier-Regiment 2, after which they would reach and secure the highway between Shitomir and Berditschev and would then be able to surround Berditschev itself and attack the city.

This large attack began on December 28, 1943, at 0230 hours with an advance of 15 T-34s, carrying infantry. The tanks advanced into the open left flank of the Regiment from Toruvez. With a counter-advance by the Panzer group which was subordinated to the Regiment, the attack was beaten back. About an hour later came a further attack of 35 tanks carrying infantry, which penetrated the left flank of the Regiment and the regimental headquarters in Volossovo. The Panzer Group of the regiment and its anti-tank weapons annihilated 19 T-34s together with the tank close-combat troops. Many enemy casualties were counted. The regimental commander, SS-Obersturmbannführer Kraas, with the men of his regimental staff, personally led a counter-attack against the right flank of the attacking enemy infantry. During this attack, his men were able to annihilate the majority of the enemy infantry.

After this unsuccessful attack which claimed many Russian casualties, the enemy tanks pulled back to the railway to regroup. Their new plan was to attack at 1230 hours in a strength of two regiments with 40 tanks and in a strength of two regiments and 20 tanks from the North and the East out of the area between the villages of Schubarovka, Toruvez, Jusofovka to Staraja-Kotelnja. Even though the Division and Korps both foresaw a retreat of the Regiment to the southern bank of the Guiva section, SS-Obersturmbannführer Kraas was able to hold up the enemy by building up a new main fighting line directly south of the street intended to be used by the attacking Russian forces.

Through this decision, his personal action by the build-up of the main fighting line and his decisive engagement at the defense of this attack, SS-Obersturmbannführer Kraas avoided the encircling of his regiment and the heavy weapons under his command.

Meanwhile, the Russians achieved a breakthrough on the left flank of the Regiment. SS-Obersturmbannführer Kraas led the men of his regimental staff and some tanks in a counterattack. Seven enemy tanks were knocked out. After successfully defending against an infantry attack, the Russians pulled back with the mass of their tanks to the Northwest.

In the meantime a divisional order arrived to retreat to the new security line south of the Guiva section. The carrying out of this order became difficult because the bridge that was foreseen to be used by the Regiment for the crossing of the heavy weapons had been destroyed.

Despite of the constantly increasing enemy pressure and the strong fire of enemy tanks and rockets from the east and the north of the crossing, SS-Obersturmbannführer Kraas was successful in bringing over all heavy weapons in the company of Panther tanks (which were driving parallel to the Russian lines) to a crossing which lay further to the west. It is without question that the decisive and meaningful leadership of SS-Obersturmbannführer Kraas, who himself was the last to remain on the bridge, must be thanked that the fighting portions of the staff and the vehicles of the heavy weapons did not fall into enemy hands, or, better said, were not surrounded by them.

During the evening of December 29, 1943, the enemy occupied the new main fighting line with tanks and infantry and won a strong bridgehead position over the Guiva section. From this strong bridgehead the Russians attacked the positions of the SS-Panzer-Grenadier-Regiment 2 with strong infantry forces and 20 tanks on numerous occasions during the late morning hours.

Fully utilizing a basin northwest of Voroschino, the opponent attacked the village directly with tanks, during which the first portions of the enemy infantry managed to push their way into the northern sector of the village. That caused a battle crisis, as portions of I.Bataillon pulled back to the village following the death of the battalion commander and almost all of its NCOs, during which the enemy went directly to the west and around Voroshino, then around our positions and advanced to the south. In this critical situation, SS-Obersturmbannführer Kraas pulled together all available forces, writers, signals men, radio men, drivers, medics, etc. Himself armed with a machine pistol and later a machine gun, he accompanied them, and along the row of houses to the north and northwest, he threw back the enemy units which had broken through and built a new main fighting line directly there on the edge of the village. All further enemy attacks were beaten off, and, with that an orderly withdrawal was secured for the entire regiment before the coming sunset.

By holding this village and by inflicting an extraordinary amount of casualties upon the opponent during the defensive fighting of the previous day, SS-Panzer-Grenadier-Regiment 2 depleted the spearhead of the Russian tank army heading to the southwest of the majority of its attack forces. They also

SS-Standartenführer Hugo Kraas is privately awarded the Oakleaves to the Knight's Cross at the Führer's headquarters. He was among the best commanders to come from the SS officer school system.

enabled the withdrawal of all portions of the division to the new main fighting line northeast of Berditschev and enhanced their ability to establish their positions there.

Under the leadership of SS-Obersturmbannführer Kraas, the SS-Panzer-Grenadier-Regiment 2 either captured or destroyed the following:

91 enemy tanks, almost all which were T-34s, of which 29 were taken in close combat
63 anti-tank guns
15 cannons
36 trucks
49 hand held anti-tank
118 machine guns
31 grenade launchers
3 airplanes
6 field kitchens
8 limbers (horse drawn artillery ammunition wagons)
29 horse and carriage teams
3200 enemy killed
900 prisoners

SS-Obersturmbannführer Kraas proved himself as a fighter, teacher and leader at all times and in the highest manner. His personal courage, his decisiveness and his composure are exceptional and remain a shining example for his men.

I hold SS-Obersturmbannführer Kraas as worthy of the award of the Oakleaves to the Knight's Cross of the Iron Cross because of his excellent leadership, his spirit of adventure as well as his exemplary personal bravery and his ability to remain unshakable."

The award was approved on January 24, 1944, as the 375th given to a man of the German Armed Forces, and Hitler personally presented him the decoration at his headquarters in Rastenburg. On January 30, 1944, Kraas was promoted to SS-Standartenführer.

After recovery from his wounds and following a divisional commanders course during September and early October, 1944, Kraas was transferred to the 12.SS-Panzer-Division "Hitlerjugend." When Fritz Kraemer went to the 6.SS-Panzer-Armee as Sepp Dietrich's Chief of Staff, Hugo Kraas replaced him as commander of "Hitlerjugend" from November 19, 1944, until the end of the war. As a divisional commander he was promoted to SS-Oberführer on January 30, 1945, and to SS-Brigadeführer on April 20, 1945.[8] In addition to his other awards he was also given the Infantry Assault Badge in Bronze on October 3, 1940, the Close Combat Clasp in Silver on October 15, 1943, the Eastern Front Medal on August 25, 1942, and the Wound Badge in Black on August 28, 1941. His younger brother Boris was killed with the "Totenkopf" Division, and was posthumously awarded the Knight's Cross in 1945 as commander of its Panzerjäger Abteilung.

Kraas surrendered with the remnants of his command to the U.S. Army near Linz and was released from captivity in the autumn of 1948. He died of a heart attack in Selk, Schleswig-Holstein, on February 20, 1980.[9] One of the exceptional leaders produced by the SS officer school system, he attained command rank solely through outstanding bravery and leadership abilities. In Greece he was one of the officers whose command allowed the "Leibstandarte" to capture the Corinth canal and cut off large numbers of British troops during the German capture of that country. He was very well thought-of by Sepp Dietrich, who highly recommended him for larger commands in his early evaluations. Possibly along with Albert Frey, Kraas was among the best infantry leaders from the SS officer school system to serve the majority of his career with the "Leibstandarte."

[8] Most promotions of this date were voided, but Sepp Dietrich had the authority to approve and grant General rank advances. Among those he approved were Kraas and Sylvester Stadler (both to SS-Brigadeführer).

[9] Krätschmer, "Die Ritterkreuzträger der Waffen-SS," page 416.

FRITZ KRAEMER

The son of a merchant, Fritz Kraemer was born in Stettin on December 12, 1900. After his education he joined the Army, serving with Baden Infanterie Regiment "Markgraf Ludwig Wilhelm" No. 111 from 1918 to the start of May, 1921. Upon leaving the Army as a Leutnant, he joined the Prussian police as an Leut-nant, serving in Stettin and Berlin. As a Zugführer he was posted in Koslin during 1928-1929 and then had a similar assignment in Kreuzberg until 1933. Promoted to Oberleutnant in 1931, he went to the Landespolizei in 1933 and was promoted to Hauptmann on May 1, 1935.

On October 1, 1934, he left the Polizei, rejoining the Army as an Oberleutnant. Kraemer then attended the War Academy in Berlin until May, 1935. He was then assigned to Infanterieregiment 55 beginning in May, 1935. In early October, 1936, he took command of the regiment's 5th Company and led it until early 1939.[1]

Kraemer then was assigned, by March, 1939, as Ib (2.Generalstabsoffizier) of the 13.Infanterie Division and underwent further training, following which he became a member of the General Staff.[2] On October 6, 1939, he was awarded the Iron Cross 2nd class. On October 11, 1940, Kraemer advanced to be Ia of the 13.Infanterie Division and won the Iron Cross 1st class on May 26, 1940.[3] His unit reorganized as a Panzer Division and he remained Ia until mid-December, 1942, and he was awarded the Eastern Front Medal on August 3, 1942. For that staff position during the fighting in southern Russia, Kraemer was awarded the German Cross in Gold on February 26, 1942, and the Knight's Cross on December 17, 1942. On April 1, 1942, he was promoted to Oberstleutnant. During February, 1942, Kraemer headed the command and supply center for the III.Panzerkorps. While at that post he first met Sepp Dietrich. A close working relationship and friendship resulted in Kraemer being requested by Dietrich as his Chief of Staff for the I.SS-Panzer-Korps in 1943.

Kraemer was the Quartermaster of the 1.Panzerarmee from mid-December, 1942, through most of June, 1943. Promoted to Oberst on January 1, 1943, Kraemer was loaned to the Waffen-SS and was given the rank of SS-Oberführer on September 1, 1943. From June 20, 1943, until succeeded by Rudolf Lehmann, he served as Chief of Staff to the I.SS-Panzer-Korps.[4] During August 9-16, 1944, he deputised for Dietrich as corps commander when he took over command of the 5.Panzer-Armee until the arrival of Georg Keppler. Kraemer was officially admitted into the SS on August 1, 1944, with the rank of SS-Brigadeführer. He also given the rank of Generalmajor der Waffen-SS with seniority from April 1, 1942.

Kraemer went with Dietrich to his 5.Panzer-Armee post as Chief of Staff in late August, 1944, then returned the following month to I.SS-Panzer-Korps. He succeeded Hubert Meyer as commander of the 12.SS-Panzer-Division "Hitlerjugend" from October 24, 1944, until command was given to Hugo Kraas in mid-November.[5] Kraemer then spent two weeks in reserve. For the balance of the war he served with Sepp Dietrich as Chief of Staff for the 6.Panzer-Armee, which was retitled the 6.SS-Panzer-Armee in late-January, 1945.

---

[1] "Das Deutsche Heer, Gliederung, Standote, Stellenbesetzung und Verzeichnis sämtlicher Offizier an 1.3.1939" has Kraemer in the post of Ib of 13.Infanterire Division by that date. His personnel records conflict, saying he was in command of the company until October.

[2] Evaluation with career data written by Panzerarmee-Oberkommando 1 on March 1, 1943.

[3] ibid.

[4] "Personalverfügung" dated July 12, 1943.

[5] "Personalverfügung" dated November 3 and November 17, 1944. Kraemer was transfered to the reserve effective November 13, 1944, according to "Stabsbefehl Nr. 29/44," dated December 9, 1944.

Trained as a Prussian-type staff officer, Kraemer was extremely gifted and a model officer with compassion for his troops. His understanding of the civilians in a war situation was appreciated by Heinz Guderian who thought him to be of good character as well as politically sound.

Kraemer and Dietrich were among the most successful staff officer and divisional commander combinations. Dietrich, a brave natural leader, compensated for his lack of formal training with Kraemer as his chief military planner. After the war he was tried in the Malmedy case and was given a ten-year sentence. Following his release, he lived in Höxter until his death on June 23, 1959. Fritz Kraemer was buried with full military honors.

Right: Fritz Kraemer as an Army staff officer and Knight's Cross holder.

Below: From right are Fritz Kraemer, Josef Dietrich, Theodor Wisch, Kurt Meyer and an unknown German Cross holder. Photo taken at the headquarters of the I.SS-Panzer-Korps.

KARL KREUTZ

The last commanding officer of the 2.SS-Panzer-Division "Das Reich" was born on September 20, 1909, in Bromberg. Karl Kreutz joined a precursor component of the later "Leibstandarte" in July, 1933, and served with the 4., then later the 7.Kompanie until March, 1935. On March 8, 1935, he became a platoon leader with the 13.Kompanie until transferring to a similar post with the 16.Kompanie in September, 1938. From December, 1938, until leaving the "Leibstandarte" in May, 1939, Kreutz served with the 12.Kompanie. Commissioned as an SS-Untersturmführer on November 9, 1935, he was promoted to SS-Obersturmführer on September 12, 1937.

The artillery regiment of the SS-Verfügungstruppe was formed in early June, 1939, under Peter Hansen and Kreutz became 2.Batterie commander. During the Polish campaign he was awarded the Iron Cross 2nd class on October 2, 1939. By December, 1939, he had moved to command the 6.Batterie when the regiment became part of the initial SS division to be formed and held command until April, 1941. Promoted to SS-Hauptsturmführer on January 30, 1940, he won the Iron Cross 1st class on July 30, 1940, for actions in the Western campaign. Kreutz was wounded on May 27, 1940, and was subsequently awarded the Wound Badge in Black.

Kreutz took command of the IV(s).Abteilung on April 20, 1941, and led the heavy caliber gun unit until early March, 1943. On November 9, 1941, he was promoted to SS-Sturmbannführer and on August 5, 1942, was awarded the Eastern Front Medal. In mid-March, 1943, artillery regiment commander Kurt Brassack replaced Herbert Vahl as "Das Reich" divisional commander and Kreutz took command of the artillery regiment. He held command of that unit until turning over leadership to Wolfgang Gast on April 18, 1945.[1]

On December 17, 1943, Kreutz was formally presented the German Cross in Gold (it was approved two days previously) from a recommendation submitted by "Das Reich" commander Walter Krüger that reads as follows:

"During the advance to the Dnjepr river on July 6, 1941, detachment commander SS-Hauptsturmführer Kreutz received orders to lead all detachment commanders on a reconnaissance for artillery positions in the quickly-advancing attack. Far ahead of the advance infantry and other commanders, he reached an unoccupied village. An enemy rear guard of company strength held a hill one kilometer away.

A truck with fifteen infantrymen returned to the village after seeing the car of SS-Sturmbannführer Heinz Lorenz.[2] Kreutz immediately employed the crew of his vehicle as infantry. When the enemy entered the village he was greeted and destroyed by rifle and sub-machine gun fire, partly done in close combat.

During the expansion of the Jelnja bridgehead on July 22, 1941, the infantry of the Division was deployed adjacent to the 10.Panzer-Division. Then SS-Hauptsturmführer Karl Kreutz's detachment was still marching along the road as it was positioned at the rear of the advance column. Kreutz came to the front and on his own initiative brought the 10.Batterie, guiding them to their fire positions and observation posts. Kreutz then

---

[1] The date, provided by Herrn Keutz during the author's research of the artillery regiment, would coincide with Gast assuming the command. Letter from Wolfgang Gast dated March 17, 1987 and Yerger, "Knights of Steel." Volume 1, page 219.

[2] Commander of I.Abteilung, Lorenz was awarded the German Cross in Gold on August 7, 1944, and ended the war as an SS-Obersturmbannführer. In October, 1944, he took command of the artillery regiment of the 16.SS-Panzer-Grenadier-Division "Reichsführer-SS." Yerger, "Knights of Steel," volume 1, pages 237-238.

personally coordinated the fire of his detachment. Without his dedication, the detachment could not have supported the tough fighting of the infantry that fast and effectively. Kreutz led his unit from the advance command post, continuously proving his bravery and command abilities. He skillfully managed the low stocks of ammunition so he could always provide effective support in critical situations.

During the tough armored battles at Rogan on February 12, 1943, he placed his command post on the same line as the observation units, forming an assembly line for our infantry. Using these forces, the enemy was repulsed and Kreutz personally engaged in the heavy defensive fighting. During that time he directed artillery fire as close as 50 meters from his own position. This daring action allowed our infantry to break contact with the Russian infantry, which were supported by tanks, and successfully man our defensive line.

During the attack north of Osanewa (north of Kharkov) on March 15, 1943, Kreutz coordinated the fire of the batteries which supported the attack of our tank detachment. Later, he directed the fire of the heavy artillery detachment from his armored personnel carrier. With this vehicle he drove closely behind the tank commander's vehicle and directed his artillery by radio, despite heavy tank and anti-tank fire. This earned him a decisive share of the credit for neutralizing the enemy tank and anti-tank lines."[3]

Those combats in Kharkov were the most intense experienced by Kreutz during the war.[4]

Promoted to SS-Obersturmbannführer on April 20, 1943, and to SS-Standartenführer on April 20, 1944, Karl Kreutz twice commanded "Das Reich." On August 27, 1944, He was awarded the Knight's Cross as a result of the following award proposal submitted by divisional commander Otto Baum:

"On July 9, 1944, the Americans succeeded in penetrating with tanks in the area east and southeast of Le Desert. A counterattack by the engineer battalion was ineffective since elements of I./Infantry Regiment 984, the Angers engineer school, and Fusilier Battalion 275 had been withdrawn from their deployment on the west bank of the Vire near Cavigny.

In this situation, SS-Standartenführer Kreutz, under heavy artillery fire, came forward to the battle group command post near Haut au Duc and was briefed on the situation. Seeing the danger to the entire front north of St. Lo, Kreutz immediately concentrated all the artillery detachments, positioned northwest of St. Lo, to seal off the penetration point near Chateau de

Karl Kreutz as an SS-Untersturmführer with the "Leibstandarte."

l'a Mare de Calvigny with directed fire. The sudden surprise fire prevented a further American advance to the south and southwest while forcing them to retreat in the north.

Following the crossing of the Vire canal on July 10, 1944, the enemy succeeded in cutting off parts of Division "Götz von Berlichingen," holding the line to the north near Grainges, by successfully breaking through to Haut Verney via Goucherie. At 13:15 hours, Haut Verney was taken by the enemy, followed by a further advance that proceeded south/southwest and took St. Adre then moved toward Le Port. At 17:30 hours the enemy moved out from Haut Verney towards Mesnil-Angot and took the town while some elements reached the northeast corner of Bois du Hommett. Our forces succeeded in holding up the hard-pursuing enemy.

In this dangerous situation, SS-Standartenführer Kreutz, based on a report saying that Tribehou was almost void of our troops, employed hastily-assembled elements of the 11.Batterie and the corps observation unit to secure the village and hold it

---

[3] German Cross in Gold recommendation dated dated August 21, 1943, and approved on December 15, 1943, with the date the award was actually presented via Herrn Kreutz.

[4] Letter to the author dated July 28, 1985.

(Above) Artillery officers of SS-Division "Reich" during a comedy performance. From right are Karl Kreutz, Oskar Drexler (awarded the Knight's Cross) and Kurt Brasack. Below, Kreutz's headquarters in Russia for the IV./Artillerie Regiment.

at all cost. At the same time, he created a screen in Tribehou with parts of the anti-tank detachment to intercept tanks reported there and also near La Haye, as well as supporting the exhausted infantry. Straggling infantry units were intercepted on his orders and, under his personal command, were put into position near Tribehou. With these and other portions of the artillery regiment he was successful in repulsing a penetration in the northwest sector."[5]

Kreutz led both the division and the artillery regiment from January 20, 1945, to February 10, 1945, after Heinz Lammerding left to assume a staff post under Himmler. Succeeded by Werner Ostendorff, Kreutz then replaced Rudolf Lehmann, who had been wounded, and led the division from April 13, 1945, until its com-

[5] "Kurze Begründung des Zwischenvorgesetzten" for Kreutz's Knight's Cross dated August 3, 1944, and signed by Otto Baum.

ponents surrendered.[6] During the final phase of the war, "Das Reich" fought in Hungary and Austria. On May 6, 1945, Karl Kreutz became the 863rd soldier awarded the Oakleaves to the Knight's Cross.

One of the most decorated, experienced, and tactically-skilled Waffen-SS artillery commanders, he served his entire wartime career with "Das Reich." His skills, bravery, and positive, good-natured personality endeared him to his subordinates as well as all commanders of the Division. Karl Kreutz lives today in retirement and has assisted numerous historians with research pertaining to his former division.

[6] Some junior commanders of the regiment give the 12th as the command change between Gast and Kreutz but a divisional commander was available at that time (Rudolf Lehmann). Kreutz, as he had previously, commanded both the Division as well as the Regiment until turning over artillery command to Gast. Awarded the Knight's Cross on June 4, 1944, and promoted to SS-Hauptsturmführer on November 9, 1943, Gast was previously the commander of II.Abteilung having served earlier in the war as an Abteilungsadjutant.

In December, 1943, are, from left, Sylvester Stadler ("Der Führer" commander), Hans Bissinger (III./Der Führer), Christian Tychsen (Panzer Regiment commander), Theodor Sorg (partly hidden, signals detachment commander), Hans Blume (Anti-aircraft detachment commander), unknown, Karl Kreutz (artillery regiment commander) and (in profile) Peter Sommer (1a).

(Below) From right are Sylvester Stadler ("Der Führer" Regiment commander), Theodor Sorg (signals detachment commander), Karl Kreutz, Walter Krüger (commander "Das Reich") and Dr. Carl Schlink (divisional medical officer). Right, Karl Kreutz as an SS-Standartenführer and Knight's Cross holder.

The commander of the "Das Reich" artillery regiment, SS-Standartenführer Karl Kreutz.

APPENDICES

Appendix 1: RANKS

SS	Polizei and Army	U.S.
Reichsführer-SS	Heinrich Himmler's rank as head of the SS and Polizei	(no equivalent)
SS-Oberst-Gruppenführer	Genearloberst	Colonel General
SS-Obergruppenführer	General	General
SS-Gruppenführer	Generalleutnant	Lieutenant General
SS-Brigadeführer	Generalmajor	Major General
SS-Oberführer	(no equivalent, a unique intermediate SS rank)	
SS-Standartenführer	Oberst	Colonel
SS-Obersturmbannführer	Oberstleutnant	Lieutenant Colonel
SS-Sturmbannführer	Major	Major
SS-Sturmhauptführer (early designation)	Hauptmann	Captain
SS-Hauptsturmführer	Hauptmann or Rittmeister	Captain
SS-Obersturmführer	Oberleutnant	1st Lieutenant
SS-Sturmführer (early designation)	Leutnant	2nd Lieutenant
SS-Untersturmführer	Leutnant	2nd Lieutenant
Truppführer (early designation)	Technical Sargeant	
SS-Oberscharführer	Feldwebel	Technical Sargent
SS-Scharführer (early designation)	Unterfeldwebel	Staff Sergeant
SS-Unterscharführer	Unteroffizier	Sergeant
SS-Rottenführer	Stabsgefreiter & Obergefreiter Corporal	
SS-Schütz	Schütz	Private
SS Mann	Mann	Recruit

Appendix 2: Waffen-SS Field Post Numbers - Corps and Divisions 1943

This Feldpost number list was assembled in 1943 by the SS Leadership Main Office.[1] In conjunction with the symbol based Order of Battle charts throughout the text, they allow the best understanding of the various higher commands at that time. As with many types of documentation there are conflicts and differences. One example is "Das Reich." Its entire Regiment "Langemarck" is listed when the II.Bataillon had been used in October, 1943, to create the II./Panzer Regiment. Only its I.(Kradschützen)/Battalion existed at that time. In some instances different components were subordinated differently within a command, such as the Field Post Office and War Reporters Units though their functions were the same. Individual companies could be distributed among the regiments they were subordinated to, normally being anti-aircraft, motorcycle, infantry gun or engineer units. The titles of all units have been reproduced as they are in the original document. The divisional designations, as well as Generalkommando SS Panzerkorps being the only higher formation, date the list more accurately to have been compiled in approximately February, 1943.[2] The units contained are listed as follows:

Generalkommando SS-Panzerkorps
SS-Panzer-Grenadier-Division "Leibstandarte SS Adolf Hitler"
SS-Panzer-Grenadier-Division "Das Reich"
SS-Panzer-Grenadier-Division "Totenkopf"
SS-Polizei Division
SS-Panzer-Grenadier-Division "Wiking"
SS-Gebirgs-Division "Nord"
SS-Freiwilligen-Division "Prinz Eugen"
SS-Kavallerie-Division
SS-Panzer-Grenadier-Division "Hohenstaufen"
SS-Panzer-Grenadier-Division 10 (10.SS-Div.)

Generalkommando SS-Panzerkorps became the II.SS-Panzer-Korps. All of the designated Panzer Grenadier Divisions were later upgraded and became Panzer Divisions. The SS Kavallerie Division was eventually bestowed the honor title "Florian Geyer." SS-Panzer-Grenadier-Division 10, after being briefly titled "Karl der Grosse," received the honor title "Frundsberg."

---

[1] SS-Führungshauptamt, Kommandoamt der Waffen-SS, Abt. Feldpostwessen, "Feldpostübersicht der Waffen-SS," I.Teil, Vorliegende Ausgabe enthält, Blatt I und 1-30, Berlin, 1943.

[2] "Nordland," numerically the eleventh division established, was formed in the March, 1943, and is not in the original document. See Bender/Taylor, "Uniforms, Organization and History of the Waffen-SS," volumes 3 and 4 for detail of the creation dates and title changes of individual divisions in 1943.

Generalkommando SS-Panzerkorps

SS-Generalkommando (Panzer) Stab	12 200
Kartenstelle	12 200
Kriegsberichter Kompanie	12 200B
Sicherungskompanie	48 759
Stab Artillerie Kommandeur (Arko)	14 513
Stab Korps Nachschubführer	15 621
1.Kraftwagenkolonne	17 028
2.Kraftwagenkolonne	18 445
3.(groß) Kraftwagenkolonne	19 160
Kraftwagen Werkstatt Zug	20 805
Feldgendarmerie Trupp	21 227
Feldpostamt	22 620
Gemeine Flak Kompanie	23 871

Korps Nachrichten Abteilung

Stab	18 726
1.Kompanie (Fu)	19 582
2.Kompanie (Fu)	20 939
3.Komapnie (Fe)	21 367
4.Panzer (Fu) Kompanie	22 871
leichte Nachrichten Kolonne	23 508

SS-Werfer Abteilung

Stab	00 004A
Stabskompanie	00 004A
1.Batterie	00 004B
2.Batterie	00 004C
3.Batterie	00 004D
4.Batterie	00 004E
leichte Kolonne Werfer Abteilung	00 004F

SS-Karstwehr Bataillon

Bataillon Stab	05 219A
Stabskompanie	05 219A
1.Kompanie	05 219B
2.Kompanie	05 219C
3.Kompanie	05 219D
4.Kompanie	05 219E

Sanitäts-Abteilung

1.SS-Lararett (mot)	01 593A
2.SS-Lararett (mot)	01 593B
Stab Korps Sanitäts-Abteilung	01 082
leichte Sanitäts Kolonne	02 996
1.Krankenkraftwagenzug	02 628
2.Krankenkraftwagenzug	03 014

SS-Panzer-Grenadier-Division "Leibstandarte SS Adolf Hitler"

Divisions Stab	21 825A
Kartenstelle	21 825A
Musikzug	48 548

SS-Grenadier-Regiment 1

Regiment Stab	00 933
Stabskompanie	00 933
I.Bataillon	
Stab	29 707A
1.Kompanie	29 707B
2.Kompanie	29 707C
3.Kompanie	29 707D
4.Kompanie	29 707E
5.Kompanie	29 707F
II.Bataillon	
Stab	11 150A
6.Kompanie	11 150B
7.Kompanie	11 150C
8.Kompanie	11 150D
9.Kompanie	11 150E
10.Kompanie	11 150F

III.Bataillon	
Stab	09 842A
11.Kompanie	09 842B
12.Kompanie	09 842C
13.Kompanie	09 842D
14.Kompanie	09 842E
15.Kompanie	09 842F
Flak Kompanie	01 087
Infanterie Geschütz Kompanie	02 396
Panzerjäger Kompanie	03 508

SS-Grenadier-Regiment 2

Regiment Stab	04 124
Stabskompanie	04 124
I.Bataillon	
Stab	09 088A
1.Kompanie	09 088B
2.Kompanie	09 088C
3.Kompanie	09 088D
4.Kompanie	09 088E
5.Kompanie	09 088F
II.Bataillon	
Stab	14 103A
6.Kompanie	14 103B
7.Kompanie	14 103C
8.Kompanie	14 103D
9.Kompanie	14 103E
10.Kompanie	14 103F
III.Bataillon	
Stab	08 280A
11.Kompanie	08 280B
12.Kompanie	08 280C
13.Kompanie	08 280D
14.Kompanie	08 280E
15.Kompanie	08 280F
Flak Kompanie	05 415
Infanterie Geschütz Kompanie	06 277
Panzerjäger Kompanie	07 841

Panzer Regiment 1

Regiment Stab	48 020
Stabskompanie	48 020A
I.Abteilung	
Abteilung Stab	48 477A
Stabskompanie	48 477B
1.Kompanie	48 935
2.Kompanie	48 162
3.Kompanie	48 427
II.Abteilung	
Abteilung Stab	28 129A
Stabskompanie	28 129B
4.Kompanie	29 055
5.Kompanie	30 464
6.Kompanie	31 820

schwere Panzer Kompanie	48 165
Panzer Pionier Kompanie	49 945
Panzer Werkstatt Kompanie	32 150
1.leichte Panzer Kolonne	48 196
2.leichte Panzer Kolonne	48 310

Sturmgeschütz Abteilung

Stab	08 917A
Stabsbatterie	08 917A
1.Batterie	08 917B
2.Batterie	08 917C
3.Batterie	08 917D

Aufklärungsabteilung

Stab	01 893
Nachrichten Zug	01 893
1.Kompanie	33 752
2.Kompanie	02 234
3.Kompanie	03 197
4.Panzer-Späh-Kompanie	09 909
5.Kompanie	37 359
leichte Kolonne Panzer Aufklärungsabteilung	
	10 344

Artillerie Regiment

Stab	03 903A
Stabsbatterie	03 903B
Beob Batterie	03 903C
Werfer Batterie	03 903D
I.Abteilung	
Stab	02 924A
1.Batterie	02 924B
2.Batterie	02 924C
3.Batterie	02 924D
II.Abteilung	
Stab	11 808A
4.Batterie	11 808B
5.Batterie	11 808C
6.Batterie	11 808D
III.Abteilung	
Stab	04 539A
7.Batterie	04 539B
8.Batterie	04 539C
9.Batterie	04 539D
IV.Abteilung	
Stab	41 805A
10.Batterie	41 805B
11.Batterie	41 805C
12.Batterie	41 805D

Panzerjäger Abteilung

Stab	12 611
Nachrichten Zug	12 611
1.Kompanie	13 427

2.Kompanie	14 046
3.Kompanie	15 775

Flak Abteilung

Stab	05 583
Stabsbatterie	05 583
1.Batterie	05 946
2.Batterie	06 706
3.Batterie	07 110
4.Batterie	43 772
5.Batterie	46 978
2cm Flak Zug	22 193

Pionier Battalion

Stab	05113
1.Kompanie	05 828
2.Kompanie	06 272
3.Kompanie	06 272B
4.Kompanie	06 272C
Brückenkolonne	07 604
leichte Pionier Kolonne	07 855

Nachrichten Abteilung

Stab	08 259A
1.Panzer (Fe) Kompanie	08 259B
2.Panzer (Fe) Kompanie	08 259C
leichte Panzer Nachrichten Kolonne	14 438

Wirtschafts Bataillon

Stab	43 667
Verpflegungsamt	43 667A
Bäckereikompanie	41 335
Schlächterei Kompanie	42 916
Verpflegungskolonne	43 667B

Sanitäts Abteilung

Stab	21 825E
1.Sanitäts Kompanie	11 941
2.Sanitäts Kompanie	45 487
Feldlararett	11 754
1.Krankenkraftwagen Zug	12 109
2.Krankenkraftwagen Zug	12 686
3.Krankenkraftwagen Zug	23 457
Feldpostamt	12 388
Kriegsbereichterkompanie	21 825B
Feldgendarmerie Trupp	21 825C

Nachschub-Dienste

Stab Divisions Nachschubführer	08 661
1.Kraftwagenkolonne	10 464
2.Kraftwagenkolonne	10 894
3.Kraftwagenkolonne	11 286
4.Kraftwagenkolonne	33 627
5.Kraftwagenkolonne	09 774

6.Kraftwagenkolonne	10 058
7.Kraftwagenkolonne	16 846
8.Kraftwagenkolonne	17 115
9.Kraftwagenkolonne	18 969
10.Kraftwagenkolonne	19 340
11.(groß) Kraftwagenkolonne	25 261
12.(groß) Kraftwagenkolonne	26 275
13.(groß) Kraftwagenkolonne	01 175
14.(groß) Kraftwagenkolonne	08 549
15.(groß) Kraftwagenkolonne für Betriebstoff	
	09 824
16.(groß) Kraftwagenkolonne für Betriebstoff	
	11 130
17.(groß) Kraftwagenkolonne für Betriebstoff	
	47 167
18.(groß) Kraftwagenkolonne für Betriebstoff	
	28 846
19.(groß) Kraftwagenkolonne für Betriebstoff	
	07 925

Instandsetzungs Abteilung

Stab	09 264A
1.Werkstatt-Kompanie	09 264B
2.Werkstatt-Kompanie	47 856
3.Werkstatt-Kompanie	47 077
4.Werkstatt-Kompanie	46 989
5.Werkstatt-Kompanie	27 330
Nachschubkompanie	40 456

VII.LSSAH

Bataillon Stab	09 505A
1.Kompanie	09 505B
2.Kompanie	09 505C
3.Kompanie	09 505D
4.Kompanie	09 505E
5.Kompanie	09 505F

SS-Panzer-Grenadier-Division "Das Reich"

Divisions Stab	20 092
Kartenstelle	20 092
Kommandant Divisionsstabsquartier	20 092A

SS-Grenadier-Regiment "Deutschland"

Regiment Stab	20 727
I.Battalion	
Stab	27 064A
1.Kompanie	27 064B
2.Kompanie	27 064C
3.Kompanie	27 064D
4.Kompanie	27 064E
II.Bataillon	

Stab	00 159A
5.Kompanie	00 159B
6.Kompanie	00 159C
7.Kompanie	00 159D
8.Kompanie	00 159E
III.Bataillon	
Stab	28 688A
9.Kompanie	28 688B
10.Kompanie	28 688C
11.Kompanie	28 688D
12.Kompanie	28 688E
13.Kompanie	21 687 A

SS-Grenadier-Regiment "Der Führer"

Regiment Stab	03 669
I.Bataillon	
Stab	15 807A
1.Kompanie	15 807B
2.Kompanie	15 807C
3.Kompanie	15 807D
4.Kompanie	15 807E
II.Bataillon	
Stab	11 707A
5.Kompanie	11 707B
6.Kompanie	11 707C
7.Kompanie	11 707D
8.Kompanie	11 707E
III.Bataillon	
Stab	05 452A
9.Kompanie	05 452B
10.Kompanie	05 452C
11.Kompanie	05 452D
12.Kompanie	05 452E
13.Kompanie	05 879A

Artillerie Regiment

Regiment Stab	03 311
Meßbatterie	46 253
I.Abteilung	
Stab	10 074A
1.Batterie	10 074B
2.Batterie	10 074C
3.Batterie	10 074D
II.Abteilung	
Stab	15 982A
4.Batterie	15 982B
5.Batterie	15 982C
6.Batterie	15 982D
III.Abteilung	
Stab	12 626A
7.Batterie	12 626B
8.Batterie	12 626C
9.Batterie	12 626D
IV.Abteilung	

Stab	03 504A
10.Batterie	03 504B
11.Batterie	03 504C
12.Batterie	03 504D

SS-Schützen Regiment "Langemarck"

Regiment Stab	26 292
Stabskompanie	26 292B
I.Bataillon	
Stab	41 940A
1.Kompanie	41 940B
2.Kompanie	41 940C
3.Kompanie	41 940D
4.Kompanie	41 940E
5.Kompanie	41 940F
II.Bataillon	
Stab	32 215A
6.Kompanie	32 215B
7.Kompanie	32 215C
8.Kompanie	32 215D
9.Kompanie	32 215E
10.Kompanie	32 215F

Panzer Regiment 2

Regiment Stab	48 800
Stabskompanie	48 880A
I.Abteilung	
Stab	27 310
Stabskompanie	27 310A
1.Kompanie	28 454
2.Kompanie	29 883
3.Kompanie	30 654
II.Abteilung	
Stab	48 070A
Stabskompanie	48 070B
4.Kompanie.	48 719
5.Kompanie	48 542
6.Kompanie	48 264
schwere Panzer Kompanie	48 308
Panzer Pionier Kompanie	48 326
Panzer Werkstatt Kompanie	06 606
1.leichte Panzer Kolonne	48 175
2.leichte Panzer Kolonne	48 933

SS-Sturmgeschütz Abteilung 2

Stab	48 963A
Stabsbatterie	48 963B
1.Batterie	48 963C
2.Batterie	48 963D
3.Batterie	48 963E

Aufklärungsabteilung

Stab	03 054
1.Kompanie	07 492

2.Kompanie	08 817
3.Kompanie	13 389
leichte Aufklärungskolonne	30 121

Panzer Jäger Abteilung

Stab	20 793
1.Kompanie	21 267
2.Kompanie	22 023
3.Kompanie	22 986

Flak Abteilung

Stab	23 223
Stabsbatterie	23 223A
1.Batterie	24 083
2.Batterie	24 067
3.Batterie	39 858
4.Batterie	48 124
5.Batterie	08 690
leichte Artillerie Kolonne Flak	30 077

Pionier Bataillon

Stab	14 179
1.Kompanie	02 558
2.Kompanie	19 167
3.Kompanie	10 897
Brückenkolonne	29 573
leichte Pionier Kolonne	23 313

Nachrichtenabteilung

Stab	06 146
1.Kompanie	04 359
2.Kompanie	07 874
leichte Nachrichten Kolonne	25 213

Wirtschafts Bataillon

Stab	33 882A
Verpflegungsamt	33 882
Bäckerei Kompanie	32 615
Schlächterie Kompanie	33 084

Nachschub-Dienst

Division Nachschubführer	25 089
1.Kraftwagenkolonne	25 976
2.Kraftwagenkolonne	26 436
3.Kraftwagenkolonne	27 172
4.Kraftwagenkolonne	27 812
5.Kraftwagenkolonne	29 387
6.Kraftwagenkolonne	
7.Kraftwagenkolonne	28 242
8.Kraftwagenkolonne	
9.Kraftwagenkolonne	28 955
10.Kraftwagenkolonne	00 048
11.Kraftwagenkolonne	
12.Kraftwagenkolonne	

13.Kraftwagenkolonne	30 028
14.Kraftwagenkolonne	30 365
15.Kraftwagenkolonne	30 966
Nachub Kompanie	32 275
Waffen Werkstatt Kompanie	21 460

Instandsetzungs-Abteilung

Abteilung Stab	00 197A
1.Werkstatt Kompanie	31 097B
2.Werkstatt Kompanie	31 832
3.Werkstatt Kompanie	27 173
Ersatz Kolonne	31 097C

Sanitäts-Abteilung

Abteilung Stab	29 245
Feldlazarett	35 153
1.Sanitäts Kompanie	34 192
2.Sanitäts Kompanie	34 647
1.Krankenkraftwagenzug	35 824
2.Krankenkraftwagenzug	36 411
3.Krankenkraftwagenzug	37 228
Stabskompanie	35 153A
Feldgendarmerie Kompanie	37 900
Feldpostamt	09 600
Kriegsberichter Kompanie	20 092B

SS-Panzer-Grenadier-Division "Totenkopf"

Divisions Stab	17 492
Kartenstelle	17 492
Stabskompanie Divisions Kommando	17 492A

SS-Totenkopf-Grenadier-Regiment 1

Regiment Stab	00 746
I.Battalion	
Stab	31 256A
1.Kompanie	31 256B
2.Kompanie	31 256C
3.Kompanie	31 256D
4.Kompanie	31 256E
II.Battalion	
Stab	18 249A
5.Kompanie	18 249B
6.Kompanie	18 249C
7.Kompanie	18 249D
8.Kompanie	18 249E
III.Battalion	
Stab	33 501A
9.Kompanie	33 501B
10.Kompanie	33 501C
11.Kompanie	33 501D
12.Kompanie	33 501E

13.Kompanie	38 623
14.Kompanie	14 456
15.Kompanie	00 581
16.Kompanie	01 705

SS-Totenkopf-Grenadier-Regiment 3

Regiment Stab	13 203
I.Bataillon	
Stab	07 526A
1.Kompanie	07 526B
2.Kompanie	07 526C
3.Kompanie	07 527D
4.Kompanie	07 528E
II.Bataillon	
Stab	39 153A
5.Kompanie	39 153B
6.Kompanie	39 153C
7.Kompanie	39 153D
8.Kompanie	39 153E
III.Bataillon	
Stab	22 135A
9.Kompanie	22 135B
10.Kompanie	22 135C
11.Kompanie	22 135D
12.Kompanie	22 135E
13.Kompanie	07 446
14.Kompanie	12 237
15.Kompanie	02 925
16.Kompanie	04 709

SS-Schützen-Regiment "Thule"

Regiment Stab	24 410
Stabskompanie	24 410A
I.Bataillon	
Stab	25 979A
1.Kompanie	25 979B
2.Kompanie	25 979C
3.Kompanie	25 979D
4.Kompanie	25 979E
5.Kompanie	25 979F
II.Bataillon	
Stab	10 945A
6.Kompanie	10 945B
7.Kompanie	10 945C
8.Kompanie	10 945D
9.Kompanie	10 945E

SS-Panzer Regiment 3

Regiment Stab	48 550A
Stabskompanie	48 550B
I.Abteilung	
Stab	32 238
Stabskompanie	32 238A
1.Kompanie	33 141

2.Kompanie	34 390
3.Kompanie	35 763
II.Abteilung	
Stab	48 279A
Stabskompanie	48 279B
4.Kompanie	48 182
5.Kompanie	48 544
6.Kompanie	48 912
schwere Panzer Kompanie	48 786
Panzer Pionier Kompanie	48 663
Panzer Werkstatt Kompanie	35 977
1.leichte Panzer Kolonne	48 407
2.leichte Panzer Kolonne	48 136

Sturmgeschütz Abteilung 3

Stab	10 003A
Stabsbatterie	10 003B
1.Batterie	10 003C
2.Batterie	10 003D
3.Batterie	10 003E

SS-Totenkopf-Artillerie Regiment

Regiment Stab	36 883
Stabsbatterie	36 883A
Beobbachter Batterie	47 438
Meßbatterie	
I.Abteilung	
Stab	39 245A
1.Batterie	39 245B
2.Batterie	39 245C
3.Batterie	39 245D
II.Abteilung	
Stab	36 053A
4.Batterie	36 053B
5.Batterie	36 053C
6.Batterie	36 053D
III.Abteilung	
Stab	08 014A
7.Batterie	08 014B
8.Batterie	08 014C
9.Batterie	08 014D
IV.Abteilung	
Stab	11 020A
10.Batterie	11 020B
11.Batterie	11 020C
12.Batterie	11 020D

SS-Totenkopf-Aufklärungsabteilung

Stab	34 404
1.Kompanie	33 755
2.Kompanie	15 101
3.Kompanie	00 223
4.Kompanie	04 262

SS-Totenkopf-Flak-Abteilung

Stab	34 963
1.Batterie	35 335
2.Batterie	35 601
3.Batterie	35 957
4.Batterie	48 014
Flak Kolonne	36 508

SS-Totenkopf-Panzerjäger Abteilung

Stab	26 460
1.Kompanie	35 354
2.Kompanie	32 287
3.Kompanie	07 094

SS-Totenkopf-Nachrichten Abteilung

Stab	16 224
1.(Fe)Kompanie	06 994
2.(Fu)Kompanie	31 110
leichte Nachrichten Kolonne	28 167

SS-Totenkopf-Pionier Bataillon

Stab	16 192
1.Kompanie	19 103
2.Kompanie	10 014
3.Kompanie	36 091
Brückenkolonne	24 068
leichte Pionier Kolonne	27 713

Instandsetzungs-Abteilung

Stab	31 135A
1.Werkstatt Kompanie	31 135
2.Werkstatt Kompanie	18 782
3.Werkstatt Kompanie	16 343
Ersatzteil und Reifenstaffel	19 606

Wirtschafts Bataillon

Stab	26 365B
Verpflegungsamt	26 365
Bäckerei Kompanie	39 301
Schlächterei Kompanie	36 178

Sanitäts Dienste

1.Sanitäts Kompanie	29 199
2.Sanitäts Kompanie	10 012
Feldlazarett	11 896
1.Krankenkraftwagenzug	03 383
2.Krankenkraftwagenzug	39 133
3.Krankenkraftwagenzug	38 263

Ordungs Dienste

Feldgendarmerie Trupp	35 423

Feldpost

Feldpostamt	32 052

Nachschub-Dienste

Stab Division Nachschubführer	22 404
1.Kraftfahrkompanie	35 106
2.Kraftfahrkompanie	11 968
3.Kraftfahrkompanie	27 730
4.Kraftfahrkompanie	29 242
5.Kraftfahrkompanie	05 623
6.Kraftwagenkolonne für Betriebstoff	39 901
7.Kraftwagenkolonne für Betriebstoff	34 011
8. (groß) Kraftwagenkolonne für Betriebstoff	24 211
Waffen-Werkstatt Kompanie	36 912
Nachschub Kompanie	06 744

SS-Polizei-Division

Divisions Stab	00 386
Kartenstelle	00 386

SS-Polizei-Grenadier-Regiment 1

Regiment Stab	11 376
I.Bataillon	
Stab	12 658A
1.Kompanie	12 658B
2.Kompanie	12 658C
3.Kompanie	12 658D
4.Kompanie	12 658E
II.Bataillon	
Stab	16 982A
5.Kompanie	16 982B
6.Kompanie	16 982C
7.Kompanie	16 982D
8.Kompanie	16 982E
III.Bataillon	
Stab	21 354A
9.Kompanie	21 354B
10.Kompanie	21 354C
11.Kompanie	21 354D
12.Kompanie	21 354E
13.Kompanie	26 665
14.Kompaie	27 356
leichte Infanterie Kolonne	28 542

SS-Polizei-Grenadier-Regiment 2

Regiment Stab	29 428
I.Bataillon	
Stab	29 948A
1.Kompanie	29 948B
2.Kompanie	29 948C
3.Kompanie	29 948D
4.Kompanie	29 948E
II.Bataillon	

Stab	32 194A
5.Kompanie	32 194B
6.Kompanie	32 194C
7.Kompanie	32 194D
8.Kompanie	32 194E
III.Bataillon	
Stab	34 798A
9.Kompanie	34 798B
10.Kompanie	34 798C
11.Kompanie	34 798D
12.Kompanie	34 798E
13.Kompanie	37 148
14.Kompanie	37 815
leichte Infanterie Kolonne	38 083

SS-Polizei-Grenadier-Regiment 3

Regiment Stab	38 783
I.Bataillon	
Stab	39 063A
1.Kompanie	39 063B
2.Kompanie	39 063C
3.Kompanie	39 063D
4.Kompanie	39 063E
II.Bataillon	
Stab	28 274A
5.Kompanie	28 274B
6.Kompanie	28 274C
7.Kompanie	28 274D
8.Kompanie	28 274E
III.Bataillon	
Stab	31 843A
9.Kompanie	31 843B
10.Kompanie	31 843C
11.Kompanie	31 843D
12.Kompanie	31 843E
13.Kompanie	34 052
14.Kompanie	34 786
leichte Infanterie Kolonne	35 366

SS-Polizei Artillerie Regiment

Regiment Stab	01 061
I.Abteilung	
Stab	02 403A
1.Batterie	02 403B
2.Batterie	02 403C
3.Batterie	02 403D
II.Abteilung	
Stab	33 780A
4.Batterie	33 780B
5.Batterie	33 780C
6.Batterie	33 780D
III.Abteilung	
Stab	04 528A
7.Batterie	04 528B

8.Batterie	04 528C
9.Batterie	04 528D
IV.Abteilung	
Stab	05 145A
10.Batterie	05 145B
11.Batterie	05 145C
12.Batterie	05 145D

SS-Polizei-Augklärungsabteilung

Stab	10 383A
1.Schwadron	10 883
2.Schwadron	01 331
3.Schwadron	01 554

SS-Polizei Nachrichten Abteilung

Stab	20 049
1.(Fe)Kompanie	20 686
2.(Fu)Kompanie	21 087
leichte Nachrichten Kolonne	22 240

SS-Pionier Bataillon

Stab	05 429
1.Kompanie	06 516
2.Kompanie	07 537
3.Kompanie	08 812
leichte Pionier Kolonne	09 017

SS-Polizei-Panzerjäger Abteilung

Stab	01 475
1.Kompanie	02 393
2.Kompanie	03 263
3.Kompanie	04 385

SS-Polizei Flak Abteilung

Stab	44 142
1.Batterie	45 534
2.Batterie	46 745
3.Batterie	47 385
Flak Kolonne	47 915

Wirtschafts Bataillon 300

Stab	11 474B
Verpflegungsamt	11 474
Bäckerei Kompanie	26 812
Schlächterei Kompanie	10 980

Sanitäts Dienste

1.Sanitäts Kompanie	36 354
2.Sanitäts Kompanie	37 360
Feldlazarett	20 595
1.Krankenkraftwagenzug	27 397
2.Krankenkraftwagenzug	19 510
Veterinär Kompanie	07 300

Ordnungs Dienste

Feldgendarmerie Trupp	34 364

Feldpost

Feldpostamt	14 776

Nachschub Dienste

Stab Divisions Nachschubführer	34 213
1.Kraftwagenkolonne	30 016
2.Kraftwagenkolonne	00 063
3.Kraftwagenkolonne	10 354
4.Kraftfahr Kolonne	39 118
5.Kraftfahr Kolonne	34 544
6.Kraftfahr Kolonne	30 469
7.Kraftwagenkolonne für Betriebstoff	31 483
Nachschub Kompanie	36 238

Instandsetzungs Abteilung

Werkstatt Kompanie	04 725

SS Nachschub Dienste

Stab	48 560
1.Kraftwagenkolonne	48 307
2.Kraftwagenkolonne	48 849
3.Kraftwagenkolonne	48 779
4.Kraftwagenkolonne	48 988

SS-Instandsetzungs Abteilung

Werkstatt Kompanie	48 445

SS-Panzer-Grenadier-Division "Wiking"

Divisions Stab	16 284
Kartenstelle	16 284

SS-Grenadier-Regiment "Germania"

Regiment Stab	30 003
I.Bataillon	
Stab	33 576A
1.Kompanie	33 576B
2.Kompanie	33 576C
3.Kompanie	33 576D
4.Kompanie	33 576E
II.Bataillon	
Stab	30 629A
5.Kompanie	30 629B
6.Kompanie	30 629C
7.Kompanie	30 629D
8.Kompanie	30 629E
III.Bataillon	
Stab	34 002A
9.Kompanie	34 002B

10.Kompanie	34 002C
11.Kompanie	34 002D
12.Kompanie	34 002E
leichte Infanterie Kolonne	37 705E

SS-Grenadier-Regiment "Westland"

Regiment Stab	25 854

I.Bataillon

Stab	26 907A
1.Kompanie	26 907B
2.Kompanie	26 907C
3.Kompanie	26 907D
4.Kompanie	26 907E

II.Bataillon

Stab	27 026A
5.Kompanie	27 026B
6.Kompanie	27 026C
7.Kompanie	27 026D
8.Kompanie	27 026E

III.Bataillon

Stab	28 109A
9.Kompanie	28 109B
10.Kompanie	28 109C
11.Kompanie	28 109D
12.Kompanie	28 109E
13.Kompanie	29 238
14.Kompanie	30 377
16.Kompanie	32 517

SS-Grenadier-Regiment "Nordland"

Regiment Stab	17 038

I.Bataillon

Stab	18 149A
1.Kompanie	18 149B
2.Kompanie	18 149C
3.Kompanie	18 149D
4.Kompanie	18 149E

II.Bataillon

Stab	19 272A
5.Kompanie	19 272B
6.Kompanie	19 272C
7.Kompanie	19 272D
8.Kompanie	19 272E

III.Bataillon (Finn. Freiwilligen Bataillon)

Stab	46 785A
1.Kompanie	46 785B
2.Kompanie	46 785C
3.Kompanie	46 785D
4.Kompanie	46 785E
13.Kompanie	21 497
leichte Infanterie Kolonne	37 802

SS-Artillerie Regiment

Stab	20 060

Meßbatterie	25 328

I.Abteilung

Stab	21 432A
1.Batterie	21 432B
2.Batterie	21 432C
3.Batterie	21 432D

II.Abteilung

Stab	22 855A
4.Batterie	22 855B
5.Batterie	22 855C
6.Batterie	22 855D

III.Abteilung

Stab	23 604A
7.Batterie	23 604B
8.Batterie	23 604C
9.Batterie	23 604D

IV.Abteilung

Stab	24 976A
10.Batterie	24 976B
11.Batterie	24 976C
12.Batterie	24 976D
Artillerie Kolonne 36t	26 145

Sturmgeschütz Batterie | 27 203

Panzer Abteilung

Stab	08 158
1.Kompanie	09 274
2.Kompanie	10 927
3.Kompanie	11 031
4.Kompanie	48 968
Panzer Werkstatt Zug	21 429

Aufklärungsabteilung

Stab	39 688
1.Kompanie	40 546
2.Kompanie	41 487
3.Kompanie	42 366
4.Kompanie	43 213

Nachrichten Abteilung

Stab	33 631
1.Kompanie	34 759
2.Kompanie	35 883
leichte Nachrichten Kolonne	36 927

SS-Pionier Bataillon

Stab	44 189
1.Kompanie	45 054
2.Kompanie	46 029
3.Kompanie	47 118
Brückenkolonne	46 899
leichte Pionier Kolonne	47 926

SS-Panzerjäger Abteilung

Stab	45 750
1.Kompanie	44 615
2.Kompanie	43 578
3.Kompanie	42 439

SS-Flak Abteilung

Stab	40 017
1.Batterie	41 432
2.Batterie	42 640
3.Batterie	43 187
4.Batterie	25 596
Flak Kolonne	43 644

Sanitäts Abteilung

Stab	44 584A
1.Sanitäts Kompanie	44 584
2.Sanitäts Kompanie	47 064
Feldazarett	40 128
SS Lazarett (mot)	45 932

Wirtschafts Bataillon

Stab	47 772
Verpflegungsamt	39 504
Bäckerei Kompanie	39 624
Schlächterei Kompanie	36 761

Instandsetzungs Abteilung

Stab	
1.Werkstatt Kompanie	46 417
2.Werkstatt Kompanie	47 269
3.Werkstatt Kompanie	
4.Werkstatt Kompanie	43 696
Bekleidungs-Instandsetzungs Kompanie	27 016

Nachub Dienste

Divisions Nachubführer	45 601
1.Kraftwagenkolonne	46 354
2.Kraftwagenkolonne	47 807
3.Kraftwagenkolonne	40 053
4.Kraftwagenkolonne	41 266
5.Kraftwagenkolonne	41 927
6.Kraftwagenkolonne	42 195
7.Kraftwagenkolonne	
8.Kraftwagenkolonne	44 204
9.Kraftwagenkolonne	44 857
10. (groß) Kraftwagenkolonne für Betriebstoff	45 223
11. (groß) Kraftwagenkolonne für Betriebstoff	45 884
12.Kraftwagenkolonne	44 583
13.Kraftwagenkolonne	46 947
14.Kraftwagenkolonne	47 135
Nachub Kompanie	46 096

Feldpostamt	12 106	11.Kompanie	44 591B	Stab	42 216
		12.Kompanie	44 591C	1.Kompanie	42 882
		13.Kompanie	44 591D	2.Kompanie	44 791
SS-Gebirgs-Division "Nord"		14.Kompanie	44 591E	3.Kompanie	43 436
		15.Kompanie	44 591F		
Divisions Stab	05 396	17.Kompanie	23 072C	**Nachrichten Abteilung**	
Kartenstelle	05 396	18.Kompanie	24 252	Stab	06 041
		19.Kompanie	23 072B	1.Kompanie	44 906
		Schützen Bataillon		2.Kompanie	39 684
Gebirgs Jäger Regiment 6 "Reinhard Heydrich"		Stab	25 081A	3.Kompanie	47 224
		1.Kompanie	25 081B	leichte Nachrichten Kolonne	19 786
Stab	12 238	2.Kompanie	25 081C		
Stabskompanie	12 238A	3.Kompanie	25 081D	**Panzerjäger Abteilung**	
I.Bataillon		4.Kompanie	25 081E	Stab	31 530
Stab	14 040A	5.Kompanie	25 081F	1.Kompanie	31 707
1.Kompanie	14 040B			2.Kompanie	32 444
2.Kompanie	14 040C	**SS-Gebirgs-Artillerie-Regiment**		3.Kompanie	32 971
3.Kompanie	14 040D	Regiment Stab	20 068		
4.Kompanie	14 040E	Stabsbatterie	20 068A	**SS-Gebirgs-Pionier Kompanie**	
II.Bataillon		Meßbatterie	20 068B	Stab	41 174
Stab	46 672A	*I.Abteilung*		1.Kompanie	42 430
5.Kompanie	46 672B	Stab	20 690A	2.Kompanie	43 525
6.Kompanie	46 672C	Stabsbatterie	20 690B	3.Kompanie	44 443
7.Kompanie	46 672D	1.Batterie	20 690C	Brücken Kolonne	45 199
8.Kompanie	46 672E	2.Batterie	20 690D	leichte Gebirgs Pionier Kolonne	46 009
III.Bataillon		3.Batterie	20 690E		
Stab	31 072A	*II.Abteilung*		**Instandsetzungs Abteilung**	
11.Kompanie	31 072B	Stab	22 615A	Abteilung Stab	44 031A
12.Kompanie	31 072C	Stabsbatterie	22 615B	1.Werkstatt Kompanie	44 031
13.Kompanie	31 072D	4.Batterie	22 615C	2.Werkstatt Kompanie	46 778
14.Kompanie	31 072E	5.Batterie	22 615D	3.Werkstatt Kompanie	47 832
15.Kompanie	31 072F	6.Batterie	22 615E	Kraftfahrpark	45 143
17.Kompanie	12 238C	*III.Abteilung*		Kraftfahrpark Kompanie	46 799
18.Kompanie	17 307	Stab	31 497A		
19.Kompanie	12 238B	Stabsbatterie	31 497B	**Wirtschafts Bataillon**	
		7.Batterie	31 497C	Stab	45 040B
Gebirgs-Jäger Regiment 7		8.Batterie	31 497D	Verpflegungsamt	45 040
Stab	23 072	9.Batterie	31 497E	Bäckerei Kompanie	42 387
Stabskompanie	23 072A	*IV.Abteilung*		Schlächterei Kompanie	43 293
I.Bataillon		Stab	24 737A		
Stab	43 720A	Stabsbatterie	24 737B	**Sanitäts Abteilung**	
1.Kompanie	43 720B	10.Batterie	24 737C	1.Gebirgs Sanitäts Kompanie	47 888
2.Kompanie	43 720C	11.Batterie	24 737D	2.Gebirgs Sanitäts Kompanie	46 617
3.Kompanie	43 720D	12.Batterie	24 737E	1.Krankenkraftwagenzug	40 426
4.Kompanie	43 720E			2.Krankenkraftwagenzug	41 278
5.Kompanie	43 720F	**Flak Abteilung**		3.Krankenkraftwagenzug	47 401
II.Bataillon		Stab	39 307		
Stab	44 143A	1.Batterie	43 232	**Ordnungs Dienste**	
6.Kompanie	44 143B	2.Batterie	40 014	Feldgendarmerie Trupp	45 988
7.Kompanie	44 143C	3.Batterie	41 225	Feldpostamt	48 700
8.Kompanie	44 143D	4.Batterie	48 502	Kriegsberichter Zug	05 396B
9.Kompanie	44 143E	leichte Flak Kolonne	42 730		
10.Kompanie	44 143F			**Nachschub Dienste**	
III.Bataillon		**Aufklärungsabteilung**		Division Nachschubführer	43 869
Stab	44 591A				

1.(groß) Kraftwagenkolonne	44 401	Stab	44 525A	*III.Abteilung*	
2.(groß) Kraftwagenkolonne	45 554	19.Kompanie	44 525B	Stab	47 819A
3.(groß) Kraftwagenkolonne	46 693	20.Kompanie	44 525C	Stabsbatterie	47 819A
4.(groß) Kraftwagenkolonne	47 158	21.Kompanie	44 525D	leichte Artillerie Kolonne	47 819A
5.(groß) Kraftwagenkolonne	43 596	22.Kompanie	44 525E	5.Batterie	47 819B
6.(groß) Kraftwagenkolonne	45 768	23.Kompanie	44 525F	6.Batterie	47 819C
6.(groß) Kraftwagenkolonne	46 146			7.Batterie	47 819D

Freiwilligen-Gebirgs-Jäger Regiment 2

8.(groß) Kraftwagenkolonne für Betriebstoff
44 642

9.(groß) Kraftwagenkolonne für Betriebstoff
45 381

10.(groß) Kraftwagenkolonne	30 408	Regiment Stab	44 609	*IV.Abteilung*	
Waffen-Werkstatt Kompanie	43 791	Stabskompanie	44 609	Stab	18 200A
Nachschub Kompanie	44 724	*I.Bataillon*		Stabsbatterie	18 200A
SS-Lager Kuusamo	18 924	Stab	45 437A	8.Batterie	18 200B
Bekleidungs Instandsetzungs Kompanie 06 899		1.Kompanie	45 437B	9.Batterie	18 200C
		2.Kompanie	45 437C	10.Batterie	18 200D
		3.Kompanie	45 437D		

SS-Freiwilligen-Division "Prinz Eugen"

		4.Kompanie	45 437E	**Kavallerie Abteilung**	
		5.Kompanie	45 437F	1.Reiterschwadron	40 878
Divisions Stab	46 000	6.Kompanie	45 437G	2.Reiterschwadron	42 992
Kartenstelle	46 000	*II.Bataillon*			
Kommandant Divisions Stabsquartier	46 000A	Stab	45 777A	**Panzer Abteilung**	
Stabskompanie	40 787	7.Kompanie	45 777B	1.Panzer Kompanie	42 659
		8.Kompanie	45 777C	Panzer Werkstatt Zug	43 046

Freiwilligen-Gebirgs-Jäger Regiment 1

		9.Kompanie	45 777D	**Aufklärungsabteilung**	
Regiment Stab	46 936	10.Kompanie	45 777E	Stab	48 940A
Stabskomapnie	46 936	11.Kompanie	45 777F	1.Kompanie	48 940B
I.Bataillon		12.Kompanie	45 777G	2.Kompanie	48 940C
		III.Bataillon		3.Kompanie	48 940D
Stab	41 797A	Stab	46 194A	4.Kompanie	48 940E
1.Kompanie	41 797B	13.Kompanie	46 194B		
2.Kompanie	41 797C	14.Kompanie	46 194C	**Kradschützen Bataillon**	
3.Kompanie	41 797D	15.Kompanie	46 194D	Stab	48 044A
4.Kompanie	41 797E	16.Kompanie	46 194E	1.Kompanie	48 044B
5.Kompanie	41 797F	17.Kompanie	46 194F	2.Kompanie	48 044C
6.Kompanie	41 797G	18.Kompanie	46 194G	3.Kompanie	48 044D
II.Bataillon		*IV.Bataillon*			
Stab	42 643A	Stab	46 824A	**SS-Panzerjäger Abteilung**	
7.Kompanie	42 643B	19.Kompanie	46 824B	Stab	26 941
8.Kompanie	42 643C	20.Kompanie	46 824C	1.Kompanie	16 538
9.Kompanie	42 643D	21.Kompanie	46 824D	2.Kompanie	25 613
10.Kompanie	42 643E			3.Kompanie	24 286

SS-Freiwilligen-Gebirgs-Artillerie Regiment

11.Kompanie	42 643F	Regiment Stab	47 140	**SS-Flak Abteilung**	
12.Kompanie	42 643G	Stabsbatterie	47 140	Stab	31 999
III.Bataillon		*I.Abteilung*		1.Batterie	30 067
Stab	43 476A	Stab	47 323A	2.Batterie	29 136
13.Kompanie	43 476B	Stabsbatterie	47 323A	3.Batterie	28 757
14.Kompanie	43 476C	leichte Artillerie Kolonne	47 323A	leichte Flak Kolonne	27 456
15.Kompanie	43 476D	1.Batterie	47 323B		
16.Kompanie	43 476E	2.Batterie	47 323C	**Nachrichten Abteilung**	
17.Kompanie	43 476F	*II.Abteilung*		Stab	43 733A
18.Kompanie	43 476G	Stab	47 537A	1.(Fe)Kompanie	43 733B
IV.Bataillon		Stabsbatterie	47 537A	2.(Fe)Kompanie	43 733C
		3.Batterie	47 537B	3.(Fu)Kompanie	43 733D
		4.Batterie	47 537C	leichte Nachrichten Kolonne	43 733E

Pionier Bataillon

Bataillon Stab	44 516A
1.Kompanie	44 516B
2.Kompanie	44 516C
Seilbahnkommando	44 516D
Pionier Maschinen Zug	44 516E
leichte Gebirgs Pionier Kolonne	44 516F
Werkstatt Zug	44 516G
Brücken Kolonne	44 958

Radfahr Bataillon

Stab	41 781A
1.Schwadron	41 781B
2.Schwadron	41 781C
3.Schwadron	41 781D

Sanitäts Abteilung

1.Gebirgs Sanitäts Kompanie (mot)	47 199
2.Gebirgs Sanitäts Kompanie (mot)	47 444
Gebirgs Kranken Tragt. Kompanie	47 358
Krankenkraftwagenzug	46 058
Kranken Karren Zug	47 246

Veterinär Dienste

1.Gebirgs Veterinär Kompanie	45 792
Veterinär Park	45 858

Wirtschafts Bataillon

Stab	46 934B
Bäckerei Kompanie	46 649
Schlächterei Kompanie	46 711
Verpflegungsamt	46 934

Nachschub Dienste

Stab Divisions Nachschubführer	45 900
1.Kraftwagenkolonne	42 799
2.Kraftwagenkolonne	42 959
3.Kraftwagenkolonne	43 055
4.Kraftwagenkolonne	43 463
5.Kraftwagenkolonne	43 601
6.Kraftwagenkolonne	43 927
7.Gebirgs Fahrkolonne	44 497
8.Gebirgs Fahrkolonne	44 532
9.Gebirgs Fahrkolonne	44 814
10.Gebirgs Fahrkolonne	44 963
11.Gebirgs Fahrkolonne	45 571
12.Gebirgs Fahrkolonne	45 975
13.Kraftwagenkolonne für Betriebstoff	46 286

Instandsetzungs Abteilung

Stab	45 900F
Material-St. Tragt. Kolonne	45 900A
Material-St. Fuhrwerke	45 900B
Werkstattzug für Fuhrwerke	45 900C

Material-St. Für Kraftfahrzug	45 900D
Werkstatt Zug	45 900E

Ordnungs Dienste

Feldgendarmerie-Trupp (ber.)	42 896
Feldgendarmerie-Trupp (mot)	43 059

Feldpost

Feldpostamt	43 726
Zweigfeldpostamt	35 914A

SS-Kavallerie-Division

Divisions Stab	17 771
Kartenstelle	17 771

Kavallerie Regiment 1

Stab	22 771
1.Schwadron	18 364
2.Schwadron	18 650
3.Schwadron	19 320
4.Schwadron	19 555
5.Schwadron	19 660
6.Schwadron	21 753

Kavallerie Regiment 2

Stab	40 144
1.Schwadron	40 610
2.Schwadron	41 255
3.Schwadron	41 928
4.Schwadron	42 014
5.Schwadron	42 572
6.Schwadron	44 880

Kavallerie Regiment 3

Stab	16 148
1.Schwadron	17 472
2.Schwadron	18 683
3.Schwadron	19 708
4.Schwadron	20 747
5.Schwadron	21 330
6.Schwadron	22 039

Artillerie Regiment

Stab	23 886
Meßbatterie	16 533
I.Abteilung	
Stab	24 142A
1.Batterie	24 142B
2.Batterie	24 142C
3.Batterie	24 142D
II.Abteilung	
Stab	25 315A

4.Batterie	25 315B
5.Batterie	25 315C
6.Batterie	25 315D
1.leichte Artillerie Kolonne	17 475
2.leichte Artillerie Kolonne	18 229

Sturmgeschütz Batterie	48 288
Radfahr-Aufklärungsabteilung	
Stab	45 637
1.Schwadron	20 903
2.Schwadron	43 441
3.Schwadron	46 980

Panzerjäger Abteilung

Stab	48 646A
1.Kompanie	48 646B
2.Kompanie	48 646C

Flak Abteilung

Stab	27 532A
1.Batterie	27 532B
2.Batterie	27 532C
3.Batterie (Heeres Flak)	38 183
leichte Artillerie Kolonne Flak	27 532D

Pionier Bataillon

Stab	28 406
1.Kompanie	29 497
2.Kompanie	29 965
Brücken Kolonne	30 708
leichte Pionier Kolonne	31 232

Nachrichten Abteilung

1.Kompanie(Fe)	32 270
2.Kompanie(Fu)	33 441
leichte Nachrichten Kolonne	34 040

Sanitäts Abteilung

1.Sanitäts Kompanie	43 008
2.Sanitäts Kompanie	14 129
1.Krankenkfaftwagenzug	43 364
2.Krankenkraftwagenzug	36 632

Veterinär Dienste

1.Veterinär Kompanie	34 864

Divisions Nachschub Dienste

Divisions Nachschubführer	37 071
1.Kraftwagenkolonne	38 314
2.Kraftwagenkolonne	39 907
3.Kraftwagenkolonne	40 408
4.Kraftwagenkolonne	41 032
5. (Groß) Kraftwagenkolonne	42 403
6.Fahrkolonne	43 974

7.Fahrkolonne	44 366
8.Fahrkolonne	45 916
Werkstatt Kompanie	46 761
Nachschub Kompanie	47 946

Wirtschafts Bataillon

Stab	42 301A
Verpflegungsamt	42 301B
Bächerei Kompanie	41 094
Schlächterei Kompanie	41 516
Feldgendarmerie	39 013
Feldpostamt	40 197
Kriegsberichter Zug	17 771B

SS-Panzer-Grenadier-Division "Hohenstaufen"

Divisionsstab und Kartenstelle	20 046
Kriegsberichter Kompanie	20 046A
Sicherungskompanie	20 046B

Panzer Regiment

Regiment Stab	21 118
Stabskompanie	21 118A
I.Abteilung	
Stab	21 815A
Stabskompanie	21 815A
1.Kompanie	21 815B
2.Kompanie	21 815C
3.Kompanie	21 815D
4.Kompanie	21 815E
leichte Panzer Kolonne	21 815F
II.Abteilung	
Stab	22 336A
5.Kompanie	22 336B
6.Kompanie	22 336C
7.Kompanie	22 336D
Panzer Pionier Kompanie	20 183
Panzer Werkstatt Kompanie	22 490

Panzer-Grenadier-Regiment 1

Regiment Stab	21 770
Stabskompanie	21 770A
I.Bataillon	
Stab	23 295A
1.Kompanie	23 295B
2.Kompanie	23 295C
3.Kompanie	23 295D
4.Kompanie	23 295E
II.Bataillon	
Stab	23 940A
5.Kompanie	23 940B
6.Kompanie	23 940C

7.Kompanie	23 940D
8.Kompanie	23 940E
III.Bataillon	
Stab	24 111A
9.Kompanie	24 111B
10.Kompanie	24 111C
11.Kompanie	24 111D
12.Kompanie	24 111E
13.Kompanie (Infanterie Geschütz)	23 324
14.Kompanie (Flak Kompanie)	24 489
15.Kompanie (Kradschützen)	24 005
16.Kompanie (Pionier Kompanie)	24 337

Panzer-Grenadier-Regiment 2

Regiment Stab	20 340
Stabskompanie	20 340A
I.Bataillon	
Stab	25 122A
1.Kompanie	25 122B
2.Kompanie	25 122C
3.Kompanie	25 122D
4.Kompanie	25 122E
II.Bataillon	
Stab	25 405A
5.Kompanie	25 405B
6.Kompanie	25 405C
7.Kompanie	25 405D
8.Kompanie	25 405E
III.Bataillon	
Stab	23 474A
9.Kompanie	23 474B
10.Kompanie	23 474C
11.Kompanie	23 474D
12.Kompanie	23 474E
13.Kompanie (Infanterie Geschütz)	21 247
14.Kompanie (Flak Kompanie)	22 535
15.Kompanie (Kradschützen)	21 991
16.Kompanie (Pionier Kompanie)	24 297

Kradschützen Regiment

Regiment Stab	22 663A
Stabskompanie	22 663B
Panzerspähkompanie	22 663C
leichte Kolonne	22 663D
I.Bataillon	
Stab	25 218A
1.Kompanie	25 218B
2.Kompanie	25 218C
3.Kompanie	25 218D
II.Bataillon	
Stab	26 584A
4.Kompanie	26 584B
5.Kompanie	26 584C
6.Kompanie	26 584D

Sturmgeschütz Abteilung

Stab	23 565A
Stabsbatterie	23 565A
1.Batterie	23 565B
2.Batterie	23 565C
3.Batterie	23 565D

Artillerie Regiment

Stab	24 537A
Stabsbatterie	24 537B
Beobachtungs Batterie	24 537C
Flak Kompanie	24 537D
I.Abteilung	
Stab	20 488A
Stabsbatterie	20 488A
1.Batterie	20 488B
2.Batterie	20 488C
3.Batterie	20 488D
II.Abteilung	
Stab	21 339A
Stabsbatterie	21 339A
4.Batterie	21 339B
5.Batterie	21 339C
6.Batterie	21 339D
III.Abteilung	
Stab	22 728A
Stabsbatterie	22 728A
7.Batterie	22 728B
8.Batterie	22 728C
9.Batterie	22 728D
IV.Abteilung	
StabBatterie	21 419
StabsbatterieBatterie	21 419
10.Batterie	21 419
11.Batterie	21 419
12.Batterie	21 419

Flak Abteilung

Abteilung Stab	20 565A
Stabsbatterie	20 565A
1.Batterie	20 565B
2.Batterie	20 565C
3.Batterie	20 565D
4.Batterie	20 565E
leichte Kolonne Flak	20 565F

Panzerjäger Abteilung

Stab	24 600A
1.Kompanie	24 600B
2.Kompanie	24 600C
3.Kompanie	24 600D

Panzer Pionier Bataillon

Bataillon Stab	21 649A

Pionier Erkundungszug	21 649A
1.Kompanie (Panzer Pionier Kompanie)	21 649B
2.Kompanie	21 649C
3.Kompanie	21 649D
Brücken Kolonne	21 649E
leichte Pionier Kolonne	21 649F

Panzer Nachrichten Abteilung

Abteilung Stab	24 742A
1.(Fe)Kompanie	24 742B
2.(Pz.Fu)Kompanie	24 742C
leichte Panzer Nachrichten Kolonne	24 742D

Division Nachschub Führer

Stab	20 636
1.Kraftfahr Kompanie	22 093
2.Kraftfahr Kompanie	23 648
3.Kraftfahr Kompanie	22 806
4.Kraftfahr Kompanie	23 083
5.(groß) Kraftwagenkolonne	20 856
6.(groß) Kraftwagenkolonne für Betriebstoff	24 908
7.(groß) Kraftwagenkolonne für Betriebstoff	22 157
8.(groß) Kraftwagenkolonne für Betriebstoff	25 096
9.(groß) Kraftwagenkolonne für Betriebstoff	25 341
Nachschub Kompanie	23 793
Waffen-Werkstatt Kompanie	22 271

Instandsetzungs Abteilung

Stab	21 520A
1.Werkstatt Kompanie	21 520B
2.Werkstatt Kompanie	21 520C
3.Werkstatt Kompanie	21 520D
Ersatz Teil und Reifenstaffel	21 520E

Wirtschafts Bataillon

Stab	12 4092A
Bäckerei Kompanie	12 402B
Schlächterei Kompanie	12 402C
Verpflegungsamt	12 402D
Feldpostamt	08 801
Feldgendarmerie Trupp	22 938

Sanitäts Abteilung

Stab	23 176A
1.Sanitäts Kompanie	23 176B
2.Sanitäts Kompanie	23 176C
Feldlazarett	23 176D
1.Krankenkraftwagenzug	23 176E
2.Krankenkraftwagenzug	23 176F

3.Krankenkraftwagenzug	23 176G

SS-Panzer-Grenadier-Division 10 (10.SS-Div.)

Divisionsstab und Kartenstelle	21 003
Kriegsberichter Kompanie	21 003A
Sicherungskompanie	21 003B

Panzer Regiment

Regiment Stab	25 520
I.Abteilung	
Stab	27 732a
Stabskompanie	27 732A
1.Kompanie	27 732B
2.Kompanie	27 732C
3.Kompanie	27 732D
4.Kompanie	27 732E
leichte Kolonne	27 732F
II.Abteilung	
Stab	26 006A
5.Kompanie	26 006B
6.Kompanie	26 006C
7.Kompanie	26 006D
leichte Kolonne	26 006E
Panzer Pionier Kompanie	26 427
Panzer Werkstatt Kompanie	28 113

Panzer-Grenadier-Regiment 1

Regiment Stab	27 001
Stabskompanie	27 001
I.Bataillon	
Stab	25 685A
1.Kompanie	25 685B
2.Kompanie	25 685C
3.Kompanie	25 685D
4.Kompanie	25 685E
II.Bataillon	
Stab	26 966A
5.Kompanie	26 966B
6.Kompanie	26 966C
7.Kompanie	26 966D
8.Kompanie	26 966E
III.Bataillon	
Stab	28 227A
9.Kompanie	28 227B
10.Kompanie	28 227C
11.Kompanie	28 227D
12.Kompanie	28 227E

13.Kompanie (Infanterie Geschütz)	28 683
14.Kompanie (Flak Kompanie)	27 121
15.Kompanie (Kradschützen)	29 562
16.Kompanie (Pionier Kompanie)	28 829

Panzer-Grenadier-Regiment 2

Regiment Stab	25 706
Stabskompanie	25 706
I.Bataillon	
Stab	29 638A
1.Kompanie	29 638B
2.Kompanie	29 638C
3.Kompanie	29 638D
4.Kompanie	29 638E
II.Bataillon	
Stab	28 588A
5.Kompanie	28 588B
6.Kompanie	28 588C
7.Kompanie	28 588D
8.Kompanie	28 588E
III.Bataillon	
Stab	28 383A
9.Kompanie	28 383B
10.Kompanie	28 383C
11.Kompanie	28 383D
12.Kompanie	28 383E
13.Kompanie (Infanterie Geschütz)	26 549
14.Kompanie (Flak Kompanie)	29 708
15.Kompanie (Kradschützen)	27 274
16.Kompanie (Pionier Kompanie)	29 899

Kradschützen Regiment

Regiment Stab	28 747A
Stabskompanie	28 747B
Panzerspähkompanie	28 747C
leichte Kolonne	28 747D
I.Bataillon	
Stab	27 869A
1.Kompanie	27 869B
2.Kompanie	27 869C
3.Kompanie	27 869D
II.Bataillon	
Stab	29 022A
4.Kompanie	29 022B
5.Kompanie	29 022C
6.Kompanie	29 022D

Sturmgeschütz Abteilung

Stab	28 913A
Stabsbatterie	28 913A
1.Batterie	28 913B
2.Batterie	28 913C
3.Batterie	28 913D

Artillerie Regiment

Stab	26 606A
Stabsbatterie	26 606B
Beobachtungs Batterie	26 606C
Flak Kompanie	26 606D

I.Abteilung

Stab	27 311A
Stabsbatterie	27 311A
1.Batterie	27 311B
2.Batterie	27 311C
3.Batterie	27 311D

II.Abteilung

Stab	25 836A
Stabsbatterie	25 836A
4.Batterie	25 836B
5.Batterie	25 836C
6.Batterie	25 836D

III.Abteilung

Stab	22 513A
Stabsbatterie	22 513A
7.Batterie	22 513B
8.Batterie	22 513C
9.Batterie	22 513D

IV.Abteilung

Stab	29 135A
Stabsbatterie	29 135A
10.Batterie	29 135B
11.Batterie	29 135C
12.Batterie	29 135D

Flak Abteilung

Abteilung Stab	27 480A
Stabsbatterie	27 480A
1.Batterie	27 480B
2.Batterie	27 480C
3.Batterie	27 480D
4.Batterie	27 480E
leichte Kolonne Flak	27 480F

Panzerjäger Abteilung

Stab	29 343A
1.Kompanie	29 343B
2.Kompanie	29 343C
3.Kompanie	29 343D

Panzer Pionier Bataillon

Bataillon Stab	28 028A
Pionier Erkundungszug	28 028A
1.Kompanie (Panzer Pionier Kompanie)	28 028B
2.Kompanie	28 028C
3.Kompanie	28 028D
Brücken Kolonne	28 028E
leichte Pionier Kolonne	28 028F

Panzer Nachrichten Abteilung

Abteilung Stab	45 215
1.(Fe)Kompanie	45 648
2.(Pz.Fu)Kompanie	46 239
leichte Panzer Nachrichten Kolonne	47 338

Division Nachschub Führer

Stab	25 920
1.Kraftfahr Kompanie	26 751
2.Kraftfahr Kompanie	20 798
3.Kraftfahr Kompanie	29 205
4.Kraftfahr Kompanie	26 177
5.(groß) Kraftwagenkolonne	28 499
6.(groß) Kraftwagenkolonne für Betriebstoff	27 510
7.(groß) Kraftwagenkolonne für Betriebstoff	23 363
8.(groß) Kraftwagenkolonne für Betriebstoff	24 045
9.(groß) Kraftwagenkolonne für Betriebstoff	20 905
Nachschub Kompanie	25 161
Waffen-Werkstatt Kompanie	27 908

Instandsetzungs Abteilung

Stab	26 218A
1.Werkstatt Kompanie	26 218B
2.Werkstatt Kompanie	26 218C
3.Werkstatt Kompanie	26 218D
Ersatz Teil und Reifenstaffel	26 218E

Wirtschafts Bataillon

Stab	27 654A
Bäckerei Kompanie	27 654B
Schlächterei Kompanie	27 654C
Verpflegungsamt	27 654D
Feldpostamt	26 310
Feldgendarmerie Trupp	26 817

Sanitäts Abteilung

Stab	29 491A
1.Sanitäts Kompanie	29 491B
2.Sanitäts Kompanie	29 491C
Feldlazarett	29 491D
1.Krankenkraftwagenzug	29 491E
2.Krankenkraftwagenzug	29 491F
3.Krankenkraftwagenzug	29 491G

Appendix 3: GLOSSARY

Abschnitt	District
Abteilung	branch, section or detachment
Allgemeine-SS	General SS
Amt	office
Arko	corps artillery commander
Armee	Army
Artillerie	artillery
Aufklärungsabteilung	reconnaissance detachment
Ausbildungs und Ersatz	training and replacement
Bäckerei	bakery
Bataillon	battalion
Batterie	battery
Betriebstoff	fuel
der Reserve (d.R.)	reserve rank
Divisionsstabsquartier	divisional staff quarters
Einsatzgruppen	Action Groups
Ersatz	replacement
Feldgendarmerie	field police
Feldpostamt	field post office
Flak	anti-aircraft
Freikorps	Free Corps
Führer	Leader
Führerschule	leader school
Führungshauptamt	Main Operational Office
Gau	area (Party term)
Gauleiter	area leader
Gestapo	Secret State Police
Gebirgs	mountain
Gemeindepolizei	Municipal Police
Gendarmerie	Rural Police
Grenadier	infantry
Grenzpolizei	Border or Frontier Police
Gruppe	group
Hauptamt	Main Office
Höherer SS und Polizeiführer (HSSPF)	Higher SS and Police Leader
Infanterie	infantry
Inspektor	inspector
Junkerschule	cadet school
Kampfgruppe	battle group
Kartenstelle	cartographic section
Kavallerie	cavalry
Kolonne	column
Kommandant	commander
Kommandoamt	Command Office
Kompanie	company
Korps	corps
Krankenkraftwagenzug	ambulance platoon
Kraftwagenkolonne	transport column
Kriegsberichter	war reporter
Kreis	province
Land	state

Landespolizei	Land Police
Lazarett	hospital
leichte	light
(mot)	motorized
Nachrichten	signals
Nachschubführer	transport leader
NSDAP or Party	the Nazi Party
Oberabschnitt	Main District
Ordnungspolizei (Orpo)	Order Police
Panzer	armor
Panzergrenadier	armored infantry
Panzerjäger	anti-tank
Personalhauptamt	Personnel Main Office
Pionier	engineer
Polizei	police
Rasse und Siedlungshauptamt (RuSHA)	Race and Settlement Main Office
Reichsführer-SS	Reich Leader of the SS
Reiterstandarte	mounted regiment (Allgemeine-SS)
Rittmeister	Captain (cavalry)
Sanitäts	medical
Schlächterei	butcher
Schützen Regiment	fast regiment
Schutzpolizei	Protection Police
schwere	heavy
Selbschutz	Self Police
Sicherheitsdienst (SD)	Security Service
Sicherheitshauptamt	Central Security Office
SS und Polizeiführer (SSPF)	SS and Police Leader
Stab	staff
Stabskompanie	staff company
Stabswache	the original NSDAP guard detachment
Stahlhelm	Steel Helmet
Standarte	regiment (Allgemeine-SS)
Stopi	corps engineer commander
Sturm	platoon (Allgemeine-SS)
Sturmabteilung (SA)	Storm Troops
Sturmgeschütz	assault gun
Totenkopf	Death's Head
Trupp	platoon
Verfügungstruppe (SS/VT)	Special Purpose Troops (the pre-war units that became the Waffen-SS)
Verpflegungsamt	feeding/food office
Volksdeutsche	ethnic Germans
Waffen-SS	armed SS
Werfer	rocket
Werkstatt	repair or maintenance
Zug	platoon

BIBLIOGRAPHY

Archives

Bundesarchiv, Berlin   National Archives, Washington D.C.
Vojensky Historiki Archiv, Prague Imperial War Museum, London

Private research collections and organizations

Ignacio Arrondo   Phil A. Nix
Allen Brandt   Ruth Sommers
Kurt Imhoff   Truppenkameradschaft "Der Führer"
Christian Kusche   Truppenkameradschaft "Dresden"
Jess T. Lukens   Truppenkameradschaft "Panzer
John Moore   Regiment 5"
George Nipe   Lennart Westberg

Interviews, correspondence and personal papers/documents/photographs

Otto Baum   Gustav Lombard
Gerd Bremer   Heinz Macher
Hermann Buch   Georg Maier
Leon Degrelle   Hubert Meyer
Ernst Deutsch   Otto Kumm
Hans Göhler   Richard Schulze-Kossens
Heinz Harmel   Arthur Silgailis
Hans Hauser   Armin Sohns
Willi Hein   Ruth Sommers
Horst Herpolsheimer   Sylvester Stadler
Hans Kempin   Albert Stückler
Ernst August Krag   Ralf Tiemann
Karl Kreutz   Karl Ullrich
Josef Lainer   Otto Weidinger
Fritz Langanke   Theodor Wisch
Frau Tutti Lehmann   Max Wunsche
Heinz Lindner
Jakob Lobmeyer

Pre-1945 documentation
(Berlin Document Center Personnel Files)

Franz Augsberger   Karl Gesele
Adolf Ax   Herbert Otto Gille
Erich von dem Bach   Curt von Gottberg
Otto Baum   Josef Grassy
Hellmuth Becker   Werner Hahn
Otto Binge   Desiderius Hampel
Wilhelm Bittrich   Peter Hansen
Georg Bochmann   Heinz Harmel
Friedrich-Wilhelm Bock   Walter Harzer
Alfred Borchert   Paul Hausser

Kurt Brasack   Nikolaus Heilmann
Karl Brenner   Constantin Heldmann
Karl Burk   Richard Herrmann
Lothar Debes   Friedrich Jeckeln
Leon Degrelle   Otto Jungkunz
Eduard Deisenhofer   Hans Kempin
Carl-Maria Demelhuber   Georg Keppler
Josef Dietrich   Matthias Kleinheisterkamp
Helmut Dörner   Fritz Klingenberg
Theodor Eicke   Hugo Kraas
Hermann Fegelein   Fritz Kraemer
Fritz Freitag   Karl Kreutz

"Das Schwarze Korps," München, 1939-1945
"Dienstalterliste der Schutzstaffel der NSDAP," issues of 1934, 1935, 1936, 1937, 1938, 1939 (addendum to 1938), October 1942, May 1943, October 1943, January 1944, July 1944, October 1944, November 1944.
"Feldpostübersicht der Waffen-SS," I.Teil, SS-Führungshauptamt, Berlin, 1943
National Archives Captured German Records, microfilm document collections: T-175 (Records of the Reichsführer-SS and Chief of the German Police), T-354 (Records of the Waffen-SS), T-611 (Schumacher Collection), A3343SSO (partial Berlin Document Center Records), RG238 (Records of War Crimes Trials)
    SS Personalbefehl
    SS-Personalverordnungsplatt
    SS-Stabsbefehle
    SS-Verordnungsblatt
    Verordnungsblatt der Waffen-SS

Post-1945 Unpublished Material

Buch, Hermann: "Die Geschichte des Kradschützen Bataillon SS-Reich," undated
Gelwick, R.A.: "Personnel Policies and Procedures of the Waffen-SS," University of Nebraska PhD thesis, 1971
Grill, Jonpeter Horst: "The Nazi Party in Baden 1920-1945," University of Michigan PhD thesis, 1975
Imhoff, Kurt: privately researched histories of the 38 individual Waffen-SS Pionier Bataillone, four Pionier Ausbildungs und Ersatz Battalione and the SS/VT Pionier Battalion, all titled by unit designation, Pionierkameradschaft "Dresden"
Thompson, Larry V.: "Nazi Administrative Conflict: The Struggle for Executive Power in the General Government of Poland, 1939-1943," University of Wisconsin PhD thesis, 1967

Published material
Angolia, John R: "Cloth Insignia of the NSDAP and SA," R. James Bender, 1985
Angolia, John R: "Cloth Insignia of the SS," R. James Bender, 1983

Bayer, Hannes: "Die Kavallerie Der Waffen-SS," Selbstverlag, Stuttgart, 1980

Bayer, Hannes: "Kavallerie Divisionen der Waffen-SS im Bild," Munin Verlag, 1982

Bender, Roger James and Taylor, Hugh Page: "Uniforms, Organization and History of the Waffen-SS," 5 volumes, R. James Bender Publishing, 1970-1982

Berben, Paul: "Dachau, The Official History 1933-1945," Norfolk Press, 1975

Deutsch, Ernst: "N, 1936-1939, Eine Dokumentation," Selbstverlag, 1988

Fürbringer, Herbert: "9.SS-Panzer-Division Hohenstaufen, 1944: Normandie, Tarnopol, Arnheim," Editions Heimdal, 1984

Hausser, Paul: "Soldaten wie andere auch," Munin Verlag, 1966

Hausser, Paul: "Waffen-SS im Einsatz," Plesse Verlag, 1953

"Historical Atlas of the World," Barnes and Noble Inc., 1981.

Höffkes, Karl: "Hitlers politische Generale, Die Gauleiter des Dritten Reiches," Grabert Verlag, 1986

Höhne, Heinz: "The Order of the Death's Head," Secker and Warburg, 1969

Husemann, Friedrich: "Die guten Glaubens waren," 2 volumes, Munin Verlag, 1971, 1972

International Military Tribunal, "Trials of the Major War Criminals Before the International Military Tribunal," 42 volumes, 1949

Jones, Nigel H.: "Hitler's Heralds, The Story of the Free Corps 1918-1923," John Murray, 1987

Jurs, August: "Estonian Freedom Fighters in World War Two," Voitleja Relief Foundation Book Committee, undated

Kaltenegger, Roland: "Die Gebirgstruppe der Waffen-SS 1941-1945," Podzun Pallas Verlag, 1994

Kannapin, Norbert: "Die Deutsche Feldpost Organisation und Lokalisation 1939-1945," 3 volumes, Biblio Verlag, 1979

Kersten, Felix: "The Kersten Memoirs 1940-1945," Hutchinson, 1956

Klapdor, Ewald: "Mit dem Panzerregiment 5 Wiking im Osten," Selbstverlag, 1981

Klietmann, Dr. K.G.: "Die Waffen-SS, Eine Dokumentation," Verlag "Der Freiwillige," 1965

Koehl, Robert Lewis: "The Black Korps, The Structure and Power Struggles of the Nazi SS," University of Wisconsin, 1983

Krätschmer, Ernst-Günther: "Die Ritterkreuzträger der Waffen-SS," Verlag K.W. Schütz, 1982

Krausnick, Helmut et al: "Anatomy of the SS State," Walker, 1968

Kumm, Otto: "Prinz Eugen, The History of the 7 SS Mountain Division Prinz Eugen," J.J. Fedorowicz, 1995

Lehmann, Rudolf and Tiemann, Ralf: "Die Leibstandarte," 5 text volumes and 1 photographic volume, Munin Verlag, 1977-1987

Littlejohn, David: "The Hitler Youth," Agincourt Publishers, 1988

Littlejohn, David: "Foreign Legions of the Third Reich," 4 volumes, R. James Bender Publishing, 1979-1987

Lucas, James: "Hitler's Enforcers," Arms and Armour, 1996

Mabire, Jean and Lefevre, Erich: "Leon Degrelle et la Legion Wallonie 1941-1945," Art et Historie d'europe, 1988

Messenger, Charles: "Hitler's Gladiator, The Life and Times of Oberstgruppenführer and Panzergeneral-Oberst der Waffen-SS Sepp Dietrich," Brassey's Defense Publishers, 1988

Meyer, Kurt: "Grenadiers," J.J. Fedorowicz, 1994

Mollo, Andrew: "Uniforms of the SS," 7 volumes (volume 2 by Taylor, Hugh Page), Historical Research Unit, 1969-1976

Meyer, Hubert: "The History of the 12.SS-Panzerdivision Hitlerjugend," J.J. Fedorowicz, 1994

Nipe, George: "Decision in the Ukraine, Summer 1943, II.SS-Panzerkorps and III.Panzerkorps," J.J. Fedorowicz, 1997

Padfield, Peter: "Himmler," Henry Holt & Company, 1990

Puntigam, Josef Paul: "Vom Plattensee bis zum Mur," Hannes Krois, 1993

Reitlinger, Gerhard: "The SS, Alibi of a Nation 1922-1945," Viking Press, 1968

Scheibert, Horst: "Die Träger des Deutschen Kreuzes in Gold," Podzun Pallas Verlag, undated

Schneider, Jost: "Their Honor Was Loyalty," R. James Bender Publishing, 1993

Schreiber, Franz: "Kampf unter dem Nordlicht," Munin Verlag, 1969

Schulz-Kossens, Richard: "Die Junkerschulen, Militärischer Führernachwuchs der Waffen-SS," Munin Verlag, 1982

Silgailis, Arthur: "Latvian Legion," R. James Bender Publishing, 1986

Strassner, Peter: "Europäische Freiwillige, Die Geschichte der 5.SS-Panzer-Division Wiking," Munin Verlag, 1968

Stein, George: "The Waffen-SS, Hitler's Elite Guard at War 1939-1945," Cornell University, 1966

Stöber, Hans: "Die Flugabwehrverbände der Waffen-SS," K.W. Schütz Verlag, 1984

Tessin, Georg: "Deutsche Verbände und Truppen 1918-1939," Biblio Verlag, 1974

Tessin, Georg: "Die Stäbe und Truppeneinheiten der Ordnungspolizei," Koblenz, 1957

Tieke, Wilhelm: "Korps Steiner, Nordland-Nederland, Nachträge zu den Truppengeschichte," Kameradwerk Korps Steiner, 1987

Tieke, Wilhelm and Rebstock: "...im letzten Aufgebot 1944-1945," Truppenkameradschaft 18/33, 1994

Tiemann, Ralf: "7.Panzerkompanie," Selbstverlag, Truppenkameradschaft 7.Panzerkompanie "Leibstandarte," 1992

United States, Chief Counsel for Prosecution of Axis Criminality: "Nazi Conspiracy and Aggression," 8 volumes, 1946-1948

United States, Chief Counsel for War Crimes: "Trial of War Criminals Before the Nuremberg Military Tribunals," 15 volumes, 1949-1953

"Unsere Ehre Heist Treue, Kriegstagbuch des Kommandostabs Reichsführer-SS etc.," Europa Verlag, 1965

von Seemen, Gerhard: "Die Ritterkreuzträger," Podzun Verlag, 1965

Vopersal, Wolfgang: "Soldaten, Kämpfer, Kameraden," 8 volumes, Selbstverlag Truppenkameradschaft der 3.SS-Panzer-Division e.V., 1983-1991

Waite, Robert G. L.: "Vanguard of Nazism, The Free Corps Movement in Postwar Germany 1918-1923," Harvard University, 1952

Wegner, Bernd: "The Waffen-SS," Basil Blackwell, 1990

Weidinger, Otto: "Kamaraden bis zum Ende, Der Weg des SS-Panzer-Grenadierregiments 4 DF," Plesse Verlag, 1962

Weidinger, Otto: "Division Das Reich," 5 text volumes, Munin Verlag, 1967-1982

"Wiking Ruf/Der Freiwillige," Munin Verlag, 1951-1997

Yerger, Mark C.: "Allgemeine-SS, The Commands, Units and Leaders of the General SS," Schiffer Publishing, 1997

Yerger, Mark C.: "Ernst August Krag," Schiffer Publishing, 1996

Yerger, Mark C.: "Images of the Waffen-SS, A Photo Chronicle of Germany's Elite Troops," Schiffer Publishing, 1996.

Yerger, Mark C.: "Knights of Steel, The Structure, Development and Personalities of the 2.SS-Panzer-Division "Das Reich," volume 1, Horetsky, 1989

Yerger, Mark C.: "Knights of Steel, The Structure Development and Personalities of the 2.SS-Panzer-Division Das Reich," volume 2, author-published, Box 4485, Lancaster, PA 17604, 1994

Yerger, Mark C.: "Otto Kumm," J.J. Fedorowicz, 1990

Yerger, Mark C.: "Otto Weidinger," J.J. Fedorowicz, 1989

Yerger, Mark C.: "Riding East, The SS Cavalry Brigade in Poland and Russia 1939-1942," Schiffer Publishing, 1996

"Zwölf Jahre 1.Kompanie Leibstandarte SS Adolf Hitler," Verlag K. W. Schütz, 1990

ILLUSTRATION CREDITS

Photographic, cartographic and artist credits:

Author's archive: Front cover, 5, 16, 32, 34-35, 38 (bottom), 41, 52, 54, 55, 57-58, 61, 63-64, 66-69, 73 (left), 80, 88, 90 (right), 97-98, 99 (top and bottom), 118-119, 121-122, 132-133, 138, 215-216, 217 (bottom) (bottom), 155-156, 166-168, 180 (top), 192, 195 (top), 222 (left), 234 (bottom), 235, 243, 248 (bottom), 256 (top), 259, 270, 273, 275, 281-286, 289, 291 (top), 292, 293 (top), 294, 297 (left), 304-305, 308

Otto Baum: 40 (left), 42, 44-49, 53 (bottom), 56, 59 (top left and right), 60 (left top and bottom), 138 (top)

Roger James Bender: 82, 321 (left)

Berlin Document Center: 26, 27 (left), 31, 40 (right), 87 (left), 101, 113 (left), 154, 165 (left), 179 (left), 188, 214, 274 (left), 280

Bob Biondi: 71 (top), 72

Allen Brandt: 27 (right), 312, 317 (top left)

Hermann Buch: 145 (bottom), 246, 248 (top), 315 (top right)

Jen Hayes: 62

Heinz Harmel: 224-229, 231-233, 234 (top), 295, 297 (right),

Kurt Imhoff: 77, 94, 106, 111, 151, 158, 206, 237, 239, 247, 264-265, 298 (top)

Hans Kempin: 287-288

Ernst August Krag: 191 (top)

Karl Kreutz: 60 (right), 329-330, 332 (top)

Otto Kumm: 221 (top)

Fritz Langanke: 251-252

Jess Lukens: 33, 71, 81, 90 (left), 91, 113 (right), 114, 115 (bottom), 125, 136-137, 139-140, 142-143, 145 (top), 179 (right), 185, 189, 195 (bottom left), 197, 202 (top), 210, 260, 296 (bottom), 300, 309, 315 (bottom), 321 (right), 327 (top), 333

Heinz Macher: 254, 257 (top), 319-320, 322

John Moore: 194

Munin Verlag via Thöle: 216 (bottom), 253, 258 (top left), 299

George Nipe: 22-23, 65, 180 (bottom)

Phil Nix: 102, 274 (right)

Jost W. Schneider: 38 (top), 74, 79, 99 (center), 110, 116 (top), 152, 157, 159, 184, 202 (bottom), 221, 256 (bottom), 315 (top left), 317 (bottom), 332 (bottom)

Ruth Sommers: 313

Jakob Tiefenthäler: 126-131, 242,

Ullstein: 204

U.S. National Archives: 28, 37, 53 (top), 59 (bottom), 73 (right), 83-84, 87 (right), 105, 115 (top), 116 (bottom), 123-124, 134, 141, 144, 146-149, 160-163, 165 (right), 169-170, 172-177, 182, 186, 190, 191 (bottom), 193, 195 (bottom right), 196, 198-200, 211-212, 218-219, 244-245, 250, 257 (bottom), 258 (right and bottom left), 261-262, 271, 291 (bottom), 294 (bottom), 298 (bottom), 301-302, 307, 310, 316, 317 (top right), 324, 327 (bottom)

Otto Weidinger: 255, 331, back cover

Wisliceny family: 222 (right), 230

NAME INDEX

REQUEST

I continue to request the loan, exchange of, or opportunity to buy SS related reference material. Published texts or periodicals (pre-war and post-war), copies of any type of original documents to include award material and photographs of all aspects are needed for a variety of ongoing projects. Especially sought are photographs of SS holders of the German Cross in Gold or Silver. Correspondence is, as always, also welcome from other researchers of the SS and Polizei. The author also asks that persons having reproduction 1/2 liter steins for sale with SS or any other Third Reich motif (to include those issued by Waffen-SS veteran groups) to send a description and price to the address below.

Mark C. Yerger
P.O. Box 4485
Lancaster, PA 17604
USA

NOTES

NOTES

NOTES

NOTES

NOTES

Also from the Publisher

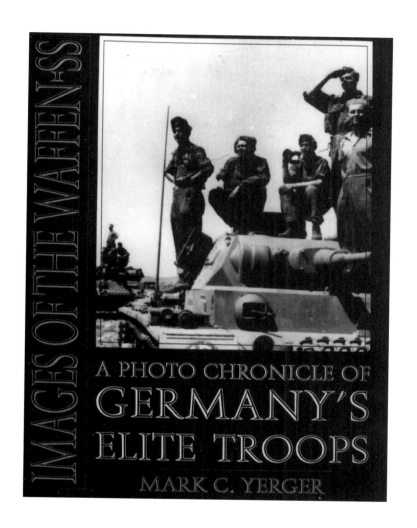

IMAGES OF THE WAFFEN-SS
A Photo Chronicle of Germany's Elite Troops
Mark C. Yerger

Images of the Waffen-SS gives its readers over 320 rare or new photos in large format on a variety of Waffen-SS topics from the photo collection of SS historian Mark C. Yerger. During more than fifteen years of researching the SS he has gathered material from a wide range of archives, collectors and veterans. Responding to requests from readers of his previous books, this new photo album provides material for the model builder, vehicle enthusiast, memorabilia collector and those interested in SS holders of the Knight's Cross.

Size: 9" x 12" over 320 b/w photographs
176 pages, hard cover
ISBN: 0-7643-0078-4 $49.95

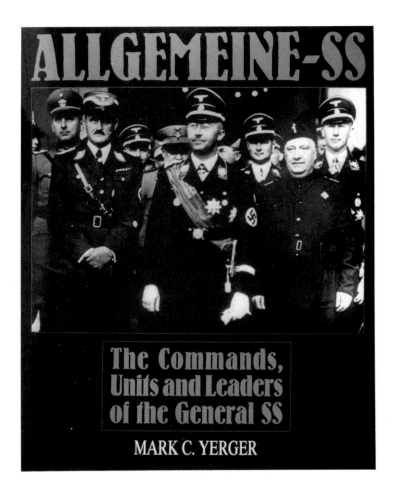

ALLGEMEINE-SS
The Commands, Units and Leaders of the General SS
Mark C. Yerger

The commands, units and leaders of the General SS are finally compiled into a single detailed reference book for both the historian and SS memorabilia collector. This complete volume begins with an explanation of the twelve administrative and command main offices involving the SS to include the development, components and functions of each as well as their respective office chiefs. The following section explores the most powerful posts in the SS, the Higher SS and Police Leaders, along with the subordinate SS and Police Leaders found in occupied territories – both the commands and the individual holders of these posts are examined in depth. The SS Main Districts are covered next including all their various subordinate components, title changes, development, commanders and chiefs of staff. The more than forty SS Districts follow, detailed in a similar format. Examining the more than one-hundred and twenty-five SS Foot Regiments in the General SS, the names and ranks of the hundreds of commanders, as well as details of unit location changes, popular and honor titles as well as other data for each are within a separate chapter. Finally, the elite SS Riding Districts and Regiments are covered similarly. Career biographies are included for more than two hundred senior SS commanders, many of whom served portions of their career in the Waffen-SS, Polizei, SD and other facets of Himmler's commands. The biographical data for individuals alone adds vast detail to this fascinating topic. Along with more than 120 rare photos of SS senior ranking officers and seven maps, a detailed index allows referencing of individual commands or personalities.
Size: 8 1/2" x 11", over 120 b/w photographs, maps, fully indexed.
256 pages, hard cover
ISBN: 0-7643-0145-4 $49.95

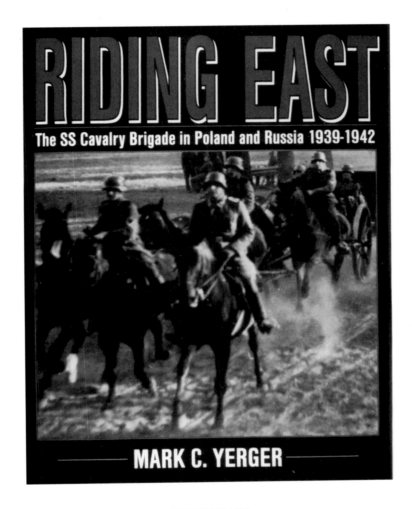

RIDING EAST
The SS Cavalry Brigade in Poland and Russia 1939-1942
Mark C. Yerger

RIDING EAST details the history of the previously unexamined SS Cavalry Brigade. Beginning with a background of the General SS mounted units, from which personnel formed part of the Brigade's cadre, the author details the organization, units and commanders of these pre-war formations. A detailed biography of Hermann Fegelein, commander of the Brigade, is followed by a chapter devoted to the SS command in Poland where the Brigade operated during 1939-40 as an occupational force. The units themselves are next examined from first creation in 1939 until they divided into two regiments in 1941, including all duties and operations in Poland. Assigned to the Headquarters Staff "Reichsführer-SS" at the start of the invasion of Russia, the regiments then combined with other units to form the SS-Cavalry Brigade and conducted anti-partisan warfare operations for most of the remainder of 1941. All the summer 1941 operations are examined in depth, including the massive Pripet marshes actions, using original documents from American and European archive sources. Subordinated in 1942 to Army Group "Center," the SS-Cavalry Brigade fought at the front during the massive Russian offensive in 1942 and was almost completely annihilated in the Rshev area before finally being withdrawn and used as cadre for the new SS-Kavallerie-Division. Heavily documented, the detailed text is supplemented by 109 photographs, most of which are previously unpublished. In addition, six maps, six Order of Battle charts, complete officer rosters 1939-1942, Feldpost numbers, details of primary commanders within the Brigade, as well information on the units and commanders it was subordinated to, complete a comprehensive history of the first combat mounted unit of the SS.
Size: 8 1/2" x 11" b/w photographs, documents
224 pages, hard cover
ISBN: 0-7643-0060-1 $59.95

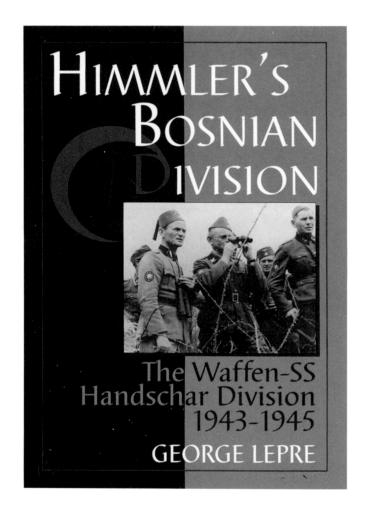

HIMMLER'S BOSNIAN DIVISION
The Waffen-SS Handschar Division 1943-1945
George Lepre

During the Second World War, Bosnia's Muslims stood alone in the face of imminent physical annihilation. In desparation, their leaders turned to an unlikely source for help – Nazi Germany – and by 1944, thousands of Muslims were serving within the ranks of the Waffen-SS. *Himmler's Bosnian Division* is the story of the "Handschar," a Muslim combat formation created by the Germans to "restore order in Bosnia." What actually transpired was quite different. Winner of Rutgers University's Sydney Zebel History Award, *Himmler's Bosnian Division* provides a unique look at this little known facet of modern military history.
Size: 6" x 9", over 250 b/w photographs
384 pages, hard cover
ISBN: 0-7643-0134-9 $39.95

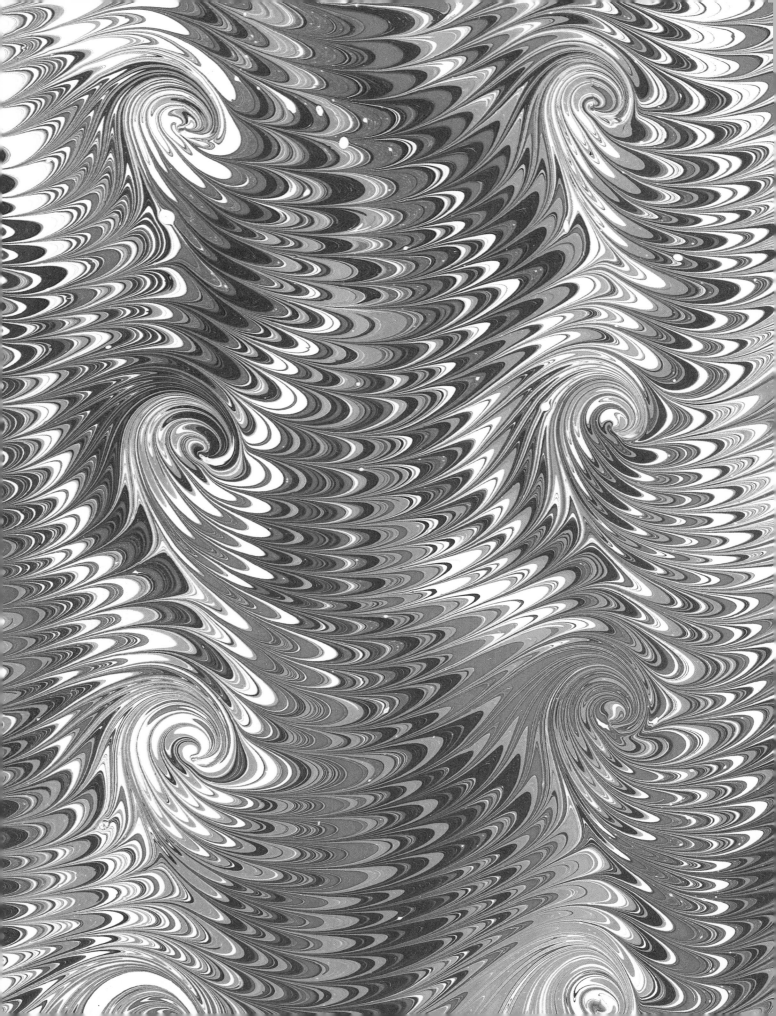